D1556973

Land and Racial Domination in Rhodesia

Perspectives on Southern Africa

1. THE AUTOBIOGRAPHY OF AN UNKNOWN SOUTH AFRICAN, by Naboth Mokgatle (1971)
2. MODERNIZING RACIAL DOMINATION: *South Africa's Political Dynamics*, by Heribert Adam (1971)
3. THE RISE OF AFRICAN NATIONALISM IN SOUTH AFRICA: *The African National Congress, 1912–1952*, by Peter Walshe (1971)
4. TALES FROM SOUTHERN AFRICA, by A. C. Jordan (1973)
5. LESOTHO 1970: *An African Coup Under the Microscope*, by B. M. Khaketla (1972)
6. TOWARDS AN AFRICAN LITERATURE: *The Emergence of Literary Form in Xhosa*, by A. C. Jordan (1972)
7. LAW, ORDER, AND LIBERTY IN SOUTH AFRICA, by A. S. Mathews (1972)
8. SWAZILAND: *The Dynamics of Political Modernization*, by Christian P. Potholm (1972)
9. THE SOUTH WEST AFRICA/NAMIBIA DISPUTE: *Documents and Scholarly Writings on the Controversy Between South Africa and the United Nations*, by John Dugard (1973)
10. CONFRONTATION AND ACCOMMODATION IN SOUTHERN AFRICA: *The Limits of Independence*, by Kenneth W. Grundy (1973)
11. THE RISE OF AFRIKANERDOM: *Power, Apartheid, and the Afrikaner Civil Religion*, by T. Dunbar Moodie (1975)
12. JUSTICE IS SOUTH AFRICA, by Albie Sachs (1973)
13. AFRIKANER POLITICS IN SOUTH AFRICA, 1934–1948, by Newell M. Stultz (1974)
14. CROWN AND CHARTER: *The Early Years of the British South Africa Company*, by John S. Galbraith (1975)
15. POLITICS OF ZAMBIA, edited by William Tordoff (1975)
16. CORPORATE POWER IN AN AFRICAN STATE: *The Political Impact of Multinational Mining Companies in Zambia*, by Richard Sklar (1975)
17. CHANGE IN CONTEMPORARY SOUTH AFRICA, edited by Leonard Thompson and Jeffrey Butler (1975)
18. THE TRADITION OF RESISTANCE IN MOZAMBIOUE: *The Zambesi Valley 1850–1921*, by Allen F. Isaacman (1976)
19. BY RIGHT OF RACE: *The Evolution of Black Power Politics in South Africa, 1934–1976*, by Gail Gerhart (1977)
20. THE RHINOCEROS AND THE UNICORN: *Gore-Brown and the Politics of Multiracial Zambia*, by Robert I. Rotberg (1977)
21. THE BLACK HOMELANDS OF SOUTH AFRICA: *The Political and Economic Development of Bophuthatswana and KwaZulu*, by Jeffrey Butler, Robert I. Rotberg, and John Adams (1977)
22. AFRIKANER POLITICAL THOUGHT, by Herman Giliomée and André du Toit (1977)
23. PORTUGUESE RULE IN ANGOLA: *A Study in Racial Domination*, by Gerald Bender (1977)
24. LAND AND RACIAL DOMINATION IN RHODESIA, by Robin Palmer (1977)
25. THE ROOTS OF RURAL POVERTY IN CENTRAL AND SOUTHERN AFRICA, edited by Robin Palmer and Neil Parsons (1977)

Land and Racial Domination in Rhodesia

ROBIN PALMER
Senior Lecturer in History
University of Zambia

UNIVERSITY OF CALIFORNIA PRESS
BERKELEY AND LOS ANGELES

To Judy, Jocelyn, Joanna
and
'the people of Rhodesia as a whole'

University of California Press
Berkeley and Los Angeles, California

First published 1977

ISBN 0–520–03255–1
Library of Congress Catalog Card Number 76–14300

Printed in Great Britain

Contents

List of Tables

List of Maps

Acknowledgements

I wish to acknowledge, chronologically, those from whom I have received financial assistance: the Rhodesia Fairbridge Memorial College, the former University College of Rhodesia, the University of London Convocation Trust Fund, and the University of Malawi.

I am most grateful to David Beach, Richard Brown, Sholto Cross, Keith Rennie, Leroy Vail, and Jaap van Velsen for their critical and perceptive comments on an early draft of this book. I am also grateful to B. N. Floyd and A. J. Christopher for permission to use their maps.

Others, who over the years have rendered diverse kinds of help and encouragement, include Peter Emmerson, Ian Henderson, Judy Palmer, Neil Parsons, Ian Phimister, Terence Ranger, Eric Stokes, the staff of the National Archives of Rhodesia, and my former students at the Universities of Malawi and Zambia.

Plates 1–6 and the cover photograph are reproduced with the permission of the National Archives of Rhodesia. Plate 7 is reproduced from Federation of Rhodesia and Nyasaland, *An Agricultural Survey of Southern Rhodesia* (Salisbury, 1961). Plate 8 is reproduced from *The African in Southern Rhodesia, No. 3: Agriculture* (Glasgow, 1952). Map 1 has been redrawn from B. N. Floyd, *Changing Patterns of African Land Use in Southern Rhodesia*, Vol. 3 (Lusaka, 1961), and Maps 2–5 have been reproduced from A. J. Christopher, 'Land Tenure in Rhodesia', *South African Geographical Journal*, **53**, 1971, with the permission of the authors and publishers.

Finally, I wish to pay tribute to my indefatigable one-fingered typist, who shall remain nameless.

Robin Palmer

ABBREVIATIONS

APS	Anti-Slavery and Aborigines' Protection Society
BSA	British South Africa (Company)
CNC	Chief Native Commissioner
Hist. MSS.	Historical Manuscripts
H.C. DEB.	House of Commons Debates
H.L. DEB.	House of Lords Debates
ICU	Industrial and Commercial Workers' Union
LAA	Land Apportionment Act
LC	Land Commission
NADA	Native Affairs Department Annual
N/C	Native Commissioner
NPA	Native Purchase Area
NRC	Native Reserves Commission
RBVA	Rhodesian Bantu Voters' Association
S/N	Superintendent of Natives
UDI	Unilateral Declaration of Independence

Note on Archival Sources

Three main archives have been used in the preparation of this book: those of the Public Record Office in London; the National Archives of Rhodesia in Salisbury; and Rhodes House, Oxford.

All Public Record Office material bears the prefix C.O. or D.O., and comprises the original correspondence of the Colonial and Dominions Offices for the years 1890–1946. Almost all the correspondence cited comes from one of five different series: C.O. 417 (Africa, South, 1884–1925); C.O. 767 (Southern Rhodesia, 1923–5); D.O. 9 (Africa, South, 1926–9); D.O. 63 (Southern Rhodesia, 1926–9); and D.O. 35 (Dominions, 1930–46).

There are now three detailed, published guides to part of the holdings of the Rhodesian Archives. They are: V. W. Hiller (Ed.), *A Guide to the Public Records of Southern Rhodesia under the Regime of the British South Africa Company 1890–1923* (Cape Town 1956), updated by T. W. Baxter (Ed.); *Guide to the Public Archives of Rhodesia, Vol. 1: 1890–1923* (Salisbury 1969); and finally T. W. Baxter and E. E. Burke, *Guide to the Historical Manuscripts in the National Archives of Rhodesia* (Salisbury 1970). As yet, there is no published guide to the post-1923 period, though the files are now open to c. 1943.

The main Rhodesian records used during the British South Africa Company period are those of the Chief Native Commissioner (N), the Chief Native Commissioner, Matabeleland (NB), the Administrator (A), the Resident Commissioner (RC), the Land Settlement Department (L), the Commercial Branch and Estates Office (LB), the Surveyor-General (S), and the Treasury (T), together with the evidence submitted to the 1914–15 Native Reserves Commission (ZAD) and to the 1925 Land Commission (ZAH). In the post-1923 period, the bulk of the citations come from the correspondence of the Chief Native Commissioner (S 138, S 235, S 1542 and S 1561 series), and from the Native [Purchase] Area Administration (S 924). The papers most frequently used from the extensive Historical Manuscripts Collection have been those of W. J. Atherstone (Hist. MSS. AT 1), Sir Drummond Chaplin (Hist. MSS. CH 8), Sir William Milton (Hist. MSS. MI 1), and Sir Francis Newton (Hist. MSS. NE 1).

The papers cited from the Rhodes House, Oxford collection are those of Cecil Rhodes (MSS. Afr. s. 77 and s. 228), Sir Robert Coryndon (MSS. Afr. s. 633), Sir John Chancellor (MSS. Brit. Emp. s. 284), and the Aborigines' Protection Society (APS Papers, G 163, 166–8).

At the end of the book there is a select bibliography of the published material consulted.

Plate 1—Ndebele Village, c. 1897 (*National Archives of Rhodesia*).

Plate 2—Shona Village, c. 1892 (*National Archives of Rhodesia*).

Plate 3—Some Shona Trading with Europeans, c. 1890 (*National Archives of Rhodesia*).

Plate 4—'Mowing', c. 1912 (*National Archives of Rhodesia*).

Plate 5—Tobacco Growing on the Marandellas Estate, c. 1926 (*National Archives of Rhodesia*).

Plate 6—Pedigree Cattle Stables on the Shangani Ranch, c. 1930 (*National Archives of Rhodesia*).

Plate 7—European land in the 'Maize Belt'. (*An Agricultural Survey of Southern Rhodesia, 1961.*)

Plate 8—E. D. Alvord Addressing a 'Before Harvest Meeting' in a Native Reserve, 1940s. (*The African in Southern Rhodesia, 1952.*)

Introduction

Loss of land ... means losing the graves of one's fathers and the home of one's childhood; the sense of community, of the ordered pattern of nature, of the continuity and meaning of life, are destroyed. When people lose their land, there can only be deep and bitter resentment.

Director, British Institute of Race Relations, 1969.[1]

The thesis on which the present study is based was written in 1968.[2] The transition from thesis to book has, not untypically, been a slow one for a variety of reasons, including congenital laziness and heavy but enjoyable teaching commitments at the Universities of Malawi and Zambia. Hopefully the long time-lag has not been without its compensations, for a more profound knowledge of land and labour problems in Rhodesia's two northern neighbours, coupled with maturer consideration and the opportunity to pick a large number of fertile brains, have all contributed to making this study a more substantial, and certainly a more readable, work than the original thesis.

There is very little need to justify a study of the land question in Rhodesia (formerly Southern Rhodesia, or Zimbabwe, as it is now called by African nationalists). Writers of almost every spectrum of opinion are agreed that land has always provided the life-blood of Rhodesian politics, and that few issues have been as consistently contentious. Right from the first days of the European occupation of Mashonaland in September 1890, when land was immediately parcelled out to the incoming settlers, to the present (1976) situation of full-scale guerrilla war, one can discern the importance of the land question as a major factor determining black–white relations. Indeed, the main theme of this book is the way in which Europeans have used their control over land to secure for themselves a position of economic and political dominance which has only very recently begun to be seriously challenged.

As land has come to play a more and more prominent role in political debate in the years since 1945 influencing the result of at least one general election in Rhodesia, so a considerable mythology, both African and European, has grown up.[3] While conscious of this mythology, I have felt it best to ignore it as far as possible, and to attempt to produce a sober, dispassionate study which will withstand (as well as such things can ever withstand) the ravages of time and the changes of political climate, and one which perhaps will permit future mythologies to have a somewhat firmer basis in reality.

Within the overall framework of 'land and racial domination', some of the main themes with which this book is concerned include the triumph of European over African farmers and the inter-related rise and fall of the African peasantry; the nature and effects of the racial division of land into European farms and native reserves; the long-term influence of the decade of fortune-hunting in the 1890s; the wholesale evictions from European land and the associated rise of segregation; the attempts to 'develop' the native reserves and to foster the growth of a land-owning capitalist African middle class; the impact of the land issue on African political consciousness; the attempted 'solutions' of the most important land commissions; and finally the inevitable conflicts between enunciated policies and realities on the ground. Following an introductory chapter 1 on 'The Land and Its People', these various themes are developed in chapters 2 to 8, which cover the period 1890–1936, while a short conclusion brings them up to the present day. For the sake of clarity, chapters 2 to 8 are divided into four main sections: background, policy, actuality, and conclusion. The first of these presents the general context within which developments take place; 'policy' examines how policies were created and by whom; 'actuality' looks at what actually happened; and the conclusions hopefully tie each chapter neatly together.

This book is written exclusively from archival material. I am well aware, from my own subsequent work and from the work of students whom I have supervised,[4] that such an archival-bound study would today be considered inappropriate. To this I can only reply that in the years 1964–5, when I was working in Rhodesia, fieldwork into this particular topic would not have been possible, and that in later years when such work might have been conceivable for others, it was not so in my own case. While fully conscious of the limitations imposed by my sources, I feel, and have been encouraged by others to feel, that what I have to say is worth saying.[5] I very much hope that in the future it will stimulate others to test and amend my hypotheses on the basis of the fieldwork which I myself was unable to carry out.

Finally, an important caveat needs to be lodged concerning the use of statistics relating to population and to land areas. As Kuczynski convincingly demonstrated in 1948–9 for the then British Empire as a whole, a great many apparently precise figures trotted out by British colonial administrators were often appallingly inaccurate.[6] So it was in Rhodesia, where the local Native Commissioners who were responsible for compiling such statistics, were neither trained census-takers nor surveyors. As a result, virtually every census in Rhodesia has commented on the unreliability of previous estimates and the African population has, over the years, been consistently underestimated. Similarly, estimates of the amounts of land alienated to Europeans or assigned as native reserves, especially for the period before c. 1920, are highly unreliable because of the limitations of the prevailing topographical knowledge.

Some random examples will suffice to illustrate the point. In 1908 the CNC (Chief Native Commissioner) Mashonaland stated that: 'Until a complete census is taken of the indigenous and alien natives in the Province, it is almost impossible to arrive at accurate figures', and in the following year he admitted that his figures were 'purely approximate'. In 1914 the CNC Southern Rhodesia revealed that the population was calculated by multiplying the number of tax-payers by three and a half, while in 1920 he wrote that the numbers of African-owned cattle had been 'considerably under-estimated in the past'. In 1933 the N/C (Native Commissioner) Bulalima-Mangwe complained that 'without a complete census, it is obviously very difficult to frame any estimate of the population which is likely to reflect, even approximately, correctly the actual position'; and in 1936 the CNC explained away an apparent decrease in population by admitting that 'for many years past we have estimated Native population by a rule-of-thumb method which is now being found to be inaccurate'. The 1944 Report on Native Production and Trade mentioned that at one time Native Commissioners had tended to multiply by three and a half, but some of them

> have, in recent years, preferred to multiply the number of tax-payers by four or four-and-one-half. Test counts recently made in defined areas suggest that five may be the more correct figure, but further uniform tests will be needed in different parts of the country before a revised universal factor could be adopted, and even then the estimates would not be very satisfactory.

Finally, the 1962 census 'revealed... that the previous official estimate of the African population was about 20 per cent too low'.[7]

What is one to make of all this? Clearly, all figures, such as those in table I and the subsequent tables, need to be treated with the greatest caution and I have drawn attention to this in the text at various times. Thus, spuriously accurate figures have been rounded, figures that were rough guesses have been identified as such, and my own estimates have been substituted for official ones where this seemed necessary—as in the case of assessing the degree of pressure on land at the time of the European arrival in 1890. I have, however, used official figures with due caution in estimating the approximate numbers of Africans turned off European land at different times, on the grounds that although these figures are undoubtedly wrong, they are consistently wrong for all categories of land, and hence one can use them to deduce the approximate number of people moved from one type of land to another.

Philip Mason, in his general survey, *Patterns of Dominance*, has written that: 'The relationship, where a group of newcomers means to possess the land and expropriate the former holders, is usually quite simple; it is one of unmitigated hostility until one group is in a position to impose its will on the other.'[8] What follows will show whether or not Rhodesia conforms to the expected pattern.

NOTES

1. P. Mason, *Patterns of Dominance* (London 1971), 106.
2. R. H. Palmer, 'The Making and Implementation of Land Policy in Rhodesia, 1890–1936', Ph.D. thesis, University of London, 1968.
3. See, for example, the summary of conflicting mythologies in T. Bull (Ed.), *Rhodesian Perspective* (London 1967), 141–3; P. Mason, *The Birth of a Dilemma* (London 1958), 329–30. See also the various arguments by Roder, Oliver, Mason and Floyd in W. Roder, 'The Division of Land Resources in Southern Rhodesia', *Annals of the Association of American Geographers*, **54**, 1964, 41–2, 53–8. R. C. Haw, speaking on behalf of the Rhodesia Information Service, noted that: 'Both here and abroad there is a tendency, which is being actively fostered, to believe that Africans have had a raw deal over land. There is no doubt that this is one of their most deeply emotional grievances and agitators have used it to stir up opposition against the Government.' He went on to acknowledge that 'the Africans' grievances are not, of course, entirely without substance', but then proceeded to demonstrate, to his own satisfaction, that such grievances were ill-founded and lacked historical perspective. Rhodesia Information Service, *Land Apportionment in Rhodesia* (Salisbury 1965), 1.
4. Some of this work has been published: R. H. Palmer (Ed.), *Zambian Land and Labour Studies, Vol. 1*, National Archives of Zambia Occasional Paper 2 (Lusaka 1973); Palmer (Ed.), *Zambian Land and Labour Studies, Vol. 2*, National Archives of Zambia Occasional Paper 3 (Lusaka 1974); Palmer (Ed.), *Zambian Land and Labour Studies, Vol. 3*, National Archives of Zambia Occasional Paper 4 (Lusaka 1977).
5. T. O. Ranger, 'The Historiography of Southern Rhodesia', *Transafrican Journal of History*, **1**, 2, 1971, 70–1.
6. R. R. Kuczynski, *Demographic Survey of the British Colonial Empire*, Parts I and II (London 1948/9). Unfortunately Kuczynski did not cover Southern Rhodesia.
7. *Report of the Chief Native Commissioner Mashonaland for the year 1908* (Salisbury 1909), 4; *CNC Mashonaland Report 1909*, 6; *CNC Report 1914*, 2; *CNC Report 1920*, 4; *CNC Report 1936*, 2; *CNC Report 1962*, 5; S 235/511, Report of the N/C Bulalima-Mangwe for the year 1933; Southern Rhodesia, *Report of Native Production and Trade 1944* (Salisbury 1945), 10.
8. Mason, *Patterns of Dominance*, 106.

CHAPTER 1

The Land and its People

Omnia Rhodesia in tres partes divisa est.[1]

This chapter, like Rhodesia itself, is divided into three parts: 'The Land', 'The People', and 'Agricultural History'. The first of these provides a very brief geographical introduction to Rhodesia; the second examines, from the standpoint of 1890, the recent history of the Shona, the Ndebele, and the Europeans; while the third looks at their different agricultural systems. The purpose of the chapter is to provide a background which will make intelligible much of what follows: for example, the alienation of certain parts of the country to Europeans and its consequences, the interaction between different concepts of land tenure, and the eventual triumph of European over African farmers.

1. THE LAND

Rhodesia's present boundaries, though recent in origin, make a great deal more geographic and ethnographic sense than those of many of her neighbours. The rivers Zambezi to the north and Limpopo to the south, the dry zones around them, and the Kalahari Desert to the west and the Eastern Highlands in the east, have all acted to some extent as barriers to movement though they have not entirely impeded it. Ethnographically, Rhodesia is dominated by the Shona, who comprise nearly 80 per cent of the total population. They are followed by the Ndebele (15 per cent) and a number of small minorities: Sena, Hlengwe, Sotho, and Tonga, who inhabit the peripheral areas of the country and are to be found more numerously in neighbouring territories. A more important minority is the European community, whose continued retention of political power since its Unilateral Declaration of Independence in 1965 has thrust Rhodesia into world prominence.

Rhodesia is a landlocked country lying wholly within the tropics, approximately 450 miles (725 km) long and 520 miles (835 km) wide and covering an area of about 150,000 square miles (389,000 sq. km), or some 96 million acres. It is therefore nearly twice the size of Great Britain, though only one-third the size of South Africa and half that of Zambia. Under the 1969 Land Tenure Act, the land is divided equally between Europeans and Africans, though the latter outnumber the former by some twenty to one. As in South Africa, Kenya and Algeria, the alienation of large areas of land to Europeans, together with the firm belief that the Europeans have taken all the best land, has been felt as a major source of grievance by the African majority.

Geographically, Rhodesia is divided into three main regions (see map 1). Running approximately north-east to south-west through the middle of the country, with an off-shoot to the north-west of Salisbury, is the predominantly flat *high veld*, land over 4,000 feet (1,220 m) which forms the watershed between the Zambezi, Limpopo and Sabi rivers, and comprises some 25 per cent of the country. This is a cool, well-watered and fertile area which attracted first the Ndebele and later the European settlers. To the west and to the east the land falls away to form the *middle veld*, between 3,000 and 4,000 feet (915 and 1,220 m), which covers about 40 per cent of the country. This is a more dissected, undulating area than the subdued *high veld*, though in the west it flattens out and becomes remarkably featureless, to the extent that the Victoria Falls railway runs for seventy miles from Gwai to Dett in a perfectly straight line. Many of the native reserves (now tribal trust lands) are situated within the *middle veld*. Finally, beyond the *middle veld* lies the hot, dry *low veld*, land below 3,000 feet (915 m), mostly in the Sabi-Limpopo and Zambezi valleys, which constitutes the remaining 35 per cent of Rhodesia. In the Sabi-Limpopo the country is extremely flat, while in the Zambezi it is much more broken and rugged, with precipitous slopes along the escarpment. Neither valley has proved attractive to human settlement and their present sparse populations were probably at one time pushed there by stronger peoples who dominated the *middle veld* and *high veld*. The tsetse fly, still prevalent in large parts of Zambia, has been confined to the two *low veld* valleys and today affects only 10 to 12 per cent of the country, though in the past it was far more widespread.[2]

The climatic feature which most influences farming in Rhodesia is, of course, that of rainfall. For over half the year, from April to October, there is virtually no rain throughout the country. Towards the end of the dry season the weather becomes progressively more humid and oppressive—October is traditionally suicide month—until the rains break with devastating force in November. One white Rhodesian farmer described the coming of the rains in the following words:

> The atmosphere was tense—the veld silent, for even the birds seemed to scent the approach of a storm. After seven months of drought the rains were breaking over the country, and again the gardens and the veld would awaken from their long, sleepy rest under the scorching sun. The storm rumbled closer ... the hills were no longer visible, for a thick veil of water gradually enveloped the landscape—rushing with hissing fury to embrace the house in its angry folds. [The wind] springing up again with cyclonic force in the north ... swept the blackening mass forward in its wild onslaught

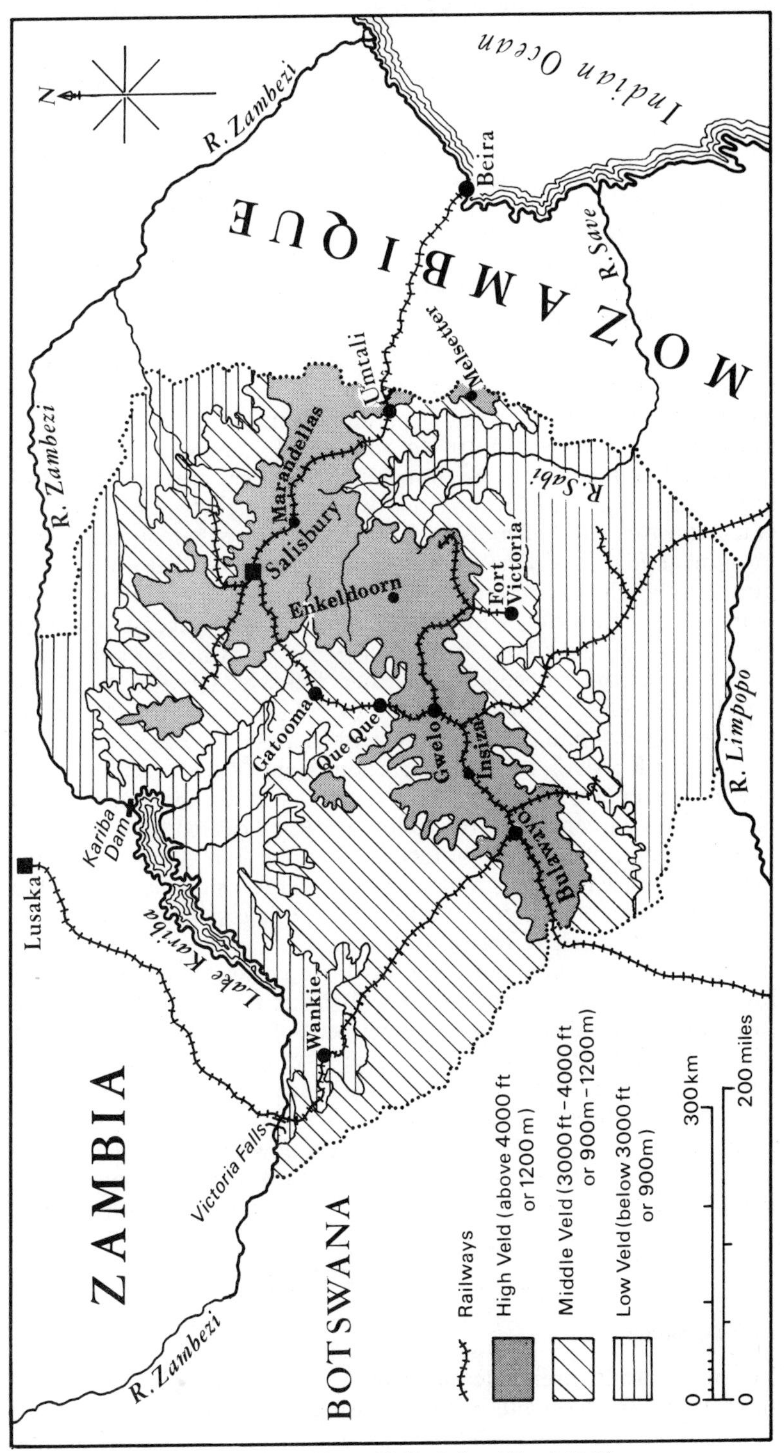

Map 1—The Three Velds (*after Floyd 1961*).

towards the farm. Flashes of lightning pierced the surrounding *kopjes*, while deafening claps of thunder crashed overhead—the rains poured down in torrents, forming an impregnable swirling barrier around the house; the wind died away, its work done, leaving the homestead and surrounding country to the deluge of tropical rain. Outside, the gravel became a racing waterway and the dried-up lawn a pool ... For hours the rain continued, while the thunder rolled away until only a distant grumble could be heard. And then the sun came out again and all was peace.[3]

Such rain is very fickle and deceptive. Only about one-third of Rhodesia enjoys an average rainfall of over 28 in. (712 mm), while about half the country has between 20 in. and 28 in. (508 and 712 mm). In general, as one moves north to south and from east to west, so the annual average decreases, though there are very great regional and annual variations. But the rain tends to come in torrents: 'Over a period of ten years at both Salisbury and Bulawayo, more than 30 per cent of the total annual rainfall fell at rates exceeding one inch per hour. Four-inch to five-inch falls during a single storm are not uncommon.'[4] Consequently a great deal of Rhodesia's rainfall—Kay suggests as much as 65 per cent[5]—is wasted in run-off. Some years however the rains fail altogether, drought conditions ensue, church leaders and traditional rain-makers alike pray for rain, and everyone suffers. In other years there is too much rain, and crops are washed away or severely damaged. Farming in Rhodesia is thus a hazardous occupation for everyone, as one European farmer of the 1930s testified with feeling: 'In England there is no real parallel to the ruin that can be caused in Africa by a black drought, or a plague of locusts, or cloud bursts. And when the main crop is a leaf crop, like tobacco, and so exceptionally susceptible, there are occasions when a year's hard work can be wiped out in twenty minutes, as I've reason to know.'[6]

Finally, though there are a number of sophisticated soil surveys of Rhodesia,[7] for present purposes it will suffice to distinguish between two major types of soil. About 70 per cent of the country is covered with light sandy soils, *sand veld*, of low inherent fertility. Most of the native reserves are situated in these areas. Heavier loam and clay soils, usually red or brown, with a much higher fertility cover some 7 per cent of Rhodesia.[8] Nearly all these areas are now European land, and it has been argued with some justification, that the Shona had made comparatively little use of such soils before the coming of the Europeans.[9]

2. THE PEOPLE

(i) The Shona

The numerically preponderant Shona-speaking peoples are found throughout Rhodesia and in neighbouring Mozambique.[10] Today the

Shona are divided into a number of groups—Korekore, Zezuru, Karanga, Kalanga, Manyika, Ndau, and Rozvi—who speak different, but mutually intelligible, dialects. Until 1820 the people whom we now refer to as Shona were undisputed masters of the *middle veld* and *high veld* of 'Rhodesia', and were also 'descendants of the creators of the most impressive Iron Age material culture in southern Africa, the Zimbabwe-Khami culture',[11] though they lacked political unity. The early history of the various Shona kingdoms and dynasties is now in the process of being written.[12]

During the nineteenth century, however, the Shona were subjected to two waves of invasion from the south. The first arrivals were the various Nguni groups thrust north by the explosive *Mfecane*. Then, half a century later, came the European settlers in the wake of the South African mineral revolution. The *Mfecane* was a revolutionary movement, in terms of social organization rather more than military techniques, and the various Nguni groups which moved through the present Mozambique, Rhodesia, Malawi, Tanzania, and Zambia often wrought profound changes on the local peoples they encountered.

In the 1820s, Soshangane settled his Shangaan people in Gazaland and began raiding the eastern districts of what was to become Rhodesia. He defeated his Ngoni rivals, Zwangendaba and Nxaba, who turned west and passed destructively through 'Rhodesia', to be followed in 1837–8 by Mzilikazi's Ndebele, who, after a long period of wandering, eventually came to rest at Bulawayo and began their attempts to dominate the surrounding Shona.

The history of Shona–Ndebele relations in the nineteenth century has recently been rewritten by Beach, and much of the earlier mythology has been destroyed as a result. Beach has shown that the most concerted Ndebele attempt to dominate the Shona took place in the years 1860–73, in which period a number of Shona groups fell tributary to the Ndebele; but that after 1877 Ndebele power was on the wane, while a massive influx of guns, common to virtually all of East and Central Africa at that time, greatly strengthened the Shona capacity to resist. This was particularly the case in central and northern Mashonaland, where the Shona were virtually impregnable and the Ndebele were afraid to go. In 1889–90 Portuguese agents entered northern and eastern Mashonaland and distributed large quantities of guns in exchange for a series of alliances with Shona chiefs.[13] The Shona clearly hoped to turn these guns on the Ndebele, but the arrival, towards the end of 1890, of the Rhodesian Pioneer Column added an entirely new dimension to Shona–Ndebele relations.

The Europeans were almost totally ignorant of the Shona past. They quickly stereotyped the Shona as a weak, cowardly people who would obviously welcome them as protectors against the supposedly dominant Ndebele, and whose susceptibilities did not therefore merit very great consideration. But while it was certainly true that the Shona were, and always had been, a politically fragmented people, they nevertheless retained in the *Mwari* cult and through their spirit mediums, a degree of religious cohesion which, so Ranger has argued, was able to provide a vehicle for commitment to resistance during their Rising of 1896–7,[14] in a manner paralleled later by the 1905–7 Maji Maji Rising in Tanzania.[15] The Shona were thus a good deal more resilient than the Europeans supposed.

(ii) The Ndebele

Mzilikazi's Ndebele settled on the Matabeleland *high veld* around Bulawayo in 1838. The history of the state which grew up there has been thoroughly revised in a recent thesis by Cobbing. In the work which he has published thus far, Cobbing has been concerned to 'demilitarize' and 'decentralize' Ndebele society, and to show how earlier writers have, often unconsciously, adopted the prejudices of nineteenth-century European observers. The Ndebele state was not a 'military state' terrorizing Shona societies at will, while its supposedly rigid caste system—*zansi*, *enhla* and *holi* in descending order—has also been much exaggerated. The Ndebele area of settlement, on the headwaters of the Umgusa, Bembesi, Umzingwani, and Gwai rivers was small, with no village being further than seventy miles from the approximate centre. Again in contrast to the standard view:

> The majority of Ndebele settlements in the pre-colonial era were small-scale, probably averaging from about fifty to two hundred people. Villages were collected together into clusters and the outlying political unit of the state was not the 'regimental' town, but the partially decentralized chieftaincy or *isigaba* (lit. sub-division), which contained several villages. One family supplied a succession of chiefs within an *isigaba* according to strict laws of patrilineality, which even the king was rarely able to disturb.[16]

Given the fact that the Shona peoples who were either forcibly or voluntarily incorporated within the Ndebele state—the so-called *holi* or 'serf' caste—comprised a numerical majority and exerted a significant influence on Ndebele society,[17] it was perhaps somewhat ironic that the British held the Ndebele in far higher esteem than the Shona; they feared and respected their military prowess, and did not feel secure until they had overthrown the Ndebele state in 1893.

For their own, quite conflicting, purposes both Lobengula and Cecil Rhodes' British South Africa Company assumed that the Ndebele were in complete control of the whole of present-day Rhodesia. From the European point of view the advantage of such a pretence was that any concessions which could be wrung from Lobengula would cover as large an area as possible. Identical tactics were employed by the Company in Barotseland, now the Western Province of Zambia, where an exaggeration of Lewanika's 'sphere of influence' was ultimately responsible for the Company acquiring the mineral rights to the Copperbelt. The reality in Rhodesia, as in Zambia, was very different from the legal fiction.

The absolute limits of the Ndebele state were in fact the Zambezi in the north-west, the Hunyani in the north-east, and the Mtilikwe in the east—not the Sabi as the Europeans and the Ndebele themselves often claimed. Within this area lay a number of Shona chiefdoms which sometimes paid tribute to the Ndebele, usually in the form of articles 'of partly symbolic value, such as skins, feathers, hoes, tobacco or spears, or the provision of services, such as labour for hut-building'.[18] But, as Beach points out

> The dividing-line between those who were tributaries and those who were not was not absolutely rigid. Some groups occasionally paid tribute in order to escape being raided, but generally resisted. Others who paid tribute were occasionally raided in spite of this by raiders not under the overlord's control.[19]

Outside this area, as many of the Company officials well knew, the Ndebele held no sway at all, and there existed many quite independent Shona chiefdoms in northern and eastern Mashonaland which had never witnessed a Ndebele raid, much less paid tribute. Indeed, when the renowned and widely travelled hunter, F. C. Selous, was on the point of revealing the truth about the situation in Mashonaland, Rhodes hurriedly bought his silence with a 'gift' of £2,000, and Selous proceeded to write what the Company wanted him to write.[20] Beach suggests that it was precisely because Lobengula no longer controlled central Mashonaland that he refrained from attacking the Pioneer Column of 1890 during its advance on Salisbury.[21]

(iii) The Europeans

The European occupation of Rhodesia in the 1890s was remarkable in two ways. Firstly, the country was 'pacified' by settlers rather than administrators; and secondly, a very large number of Europeans descended on the country during the initial decade of colonisation. The Pioneer Column itself comprised some 196 pioneers accompanied by 500 police; by 1896 there were approximately 5,000 Europeans in the country, and by 1901 the number had grown to 11,100 (see table I on page 12).[22] Compare this with the 850 Europeans in Northern Rhodesia in 1904 and the 314 Nyasaland in 1901.

Two important consequences stem from these facts. First there is the psychological point that by occupying the country themselves, by defeating the Ndebele in 1893 and by crushing the Shona and Ndebele

TABLE I

Estimates of the African and European Population, 1901–73

Year	*African*	*European*
1901	500,000	11,100
1911	750,000	23,700
1921	870,000	33,800
1931	1,080,000	50,100
1941	1,430,000	69,300
1951	2,180,000	138,000
1961	2,910,000	221,000
1971	5,310,000	255,000*
1973	5,700,000	271,000*

* This figure includes (for the first time) all non-Africans, and is therefore an inflated figure.

Risings of 1896–7 at the cost of a good many white lives, the European settlers gained a 'right' to the country[23] in a manner not paralleled in Kenya, Northern Rhodesia, and elsewhere where 'pacification' was carried out by government officials and their African auxiliaries. Though today the majority of Rhodesia's white population was not born in the country, the conviction that 'we' have conquered it is used to justify the continuation of white political dominance. Secondly, the sudden arrival of so many Europeans, searching for gold and largely unchecked in their activities, inevitably placed great stresses on Shona and Ndebele societies, which was in marked contrast to the gradual, piecemeal way in which Africans elsewhere, notably in Northern Rhodesia and Nyasaland, were brought under administrative control. The advantage from the European point of view of the latter process, was that it often took Africans a long time to realize what was happening, and those who chose to resist generally did so in isolation and were therefore defeated in isolation.

The event which ultimately precipitated the European drive from the south was the discovery in 1886 of the Witwatersrand gold deposits in the Transvaal. This portentous event, by potentially placing great economic power in the hands of the Afrikaners, theatened to dismantle the carefully woven fabric of British supremacy in South Africa, and in these circumstances the expansionist yearnings of Cecil Rhodes took on a new significance.

Rhodes looked north, to the 'Mashona goldfields' of which Henry Hartley and Carl Mauch had written so extravagantly in the late 1860s.[24] No concerted effort had been made to follow up their discoveries, partly because once Lobengula had been firmly established on the throne by 1870 he represented a formidable obstacle, and partly because of the discovery of the more accessible diamond fields at Kimberley. But the development of the Rand profoundly altered the situation, for it brought political as well as economic motives into play. Rhodes began to argue that continued British supremacy in South Africa could only be guaranteed by the discovery and exploitation of a 'Second Rand' to the north. He added pertinently that if Britain did not act soon others certainly would, notably the Afrikaners from the Transvaal and the Portuguese from Mozambique, and indeed both were active in 'Rhodesia' in the late 1880s. Rhodes had the men and the money. The British Government had neither, tied even in the 'Scramble' era by tight Treasury purse-strings, but it was not prepared to allow Mashonaland to fall into alien hands. Thus Rhodes obtained a Royal Charter for his British South Africa Company, which commenced its administration of Mashonaland on 12 September 1890. There is little ambiguity about the motives of the settlers who were attracted by the Company's venture; as the *Bulawayo Sketch* put it, the 'main reason we are all here is to make money and lose no time about it'.[25]

3. AGRICULTURAL HISTORY

(i) The Shona

A striking feature of many travellers' accounts of East and Central Africa in the nineteenth century is the evident agricultural prosperity of many—though not all—of its peoples and the great variety of produce grown, together with the volume of local, regional, and long-distance trade and the emergence of a wide range of entrepreneurs. An equally striking feature of accounts written in the 1920s and 1930s is the picture of widespread stagnation and decay which emerges, with a greatly reduced number of crops being grown, an almost complete cessation of inter-African trade, and an increasing cycle of rural poverty driving more and more people away to the towns.[26] By 1939 virtually all vestiges of African economic independence have been shattered; African cultivators have become tied to a world market over which they have no control and a pattern of underdevelopment has been firmly established. The Shona provide a classic example of this general pattern.

Though there were naturally great regional variations, the Shona were in general skilled agriculturalists who enjoyed a degree of prosperity which belies the standard (though as we have seen palpably false) picture of a people utterly demoralized by Ndebele raids. However, Shona agriculture was vulnerable to *shangwa* (droughts or disasters) which periodically ravaged the country, and against which there was no assured defence since it was not possible to store surplus grain for more than two to three years. Both their agricultural skill and their vulnerability in the face of a harsh environment, explain the eagerness and rapidity with which the Shona availed themselves of the opportunity to become peasant producers at the end of the nineteenth century.

'In my opinion', wrote the N/C Umtali in 1897, 'the Mashona works his lands better than any other native tribe I know'.[27] Certainly nineteenth-century Shona farmers produced a wide variety of crops. The basic grain staples were finger millet (*Eleusine coracana*), known as *rapoko* or *rukweza*, and bulrush millet (*Pennisetum typhoideum*) known as *mhunga*. Also widely grown were sorghum, known as *mapfunde* or 'kaffir corn' in white Southern African terminology, and maize, *magwere* or *chibagwe*, which became very popular in the twentieth century and was grown especially in the drier areas. In the wetter, eastern districts in particular, rice was grown by the Ndau group of Shona-speakers, though it could also be grown on a small scale in any *vlei*.[28] These staples were supplemented by a variety of fruits, such as pineapples, lemons, and pawpaws; by vegetables like peas, beans, sweet potatoes, and tomatoes; and by cucurbits such as pumpkins, marrows, melons, and cucumbers. In various parts of the country tobacco, cotton, groundnuts, yams, cassava and sugar were also produced. Further variety was provided by game and fish; the Shona were excellent hunters and fishermen. Numerous wild foodstuffs were also collected from the plant and insect life. Livestock (an important insurance against *shangwa*) included cattle, goats, sheep, dogs, and fowl. Other activities included the working of iron for agricultural tools and weapons, pottery, wood carving, and the making of cloth, baskets, nets and mats. Gold had been mined and traded extensively with the east coast in previous centuries notably between the twelfth and fifteenth, and even though the volume of this trade had declined, the washing of alluvial gold continued and copper was also mined in small quantities.[29]

Long-distance trade routes, while used less extensively than in the days of the powerful Shona states, continued to run north-eastwards towards Tete and the other Portuguese settlements on the Zambezi, and many Shona felt aggrieved when British occupation gradually brought an end to the gold trade with that area.[30] There was also a very great deal of local trade, for example in the Melsetter area between the people of the drought-ridden Sabi Valley, who in bad years exchanged salt, dried fish, palm wine, mats, baskets, and cloth for grain and tobacco from the people of the more favoured uplands. Iron tools and pots were bartered throughout the Shona country, and the early Europeans, like modern tourists, were besieged by people offering them a wide range of goods.[31] In short, within the limitations of the prevailing technology, the Shona made intelligent use of their harsh environment though they never entirely mastered it, and consequently were very responsive to the new markets created by the arrival of the Europeans.[32]

Shona agricultural techniques were similar to those of many other Bantu-speaking agriculturalists. They employed a version of what was once rather loosely termed 'shifting cultivation', but which is better described in Allan's phrase 'land rotation cultivation'.[33] A typical Shona family would clear about one acre of virgin land by chopping down small trees leaving the trunks standing at a height of about four feet, and lopping the branches off the larger trees. The land was then tilled with a short-handled hoe, and after the wood had dried out it was burnt and dug into the ground as fertilizer just before the coming of the rains. The crops were planted as soon as the rains began, different crops sometimes being grown together in the same field. Most agricultural operations were carried out communally, with the head of the family offering beer to other members of the village as an incentive to work. The following year another piece of land would be brought under cultivation, until after three or four years an area of about four acres was in use. At this point the land first used was abandoned and allowed to revert to fallow for an average of fifteen years, by which time it had generally recovered its fertility and could be cultivated again. Such a system was clearly only viable while population densities remained low. One result of this system was that most villages (*misha*) moved every six to eight years, as by that time the arable land in the immediate vicinity had been used up. Shona villages were thus mobile and of a temporary nature, while the coming of the Ndebele intensified the existing tendency to site villages on easily defensible *kopjes* overlooking the lands, and since such *kopjes* could not hold many people, Shona settlements tended to be widely dispersed throughout the tribal ward (*dunhu*).[34]

The European settlers deplored this system of land rotation cultivation which they dubbed 'slash and burn', and quite failed to perceive that it was less 'a relic of barbarism' than 'a concession to the nature of the soil'.[35] It was an adaptation to an environment of relatively sparse population and abundant land, which allowed the soil ample time to recover its fertility and also prevented soil erosion. Indeed, the colonial orthodoxy of deep ploughing and the emphasis on rotation rather than fallow, had disastrous effects on soils unsuited to intensive or continuous cultivation and in fact produced yields inferior to those of peasant farmers until after the Second World War, when the agricultural revolution of manufactured fertilizers, herbicides and pesticides, of efficient motorised machinery and new crop strains, finally gave a decisive advantage to large-scale capital-intensive production.[36]

The Rhodesian settlers also denigrated Shona land tenure as

'communal', for they believed, like their Kenyan counterparts, that 'the individual freehold title was the highest form of evolution in land tenure'.[37] 'With the Bantu' [*sic*], wrote an early Rhodesian pioneer, 'removal does not entail the same degree of hardship that we contemplate in the dispossession of land in civilized communities. The natives do not hold the soil in the same sense of ownership. To them the earth is as free as the air and the water, and to be used only in ministration to their immediate wants. The occupancy of any given plot of ground is but temporary.' He went on to add for good measure that the laws of human progress were inexorable: 'By their ceaseless operation the American Indian and the Australian Bushman have in a very short space of time given place to a people who march in the van of the world's enlightenment.'[38] Such assumptions, which are still propounded in official circles in Rhodesia, were obviously highly convenient for European intruders who were busily dispossessing Africans of their land.

There were of course differences between Shona and European concepts of land tenure and the rights and obligations which went with the possession of land, and much subsequent conflict stemmed from these differences. In brief, 'Europeans thought of the grants made to them by Africans as grants of *ownership*: Africans as grants, more or less temporary, of occupational *use*'.[39] But the differences were not as great as the settler source quoted above would imply, and certainly not as great as to justify dispossession on the scale later witnessed in Rhodesia. No one anywhere in the world owns land *absolutely*. The restrictions will vary from place to place; in England, for example, a person might not be able to build a factory on 'his' land; in Rhodesia a European cannot sell 'his' land to an African; while in Shona society no one can dispose of rights to land to a third party, except to the next of kin in the case of senility or death. In terms of obligations, there are various similarities between black and white rural communities in the sense that there is very strong social pressure to be a good neighbour and to offer help and hospitality to those in need. Such obligations were rather stronger in Shona society and extended to acknowledging the authority of the land-giver, the ward headman, which did not apply to Europeans. The main difference was that Europeans tended to hold land as part of a very small community, generally the nuclear family. However sometimes, as in the case of many Afrikaners, land was held by an extended group, while Africans held land as members of a much larger community, the ward (*dunhu*), and beyond that the chiefdom (*nyika*). Nevertheless, the rights of ownership held by such communities were quite as strong and as firmly embedded in law as the 'individual' rights of the Europeans. Shona chiefdoms in fact covered virtually the whole of Rhodesia, and there were very few parts of the country where there was not one clear individual, a ward headman, who was able to give permission to settle. The chiefdoms themselves, often as a result of wars and conflicts over land, were almost always contiguous and defined by 'rivers, minor streams, ridges or imaginary lines between hills and trees'. As Beach points out: 'A chiefdom might not occupy all its land, but it would know its frontiers, and it would be most sensitive to any invasion by strangers.'[40] The Europeans chose to disregard such factors, and they were also guilty of seriously underestimating the security inherent in Shona land tenure, whereby 'because the land and its resources belong to the community, every full member of this community has an inalienable right to a reasonable share according to his requirements'.[41]

(ii) The Ndebele

Cattle undoubtedly played an important role in Ndebele society; by 1890 the herd numbered around a quarter of a million, and it is probable that the Ndebele settled on the Matabeleland *high veld* precisely because it was free of tsetse fly and was ideal cattle country. Yet, as with the supposed 'militarism', the significance of cattle-keeping among the Ndebele has been much exaggerated and it is certainly not true to depict them as pastoralists. They were not beef eaters—cattle were killed mainly on ceremonial occasions—and though milk was readily available, this was not in itself an adequate diet.

Thus the Ndebele, like the Shona, were basically agriculturalists, with much of the labour being performed by the incorporated Shona (*holi*). In a society in which socio-economic differentiation was increasing as a result of contacts with Western capitalism, all the larger villages contained 'a royal field and granary to supply the king with food whenever he visited', while the so-called *holi* 'had to hoe in the king's fields before they were allowed to start on their own'.[42] The missionary T. M. Thomas, who spent the years 1859–70 vainly endeavouring to convert the Ndebele to Christianity, wrote glowingly of 'gardens full of ripe maize, and various indigenous grains', of 'extensive fields of Indian corn and other cereals', and of some valleys 'converted into the most fruitful gardens'. He also mentioned that in some areas cotton was grown, from which the Ndebele made durable garments, and that he knew of no village without its tobacco garden. In addition to this, the Ndebele evolved a system of underground granaries—later raided by the Europeans—which were well disguised, water- and air-tight, in which 'corn is preserved sometimes for many years; and in this way the natives have occasionally stored up food enough to keep themselves active during years of scarcity'.[43] One European looter estimated that each granary could hold some thirty 200 lb bags of grain.[44] In October 1887, the concession-hunter, 'Matabele' Wilson, noted in his Bulawayo diary that 'there is more stuff about the place in the shape of cattle, sheep, goats, eggs, potatoes, rice, groundnuts, sweet potatoes, Indian corn and millet, poultry by the dozen, and milk and beer which the natives bring round to the white men's wagons for sale'.[45]

There is clear evidence too that the Ndebele were not plunderers and economic parasites, but rather were involved in a good deal of regional trade. They provided the main market for the thriving tobacco industry of the Shangwe (Shona-speaking) people of Inyoka, near Gokwe.[46] For instance, they obtained grain from the Ngwato and copper from the Lemba, and also 'had considerable traffic with the Amasili/Masarwa of the edge of the Kalahari, exchanging iron, dagga, spears, hoes, and knives for ostrich-egg-shell beads, ivory and feathers, horns, and skins'.[47] Bhebe observes that 'periodic droughts were among the most powerful forces that drove the Ndebele into trade relations with their neighbors', and at such times cattle, goats, and beads were sold to the Shona in return for grain.[48] In the early days of Ndebele settlement at Bulawayo, cattle were apparently traded out to the Rozvi in return for young people who were promptly incorporated into Ndebele society.[49] Cattle were also sold to white missionaries, traders and, after 1890, to the newly arrived settlers.[50]

Ndebele land tenure was not fundamentally different from that of the Shona. The king was trustee for the whole nation and assigned arable and grazing lands to the various villages. This assignment was then subdivided into family units by the local chiefs and headmen. Thereafter:

> The husband cleared the garden of trees and constructed a strong fence around it to keep out wild animals and cattle. The wife or wives, using a 'six or eight-pound pick,' broke up the soil just before the rainy season. When the sowing time came, the women went over the whole land again, this time sowing the seeds, while the husbands chopped down branches of large trees in the gardens or on their edges 'to prevent birds hiding themselves in harvest time, and clearing the way for the sun and rain to pour down on the sown seed'. Both the males and females joined together to harvest and thresh the crops.[51]

Ndebele villages were moved approximately every ten years, when either the arable land had become exhausted or the accumulation of cattle was too great; the people would then move and in the new villages 'they would build their huts in the relative position they occupied in the old, and the lands would be distributed in the same way. So also the grazing rights.'[52]

(iii) The Europeans

It was not until twenty years after the white occupation of Rhodesia in 1890 that European farming began to offer any serious threat to African cultivators. In part this was because most Europeans were obsessed with the notion of finding a 'Second Rand', and their energies were directed almost exclusively towards mining. But though European farming was slow to develop in Rhodesia, it did inherit a number of characteristics from South Africa since the vast majority of the settlers were either South African born or had spent some time 'down south'. It is therefore worth examining briefly some of the main features of European farming as it grew up in South Africa.

In 1654 the first land grants were made to settlers near Cape Town to encourage vegetable growing, and under the Cape Dutch system of land tenure which subsequently emerged, Europeans were virtually given a free hand to peg out their own farms. A tradition quickly grew up whereby when they managed to defeat Africans in warfare, they were allowed to parcel out the lands of the conquered among themselves. The further north white settlement extended, the larger the European farms became, partly because so much of the land was suitable only for ranching, and a general lack of water necessitated extensive farms if ranching was to be successful. Thus in the Cape interior during the seventeenth and eighteenth centuries

> it became an established custom that a man could possess all the land within half-an-hour's ride, at walking-pace, from his house on the centre of his farm. Thus farms could be spaced out at an hour's ride from one another. The area involved was 3,000 morgen (6,350 acres)[53] per farm... In time the term 'farm' and 3,000 morgen of land became synonymous.

In the Transvaal in the nineteenth century, however, square 4,000 morgen farms were found to be more economical than the circular 3,000 morgen farms of the Cape, though here 'horses were sometimes ridden at speeds greater than walking-pace and farms of up to 6,000 morgen were not uncommon'. Such expansiveness was further enhanced by the very African tradition that 'each member of the family was entitled to a farm and a farm was regarded as the birthright of every man'.[54] Afrikaners believed in having large families.

So the white frontier moved northwards, but eventually the seemingly inexhaustible supply of land began to run out and wars were waged on African societies specifically for land. During the 1880s small Afrikaner 'republics' were carved out of Bechuanaland, Zululand, and Swaziland, while new settlements were founded in South West Africa and Angola. Hence it is not surprising that the European pioneers who entered Mashonaland in 1890 were each promised farms of 1,500 morgen, which they were 'to be allowed to "ride off" ... in the Boer manner',[55] or that the trekkers from the depressed and land-short Orange Free State whom Dunbar Moodie led to Melsetter in 1892–3, were given farms of 3,000 morgen, as were those Europeans who volunteered to invade

Matabeleland in 1893. The 1893 invaders in fact refused to fight for the British South Africa Company until they had been promised land and mineral concessions and a share of the Ndebele cattle.

Before the mineral revolution of the late nineteenth century, 'land was all that South Africa had to offer the prospective colonist',[56] but on that land, to which he had helped himself so liberally, he was as yet by no means the master. Both Bundy and Denoon have clearly shown how, in all four provinces of South Africa, some African cultivators avidly seized the economic opportunities afforded by the expansion of the white frontier and became peasant farmers, producing a wide variety of crops, competing successfully with European farmers, and winning prizes in competition with them at agricultural shows.[57] As Denoon rightly says, until the early twentieth century 'African peasants were more efficient and productive than white farmers'.[58] They were able to be so despite being dispossessed of much of their land. Some simply bought the land back; others farmed as rent-paying squatters on the millions of acres held by absentee landlords and land companies; while others, largely in the Orange Free State and the Eastern Cape, became sharecroppers, surrendering half of their crop in return for seed and the use of the land. In the end it was the mineral revolution, which dramatically increased the demand for African labour and offered substantial incentives to European commercial farmers, combined with 'a sustained, several-pronged offensive... launched by white legislators and administrators... against the self-reliance and independence of the peasantry',[59] which ultimately put an end to African agricultural prosperity in South Africa. Rhodesia was to follow a not dissimilar path.

NOTES

1. L. King, 'The Geomorphology of the Eastern and Southern Districts of Southern Rhodesia', *Transactions and Proceedings of the Geological Society of South Africa*, **54**, 1951, 33. Quoted in B. N. Floyd, *Changing Patterns of African Land Use in Southern Rhodesia* (Lusaka 1961), 28.
2. J. Ford, *The Role of the Trypanosomiases in African Ecology* (Oxford 1971), 283–366.
3. R. Hoare, *Rhodesian Mosaic* (London 1934), 96–7.
4. Floyd, *Changing Patterns*, 43.
5. G. Kay, *Rhodesia: A Human Geography* (London 1970), 16–17.
6. L. Hastings, *Dragons Are Extra* (Harmondsworth 1947), 129. Hoare, who farmed at the same time, agreed that 'within a few minutes a valuable crop of tobacco may be destroyed by wind and hail'. Hoare, *Rhodesian Mosaic*, 92. The agricultural economist Yudelman noted that: 'In common with many other parts of Southern, Central and East Africa, Southern Rhodesia does not have a well-endowed resource base. More than 75 per cent of the country is subject to conditions that make crop production a risky venture.' M. Yudelman, *Africans on the Land* (Cambridge, Mass. 1964), 34.
7. Notably J. G. Thompson, *The Soils of Rhodesia and their Classification* (Salisbury 1965).

8. Floyd, *Changing Patterns*, 37–8.

9. R. H. Palmer, 'Red Soils in Rhodesia', *African Social Research*, **10**, 1970, 747–58. For a dissentient voice, see J. M. Mackenzie, 'Red Soils in Mashonaland: A Re-assessment', *Rhodesian History*, **5**, 1974, 81–8. However, as Beach points out, 'recent arguments about the soil preferences of the Shona are strictly academic, since the Shona rarely had a free choice in the matter'. D. N. Beach, 'The Shona Economy: Branches of Production', in R. H. Palmer and Q. N. Parsons (Eds.). *The Roots of Rural Poverty in Central and Southern Africa* (London 1977), 41.

10. Thus the 1917 Makombe Rising in Mozambique was in fact a Shona rising. T. O. Ranger, *The African Voice in Southern Rhodesia* (Nairobi 1970), 8.

11. D. N. Beach, 'Ndebele Raiders and Shona Power', *Journal of African History*, **15**, 1974, 646.

12. Four outstanding recent theses on Shona history are being rewritten for publication: D. N. Beach, 'The Rising in South-Western Mashonaland, 1896–7', Ph.D. thesis, University of London, 1971; H. H. K. Bhila, 'The Manyika and the Portuguese, 1575–1863', Ph.D. thesis, University of London, 1971; S. I. Mudenge, 'The Rozvi Empire and the *Feira* of Zumbo', Ph.D. thesis, University of London, 1972; J. K. Rennie, 'Christianity, Colonialism and the Origins of Nationalism among the Ndau of Southern Rhodesia, 1890–1935', Ph.D. thesis, Northwestern University, Illinois, 1973.

13. Beach, 'Ndebele Raiders', 642–50; Beach, 'The Rising', 195–6.

14. T. O. Ranger, *Revolt in Southern Rhodesia, 1896–7* (London 1967). Ranger's interpretation has been challenged by J. R. D. Cobbing. 'The Ndebele under the Khumalos, 1820–96', Ph.D. thesis, University of Lancaster, 1976.

15. One should note that religious cults were also frequently utilised in pre-colonial Africa as a means of organizing political resistance against unpopular overlords. See, for example, E. Hopkins, 'The Nyabingi Cult of Southwestern Uganda', in R. I. Rotberg and A. A. Mazrui (Eds.), *Protest and Power in Black Africa* (New York 1970), 258–336.

16. Cobbing, 'The Ndebele'; J. R. D. Cobbing, 'The Evolution of Ndebele Amabutho', *Journal of African History*, **15**, 1974, 608.

17. Beach, 'Ndebele Raiders', 634; N. M. B. Bhebe, 'Some Aspects of Ndebele Relations with the Shona in the Nineteenth Century', *Rhodesian History*, **4**, 1973, 31–8.

18. Beach, 'Ndebele Raiders', 645.

19. D. N. Beach, 'The Shona and Ndebele Power', University of Rhodesia, Department of History, Henderson Seminar No. 26, 1973, 15.

20. For the full details of this episode, see T. O. Ranger, 'The Rewriting of African History during the Scramble: The Matabele Dominance in Mashonaland', *African Social Research*, **4**, 1967, 271–82. Rhodes wrote to one of his associates: 'I saw at once the danger of our position if a series of articles appeared in the papers from a man of Selous' position claiming that Mashonaland was independent of Lobengula... I gave him personally £2,000 out of my own private fund... I consider I did the right thing with Selous.' Ranger, 'The Rewriting', 274–5. Selous then proceeded to write extravagantly about the devastating effects of Ndebele raiding and the depopulation of large tracts of country. F. C. Selous, *Travel and Adventure in South-East Africa* (London 1893), 81, 345.

21. Beach, 'The Rising', 195–6; Beach, 'Ndebele Raiders', 649. For a slightly different view, see J. R. D. Cobbing, 'Lobengula, Jameson and the Occupation of Mashonaland 1890', *Rhodesian History*, **4**, 1973, 39–56.

22. The actual number who set foot in Rhodesia must have been higher than this, for a great many abandoned the country on failing to make their fortune, 372 were killed in the 1896–7 Risings, and a good many others died of malaria etc., in the bush during the early gold rush.

23. The Ndebele headman Somabulana appeared to accept the validity of this when he told Rhodes in the post-Rising *indaba* of 1896: 'You came, you conquered. The strongest takes the land. We accepted your rule. We lived under you. But not as dogs!' V. Stent, *A Personal Record of Some Incidents in the Life of Cecil Rhodes* (Bulawayo 1970), 43.

24. Mauch recorded, 'how the vast extent and beauty of these goldfields are such that at a particular point I stood as it were transfixed, riveted to the place, struck with amazement and wonder at the sight and for a few minutes was unable to use the hammer'. Quoted in L. H. Gann, *A History of Southern Rhodesia* (London 1965), 50. Similarly, in April 1890 the *Pall Mall Gazette* wrote that 'Nature ... has also made it [Rhodesia] one of her rare storehouses of mineral wealth. She has glutted it with gold. The rocks sparkle with gold; gold peeps out from every hillside; in the bed of every stream the sand is clothed with it.' Quoted in J. S. Galbraith, *Crown and Charter* (Berkeley, Los Angeles and London 1974), 265.

25. *Bulawayo Sketch*, 20 July 1895. Quoted in H. A. C. Cairns, *Prelude to Imperialism* (London 1965), 228. For a note on the composition and economic activities of some of the early settlers, see B. A. Kosmin, 'On the Imperial Frontier: The Pioneer Community of Salisbury in November 1897', *Rhodesian History*, **2,** 1971, 25–37.

26. See, for example, J. Iliffe, *Agricultural Change in Modern Tanganyika*, Historical Association of Tanzania Paper No. 10 (Nairobi 1971), 33; W. Rodney, *How Europe Underdeveloped Africa* (London and Dar es Salaam 1972); various chapters in Palmer and Parsons, *The Roots of Rural Poverty.*

27. N 9/1/3, Report of the N/C Umtali for the year ending March 1897.

28. Selous wrote of Chief Mtoko's area in north-eastern Mashonaland: 'His people are wonderfully well supplied with all kinds of vegetable food and in no part of the country have I seen such fine rice as is here grown of very large grain and beautifully white.' Hist. MSS. SE 1/1/1, Selous to Colquhoun, 25 January 1891.

29. I. R. Phimister, 'Alluvial Gold Mining and Trade in Nineteenth-century South Central Africa', *Journal of African History*, **15,** 1974, 445–56; I. R. Phimister, 'Precolonial Gold Mining in Southern Zambezia: A Reassessment', *African Social Research*, **21,** 1976, 1–30. R. Summers, *Ancient Mining in Rhodesia*, National Museums of Rhodesia Memoir No. 3 (Salisbury 1969).

30. Though as late as 1912 some Shona were still managing to take gold to Tete—to the irritation of the settlers. C. van Onselen, *Chibaro: African Mine Labour in Southern Rhodesia, 1900–1933* (London 1976), 12, 262 n. 4.

31. I. R. Phimister, 'Peasant Production and Underdevelopment in Southern Rhodesia, 1890–1914', *African Affairs*, **73,** 291, 1974, 219. This has been revised for inclusion in Palmer and Parsons, *The Roots of Rural Poverty*, 255–67.

32. This account is based on a number of sources, the most important of which are: Beach, 'The Shona Economy'; Rennie, 'Christianity and Nationalism', 46–54; W. Roder, *The Sabi Valley Irrigation Projects*, University of Chicago, Department of Geography, Research Paper No. 99 (Chicago 1965), 42–72; H. Kuper, A. J. B. Hughes and J. van Velsen, *The Shona and Ndebele of Southern Rhodesia* (London 1954), 24–8.

33. Allan's basic objection to 'shifting cultivation' is that it has been applied uncritically to a wide range of methods, varying from semi-permanent to very extensive, and covering a great variety of soils. W. Allan, *The African Husbandman* (Edinburgh and London 1965), 5–6.

34. The ward headman was the ultimate arbiter of all land disputes; he would be called in if two villagers laid claim to the same area and the village headman was unable to resolve the conflict. It was he who allocated land to the village headman, who in turn selected suitable arable land for family heads, who then finally distributed land to individuals within the family. Only accepted members of the ward were allowed to cultivate within its boundaries, and newcomers had to ask the ward headman for permission to settle and cultivate. When land was abandoned by a family, it returned to the ward for subsequent reallocation.

35. W. M. Hailey, *An African Survey, revised 1956* (London 1957), 819.

36. Q. N. Parsons and R. H. Palmer, 'The Roots of Rural Poverty: Historical Background', in Palmer and Parsons, *The Roots of Rural Poverty*, 6–8.

37. M. P. K. Sorrenson, *Origins of European Settlement in Kenya* (Nairobi 1968), 178.

38. W. H. Brown, *On the South African Frontier* (New York 1899), 397.

39. T. R. Batten, *Problems of African Development, Part I: Land and Labour* (London 1954), 26.
40. Beach, 'The Rising', 52–3.
41. Southern Rhodesia, *Report of the Mangwende Reserve Commission of Inquiry* (Salisbury 1961), 35.
42. Kuper, Hughes and van Velsen, *The Shona and Ndebele*, 56. Cobbing's fullest discussion of the Ndebele economy to date occurs in: J. Cobbing, 'Historical Materialism and the Nineteenth Century Ndebele', University of Rhodesia, Salisbury, Political Economy Research Seminar No. 11, 1974.
43. T. M. Thomas, *Eleven Years in Central South Africa* (London 1873), 81, 84–5, 92, 180, 189–90.
44. N. Jones, *Rhodesian Genesis* (Bulawayo 1953), 116–17. Interestingly, in 1912–13 the new Bulawayo railway station was built, 'on the site of the kraal of one of Lobengula's crack regiments and underground storage bins for their grain were found when the foundations were being excavated'. A. H. Croxton, *Railways of Rhodesia* (Newton Abbot 1973), 115.
45. Jones, *Rhodesian Genesis*, 23.
46. B. A. Kosmin, 'The Inyoka Tobacco Industry of the Shangwe People: A Case Study of the Displacement of a Pre-Colonial Economy in Southern Rhodesia, 1898–1938', *African Social Research*, **17**, 1974, 554–77. This has been revised for inclusion in Palmer and Parsons, *The Roots of Rural Poverty*, 268–88.
47. Cobbing, 'Historical Materialism', 8; N. Sutherland-Harris, 'Trade and the Rozwi Mambo', in R. Gray and D. Birmingham (Eds.), *Pre-Colonial African Trade* (London 1970), 253–4.
48. N. M. B. Bhebe, 'Ndebele Trade in the Nineteenth Century', *Journal of African Studies*, **1**, 1974, 89.
49. Beach, 'Ndebele Raiders', 638.
50. P. Stigger, 'Volunteers and the Profit Motive in the Anglo-Ndebele War, 1893', *Rhodesian History*, **2**, 1971, 15–17.
51. Bhebe, 'Ndebele Trade', 88.
52. South Africa, *South African Native Affairs Commission, 1903–5, Vol. V* (Cape Town 1905), Evidence of C. D. Helm, 26 January 1904, 333.
53. One Cape morgen equals 2·11654 acres.
54. A. J. Christopher, 'Land Policy in Southern Africa During the Nineteenth Century', *Zambezia*, **2**, 1, 1971, 3, 4. See also A. J. Christopher, 'Government Land Policies in Southern Africa', in R. G. Ironside (Ed.), *Frontier Settlement* (Edmonton 1974), 208–25; W. K. Hancock, 'Trek', *Economic History Review*, **10**, 1958, 331–9.
55. A 1/2/4, Harris to Colquhoun, 20 September 1890.
56. Christopher, 'Land Policy', 7.
57. C. Bundy, 'The Emergence and Decline of a South African Peasantry', *African Affairs*, **71**, 285, 1972, 372–86; C. Bundy, 'The Transkei Peasantry, c. 1890–1914: "Passing through a Period of Stress"', in Palmer and Parsons, *The Roots of Rural Poverty*, 201–20; D. Denoon, *Southern Africa since 1800* (London 1972), 128–35.
58. Denoon, *Southern Africa*, 61. Dr. E. A. Nobbs, Rhodesia's first Director of Agriculture, 'held the opinion that the native methods of cultivation were frequently of a high order, and enabled a crop to be produced under drought conditions when a large European acreage would have failed'; while two vastly experienced Native Commissioners, J. W. Posselt and W. Edwards, believed that, 'as far as their own crops are concerned, I do not think we can teach the Natives anything. The excellence of their crops around tree stumps is indisputable', and while, 'native methods of agriculture may be primitive in our eyes ... we must remember that they are the results of many generations of experience gained by their forefathers in agriculture, with the implements at their command'. F 35/2(25), Memo by Jennings, 1927; S 138/10, N/C Charter to CNC, 23 September 1925; S 235/503, Report of the N/C Mrewa for the year 1925.
59. Bundy, 'The Emergence', 383.

CHAPTER 2

The Age of the Fortune Hunters 1890–6

Throughout the 1890s Rhodesia was a land of reckless speculation.

Gann and Duignan.[1]

Jameson has given nearly the whole country away.

Company's Administrator, 1896.[2]

1. BACKGROUND

The 'pacification' of Rhodesia in the 1890s was an unusually brutal process, even by the standards prevailing during the 'Scramble'. The peaceful occupation of Mashonaland in 1890 was followed by a series of armed clashes as the Europeans endeavoured to tax and rob the unconquered Shona; the Ndebele state was destroyed in a crude war of aggression in 1893; and finally European rapaciousness did much to provoke the spectacular Ndebele and Shona Risings of 1896–7, one of which was brought to an end by false promises, the other by savage repression. Almost as a by-product of all this activity, one-sixth of the country's 96 million acres was expropriated by the Europeans.

It is sometimes argued, for example by the 'stubbornly ... Eurocentric old-Guard Marxist' Jack Woddis,[3] that the essential reasons behind such wholesale expropriation of land in Africa were 'to prevent the African peasant from becoming a competitor to the European farmer or plantation owner; and to impoverish the African peasantry to such an extent that the majority of adult males would be compelled to work for the Europeans, in the mines or on the farms'.[4] These two motives did become apparent in Rhodesia in later years, but they cannot be used to explain the initial alienation of land in the 1890s. For an explanation of this, we must turn to the commercial and speculative nature of the European occupation, and to the South African traditions of 'war and land' referred to in the previous chapter.

It was inevitable that the whole ethos of British South Africa Company rule should differ markedly from that which characterized Colonial Office administration. For one thing, the Company was in a hurry. It had been founded in 1889, at Rhodes' insistence, expressly for the purpose of exploiting the lands to the north of the Limpopo and so compensating Rhodes and his associates for their failure to strike it rich on the Rand.[5] Rhodes also anticipated that a rich Mashonaland would act as a counterweight to the Transvaal, and so reassert British political supremacy in South Africa. The Company's attentions, therefore, were focused firmly upon the rapid discovery and exploitation of mineral resources; all else, and especially 'native policy', was of secondary consideration. Moreover the Company was able to indulge its impatience by virtue of the resources at its disposal. Its quixotic administrator, Leander Starr Jameson, could call upon 'the expansive energies of the South African economy and the private fortune and personal dreams of Cecil John Rhodes',[6] while the Pioneer Column itself represented 'an exercise of European power quite without parallel anywhere else in East and Central Africa'.[7] Yet the Company's resources were not unlimited, and it was therefore all the more eager to expend them in the hopes of showing a quick return. Finally, while the Colonial Office could draw upon a cadre of trained administrators, the Company had no such supplies available, and Rhodes was therefore obliged to employ 'the sort of men who preferred speculative fortune hunting to a sober administrative career; and he had to allow them to make their fortunes if they could'.[8]

Fortunately for the Company, it was very little embarrassed by Imperial supervision in the years before the Risings of 1896. The British Government's decision to grant Rhodes a charter itself implied a policy of minimal interference. Even had the Colonial Office wished to intervene, there were logistic and political obstacles. Cape Town, where the British High Commissioner for South Africa resided, was more than 1,600 miles from the new settlement of Salisbury, communications were at best erratic, and there was no Imperial official permanently stationed in Rhodesia. Moreover, the High Commissioner, who was theoretically responsible for exercising control over the Company was also Governor of the Cape, and from July 1890 the Prime Minister of the Cape was Cecil John Rhodes. On those few occasions when Loch, the incumbent of this difficult dual position, did urge some form of positive action, the response in Downing Street was generally chilly, for the success of the venture was by no means assured and the Colonial Office had no desire to take any steps which might ultimately lead to increased responsibility. Hence the Company in general, and Jameson in particular, enjoyed in the years 1890–6 a freedom of movement greater than that of any succeeding Rhodesian administration, including the Smith regime.

2. POLICY

(i) The Lippert Land Commission

Gold was the prime motive behind the occupation of Mashonaland, and land was regarded very much as a consolation prize, for, as one of the Company's directors put it in 1891, 'when cattle and gold were in competition for men's attention, nobody thought of cattle'.[9] Thus while each of the 196 pioneers was promised verbally a free farm of 1,500 morgen (3,175 acres) and 15 reef claims of 400 by 150 feet—'for political reasons ... no undertakings on paper could be given'[10]—it was the gold claims which were the more highly prized, and many pioneers sold their land rights for about £100 to speculators like Frank Johnson and Sir John Willoughby while still on the march to Salisbury. Indeed, within a fortnight of the Column being disbanded at the end of September 1890, there were estimated to be nearly 300 prospectors seeking their fortune in the area between Hartley and the Mazoe Valley, and by February 1891 some 7,000 claims had been marked off.[11] The results of this gold rush must have been cruelly disappointing to the participants. Not only did it rapidly become obvious that some mysterious 'ancients' had long since departed with the bulk of Mashonaland's dispersed gold deposits, but the rainy season of 1890–1 was exceptionally severe and protracted and many prospectors, inadequately equipped with clothing, food, and medicine, contracted malaria and died.[12] This was scarcely an auspicious start.

The Company's mineral rights, which ironically were to prove far less valuable than those acquired more casually in Northern Rhodesia, were based on the controversial Rudd Concession of 1888. This was upheld by the British Government, though a missionary witness, C. D. Helm, claimed that the grantees had promised verbally not to bring in more than ten white men to dig for gold.[13] The land rights proved more elusive. In July 1891, High Commissioner Loch attempted to assert some degree of Imperial control by suggesting a land settlement in favour of the Crown in order to protect African interests.[14] The Colonial Office declined the invitation. Wingfield, the assistant under-secretary, observed that such interests were adequately protected under the Company's Charter,[15] and that it was 'difficult to see why the Crown should incur a very risky responsibility in order to further the interests of the adventurers and nobodies who have gone out prospecting in Mashonaland'.[16] A quarter of a century later, when the risks were less great, the Crown entered a successful claim at the Privy Council to the ownership of the unalienated land of Rhodesia (see chapter 6, pp. 133–5).

In the absence of direct Crown intervention, Lobengula attempted to divide and rule. For some years past he had been besieged by concession hunters of one kind and another, including Renny-Tailyour, the emissary of 'one of the most unsavoury financiers in South Africa, Edouard Lippert'.[17] Lobengula decided to grant a land concession to Renny-Tailyour on the assumption, valid at the time, that Rhodes and Lippert were bitter rivals, and under the mistaken impression that Renny-Tailyour was 'a representative of the British agent in Swaziland'.[18] Lobengula clearly hoped to create confusion in the European ranks, from which he might hope to profit. The Lippert Concession was accordingly signed on 22 April 1891.

Rhodes was furious. His first reaction was to have Renny-Tailyour arrested, but more mature consideration produced a subtler approach. The chicanery that followed is perhaps best described in the dry, formal language of the Colonial Office.

> The High Commissioner and the Company were at first disposed to oppose this concession on various grounds; amongst others, on the grounds that its validity or authenticity was doubtful; but after several communications and interviews of the Company's officials with Mr Lippert, it was decided that on the whole it would be better to come to terms with him and take over the concession from him,[19] provided that such a ratification of it were obtained from Lo Bengula as would give an assurance that the concession was genuine and one on which the Company might safely proceed. With this object Mr. Renny-Tailyour, who was well known to Lo Bengula and possessed his confidence, was sent back to his kraal Buluwayo, the British Resident Commissioner, Mr. J. S. Moffat, C.M.G., being instructed to co-operate suitably with him.[20]

Naturally, the British Government did not inform Lobengula of the agreement reached between Rhodes and Lippert, while John Smith Moffat offered his co-operation with extreme reluctance, for he informed Rhodes that the whole plan was 'detestable, whether viewed in the light of policy or morality'.[21] Moffat was subsequently sent back to Bechuanaland on a reduced salary, but the Concession was ratified by Lobengula on 17 November 1891 and duly confirmed by the Colonial Secretary, Lord Knutsford, on 5 March 1892.

The 'defective and fraudulent'[22] Lippert Concession granted:

> The sole and exclusive right, power, and privilege for the full term of 100 ... years to lay out, grant, or lease ... farms, townships, building plots and grazing areas; to impose and levy rents, licences and taxes thereon, and to get in, collect and receive the same for his own benefit; to give and grant Certificates ... for the occupation of any farms, townships, building plots and grazing areas.

Lobengula, of course, had no right in customary law to make such a grant as far as the Ndebele homeland was concerned, for land was not a marketable commodity; still less did he have the right to sign away land over the whole country. But the legal fiction that Lobengula controlled the whole of Rhodesia at least saved the Company the bother of tracking down the Shona chiefs and 'persuading' them to sign farcical treaties like those obtained by Thomson and Sharpe in North-Eastern Rhodesia (now eastern Zambia) in 1890–1.[23]

Though the Lippert Concession was declared 'valueless' as a title deed by the Privy Council in 1918, Rhodes did not think so at the time, for he bought it from Lippert for 30,000 British South Africa Company shares at £1 each, 20,000 United Concessions Company shares at £1 each, and £5,000 in cash; plus land grants of 32,000 acres in Mashonaland and 48,000 acres in Matabeleland—which was still under Lobengula's control![24] A similar occurrence took place in the eastern districts of Rhodesia where land was given out to Europeans before the Gungunyana Concession had received British approval.[25] The end result of the whole exercise was that the Company was now 'legally' entitled to issue titles to the many 'provisional' grants of land which it had already made to the settlers.

(ii) The Seizure of Matabeleland

No coherent 'native policy' was evolved in Mashonaland in the years 1890–3. In part this was a result of a number of Imperial directives informing the Company that 'the natives and chiefs should be left to follow their own laws and customs without interference from the officers of the administration'.[26] Such a policy indeed conformed to Jameson's own inclinations, but it was unrealistic to expect several thousand Europeans to rush around digging for gold and pegging large farms in Mashonaland without making any contacts with the Shona, especially as the demand for labour increased. In fact the settlers frequently took the law into their own hands with disastrous consequences.[27]

In the event, the Mashonaland gold rush proved a failure. In 1892 only 779 oz were produced, showing that 'wherever the "Second Rand" was, it did not lie within Mashonaland'.[28] When independent witnesses such as Randolph Churchill[29] began pointing this out, to the Company's intense displeasure, chartered shares began to fall alarmingly on the London market. Many pioneers trekked disconsolately back to South Africa, the Company's initial capital was nearly exhausted, and there was also the constant threat of confrontation with the Ndebele, who were beginning to realize the full implications of the Company's presence in Mashonaland. In such circumstances, Rhodes turned his acquisitive eye towards Matabeleland, whose mineral resources, he hoped, would be greater than those of Mashonaland, and where the fertile, well-stocked *high veld* was an added inducement.[30] Accordingly, Jameson, 'the instinctive surgeon[who] could operate, with a few swift cuts, not only on people, but on history',[31] seized the opportunity afforded by the Victoria Incident of July 1893[32] to push matters to a head. 'We have the excuse for a row over murdered women and children now', he wired to Harris, the Company's Cape Town secretary, 'and the getting Matabeleland open would give us a tremendous lift in shares and everything else.'[33] Hence, following some border incidents concocted to appease Imperial consciences, the European invasion of Matabeleland began in October. The Company achieved a spectacular military success at a cost of only £66,000,[34] occupying Bulawayo by 4 November, driving Lobengula away to his death, and bringing the powerful Ndebele kingdom to an end.

The Company's victory was important politically and also psychologically, for it left the Europeans with a dangerous belief in their invincibility and a firm conviction that 'the natives' were not a factor meriting serious consideration.

The impact of the Matabele War on future land problems was immense. Even before battle had been joined, the economic future of Matabeleland was largely predetermined by a unilateral act on the part of the settlers. In August 1893 the Europeans in Fort Victoria refused to fight for the Company, though they were under a legal obligation to do so, until they had been granted certain concessions. Jameson had no option but to comply with their demands which were incorporated into the Victoria Agreement. This agreement, which applied both to the 414 men who invaded Matabeleland from Fort Victoria and to the 258 men of the Salisbury column, stipulated that everyone taking up arms was to be entitled to a free farm of 3,000 morgen (6,350 acres) anywhere in Matabeleland, with no obligation to occupy the land. Each man was also granted 15 reef and 5 alluvial gold claims, while the 'loot'—the Ndebele cattle—was to be shared, half going direct to the Company, and the remaining half being divided equally among the officers and men.[35] 'There was in reality nothing novel to South Africans in an agreement of this kind', wrote the Company's official historian.[36] J. M. Orpen, subsequently Surveyor-General, described what happened next, as the men, 'seized the farms wherever they wanted them, and when these were pegged out on top of each other—as they often were—they had to rearrange matters as well as they could. Only after all this had been settled could any provision be made for the Matabele natives.'[37] So the South African frontier traditions reached Bulawayo. The British Government was not informed of the terms of the Victoria Agreement, but it would probably have turned a blind eye in any event.

In the face of such activities in Bulawayo, and of the enormously increased prestige of the victorious Company, the British Government made vain attempts to exercise some control over the post-war settlement. Loch, prompted by Ripon the Colonial Secretary, demanded to take charge of all post-war negotiations, while Ripon himself asserted that the Imperial Government could not acquiesce in the parcelling out of land, and urged that the Ndebele be allowed to settle down peacefully and provided with 'good and habitable land, water, and cattle, adequate to their subsistence', and that an Imperial resident be stationed in Bulawayo to keep an eye on the Company.[38] Such intentions flew in the face of reality and infuriated Rhodes, who pointed out that the Company had won the war and was entitled to dictate the peace. Had the British insisted on taking a firm stand, they would have antagonized virtually the whole of white South African opinion at a time when they were desperately seeking to retain the loyalty of the Afrikaners in the Cape. Not surprisingly, Rhodes had his way.

(iii) The Land Commission of 1894

The extent to which the Company dictated the post-war settlement in Matabeleland is well illustrated by the negotiations over the land question.[39] It was decided to entrust the assignment of land to the Ndebele to a Land Commission, and the discussions therefore centred on its terms of reference. Rhodes successfully demanded, in defiance of Loch's earlier proposals, that the Commission's recommendations should be confined to Matabeleland and that they should be final,[40] as the Company had no intention of providing free land for Africans as their numbers increased. In the eventual agreement, the Matabeleland Order in Council of 18 July 1894, the Commission was instructed to assign without delay, 'to the natives inhabiting Matabeleland land sufficient for their occupation, whether as tribes or portions of tribes, and suitable for their agricultural and pastoral requirements, including in all cases a fair and equitable proportion of springs or permanent water'.[41]

The Land Commission was appointed on 10 September 1894 and, with a haste typical of the period, produced its report by 29 October, assigning two large native reserves, Gwaai and Shangani, estimated to be 3,000 and 3,500 square miles respectively.[42] The Commission comprised three members: Judge J. Vintcent, the chairman, and Capt. H. M. Heyman,[43] who were both chosen by the Company; and Capt. C. F. Lindsell, who was nominated by the Imperial Government.

Joseph Vintcent was the first Chief Justice of Matabeleland, and belonged to a prominent sporting family in South Africa. His father was a member of the Cape Legislative Assembly, and he himself had served as Crown Prosecutor in British Bechuanaland and the Bechuanaland Protectorate since 1886. During the Shona Rising he took charge of the administration of Mashonaland, incurred a good deal of grumbling from the settlers, and was glad to be relieved of the post by Milton at the end of 1896. He continued to serve as Chief Justice until 1901.

Herman Heyman had fought in every 'down country' war against Africans since the Gaika and Galeka campaigns of 1877–8. He was a member of the police force which escorted the Pioneer Column into Mashonaland in 1890, and was the hero of the 1891 'battle' against the Portuguese at Macequece (now Vila de Manica). He became a resident magistrate at Umtali and then served as second-in-command of the column which invaded Matabeleland from Fort Victoria in 1893. After the war he was a highly unpopular magistrate in Bulawayo, who 'managed somehow to anger and insult every one of the chiefs', and whose response to a request for food from a Ndebele headman and his people who had been waiting all day to see him, was that 'the town was full of stray dogs; dog to dog; we might kill those and eat them if we could catch them'.[44] Heyman was also chairman of the 1894 Loot Committee, which endeavoured to control the parcelling out of Lobengula's cattle. He was sacked by Rhodes in 1896, following Ndebele complaints at his behaviour,[45] and was then despatched to Johannesburg just before the Jameson Raid in a vain attempt to persuade the *uitlanders* to start their promised revolt. He became managing director of Willoughby's Consolidated, which owned over a million acres in Rhodesia much of it in Matabeleland where the Land Commission was endeavouring to look for land for the Ndebele. He sold his own 'conquest farm' near Bulawayo early in 1894 however.[46] He became a Member of the Legislative Council (1903–8, 1911–20) and obtained a knighthood in 1920—the reasons for which I have not been able to ascertain.

Charles Lindsell, the Imperial nominee, was compulsorily retired from the British Army in 1892 after a 'mundane military career'. He served as 'acting unpaid transport officer' in the Bechuanaland Border Police during the Matabele War, became a temporary magistrate in the Tati District, and was appointed to the Land Commission because he happened to be available and was about to become unemployed once more.[47] He later participated in the Jameson Raid and was one of thirteen officers sent back to England with Jameson to stand trial. He was soon discharged, but the Imperial authorities declined to offer him another appointment after receiving highly adverse reports of the Gwaai and Shangani Reserves. He returned to Rhodesia, where he lived in Umtali until 1928, the year before his death.[48]

The Land Commission's Report reflects quite clearly the extremely casual manner in which African interests were regarded by the Company at this time; even the Company's own historian described the enquiry as 'somewhat perfunctory'.[49] The commissioners were unable, for example, to hazard a guess as to the African population of Matabeleland, which must have made the provision of 'sufficient' land to them somewhat a matter of conjecture. They further decided to make no provision for those Ndebele, the great majority, who found themselves living on what had become European farms, on the grounds that they appeared 'contented, and have expressed no desire to remove elsewhere'. The commissioners then turned away from the *high veld*, 'after learning that the British South Africa Company has made numerous grants of land to Europeans in portions of the country where the natives formerly resided, and are in many cases still residing'. They therefore looked north-west to the Kalahari soils where 'no grants of land have been made'.[50] Vintcent and Lindsell were able to inspect only a small portion of the Shangani Reserve—Heyman was away getting married—while lack of time and adverse weather conditions were adduced as reasons for failing to carry out any examination of Gwaai.[51] In these circumstances, they were heavily reliant on the tainted evidence of the Native Commissioner, J. W. Colenbrander.[52] and of various Ndebele headman. It is worth noting that much of the Ndebele evidence, which apparently indicated that the Gwaai and Shangani Reserves were of good quality, was in fact so vague that it is impossible to determine whether they were actually referring to land situated within the Reserves.

The commissioners believed that the Shangani Reserve could carry a population of at least 30,000; in 1915 its actual population was under 8,000, while its boundaries, as defined by the Commission, were 'upon closer observation, found to be impossible' and were amended in 1899.[53] The Gwaai Reserve, the commissioners wrote, was 'well watered and fertile, and is regarded as being the best grazing veldt in Matabeleland, and has been, and is still being, occupied by natives'.[54] Strange indeed that not one intrepid European pioneer was interested in the best grazing veld in Matabeleland! In 1913 its population was about 2,500 and the local Native Commissioner estimated that 'about four-fifths of the Reserve is useless for native settlers at present'.[55] (See map 2.)

Finally, the Commission made a number of minor recommendations: that the distribution of cattle to the Ndebele be left in abeyance, presumably until Heyman's Loot Committee had completed its work; that a reserve of 12,000 acres be established on the Bembesi river for the wives of Lobengula, provided they exercised their right of occupation; and that the ownership of the land be vested in the Company, a matter quite outside their terms of reference.[56]

Imperial scrutiny of the Land Commission's Report cannot be described as searching.[57] Loch opined that the Ndebele had occupied an area of some 10,000 square miles before the European occupation, and that as the 'slaves' had returned north, the 6,500 square miles assigned by the Commission should suffice if the land was suitable; the commissioners, having acquired local knowledge, asserted that this was so.[58] Loch did not think to question the extent of local knowledge which had been acquired. At the Colonial Office, Graham

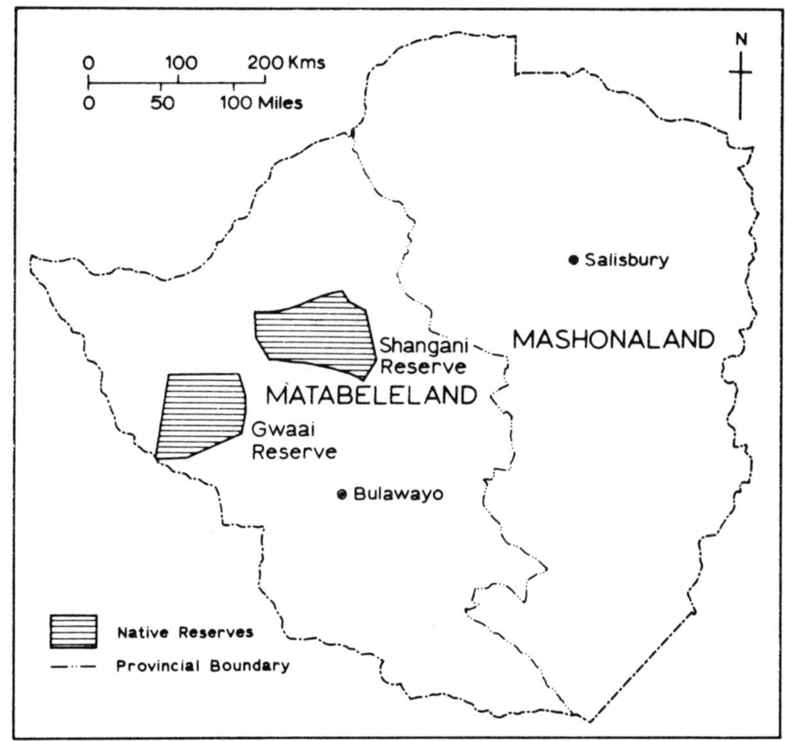

Map 2—Native Reserves, 1894 (*from Christopher 1971*).

believed that the Reserves seemed sufficient and suitable, though it appeared curious at first sight that Shangani lay entirely within the tsetse fly area, as defined by Selous in 1880. Ripon felt it worth asking for information on the point but, fortunately for the Company, Fairfield was able to report reassuringly that Jameson, no less, had stated that it would be incorrect to describe Shangani as lying wholly within the fly-belt—a party of police had recently visited the area and found no fly, and in any event the belt was constantly shifting.[59] Armed with this reassurance, Ripon was able to approve the Report formally on 25 January 1895, declaring that the commissioners 'appear to have given their best attention to the questions and arrived at well-considered conclusions'.[60] Two years later, in the wake of the Jameson Raid and the Risings, the Colonial Office was forced to concede that 'the proceedings of the Land Commission were a farce', and that 'the Imperial Government must accept their share of whatever blame attaches to the settlement, as they were represented on the Commission',[61] while Jameson's successor, Earl Grey, admitted that the Ndebele regarded the two reserves as '*cemeteries* not Homes'.[62]

Fortunately, the 1894 land settlement in Matabeleland did not survive for long. By the end of 1895 the 'Second Rand' was no more apparent in Matabeleland than it had been in Mashonaland. Thus Jameson, 'a born gambler' to whom life 'was like a game of whist',[63] determined to invade the Transvaal in an attempt to overthrow the Kruger Government and so reassert British supremacy.[64] The Raid was a complete fiasco, and it led Jameson to Pretoria Jail,[65] Wormwood Scrubs and Holloway, while it afforded the ill-treated Ndebele and Shona the opportunity to rise in armed revolt against the Company, an opportunity which they duly took in March and June 1896.

3 ACTUALITY

(i) The Scramble for Land

The land grabbing, which so typified Rhodesia during the pioneer era, was, for a few brief months in 1890, held in check. This was largely the work of the first Administrator, Archibald Colquhoun,[66] recently Deputy Commissioner for Upper Burma, a civil servant with a love of ordered administration who was very much out of place in Rhodesia,[67] and who subsequently admitted having felt 'an utter distaste for the atmosphere of mining speculation and company promoting which pervaded the country'.[68]

Colquhoun endeavoured to exercise strict control over the settlers. He refused to allow prospectors to cross the Umsweswe river, which cuts the present Salisbury–Bulawayo road roughly half-way between Hartley and Que Que. His successor, Jameson, soon pushed this 'border' further southwards.[69] Colquhoun also endeavoured to control the land settlement. Recognizing that the Company had no legal right to grant land titles, he sent a small party of surveyors to demarcate an area, approximately 25 miles by 30, between the Umfuli, Hunyani, Ruzawi, and Sabi rivers, within which the pioneers would be permitted to occupy land 'pending permission from Lo Bengulo or [Shona] independent chiefs to allot farms'.[70] Colquhoun was anxious not to provoke conflict with the Shona, and when he discovered that part of this land was in fact densely populated—it belonged to the people of Seke, Chihota, and Mudzimwema[71]—he suggested that it be exchanged for an alternative site, possibly in the vicinity of Mount Hampden, near Salisbury.[72] Such attention to detail not surprisingly earned Colquhoun the displeasure of the settlers and indeed of Rhodes himself, who by the end of 1890 had in effect promoted the swashbuckling Jameson over Colquhoun's head.

Jameson was, in the words of a subsequent Rhodesian chief justice, 'admirably fitted for the period in which rough justice was appropriate',[73] and rough justice was what he proceeded to dispense. He did not share Colquhoun's regard for Shona land rights, and after being told by numerous disgruntled pioneers that the land chosen by Colquhoun was heavily timbered and unsuitable for farming, he allowed them the right to peg their farms where they pleased, though they were told that 'no land was to be taken which was used by the natives for their villages and gardens'.[74] In practice this proviso, based more on a desire to avoid unnecessary trouble than a genuine regard for African interests, was frequently ignored, though there is one recorded case of it being effective.[75]

Having won the right to peg their farms anywhere except on the Gold Belt, which until 1903 was reserved for miners,[76] the settlers proceeded to fight for the right not to occupy them. When those who had gone off in search of gold returned to Salisbury in 1891, they found that a good deal of land had been beaconed off near Salisbury and out towards Mazoe and Umtali. Some of them formed a 'vigilance committee' under Lionel Cripps, later a Member of the Legislative Council (1914–23) and Speaker of the Legislative Assembly (1924–35). The committee interviewed Rhodes on 18 October, and informed him that the terms under which they had been recruited had not stipulated occupation, that they had gold claims to work, and that it was impossible for them to live off the land under existing conditions. Rhodes accepted Cripps' case, though he insisted on a nominal annual quit-rent of £1 per 1,500 morgen (3,175 acres).[77] Thus began a long tradition of absentee landlordism.

Also in 1891, Rutherfoord Harris, the Company's Cape Town secretary, reversed an earlier ruling that no farms could be pegged within six miles of Salisbury and proclaimed that the limit was now three miles with the land immediately surrounding the town reserved for a commonage. 'The country was therefore pegged into farms for miles, where three months earlier all had been unpossessed', noted W. H. Brown, an American member of the Pioneer Column.[78] All this activity took place before the Company had acquired the Lippert Concession. As Marshall Hole, the Company's historian, and himself a pioneer, put it, 'this deficiency was tacitly ignored'.[79]

Prominent among the early land-grabbers were quasi-aristocrats, speculative companies, fortune-hunters and missionaries. In 1896 William Milton, who arrived to salvage something from the wreck, stressed the need to 'clear out the Honourable and military elements which are rampant everywhere', and noted sadly that 'Jameson has given nearly the whole country away to the Willoughby's Whites and others of that class so that there is absolutely no land left which is of any value at all for settlement of Immigrants by Government'.[80]

Among the military elements was Major Sir John Willoughby, who had been seconded from the Royal Horse Guards to act as chief staff officer to the Pioneer Column. Though 'without any outstanding brain capacity', Willoughby had 'one eye always open for a chance of profit'.[81] He bought up a large number of land rights from gold-obsessed pioneers, was granted some 600,000 acres in Mashonaland by Jameson on the understanding that he spent £50,000 on developing the land,[82] and finally accumulated 1·3 million acres for his own Willoughby's Consolidated Company. He was also a director of seven other companies, and was allocated 8,850 head of Ndebele cattle by the Loot Committee.[83] Willoughby played a prominent role in the Jameson Raid, joined the doctor in his tour of South African and British prisons, and was compulsorily retired from the army.

Jameson also induced a number of quasi-aristocrats, such as the Honourable Henry and Robert White, sons of Lord Annaly, to come to Rhodesia and advertise the country to their well-connected friends by offering them lavish grants of land and a share in the looted Ndebele cattle.[84] It was hoped that such people would bring 'development', but in fact they rarely did so—though the Whites eagerly participated in the Jameson Raid and met the same fate as Willoughby.

Many of these 'Honourable and military elements' decided to float speculative companies in the hope of persuading others to invest money. By 1896 the total nominal capital of such companies was about £20 million.[85] W. H. Brown estimated that by the end of 1891 over half the pioneer land rights were in the hands of such syndicates,[86] and some idea of the extent of vested interests which they established can be gauged from the fact that of an estimated 15·8 million acres which had been alienated to Europeans by March 1899, some 9·3 million acres were in the hands of companies.[87] Phimister suggests that this massive speculation in land was a direct reflection of the companies' lack of confidence in the country's mineral resources,[88] while Galbraith notes that: 'This emphasis on speculation rather than production contributed to maladministration and near financial ruin for the company.'[89]

In addition to attempting to promote development through the well-connected, the Company was also obliged to employ a band of fortune-hunters to administer Rhodesia. The most notorious of these was Dunbar Moodie, who became in effect the feudal lord of the Melsetter District. Moodie 'simply laughed' at a missionary's complaint that he should not alienate land occupied by Africans; he carved out for himself a huge estate of over 60,000 acres together with an enormous herd of cattle, and, in the words of his successor, appeared 'entirely to have studied his own interests at the expense of those of the country', and to have 'considerably abused' his power by demanding bribes.[90]

The missionaries also helped themselves liberally. By the turn of the century they had acquired almost a third of a million acres, with the Catholics taking nearly half this amount. From Rhodes' point of view, it clearly made good sense to allow the various denominations to acquire such large vested interests, though in subsequent years the ambivalent position of African tenants on these 'mission lands' caused tensions with the Government as a result of their tendency to become surrogate native reserves.

The missionaries were naturally quick to deny that they were land-grabbing. Knight-Bruce, the Anglican Bishop of Mashonaland, argued that the mission lands were intended as native reserves in case Africans were ever squeezed off their lands. He admitted, however, that nearly all 'his' farms were adjacent to African villages,[91] and indeed both Jameson and Duncan, the Surveyor-General, who had been 'awarded' 640,000 acres on taking up his post,[92] encouraged the missionaries to include African villages on their farms.[93] Douglas Pelly, acting on behalf of Knight-Bruce, was exhausted by the whole process. 'The one thing I strongly object to', he wrote to his parents, 'is to go looking for more *farms*, which I hear from Upcher is the Bishop's great idea. He already has more than 40!! all over 3,000 acres! and not one of them is being worked, either as farm or station as far as I can discover.'[94] On one occasion Isaac Shimmin reported from Lomagundi District that: 'With a sublime disregard of correct measurement, which must be attributed to our early Methodist training, we marked out a farm four or five times the usual size (and afterwards got it granted from the Company).'[95]

In fairness however, one should add that missionaries with some South African experience, such as Knight-Bruce, were conscious of the possible need to protect Africans from European farmers in the future, and to provide themselves with a more captive audience than could be obtained on a white farm or in a government-controlled native reserve. As the Methodist John White wrote in 1911

> It is my experience that on the farms that we own we secure an influence over the people we cannot get on the Reserves. Among these people one of our greatest obstacles to the Gospel is drinking; on the farms we can practically prohibit its manufacture. They contribute much more generously to the work when living on Mission lands.[96]

This carefree alienation of land to all and sundry in Mashonaland[97] caused concern to the Company's London Office, which, in the light of the 'fragmentary' and 'contradictory' reports it was receiving of the scramble for land, decided in December 1892 that all future applications should be forwarded to Jameson as it had no idea how much land remained unalienated. It even gently suggested to Jameson that future grants might contain an occupation clause of one man per 3,175 acre farm. The advice was disregarded, though in April the following year Rhodes himself decided that free grants of land should cease since 'they will close up the country', and that henceforth the Company should endeavour to obtain 9d. per acre in Mashonaland and 'occupation by individual farmers.'[98] Land was a very cheap commodity during the Jamesonian era.

The seizure of land was even more ruthless in Matabeleland following the war of 1893. Here the invading Europeans were granted farms of 6,350 acres, double the size of the Mashonaland farms, and the *high veld* on which the Ndebele lived was precisely the area coveted by the invaders. 'Within a few months of the European occupation', observed a senior Native Department official, 'practically the whole of their most valued region ceased to be their patrimony and passed into the private estates of individuals and the commercial property of companies. The whole of what their term *nga pakati kwe lizwe* (the midst of the land) conveyed became metamorphosed, although they did not early realize it, into alien soil, and passed out of the direct control even of the Government.'[99] The conquerors wasted no time, 'before many weeks had passed the country for sixty miles and more around Bulawayo was located as farms',[100] and by January 1894 over 900 farm rights had been issued and over half of them pegged out.[101] Far from excluding African villages from European farms, the lands of the Ndebele were expropriated virtually *in toto.* H. J. Taylor, who as Chief Native Commissioner for Matabeleland was subsequently confronted with many of the problems bequeathed by these activities, remarked later with monumental understatement that 'the policy of the Government in throwing Matabeleland open without first having studied the native side of the question as affecting their tribal lands did create difficulties'.[102]

(ii) The Effects of the Scramble

The immediate effects of the loss of these 15·8 million acres were much less than might at first be imagined. There are two basic reasons for this. In the first place the African population was very small, and second, very few Europeans actually occupied and worked the farms which they had acquired on paper.

When the Europeans came to Rhodesia in the 1890s, they were immediately struck by the vast amount of seemingly empty land. J. T. Bent, who claimed that the Phoenicians had built Zimbabwe, wrote of 'tens of thousands of acres of fertile land entirely unoccupied' in Mashonaland;[103] John Smith Moffat, the missionary who had been so critical of the Lippert Concession, believed 'there is ample room for myriads of white people in this country without displacing a single native';[104] while Bishop Knight-Bruce observed that 'the Mashona only occupy a small part of the country, and land which they have never occupied may with justice be said not to belong to them'.[105] The examples could be multiplied. How accurate were such assessments?

The Company's first official estimate of the African population, in March 1902, was 514,813. This figure is certainly too low, and an intelligent guess of the population in 1890 would be about 750,000. There are some 150,000 square miles in Rhodesia, which means that at that time the population density was around 5 per square mile. Robinson has estimated that

> The system of shifting agriculture has an approximate carrying capacity of 20 persons per square mile of country, of which 25 per cent can be cultivated, five per cent is waste land and the remainder grazing land. It is permanent when there is no pressure of population greater than 20 persons per square mile.[106]

My own calculations would suggest that Robinson's estimate is perhaps a somewhat generous one,[107] but in any event it would seem that on average, the people had more than enough land to meet their requirements and hence the European descriptions of 'vacant lands' had some validity. But one needs to remember that Shona–Ndebele and inter-Shona warfare in the nineteenth century had the effect of compressing settlement patterns and forcing many people to seek safe strongholds, thus resulting in relatively dense populations in some areas and the reverse in others. This no doubt explains why so many of Beach's Shona informants frequently refer to 'land pressure' as an explanation for migration in the nineteenth century and before.[108]

Yet if a great deal of land was physically unoccupied, hardly any at all was unclaimed, for Shona chiefdoms covered the greater part of the country and their boundaries were normally well defined and contiguous. These 'vacant lands' were therefore deceptive, and dangerous errors were made by early colonial administrators in the Kikuyu country of Kenya and in the Shire Highlands of Nyasaland, when they failed to take account of tribal claims to the land – easily ascertainable from the people—and the full implications of land rotation.

Into this sparsely populated country poured the Rhodesian fortune-hunters. They were abundantly rewarded with land, as we have seen, and by March 1899 an estimated 7·3 million acres had been alienated in Mashonaland, principally around the main centres of Salisbury, Umtali, and Fort Victoria, and along the main roads linking them, and at Enkeldoorn and Melsetter, which attracted Afrikaners from the Transvaal and the Orange Free State. In Matabeleland, 8·5 million acres were alienated, principally on the *high veld* around Bulawayo. At first land had been despised in favour of gold—160,000 mining claims were registered by 1898[109]—but as the absence of a 'Second Rand' became more apparent year by year, so more attention was paid to the land claims. Even so, land was regarded as a speculative asset, whose value would increase as the country gradually settled down rather than something of immediate value.[110] Hence very little active farming was undertaken.

There were at this stage numerous obstacles to the development of European commercial farming: the lack of capital, equipment, and a regular supply of labour, the rinderpest and later the east coast fever, which decimated the cattle, and the locusts and drought which preceded the Risings. Moreover, with no mining boom and no railway until the turn of the century, and consequently with a highly limited internal and a non-existent external market, the early European farmers were 'subsistence cultivators indistinguishable (by style of life, techniques of production, and crops cultivated) from the African peasantry'.[111] This is nicely illustrated in a report of the Civil Commissioner, Bulawayo, for March 1895, in which he says that only 'about 150' of the 1,070 white farms in his area were occupied and that the white farmers were cultivating only 'about 900 acres', or six acres per farm.[112] As one white settler wrote of the 1890s: 'In those days ... no farmers grew grain, it being cheaper to trade the country's requirements from the natives.'[113] Early European agriculture was thus little more than market gardening for Salisbury and Bulawayo and the small mining centres. Most 'farmers' were primarily transport riders,[114] storekeepers or traders, who bought—and sometimes stole—food from their African neighbours, while even 'the most elaborate farm consisted of little more than a collection of thatched huts and up to ten ploughed acres of land'.[115] Moreover, not only were the early settlers

> completely ignorant of local conditions and potential for agriculture—but few of [them] had much agricultural background and experience in a practical sense. Even the Dutch Boer trekkers were to experience new hazards and many of them were content to live a semi-subsistence existence rather than actually develop their farms.[116]

Thus in the Fort Victoria District, which was one of the more important European centres in Mashonaland, of a total of 70 registered farms in 1897, '20 are now more or less occupied being used by traders for grazing purposes and on a few of these 5 or 6 acres of land have been ploughed up', while 'the land owned by Companies is not occupied at all'.[117] In Hartley, '21 farms were pegged between 1891 and 1896, but only three appear to have been worked ... and only one had more than a single occupant at any one time'.[118] Similarly in the Umtali District, where some 224 farms had been alienated by 1895, the local newspaper complained that 'there are but two ... holders of land in this rich district who are actually doing beneficial work on their farms'.[119] At Mazoe, subsequently an important European farming centre, 'there was little occupation' and the voters' list of 1899 revealed a total of 13 Europeans, none of whom identified himself as a farmer.[120] Around Enkeldoorn, a few Afrikaners from the Transvaal 'had some lands planted before the rising, but many other[s] were content to grow just enough to keep themselves for the near future, and some ... left their farms and took up transport-riding'.[121]

The most extensive alienation in Mashonaland took place in the Melsetter District where, following the evacuation of the Gaza leader Gungunyana in 1889, the Company was anxious to occupy the land before 'the natives ... come in and fill it up again'.[122] Thus, following the Moodie Trek of 1892–3, and under the watchful eye of Dunbar Moodie, Europeans 'were allowed to peg off farms [of 6,350 acres] whenever they chose, and apparently without respect to the rights of the Natives. In fact, the very spots on which the [Ndau] Natives were most thickly situated, were, to a great extent, selected as farms.'[123] Melsetter was clearly one district where the Shona did feel land pressures at a very early date, for the rapacious Dunbar Moodie was nicknamed *Dabuyazizwe*, the one who divides the land, and such was his brutality that a report of 1895 revealed that 'the natives are running away from G. B. D. Moodie's farms as fast as they can'.[124] It is thus interesting to note that in 1895/6 the local Native Commissioner, T. B. Hulley, responded to this situation by proposing, on his own initiative, the creation of a native reserve to protect Africans in the likely event of their being evicted from European farms in the future, and perhaps also with an eye to avoiding a possible African uprising.[125]

Melsetter was very much the exception however, for elsewhere in Mashonaland the vast estates granted to speculative companies inevitably meant thst such land would neither be closely occupied[126]—'many of the land owners in this country ... do not know the location of their land'[127]—nor greatly developed, and they at least prevented other Europeans from acquiring the land. In addition, many settlers owned a number of farms, and obviously could not hope to occupy them all. Company officials, well rewarded with land, rarely found the time to use it. Afrikaners at Enkeldoorn bought family blocks of farms, but the families tended to live together and even they 'who intended to live on their farms and were not speculators, did relatively little farming work prior to 1896'.[128] Europeans who did take up farms tended to choose the heavy red soils which the Shona were inclined to neglect in favour of the lighter, more easily manageable, sandy soils.[129] Shona settlement was more widely dispersed than that of the Ndebele, which worked to their advantage, as did the fact that after the Matabele War of 1893, 'Mashonaland settled down to a period of utter stagnation, for all interest was concentrated on the new province. The bulk of our fellow-settlers', Marshall Hole recalled, 'had gone with Jameson to the front and, as they were well rewarded with farms and gold claims, they had every temptation to remain in Matabeleland.'[130]

The Ndebele were naturally more immediately conscious of the land problem for, unlike the Shona, it was precisely the land on which they were living with its fertile red and black soils, which was coveted by the Europeans. But though the white invaders fell over each other pegging out their farms, and though the Ndebele were no doubt aware of their future intentions,[131] many of the features which were apparent in Mashonaland applied equally to Matabeleland. Absentee landlordism was the rule rather than the exception, since it was gold, rather than land, which had brought the Europeans to Bulawayo, and thus only about 150 out of over 1,000 farms were being worked—at a subsistence level. Again vast areas were locked up in the hands of companies, as many Europeans quickly sold their farm rights for between £10 and £60, a sure indication of a loss of confidence in Rhodesia, since the Mashonaland claims for only half the acreage had fetched an average price of £100 in 1890. Thus over half the Umzingwane District, near Bulawayo, passed into the clutches of Willoughby's Consolidated. Moreover, no attempt was ever made to force the Ndebele into the distant Gwaai and Shangani Reserves, as they were far too highly prized as a potential pool of labour.[132]

Hence, though the Ndebele had in fact lost their land, they were not as yet fully conscious of this, for in the European view:

> The position in 1895 was that practically the whole of the Matabele tribe continued to cultivate and occupy land previously allotted to them by their chiefs, but they had no legal rights to this land, it was entirely at the will of the landowner that they remained there. Farming at this time was in its infancy. The landowner had a vague idea that the Matabele were living on his land, he took no interest in the matter, and did not trouble to ascertain particulars regarding them.[133]

Such indifference proved costly when the Ndebele rose in revolt the following year and a high proportion of Europeans in the outlying districts were killed.

In conclusion, therefore, whilst the future tenure of the Shona and particularly the Ndebele was greatly prejudiced by the alienation of so much land, their immediate tenure, except for a few isolated cases such as Melsetter, was very largely undisturbed. It is therefore not correct to argue, as I once did, that the Risings of 1896 should be seen 'essentially as a struggle for lost land'.[134]

(iii) Other Pressures

There were a number of much more potent pressures than loss of land, notably forced labour and taxation. The Ndebele, after the War of 1893, were treated as a conquered people. Perhaps as much as 80 per cent of their cattle was first looted by Company, Shona and South African freebooters, and then decimated by rinderpest;[135] forced labour was widespread and much resented, while the African police, deliberately recruited from the crack regiments of Lobengula's former army, acted with great brutality and paid off a number of old scores.[136]

Forced labour was common in both provinces. The N/C Hartley observed in 1895, 'I am at present forcing the natives of this district to work sorely against their will, using such methods as I think desirable'; while an early pioneer wrote home in 1892, 'we have great trouble in getting native labour up here, the only way we can do it is to go and catch them at dawn and compel them to work'.[137] Conditions of work were generally appalling. Not only was there frequent recourse to the *sjambok* or *chikoti*, the hide whip, both by employers and the young inexperienced Native Commissioners (the N/C Mazoe 'had a reputation for flogging indiscriminately'[138]) but there were also numerous fatalities in the small primitive mines, and many employers were not above picking quarrels with their workers towards the end of the month with the predictable, and intended, result that workers fled their employment unpaid.[139] Severe punishments were also handed out to recalcitrants; one headman who failed to deliver the required quota of labourers was given fifty lashes, fined six goats and three head of cattle, and had his rifle confiscated.[140] Labour thus became scarcer and people took to fleeing at the approach of the police, which in turn provoked even greater brutality.

The imposition of a hut tax on the undefeated Shona was bitterly resented. The idea of a tax was first suggested by Rhodes in 1892, but was turned down by Jameson on the less than philanthropic grounds that he did not have an administration capable of collecting it.[141] The matter was raised again the following year, the Company gently suggesting that taxation would 'to a certain extent furnish an incentive to labour which might otherwise be wanting'.[142] Her Majesty's Government demurred, pointing out with unusual percipience that 'the natives are probably in law and equity the real owners of the land they occupy', that the proposed tax amounted to a 'charge ... for the occupation of their own lands',[143] and that it would arouse 'great antagonism on the part of the natives or of Lobengula or of both'.[144] And indeed it would, since Lobengula continued to regard many of the Shona as his vassals, while the Shona themselves had neither ceded, nor been asked to cede, any authority to the Company. The dispute was not pushed to a conclusion, for the war intervened and this radically altered the whole situation since the Company then regarded itself as master of Rhodesia by right of conquest.

Though in fact 'nothing had happened to make the Shona feel any more subject to the whites',[145] the Company began collecting a 10/– hut tax in Mashonaland in 1894 six months before it was legally entitled to do so. In Matabeleland, tax was in effect collected by confiscating the greater part of the Ndebele cattle. Collection of the tax proved so difficult that towards the end of the year it was decided to set up a Native Department specifically for the purpose, a scarcely auspicious beginning to Rhodesian 'native policies'.[146] The tax, 'more like the levy of a tribute than the collection of a civil tax',[147] was collected in cash, or in grain, cattle, or even alluvial gold,[148] or in labour, usually of two months' duration. An attempt was made to 'encourage' payment in cash through the simple expedient of pricing cattle and grain below their market value,[149] and refusing to give credit for the following year when more than ten shillings' worth of goods were handed in.[150] By 1895 the Native Department was managing to collect about £5,000, and in some districts as much as one-third of the Shona cattle, sheep, and goats were rounded up, often by force.[151] This represented a substantial attack upon the material wealth of the Shona. The Native Commissioners were unwisely allowed great latitude, and were given no definite instructions on how to go about collecting the tax. Inevitably highly arbitrary methods were employed, and they and their African helpers roamed the country like Ndebele raiders, while some pocketed the tax for themselves. Such actions provoked sporadic resistance from the Shona, resistance which the Native Commissioners were at pains to conceal from Jameson. In all the circumstances, it is scarcely surprising that the Africans of Rhodesia broke out into armed revolt in 1896.

4 CONCLUSION

'The blacks have been scandalously used', wrote Sir Alfred (later Lord) Milner,[152] himself a high imperialist and firm advocate of forced labour.[153] Few would now quibble with this judgement, and the Risings of 1896 should be seen as the desperate response of men who had been greatly abused and had come to realize that the Rhodesian settlers, unlike earlier Europeans, had come to stay. I have argued, however, that the loss of land was not a major African grievance at this time. Evidence to support this conclusion lies in the fact that no direct correlation can be drawn between the extent of land alienated and the outbreak of resistance in 1896, since some people who had suffered great loss of land did not join the Rising, while others who had lost no land came out in revolt.[154] In Melsetter there was no rising, partly because the Gaza evacuation left no clear political authority in the region and partly because it escaped the rinderpest; in Fort Victoria, Chiefs Zimuto and Chikwanda, whose lands had been alienated, did not rise; while at Enkeldoorn, Chief Chirumanzu, who had lost land, stayed out, and Chief Mutekedza, who had not, became a leading 'rebel'. Indeed, the crucial decision of whether or not to join the Rising appears often to have been taken more as a result of internal

Shona politics than in direct response to the severity of European pressures.[155]

Finally, although the immediate effects of land alienation may not have been severe, and although the original settler motives for grabbing land stemmed more from uncertainty about the extent of Rhodesia's gold deposits than a conscious desire to dominate and exploit, the long-term effects were to prove very great. Vested interests were established which proved impossible to undo, and the control of land subsequently became the key mechanism in ensuring European political and economic dominance over Africans. Hence, 'from that day to this Rhodesian governments have been faced with the legacy of the age of the fortune hunters'.[156]

NOTES

1. L. H. Gann and P. Duignan, *White Settlers in Tropical Africa* (Harmondsworth 1962), 54.
2. Hist. MSS. MI 1/1/2, Milton to his wife, 25 September 1896.
3. I. Henderson, 'Wage-earners and Political Protest in Colonial Africa: The Case of the Copperbelt', *African Affairs*, **72,** 1973, 288, 290.
4. J. Woddis, *Africa: The Roots of Revolt* (London 1960), 8.
5. I. R. Phimister, 'Rhodes, Rhodesia and the Rand', *Journal of Southern African Studies*, **1,** 1974, 75–6.
6. T. O. Ranger, *Revolt in Southern Rhodesia, 1896–7* (London 1967), 46.
7. T. O. Ranger, 'African Reaction and Resistance to the Imposition of Colonial Rule in East and Central Africa', in L. H. Gann and P. Duignan (Eds.), *Colonialism in Africa, 1870–1960, Vol. 1, The History and Politics of Colonialism 1870–1914* (Cambridge 1969), 294.
8. T. O. Ranger, 'The Last Word on Rhodes?', *Past and Present*, **28,** 1964, 119. Similarly, Galbraith notes that: 'The limitation of funds also imposed the necessity of using the resources of the country rather than money as a means of rewarding services.' J. S. Galbraith, *Crown and Charter* (Berkeley, Los Angeles and London 1974), 278.
9. C.O. 417/61, Minute by Wingfield, 28 July 1891. The director was Rochfort Maguire.
10. N. Jones, *Rhodesian Genesis* (Bulawayo 1953), 55.
11. A 1/2/4, Pennefather to Colquhoun, 11 October 1890. Quoted in E. E. Burke, 'Twenty-eight Days in 1890: Two Reports by Lieut.-Colonel E. G. Pennefather', National Archives of Rhodesia, *Occasional Paper 1*, 1965, 28; Galbraith, *Crown and Charter*, 258.
12. A. R. Colquhoun, 'Matabeleland', *Proceedings of the Royal Colonial Institute*, **25,** 1893–4, 82.
13. Helm to London Missionary Society, 29 March 1889. Quoted in V. W. Hiller (Ed.), *The Concession Journey of Charles Dunell Rudd, 1888* (London 1949), 227. The question is discussed fully in R. Brown, 'Aspects of the Scramble for Matabeleland', in E. Stokes and R. Brown (Eds.), *The Zambesian Past* (Manchester 1966), 81–2; Galbraith, *Crown and Charter*, 71–4; J. R. D. Cobbing, 'Lobengula, Jameson and the Occupation of Mashonaland 1890', *Rhodesian History*, **4**, 1973, 39–56.
14. C.O. 417/61, Loch to Knutsford, 8 July 1891.
15. Article 14 of the Charter stated that: 'Careful regard should always be had to the customs and laws of the ... tribe ... especially with respect to the holding, possession, transfer and disposition of land and goods.'

16. C.O. 417/61, Minute by Wingfield, 28 July 1891.

17. Galbraith, *Crown and Charter*, 271.

18. Cobbing, 'Lobengula', 54–5.

19. 'There is Mr. Rhodes fears, little possibility of this Company being successful in obtaining from Lobengula a cession of his land, for, in Mr. Rhodes' opinion, Lobengula is disturbed at the power of the Company within his dominions and his policy is to weaken such power by the grant to ... another white power of authority to deal with the land as opposed to the Company's power to deal with the minerals.' CT 2/6/3, Cape Town Office to (?) London Office, 12 August 1891.

20. C.O. 417/68, Colonial Office to Foreign Office, 4 December 1891.

21. Moffat to Rhodes, 9 October 1891. Quoted in R. U. Moffat, *John Smith Moffat* (London 1921), 258.

22. Galbraith, *Crown and Charter*, 273.

23. In 1930 the Colonial Office, making enquiry into the BSA Company's alleged land concession in northern Nyasaland, noted that 'there are always new depths to be plumbed when we look into these old Central African land questions', and that 'justice [was] not a consideration suited to the interpretation of documents in which illiterate chiefs signed away lands that did not belong to them in exchange for a few guns and a bale of cloth'. C.O. 525/135, Minutes by Bottomley and Green, 2 and 8 July 1930.

24. J. S. Galbraith, 'Engine without a Governor: The Early Years of the British South Africa Company', *Rhodesian History*, **1**, 1970, 13; Galbraith, *Crown and Charter*, 275.

25. J. K. Rennie, 'Christianity, Colonialism and the Origins of Nationalism among the Ndau of Southern Rhodesia, 1890–1935', Ph. D. thesis, Northwestern University, Illinois, 1973, 168–9.

26. C.O. 417/72, Imperial Secretary to Company, 5 June 1891. See also C.O. 417/72, Knutsford to Loch, 15 May 1891, Colonial Office to Company, 29 May 1891, High Commissioner's Proclamation of 10 June 1891.

27. In the Ngomo (Nenguwo) incident of 1892, twenty-three Africans were killed in retaliation for the alleged theft of goods from a trader's store, a punishment which the Imperial authorities considered 'utterly disproportionate to the original offence'. *African (South) 426*, Imperial Secretary to Company, 26 April 1892. One of the Company's directors took a somewhat different view however; he told Jameson: 'I am thundering glad you gave the Mashonas a lesson, they will not be so cheeky in future.' A 1/3/4, Gifford to Jameson, 1 April 1892.

28. Phimister, 'Rhodes, Rhodesia and the Rand', 78.

29. R. Churchill, *Men, Mines and Animals in South Africa* (London 1893).

30. P. Stigger, 'Volunteers and the Profit Motive in the Anglo-Ndebele War, 1893', *Rhodesian History*, **2**, 1971, 11–23. 'I am off on the war path', wrote one of the settlers in August 1893, 'as we intend to fight the Matabele, the best fighting niggers in South Africa. They are going to give us a farm of 6,000 acres and the right to 20 gold claims for going but it is not that which induces me but the love of sport.' Hist. MSS. GR 7/1/1, Graham to Gaukroger, 18 August 1893.

31. S. G. Millin, *Rhodes* (London 1937), 258.

32. In which a Ndebele raiding party killed a number of Shona who were working for the settlers in Forth Victoria, intimidated the remainder, and so brought the economic life of the 'town' to a standstill.

33. Rhodes House, Oxford, Rhodes Papers, MSS. Afr. s. 228, C.3B, Jameson to Harris, 19 July 1893.

34. Galbraith, *Crown and Charter*, 308.

35. In like manner, the cattle of Mpezeni's Ngoni in Northern Rhodesia was looted following the war of January 1898.

36. H. M. Hole, *The Making of Rhodesia* (London 1926), 302.

37. Hist. MSS. MISC/OR 1/1/1, Orpen to Harris, 26 January 1915.

38. C.O. 417/104, Ripon to Loch, 2 December 1893; C.O. 417/105, Ripon to Loch, 10 December 1893. In a private letter to Gladstone at this time, Ripon wrote: 'I regard

the system of administration by Chartered Companies as essentially bad. These companies are really speculative, got up mainly for Stock Exchange purposes, and a good deal blown up in that aspect of their existence. The B.S.A. Coy. has been very near bankruptcy—from which probably their success in Matabeleland will save them for a time. But anyhow they are not pleasant instruments of administration.' Quoted in Galbraith, *Crown and Charter*, 330–1.

39. Details of these negotiations are to be found in C.O. 417/111–21. For a discussion of the general post-war negotiations, see Galbraith, *Crown and Charter*, 326–39.

40. Attempts to achieve 'final' settlements were an almost constant theme of colonial decision making; Harry Johnston sincerely believed that he had produced a final solution to the land question in Nyasaland as early as 1892.

41. C.O. 417/121, Matabeleland Order in Council, 18 July 1894.

42. C. 8130, Matabeleland, *Report of the Land Commission of 1894, and Correspondence relating thereto* (London 1896).

43. In C. 8130 Heyman's initials were recorded as 'J.W.', but this is a printing error, possibly the result of inaccurate transcription. Personal communication from Peter Emmerson and Digby Hartridge, National Archives of Rhodesia.

44. V. Stent, *A Personal Record of Some Incidents in the Life of Cecil Rhodes* (Bulawayo 1970), 46–7.

45. P. Stigger, 'The Emergence of the Native Department in Matabeleland, 1893–1899', unpublished 1974, 26.

46. Stigger, 'Volunteers', 13–14.

47. P. Stigger, 'The Membership and Proceedings of, and the Evidence before, the Land Commission of 1894', unpublished 1974, 6–11.

48. Personal communication from Peter Emmerson and Digby Hartridge, National Archives of Rhodesia.

49. Hole, *The Making*, 335.

50. C. 8130, 5.

51. Stigger claims that Vintcent and Lindsell were deliberately led by Colenbrander on a long, slow journey through uninhabited country, Colenbrander knowing that the rains were due soon and that the Report had to be written before Vintcent went off to open the High Court in Salisbury in mid-November. Stigger, 'The Membership', 18–19.

52. Colenbrander 'represented the king [Lobengula] in negotiations with the company even though he was paid by the company'. His 'loyalty in 1893 was entirely given to the company which he served and from which he hoped to derive benefits'. He duly became a company promoter, acquiring, among other things, a £16,000 house. Galbraith, *Crown and Charter*, 304; Stigger, 'The Emergence', 11.

53. L 2/2/117/10, CNC Matabeleland to Secretary, Department of Administrator, 9 March 1899.

54. C. 8130, 6.

55. LB 2/1/15, N/C Nyamandhlovu to CNC Matabeleland, 16 May 1913.

56. C. 8130, 6–7.

57. Lord Olivier, who was a young official at the Colonial Office during this time, later wrote that his superiors 'looked on hypnotized by the aura of impeccable personages whose figures decked the Company's office-window'. S. H. Olivier, *The Anatomy of African Misery* (London 1927), 51. Quoted in Galbraith, 'Engine without a Governor', 15.

58. C. 8130, Loch to Ripon, 19 November 1894, 3.

59. C.O. 417/130, Minutes by Graham, Ripon and Fairfield, 20 and 26 December 1894, 18 January 1895.

60. C. 8130, Ripon to Loch, 25 January 1895, 14.

61. C.O. 417/209, Minutes by Graham and Just, 26 and 24 June 1897.

62. Rhodes House, Oxford, Rhodes Papers, MSS. Afr. s. 228. 1., Grey to Rhodes, 26 May 1897.

63. O. Ransford, *The Rulers of Rhodesia* (London 1968), 185.

64. Milton, who arrived in 1896, thought that 'Jameson must have been off his head for some time before the Raid'. Hist. MSS. MI 1/1/2, Milton to his wife, 25 September 1896.

65. The Colonial Office presumed that the Company would 'at once remove from office... their present Administrator (who is lodged in Pretoria Gaol) and will appoint a properly qualified and prudent person in his place'. The words in parenthesis were excised at the request of Chamberlain, who was himself implicated in the Raid. C. Palley, *The Constitutional History and Law of Southern Rhodesia, 1888–1965* (Oxford 1966), 149 n. 3.

66. See J. A. Edwards, 'Colquhoun in Mashonaland: A Portrait of Failure', *Rhodesiana*, **9**, 1963, 1–17, and Colquhoun's own works: *Matabeleland: The War and Our Position in South Africa* (London 1894) and *Dan to Beersheba* (London 1908).

67. Colquhoun appears to have been heartily disliked by the leading fortune-hunters in the Company's employ, most notably by Jameson himself.

68. Colquhoun, *Dan to Beersheba*, 294.

69. D. N. Beach, 'The Rising in South-Western Mashonaland, 1896–7', Ph.D. thesis, University of London, 1971, 217. The 'border' was not, however, recognized by Lobengula.

70. LO 5/2/4, Pennefather to Kimberley Office, 23 September 1890. Quoted in Burke, 'Twenty-eight Days', 25.

71. Beach, 'The Rising', 261.

72. A 1/2/4, Pennefather to Colquhoun, 11 October 1890. Quoted in Burke, 'Twenty-eight Days', 29–30.

73. R. C. Tredgold, *The Rhodesia that was My Life* (London 1968), 61.

74. W. H. Brown, *On the South African Frontier* (New York 1899), 120; J. E. S. Green, *Rhodes Goes North* (London 1936), 221–2.

75. In 1893 George Grey, of the Northumberland Mining Syndicate, was told to go and peg his farms somewhere else by the conscientious Civil Commissioner Victoria, as: 'It was found that the land chosen by you had very large numbers of native lands. The natives complained that the whiteman was taking away all their fields and would in time do away with their means of subsistence. That is the reason why that part of the country was reserved for them.' DV 2/2/1, C/C Victoria to G. Grey, 28 August 1893. I am indebted to David Beach for this reference.

76. After 1903 special 'Gold Belt titles' were issued, with 'almost prohibitive' terms restricting the farmers' use of timber and water. E. T. Jollie, *The Real Rhodesia* (London 1924), 130; P. F. Hone, *Southern Rhodesia* (London 1909), 290–7.

77. Hist. MSS. CR 1/2/8, Cripps to Editor, *Rhodesia Herald*, 23 May 1930.

78. Brown, *South African Frontier*, 174.

79. Hole, *The Making*, 277. Lobengula protested in vain to the Imperial Government: 'I have heard that my land is being cut up and given out. Why is my Country to be cut up without my word ... This is bad!' Hist. MSS. CO 4/1/1, Lobengula to Loch, 30 December 1890.

80. Hist. MSS. MI 1/1/2, Milton to his wife, 25 September 1896.

81. H. M. Hole, *The Jameson Raid* (London 1930), 16.

82. Galbraith, 'Engine without a Governor', 13; Galbraith, *Crown and Charter*, 279.

83. Stigger, 'The Emergence', 16.

84. Milton wrote disgustedly that: 'Lady Dudley's son, a youngster of the la-di-da class, has just been sent up here probably with an expression of Jameson's wish that half a country may be given to him ... it is perfectly sickening to see the way in which the country has been run for the sake of hobnobbing with Lord this and the Honble. that.' Hist. MSS. MI 1/1/2, Milton to his wife, 25 September 1896.

85. Galbraith, *Crown and Charter*, 126.

86. Brown, *South African Frontier*, 174.

87. Of the 948 Victoria Agreement farms, 493 had passed into the hands of companies, while a further 147 were owned by individuals in blocks of farms. 'Report of the

Surveyor General for the Two Years ending 31st March, 1900', in British South Africa Company, *Reports on the Administration of Rhodesia, 1898–1900* (London 1901), 175–6. One early settler recalled that individual enterprise was not encouraged at this time: 'The Administration appeared to be Company-minded to the exclusion of all else. Large blocks of land were given to Companies who were making no development on them whatsoever'. Hist. MSS. SO 5/2, Reminiscences of an Early Settler in Rhodesia [C. W. R. Southey], January 1943.

88. Phimister, 'Rhodes, Rhodesia and the Rand', 82.

89. Galbraith, *Crown and Charter*, 127.

90. L 2/2/95/21, Bates to Surveyor General, 14 November 1893; L 2/2/95/22, Magistrate Melsetter to Acting Administrator, 12 April 1896.

91. G. W. H. Knight-Bruce, *Memories of Mashonaland* (London 1895), 99.

92. Galbraith, 'Engine without a Governor', 14; Galbraith, *Crown and Charter*, 281.

93. Jameson advised the Methodist Shimmin: 'To include some large native village in any other farm I may select. This is an important point as it is against the law of the Company for any "pegger out" to take in any native dwellings, but Dr. Jameson was anxious to let me clearly see that our efforts amongst the natives would have his strongest support.' Duncan said that: 'Instead of granting me three or even six farms ... he would willingly give *thirty* or *sixty* if I wanted them. His idea is briefly this. Wherever we find native towns or villages of any importance we can there make out a farm including those towns, and such farms will be registered and handed over to us for missionary work.' Methodist Missionary Society Archives, Mashonaland 1891–9, Shimmin to Hartley, 29 November 1891 and 26 February 1892.

94. Hist. MSS. PE 3/1/1, Pelly to his parents, 22 October 1892.

95. Methodist Missionary Society Archives, Shimmin to Hartley, c. October 1892.

96. Methodist Missionary Society Archives, White to Lamplough, 23 December 1911.

97. Even the early railway builders found themselves rewarded with farms of 3,175 acres. A. H. Croxton, *Railways of Rhodesia* (Newton Abbot 1973), 40–1.

98. CT 1/11/2/3, London Office to Cape Town Office, 5 February and 16 December 1892; CT 2/6/3, Cape Town Office to London Office, 26 April 1893; Galbraith, *Crown and Charter*, 280.

99. N 3/16/9, S/N Bulawayo to CNC, 1 June 1920.

100. A. Boggie, *From Ox-Wagon to Railway* (Bulawayo 1897), 26.

101. C. L. N. Newman, *Matabeleland and How We Got It* (London 1895), 147. Nine hundred farms represented some 5·7 million acres.

102. D.O. 63/3, Memo by CNC, February 1927.

103. J. T. Bent, *The Ruined Cities of Mashonaland* (London 1896), 269.

104. Moffat's diary, 6 December 1891. Quoted in Moffat, *John Smith Moffat*, 237.

105. Knight-Bruce, *Memories*, 98.

106. D. A. Robinson, 'Land Use Planning in Native Reserves in Southern Rhodesia', *Rhodesia Agricultural Journal*, **50**, 1953, 328. Both Floyd and Garbett, in their calculations appear to have misread Robinson. B. N. Floyd, *Changing Patterns of African Land Use in Southern Rhodesia* (Lusaka 1961), 100; G. K. Garbett, 'The Land Husbandry Act of Southern Rhodesia', in D. Biebuyck (Ed.), *African Agrarian Systems* (London 1963), 188–9.

107. This is based on the Shona system, described more fully in the previous chapter. A Shona family cultivated about 4 acres at a time, bringing one new acre under cultivation each year, and allowing one old one after three or four years' use to revert to fallow for 15 years. They would therefore require some 20 acres for cultivation in order to maintain this subsistence system. Using Robinson's estimate of 25 per cent cultivable land, the family would require about 80 acres in all. Assessing a 'family' conservatively at four members, this gives an average requirement of 20 acres per head, which is less than Robinson's 32 acres (=20 to the square mile). Accepting my figure, the estimated African population of 750,000 in 1890 would have required some 15 million acres;

using Robinson's, they would have needed 24 million acres. The total area of Rhodesia is 96 million acres.

108. Personal communication from David Beach.

109. G. Kay, *Rhodesia: A Human Geography* (London 1970), 43.

110. Brown, *South African Frontier*, 307–8.

111. G. Arrighi, 'Labour Supplies in Historical Perspective: A Study of the Proletarianization of the African Peasantry in Rhodesia', *Journal of Development Studies*, **6**, 1970, 209.

112. British South Africa Company, *Report, 1894–5*, 67; Stigger, 'Volunteers', 14.

113. Jones, *Rhodesian Genesis*, 116. A Government report of 1961 noted that: 'Native agriculture was of great importance to the European settlers at this early stage, as the Natives supplied them with their grain and vegetable requirements for much of the year, and, in addition, native cattle formed the basis of many new European-owned cattle.' Federation of Rhodesia and Nyasaland, *An Agricultural Survey of Southern Rhodesia, Part II, Agro-Economic Survey* (Salisbury 1961), 14.

114. 'The majority of the so-called early "farmers" were employed solely in transport riding—their farms merely serving as bases where they maintained a rough homestead and kept a few spare oxen.' M. G. B. Rooney, 'European Agriculture in the History of Rhodesia, 1890–1907', M.A. thesis, University of South Africa, 1968, 70.

115. Beach, 'The Rising', 291.

116. Rooney, 'European Agriculture', 73.

117. D.O. 119/520, Gazeteer by the C/C Victoria, 11 November 1897; D.O. 119/586, Report of the N/C Victoria for the year ending June 1900.

118. Beach, 'The Rising', 262.

119. Rooney, 'European Agriculture', 44.

120. E. E. Burke, 'Mazoe and the Mashona Rebellion; 1896–97', *Rhodesiana*, **25**, 1971, 23.

121. D. N. Beach, 'Afrikaner and Shona Settlement in the Enkeldoorn Area, 1890–1900', *Zambezia*, **1**, 2, 1970, 28. The missionary John White reported travelling some 250 miles in 1904 and passing only two *bona fide* European farmers. *South African Native Affairs Commission, Vol. IV* (Cape Town 1905), Evidence of J. White, 1 September 1904, 92.

122. L 2/2/95/21, Cape Town Office to Jameson, 27 January 1892.

123. NUE 2/1/2, Report of the N/C Melsetter for the half-year ending September 1897. Quoted in Rennie, 'Christianity and Nationalism', 177–8.

124. NUE 2/1/1, N/C Melsetter to CNC Mashonaland, 13 October 1895. Quoted in Rennie, 'Christianity and Nationalism', 183.

125. NUE 2/1/1, N/C Melsetter to CNC Mashonaland, 2 April 1896. A similar plea was made by the N/C for Chibi-Chilimanzi: N 9/1/1, Report of the N/C Chilimanzi for the year 1895.

126. 'In the case of the great land companies, one "ranger" sufficed to "occupy" an area of up to 170,000 morgen.' Beach, 'Afrikaner and Shona', 26.

127. *South African Native Affairs Commission, Vol. V*, Written reply of Miss H. F. Davidson, 1903, 321.

128. Beach, 'The Rising', 264.

129. R. H. Palmer, 'Red Soils in Rhodesia', *African Social Research*, **10**, 1970, 747–58.

130. H. M. Hole, *Old Rhodesian Days* (London 1928), 97–8.

131. Julian Cobbing has come across an instance of the Ndebele ripping up boundary posts prior to 1896, and the Europeans deluding themselves that this was because the posts were thought to be 'bad medicine'. Personal communication from David Beach.

132. Frank Johnson, the organizer of the Pioneer Column, was moved to comment that: 'We have excellent labourers in the Matabele, and from the mining and commercial point of view I regret the loss of the 2,000 odd Matabele killed in the late war very much.' In Colquhoun, 'Matabeleland', 98.

133. D.O. 63/3, Memo by CNC, February 1927.

134. R. H. Palmer, *Aspects of Rhodesian Land Policy, 1890–1936*, Central Africa Historical Association, Local Series Pamphlet **22**, 1968, 12.

135. One should note Ford's comment that Ranger's account of the confiscation of the cattle is misleading, since: 'We should expect to find that a population of 250,000 cattle in February 1895 would have been reduced [by rinderpest] to about 13,000 by the end of the year. Rhodesian pioneers did commandeer the cattle of the defeated natives, but the *panzootic* can have left very few of them to take.' J. Ford, *The role of the Trypanosomiases in African Ecology* (Oxford 1971), 350. But this ignores the fact that a great deal of the looted cattle—Stigger estimates 73 per cent—'left' Matabeleland for Kimberley and Johannesburg before the rinderpest struck. Stigger, 'Volunteers', 22.

136. The Ndebele headman Somabulana told Rhodes in the 1896 *indaba* about 'the brutality of the Zulu police, who ravished their daughters, and insulted their young men, who tweaked the beards of their chieftains and made lewd jokes with the elder women of the Great House, who abused the law they were expected to uphold, who respected none but the Native Commissioners and officers of police, who collected taxes at the point of their assegais, and ground the people in tyranny and oppression'. Stent, *A Personal Record*, 46–7. A similar picture is drawn in L. Vambe, *An Ill-Fated People* (London 1972), 107–9.

137. N 1/2/2, N/C Hartley to CNC Mashonaland, 30 November 1895; Hist. MSS. MA 9/1/1, Mallett to his father, 3 July 1892. Quoted in J. M. Mackenzie, 'African Labour in the Chartered Company Period', *Rhodesian History*, **1**, 1970, 46 n. 13.

138. C. G. Chivanda, 'The Mashona Rebellion in Oral Tradition: Mazoe District', University College of Rhodesia, Department of History, undergraduate seminar paper, 1966, 7.

139. The N/C Lomagundi, commenting on such employers in 1899, mentioned that they 'also interfere in other ways with natives, thinking that because they came up with the pioneers, or in the early days, they are entitled to treat the natives as they please, and as apparently they have done hitherto'. N 9/1/5, Report of the Acting N/C Lomagundi for the year ending March 1899.

140. DS 1/1/1, Mining Commissioner Mazoe to Resident Magistrate Salisbury, 8 and 16 March 1893.

141. A 1/5/10, Memo of a conversation between Rhodes and Jameson, 15 May 1892.

142. *African (South) 454*, Company to Colonial Office, 7 July 1893. Even Edward Fairfield, a Colonial Office official notably sympathetic to the Company, pointed out that: 'Rhodes' argument that the necessity of paying the tax will compel the Mashonas to work for the mining industry is all well enough in a Stock Exchange Luncheon Room, but it is hardly a *parliamentary* argument.' CT 1/3/1, Fairfield to Hawksley, 29 July 1893.

143. *African (South) 441*, Imperial Secretary to Company, 29 August 1892. Olivier observed tartly that: 'The usual inclination is of course to kill two birds with one stone, and to appropriate the land with a view to starving the natives into working for the white expropriator on their own former property.' C.O. 417/110, Minute by Olivier, 7 July 1893.

144. *African (South) 441*, Colonial Office to Company, 29 June 1893.

145. Ranger, *Revolt*, 69.

146. The missionary Carnegie pointed out at the end of 1896 that 'up till now there has been really no native policy whatever'. Hist. MSS. LO 6/1/5, Carnegie to Thompson, 12 December 1896.

147. Ranger, *Revolt*, 77.

148. I. R. Phimister, 'Alluvial gold mining and Trade in Nineteenth-Century South Central Africa', *Journal of African History*, **15**, 1974, 453.

149. The N/C Chilimanzi reported that: 'Selling of the natives' cattle at the hut tax valuation has been a great inducement to make them work and has proved to be a most successful policy in this district.' N 9/1/1, Report of the N/C Chilimanzi for the year 1895.

150. J. J. Taylor, 'The Origins of the Native Department in Southern Rhodesia, 1890–98', University of Rhodesia, Department of History, Henderson Seminar No. 7, 1968, 10. See also J. J. Taylor, 'The Native Affairs Department in Southern Rhodesia, 1894–1914', Ph.D. thesis, University of London, 1974.

151. D. N. Beach, 'The Politics of Collaboration: South Mashonaland, 1896–97', University of Rhodesia, Department of History, Henderson Seminar No. 9, 1969, 19.

152. Milner to Asquith, 18 November 1897. Quoted in C. Headlam (Ed.), *The Milner Papers, South Africa, 1897–99, Vol. 1* (London 1931), 178.

153. P. Mason, *The Birth of a Dilemma* (London 1958), 219–20.

154. Beach, 'The Rising', 250.

155. Beach, 'Politics of Collaboration', 9; Beach, 'Afrikaner and Shona', 28.

156. Ranger, 'The Last Word', 122.

CHAPTER 3

The Imperial Awakening 1896–1908

You will give us land in our own country! That's good of you!

Ndebele headman to Rhodes, Matopos Hills, 1896.[1]

1 BACKGROUND

The period 1896–1908 opened dramatically with the Jameson Raid and *ChiMurenga*, the African Risings; it witnessed much tighter British control over Rhodesia than hitherto, and ended with formal Imperial approval of the new native reserves and the Company's decision to turn its attention from gold to land.

The Jameson Raid and the Risings in Matabeleland and Mashonaland at last goaded the Imperial Government into action, and for the next decade Downing Street kept a close surveillance over the Company's affairs in general,[2] and over its administration of Africans in particular. Once again Treasury principles were invoked to preclude direct annexation, though Chamberlain's complicity in the Jameson Raid must have been a weighty additional factor. But with the Company's morale at its lowest ebb—Rhodes was forced to resign the Premiership of the Cape, and Jameson, Willoughby and others were in gaol[3]—the British Government was able, and willing, to step in decisively, take control of the military operations against the 'rebels', and dominate, though not always intelligently, the political settlement that followed. The really decisive step was the appointment, successfully resisted by Rhodes in 1894, of an Imperial Resident Commissioner, who was to be permanently based in Rhodesia. The first incumbent of the post, Sir Richard Martin, was empowered to take charge of the post-Risings political settlement, and Martin's successors, though not brilliant men, continued to act as the 'eyes and ears' of the British Government until the Company handed over power to the settlers in 1923.[4]

Although Rhodesia could never be divorced from the wider focus of South African politics, and hence, as Milner admitted, the British Government could not 'be seen taking a strong line against the Company for the protection of the blacks',[5] the existence of an Imperial resident in Salisbury gave teeth to British good intentions. Among other things, it ensured that forced labour was curbed, that the hut tax was not raised from 10/– to £2 or even £4 in 1903, that the appointment of Native Commissioners was more carefully vetted,[6] that the Company's attack on the native reserves in 1908–14 was temporarily beaten off, and that the beginnings of a coherent African land policy, as opposed to simple expropriation, were at last laid down.[7]

The Company itself acknowledged the need for reform. It realized that its charter was in danger and that unless it established a more regular and ordered administration, there was a possibility of further African risings. Such a prospect could scarcely have commended itself to the Company, since the cost of suppressing the 1896–7 Risings had amounted to over £7 million. The men appointed to take Jameson's place were Albert, Earl Grey, one of the Company's well-connected directors,[8] and William Milton, a senior Cape civil servant and expert in 'native affairs',[9] seconded at Rhodes' urgent request. Both were horrified at the legacy of the Jamesonian era. 'Every thing here is in an absolutely rotten condition' noted Milton on arrival,[10] while Grey lamented that: 'Land is our great difficulty. It has all been given away. I will not give away another acre until the Native Q[uestion] has been settled.'[11]

Together Milton and Grey determined, with gentle prompting from Imperial officials but also acting on their own beliefs, on a threefold programme of reform. Firstly the Native Department was reorganized and put on a more regular footing, with Milton recruiting a number of young and tolerably well qualified recruits from Natal who could speak Zulu and hence get by in SiNdebele, and who brought with them 'the firm paternalism and close supervision of Africans that characterised the Natal system'.[12] Many of these officials served for long periods, some of them for twenty or thirty years, and they therefore provided a degree of continuity which was frequently lacking in territories to the north administered by expatriate District Commissioners.[13]

The other two planks of the reform programme comprised the creation of native reserves throughout the country and an attack on the absentee landlords. These will both be analysed shortly, together with the Company's policy towards Africans who were living on European farms and those, few in number, who aspired to become landowners themselves. The declared policies will then be contrasted with the reality, both within and without the reserves, and this chapter will conclude with an examination of the response of the African peasantry to their new situation.

2 POLICY

(i) Introduction

At the end of 1895 Jameson invaded the Transvaal in an attempt to overthrow the Kruger Government. The Raid was a complete fiasco which, by denuding the country of white troops, afforded the Ndebele and Shona the opportunity to rise up in armed revolt in March and June of 1896.

The Risings, or *ChiMurenga* as they were called by the people, were the most violent, sustained, and highly organized instance of resistance to colonial rule anywhere in Africa. They were a genuine people's war, in which individuals fought because they chose to, not because they were ordered to by their leaders. A wide cross-section of society was involved, not merely, as so often elsewhere, simply the official army. The European casualties were much higher than in any comparable revolt; 372 were killed and 129 wounded, representing about 10 per cent of the entire white population. During 'Mau Mau' 68 Europeans were killed. The African casualty figures in 1896–7 will never be known, for the Shona Rising was put down with appalling ferocity and indifference to suffering. Today, eighty years later, as the guerrilla campaign inside Rhodesia intensifies, the people look back to *Chi-Murenga* with pride and as an inspiration for the long struggle ahead.

Terence Ranger's masterly study of the Risings, published in 1967,[14] which in itself did much to revive memories of that period, has undergone a certain amount of revision in recent years. In particular, it is argued, Ranger paid insufficient attention to those who did not resist, an important omission, since the 'collaborators' were ultimately responsible for the failure of the Risings, though any 'success' achieved by Africans in 1896 would almost certainly have been of short duration. But in Matabeleland, for example, the Ndebele headman Gambo, influenced by the attitude of the Mwari shrine at Umkombo, remained 'loyal' and refused to cut the vital road to the south with the result that supplies and reinforcements were able to reach the besieged *laager* in Bulawayo. In Mashonaland too, 'collaborators' played a vital role for they influenced the spatial expansion of the Rising and also limited the possibilities of combined 'rebel' military operations. David Beach, in his local study of south-west Mashonaland, has unravelled a complex pattern of resistance, collaboration, and neutrality, in which traditional Shona political rivalries, fears of an Ndebele resurgence, and realistic assessments of the likely outcome of the fighting all played a part.[15] The politics of resistance and collaboration were also to play an important role, as we shall see, in the post-Risings land settlement.

By the end of June 1896 the Ndebele siege of Bulawayo had been beaten off, and the Europeans cautiously began to take the offensive. It therefore became possible to think in terms of a peace settlement and to plan a basis for future land policies. The Imperial Government had two major objectives: to ensure that adequate native reserves were established throughout the country; and to protect Africans who found themselves living on European land. Imperial thinking was however dominated by two major assumptions, both of which turned out to be mistaken. Firstly, it believed that native reserves were merely a temporary expedient destined to disappear as the country developed; and secondly it thought that there would be no wholesale evictions of Africans from European farms in the future.[16] The Company broadly accepted the two Imperial objectives; it initiated a system of locations on white farms, entrusted the task of assigning reserves to the new Native Commissioners, and attempted to enforce a policy of 'beneficial occupation or surrender' on the absentee landlords in an attempt to undo some of the damage caused by Jameson's liberality. Each of these policies will be examined in turn.

(ii) Africans on European Farms

The main problem facing Grey and Resident Commissioner Martin in the middle of 1896 was that of inducing the Ndebele to leave their strongholds in the Matopos Hills whence they had retired in the course of the Rising, and begin planting their crops as soon as possible to avert the danger of starvation the following year. Grey admitted that the Company was left with only 'a few farms, which may almost be termed the refuse of the country, as they ... are generally without water and unsuitable for cultivation'. He suggested that Africans who surrendered to the administration could either be settled in the Gwaai and Shangani Reserves, or else remain as tenants and make their own arrangements with the white farmers, as in the Cape.[17] Imperial pressure however forced Grey to acknowledge that Gwaai and Shangani were unsuitable, and that legislation similar to the Cape Location Acts was necessary to regulate the position of Africans on European farms.

The final result of these negotiations[18] was the High Commissioner's Proclamation No. 19 of 14 October 1896, which, in order to lessen the prospect of an immediate recurrence of violence, allowed the Ndebele a two-year period of grace, during which time no rents were to be charged and no tenants were to be evicted. Thereafter, rents were to be arranged between landlords and tenants and approved by the Chief Native Commissioner, who was to act as arbiter in the event of disputes. Where labour agreements were imposed, these too had to receive the sanction of the Chief Native Commissioner and, at the insistence of Martin, were not to last for more than one year at a time. Whilst forced labour was specifically outlawed, Native Commissioners were not to allow tenants to work elsewhere if the landlord needed their labour and could offer a comparable wage. Finally, at the suggestion of Grey who believed that the Ndebele should not be permitted to gather in numbers large enough to threaten the peace, the number of tenants was to be limited to 7 family heads for each farm of 3,175 acres.[19] This compares with the 5 heads of families permitted in the Transvaal and Orange Free State under the *Plakkers Wet* (Squatters Law) of 1895.[20]

The High Commissioner's Proclamation, which was a permissive piece of legislation in that it did not compel landlords to come under its aegis, was essentially a response to the immediate situation existing in Matabeleland in 1896. It endeavoured on the one hand to encourage the Ndebele to return to their homes and start planting their crops, while at the same time providing those few Europeans who were actually farming with a readily available supply of labour. Not surprisingly, the Proclamation had a relatively short life, being replaced by the Private Locations Ordinance in 1908.

(iii) The Making of the Reserves

The second question which required an urgent solution was that of the provision of land for African use. Since so much land had already passed into European hands, the most obvious solution was to follow the South African precedent and create 'native reserves' which would afford some degree of protection against European acquisitiveness. Reserves had originally been designed to protect dispossessed 'Hottentots' in the Cape, and were later extended to Africans in Natal and the Transkei. Their appearance in Southern Rhodesia— and later in Kenya and Northern Rhodesia—was an indication of the extent of alienation which had already taken place, for reserves usually carry the connotation of land left over after the Europeans have helped themselves. In countries where alienation to Europeans was on a small scale, the bulk of the land was normally secured for African use—in Nyasaland as native trust land and in Tanganyika as public land—while non-African holdings were confined to small enclaves of Crown Land, which were, in effect, European reserves. A policy of native reserves meant in essence therefore that Africans had lost control over much of their land. In Northern Rhodesia an attempt was made to follow the Southern Rhodesian policy of reserves in the 1920s but the results proved disastrous,[21] whilst the Jackson Land Commission of 1920–1 in Nyasaland believed 'the institution of Native Reserves would be an unwarrantable interference with the free occupation by the people of their native land and would in addition be totally unsuited to their manner of life ... Their movements in large numbers from the sites on which they have already settled would be a great hardship'.[22]

The native reserves which were created in Rhodesia at the turn of the century are important precisely because they have survived—with a good deal of amendment but recognizably in the same pattern—down to the present. This was certainly not foreseen at the time. H. J. Taylor, the CNC Matabeleland, was by no means alone when in 1904 he expressed the view that reserves 'involve the negation of all progress, and should be regarded only as a temporary makeshift'.[23] The reserves therefore were not initially designed to be the Africans' share of the land; they were essentially *ad hoc* creations intended to solve the post-Risings refugee problem, and 'to provide some place or other where the Natives can escape being rack rented'.[24] Indeed the general expectation, shared by Company and Imperial officials alike, was that as the country developed and Africans were sucked into the money economy, so the need for reserves would disappear. As Wilson Fox, the Company's General Manager, put it, 'the true aim should be that the natives should be absorbed as live members of the social organism';[25] or, in Philip Mason's words, that they 'would gradually come to be integrated into an economic structure based in class instead of race'.[26] The object clearly was to turn Africans into wage-labourers as rapidly as possible. Such was 'the Doctrine'[27] which was generally accepted in the years before the serious development of European farming and settler political power, which between them led to the espousal of a new doctrine based on segregation.

The agreed policy in 1896 was that reserves should be established throughout the country, and this was in fact written into the post-Risings settlement, the Southern Rhodesia Order in Council of 1898, which stipulated that: 'The Company shall from time to time assign to the natives inhabiting Southern Rhodesia land sufficient for their occupation, whether as tribes, or portions of tribes, and suitable for their agricultural and pastoral requirements, including in all cases a fair and equitable proportion of springs or permanent water.'[28] This was the same injunction as that given to the 1894 Land Commission, except that it now applied to the whole country rather than to Matabeleland alone, and it included the words 'from time to time' which Rhodes had successfully resisted in 1894. The implication was that the Imperial Government could at any time call upon the Company to provide more land if it believed the current assignment to be inadequate.

The task of demarcating the reserves fell to the Native Commissioners. Those in Matabeleland began work in 1897, while their colleagues in Mashonaland, where the Rising took much longer to subdue, could only start in the following year. Progress was slow however, for the necessary surveys took longer than anticipated, while the South African War diverted the attention of Imperial officials who in any event were cautious and anxious not to repeat their earlier mistakes.

Following Martin's damning reports on the Gwaai and Shangani Reserves in April 1897,[29] the Acting CNC Matabeleland was able to submit in July a list of 18 new reserves throughout the province. They were alleged to contain 'a great deal of the very best land in Rhodesia', a somewhat dubious claim in the light of Grey's belief that the Company was left with the refuse of the country, and were held to be more than sufficient for the next twenty years.[30] They totalled approximately 5·5 million acres, of which Gwaai and Shangani accounted for 4·2 million. Martin took the view that twenty years was rather a short time, but the general opinion in London was that such an attitude 'exhibits a little *too* much zeal in favour of the natives'.[31] As far as Milner was concerned, after his visit to Rhodesia in 1897, the reserve system was essentially transitional[32] and locations on farms were much more promising. The new reserves, he felt, were an immense improvement on the 1894 assignment, but since these were early days any settlement would require considerable modification later and if the reserves in time proved inadequate, they could always be added to. This view was upheld at the Colonial Office, and the reserves were approved in February 1898.[33]

This approval was somewhat premature however since the reserves had not been properly surveyed, and it was not until December 1899 that more accurate descriptions could be furnished. By this time the number of reserves in Matabeleland had been reduced from 18 to 16, but the total area increased from 5·5 million to an estimated 6·1 million acres. Commenting on the revised selection, Sir Marshal Clarke (Martin's successor as Resident Commissioner), observed that it did not seem a fair exchange for much of the new land was adjacent to the Gwaai Reserve, while much of that taken away was from centres of long established African settlement.[34] But by this time the South African War had broken out and Milner put the question aside together with a great deal of other correspondence, somewhat to the irritation of the Colonial Office.

The war did at least give the Native Commissioners and surveyors sufficient time in which to conduct their deliberations, and by the end of 1902 they had completed their task. The Mashonaland reserves, 80 in number plus most of the Mtoko District, totalling an estimated 17·1 million acres, were formally approved by the Administrator in Executive Council on 27 October; and the 16 Matabeleland reserves, now thought to be 7·7 million acres, were similarly approved on 2 December. Many of the estimates made of the size of the reserves at this time were subsequently found to be inaccurate. Clarke immediately recommended the approval of the new reserves,[35] but Milner contrived to lose the relevant despatches in his office until July 1904, thus leaving the Colonial Office in total ignorance of what had been done.[36]

When the despatches were finally forwarded to London, Colonial

Office officials remained firm in their belief that the reserves were only temporary and were oases of barbarism compared to the civilizing influence of locations on farms. They also believed that there was no real prospect of substantial movements of people off the farms and into the reserves, whilst admitting that 'we are almost entirely in the hands of our local advisers'.[37] Under the flexible 'from time to time' policy adopted, the question of Imperial approval of the reserves was neither urgent nor actively sought by the Company. Hence it was not until March 1907 that the Colonial Office asked for a further report from the Resident Commissioner, now Chester-Master. He duly reported that the reserves 'were not only sufficient but liberal, and will prove to be ample for the requirements of the native inhabitants for many years to come, even taking into consideration the rapid rate at which they and their stock increase, as well as their extensive methods of cultivation'. The time had not arrived for a final delimitation, but when this was required, a commission should be appointed.[38] The Colonial Office accepted this advice, and hence on 11 July 1908, the Colonial Secretary, the Earl of Crewe, formally approved the reserves, though 'upon the understanding that my approval is to be regarded as provisional and not to preclude their further consideration'.[39]

It was twelve years since Martin and Grey had first opened negotiations on the reserves question. Almost immediately the Company launched an attack on the reserves in an attempt to recover the best land for European settlement.

(iv) The Attack on the Absentee Landlords

When Grey and Milton arrived in Rhodesia in 1896, they were appalled to discover how much land had been given away indiscriminately by Jameson. Not only did this make the task of selecting suitable reserves exceedingly difficult, but also there was 'absolutely no land left which is of any value at all for settlement of Immigrants by Government'.[40] The Company therefore decided to attack the absentee landlords, in particular the large land companies and syndicates,[41] and it determined upon a policy of 'beneficial occupation or surrender'. In doing so, however, it came into direct conflict with the settler representatives in the new Legislative Council set up under the 1898 Order in Council. Interestingly, Rhodes had pressed for settler representation in the LegCo in an attempt to check Imperial influence, while the British Government had done the same in the hopes of curbing the Company! The appointment of settler representatives at such an early stage in the country's development was to be fraught with momentous consequences.[42] The early settler members elected to the LegCo, and in particular Colonel Raleigh Grey,[43] all had close connexions with the large, land-owning companies and were therefore strongly opposed to the new, post-Jameson, policy.

The first essential was to prevent any further casual granting of land, and hence in December 1896 the Administrator's Council resolved that 'henceforth no land shall be parted with otherwise than by sale or lease at public auction except with the special consent of the Council'. The following year it was agreed that anyone who had been promised land in the past should not be granted title until it was ascertained that such land was not required for native reserves.[44] It was easy enough to enforce such defensive methods. The difficulty came when Grey and Milton went into the attack.

The first attempted reform, Government Notice No. 154 of 7 September 1897, called on all who had been granted land on terms of beneficial occupation to comply with those terms by 1 August 1898, or face the threat of forfeiture. The settlers complained to Rhodes, who at the time was courting settler support against the post-Raid pressures being applied by the Imperial Government, and he therefore upheld their appeal. A similar fate befell the Land Ordinance of 1899, which brought forth strong protests from a body calling itself the Representatives Association, and from the settler members in the LegCo who claimed that it was typical of legislation passed in pre-1861 Russia. This time it was Milner who upheld the objection; he needed settler support during the South African War. The Company tried yet again in 1900, with the Land Occupation Conditions Ordinance, but settler opposition was once again manifest and succeeded in emasculating the occupation conditions.[45] The failure to push through genuine reform eventually led Milton to adopt a compromise solution. This took the form of Government Notice No. 274 of 29 October 1903, which stipulated that landlords could, by surrendering one-third of their holdings, receive title free of occupation to the remainder.[46] By 1914 some 954,210 acres had been surrendered in this way, of which 358,015 acres had been re-sold to Europeans, and 59,263 acres assigned to the native reserves.[47] But the victory was evidently somewhat Pyrrhic, since by 1912 'development' was being carried out on only one million acres out of the total of eight million acres owned by companies; the rest was lying idle.[48] Absentee landlordism thus continued to flourish unabated.

(v) African Land Purchase

The Southern Rhodesia Order in Council of 1898 proclaimed, as had the 1894 Matabeleland Order, the right of Africans to 'acquire, hold, encumber, and dispose of land on the same conditions as a person who is not a native'. Thus while the native reserves were set aside for 'traditional' communal occupation, individual Africans with the necessary capital and expertise could buy freehold farms in exactly the same way as the white settlers. This was also the case in the Cape and in Natal.

In the very early years a number of grants were in fact made to Africans—78 farms, totalling 7,810 acres, were given in Matabeleland to black South Africans,[49] the so-called 'Cape Boys' who had helped the Company put down the Ndebele Rising. Like the Europeans, the majority of these 'Cape Boys' preferred to sell their land rights rather than occupy their farms. Rhodes also permitted the Tswana chiefs, Mphoeng and Raditladi, brothers of Khama, to settle in the Bulalima-Mangwe District of Matabeleland, where they were given reserves.[50] He hoped that such generosity would persuade the Imperial Government to hand Bechuanaland over to the Company. In addition, a party of Mfengu ('Fingos') from the Transkei were allowed to take up individual plots in the Fingo Location on the Bembesi river near Bulawayo. They had been brought up to augment the labour supply and to assist in the defence of Bulawayo in the event of a further rising. A number of other attempts to attract 'foreign' Africans by offering land in return for labour failed.[51]

These were all special arrangements, however, and it was not until 1903 that the first recorded application for land by a non-white was made to the Company. This came, somewhat surprisingly, from a black American, William Lincoln, about whom nothing is presently known—not even by George Shepperson! Lincoln applied for a farm in Bulalima-Mangwe and was promptly informed that the Company had no intention of selling it, though a general decision on the sale of land to 'such persons' was postponed.[52]

A year later, however, an application from a Mfengu minister, John N'Gono, persuaded the administration to define a general policy which could be applied to subsequent applicants. Four officials gave their verdicts. The Acting Civil Commissioner for Bulawayo, A. Honey, thought that the principle of allowing Africans to buy land next to European farms was bad, since it would not enhance the value of surrounding farms because Europeans would tend not to buy such land. Marshall Hole, then Civil Commissioner for Bulawayo, believed that the interests of white farmers and Africans were best served by keeping the latter in separate areas, and he pointed out that Africans would not improve any land which they bought. H. J. Taylor, the CNC Matabeleland, felt that the Ndebele, who had already objected to the Mfengu being given some of their best land, would further object to having foreign Africans as landlords. Moreover, he was averse to granting Africans any footing of equality with Europeans and advocated that their right to the franchise be withdrawn.[53] Finally the Surveyor-General, W. J. Atherstone, believed that no Africans should ever be allowed to own land as there was no hurry for them to rise from their position of inferiority. He warned of the dangers of stock thefts and diseases, trespass and molestation of white children, and asked: 'Why should we want contact between the two races over and above that brought about in the various spheres of labour?'[54]

Thus John N'Gono's application was rejected and a general policy was defined which was in total conflict with the terms of the Order in Council, though one might add, in fairness to the Company, that the Kenyan administration adopted precisely the same attitude.[55] This policy persisted throughout the Company's period of administration; on the one hand it refused all African applications for land though it could not prevent individual Europeans from selling to Africans, while on the other it rejected all European demands for the law to be changed arguing that there was little point in risking conflict with the Imperial Government on an issue over which it was largely in control. In fact only three further written applications were made to the Company by 1914[56] though there were also a number of informal approaches.[57]

While the question of African land purchase was at the time a small and relatively insignificant one, since very few Africans indeed were in a position to compete for land in this way, it later assumed a much wider importance and was in fact the direct precursor of the great segregation debate of the 1910s and 1920s, and of the Land Apportionment Act of 1930.

3 ACTUALITY

(i) Outside the Reserves

The two Risings of 1896 ended in markedly different ways. Whereas, in the face of strong settler opposition, Rhodes and the leading Ndebele headmen made a peace treaty as between equals, the Shona chiefs were ruthlessly hunted down and had their caves, full of people, blasted with dynamite until the last pockets of resistance were utterly crushed.[58] No peace treaty was signed in Mashonaland.

By the middle of 1896, Rhodes recognized that it would require much time and money, and cost a great many white lives before the Ndebele 'rebels' could be driven from the virtually impregnable Matopos Hills. He therefore persuaded them to accept peace terms which stipulated, *inter alia*, that they would be allowed to return to their homes. And so they were. But, as Chief Native Commissioner Taylor admitted: 'It was natural for the Matabele to assume that they would be secured in regard to their tribal lands. On this assumption they surrendered and returned to their homes.'[59] The assumption was ill-founded however, for as a result of the 1893 war their homes had become European property. It is true that the Company might have attempted to expropriate some of this land or buy it back from the settlers, but neither action was really within the bounds of political or economic feasibility.[60] Expropriation, in Rhodesia, was something that happened to Africans, but not to Europeans.

Promises were made not only to 'rebels' but also to 'loyalists'. The Ndebele headman Faku, shortly before his death, came to Rhodes to complain that his people had 'no longer any land they can call their own'. Rhodes assured him that:

> Ample land will be set aside for the whole of your nation, and I will buy all the land surrounding your kraal and also that surrounding the kraals of others of Lobengula's relatives which have been disposed of by the Government. None of you will ever be dispossessed. I pledge my word to you over this.[61]

Rhodes duly bought, 'at a high cost', the farm Sauerdale (81,000 acres) which extended southwards from Bulawayo into the Matopos Hills, on which some 4,000 people, including 'a good many former rebel chiefs "and half the dangerous characters in the land"'[62] were settled in 1897. Sauerdale was at first included in the list of reserves drawn up in 1897, but was later excluded as it was private property. After Rhodes' death, however, the people were nearly all evicted, only 400 remaining by 1947. An attempt in that year to evict the remainder to create a tourist resort led to an invocation of Rhodes' promise and a protracted legal wrangle.[63]

It is clear that in later years the Ndebele, on finding themselves at the mercy of white landlords, felt that they had been betrayed. In 1931 Chief Mdala of Insiza complained that: 'After the rebellion when we were in the "Gusu" [waterless woodland country north-west of Bulawayo] we were told to return, as we would be given land. This promise has not been carried out. The Government has sold the land to Europeans.'[64] In an almost identical tone, one Mihalihali of Umzingwane claimed in 1933, 'After the Matebele War, the Government promised to give us land, but we are still waiting'.[65] To this day the Ndebele believe that solemn promises have been broken.

Many of those who returned to their homes in 1896–7, only to find themselves living on European farms, were obliged to enter agreements under the High Commissioner's Proclamation. This allowed a two-year period of grace to the end of 1898. Thereafter landowners, both resident and absentee, began demanding rents, a demand which closely followed the imposition, for the first time in Matabeleland, of a 10/– hut tax. The rents were generally fixed at £1, though near Bulawayo they were sometimes as high as £2 or £3—the 'lack of uniformity in agreements gives rise to dissatisfaction'[66]—while Willoughby's decided to extract one bag of grain per hut.[67] The Ndebele bitterly resented paying rents for the privilege of remaining on their own land, and many of them were forced to become temporary wage labourers in order to get the necessary money. On the whole, however, the Ndebele preferred to remain on their old lands and put up with these exactions rather than move into the native reserves, which, as we shall see, were situated in inhospitable country far from the traditional areas of Ndebele settlement.

In Mashonaland the situation was rather different. A much smaller proportion of the population—about one-third, compared to two-thirds in Matabeleland—found themselves living outside the reserves, which when defined were generally much larger and contained a greater amount of 'traditional lands' than those in Matabeleland. Less use was made of the High Commissioner's Proclamation, a mere 705 people in the Chilimanzi, Gutu, Makoni, and Melsetter Districts, coming under its terms by the end of 1907, compared with some 40,000 in Matabeleland.[68] Rents were not generally imposed in Mashonaland until 1904, and verbal agreements tended to be the norm, with 'the labour condition being least popular'.[69] While in theory such verbal agreements allowed the white landlords a greater freedom of action than written agreements, in practice tenants generally had the security of knowing that a reserve was within easy reach. This meant that European farmers wishing to retain Africans on their farms as labourers were obliged to treat them with rather more deference than was the case in Matabeleland where the Ndebele tended to stay put no matter what burdens were imposed on them. Hodder-Williams cites the case of Marandellas, where Africans moved into the reserves rather than pay rent: 'A tacit agreement was struck between the European owner and the Africans that the Mashona could remain in their kraals rent free; at least, in this way, the farmer had a potential supply of labour and could actually buy maize for the labour he ultimately employed from outside.'[70] Many white farmers were in fact heavily dependent on migrant labour, from Nyasaland, Mozambique and Northern Rhodesia, as the local Shona preferred to farm on their own account.

As peace was slowly restored to Mashonaland, it became Company policy to move the Shona into the reserves where practicable,[71] and it was 'probably easier to shift the Natives and locate them where you like in Districts where there has been rebellion'.[72] It was also decided that they should be moved away from their inaccessible *kopjes* into more open country and settled in much larger villages than hitherto, thereby it was hoped, reducing the chances of a further rising and making it easier for Native Commissioners and chiefs to exercise control. The policy provoked strong reactions, for the N/Cs Chibi, Marandellas, Mazoe, Mrewa, and Ndanga all admitted that force was needed to make the Shona comply with these instructions. In fact, like the attempt in 1906 to regroup the Bemba of Northern Rhodesia into large villages, the scheme was soon abandoned as Native Commissioners found themselves unable to control effectively the movement of people, and the large villages themselves gave rise to problems of erosion and sanitation.[73] However the very attempt to enforce such a policy left little doubt that ruthless pacification was being followed up by very firm direct rule.

(ii) The Reserves

The most positive result of the armed resistance of 1896–7 was the creation of native reserves throughout the country after the restoration of the *Pax Rhodesiana.* The Risings on the one hand convinced administrators of the urgent need to assign land for African use, and on the other they helped to mould the pattern of the reserves settlement to a considerable extent. Thus although black Rhodesians lost the war, they at least achieved tangible gains from the peace. Hitherto, with the exception of the grossly inadequate Gwaai and Shangani Reserves, there was no land in Rhodesia which had been immune from the threat of instant expropriation. One might argue that the sheer impact of white settlement would in time have compelled the Company to set aside reserves for Africans, as happened subsequently in Kenya, but it was undoubtedly the Risings which made their provision a matter of urgent necessity. Had there been no violence, reserves might not have been assigned until much later, by which time, as happened in South Africa, considerably more land would have fallen into European hands.

The manner in which the reserves were created demonstrates the falsity of viewing colonial administrations as monolithic, for there were wide differences of approach among the Native Commissioners themselves, and conflicts between the Native Commissioners, the two Chief Native Commissioners and Administrator Milton. On the whole, the Native Commissioners tried to obtain as much good land as was available and were even on occasion prepared to recommend the expropriation of European land, while the Chief Native Commissioners attempted to balance the respective demands of African and Europeans. Milton always tended, in cases of conflict, to back the settlers and point out that Africans who found difficulty obtaining land could always move to other districts where there was a great abundance.

In many ways the task of the Native Commissioners was an unenviable one, and in view of the fact that it was not intended at the time that the reserves should be the Africans' share of the land, it is unreasonable to criticize them for their part in creating a division of the land which has remained fundamentally unaltered to this day.

In the first place, the Native Commissioners were given no criteria on which to base their selection of land; they were left to fend for themselves and do the best they could in the conditions obtaining in their district. Moreover, they appeared to be unaware of the value of working with their colleagues in neighbouring districts. As a result, their interpretations of what was required tended to vary enormously. The N/C Hartley, for example, made his reserves 'large enough for all purposes', on the grounds that it would be easier to reduce rather than increase them in the future; while the N/C Lower Gwelo decided, for reasons unstated, that his reserves should be 'as small as possible'. Some, like 'Wiri' Edwards at Mrewa, paid careful attention to tribal boundaries and to the needs of extensive cultivators, while others failed or were unable to make such provision.[74] A confused pattern therefore emerged in which individual inclinations were allowed to run riot.

Inclinations had to be tempered however by a solid core of reality, for it was clearly understood that certain categories of land could under no circumstances be selected for a reserve. Foremost among these were the land already alienated to Europeans, land on the Gold Belt (which was also closed to Europeans until 1903),[75] land near existing or projected railways,[76] and, in some districts, land which could easily be defended in the event of another rising.[77] Thus the extensive vested interests built up during the Jamesonian era were left untouched. The estimated 15·8 million acres granted to Europeans by March 1899,[78] representing one-sixth of the total area of Rhodesia and, quite literally, the Europeans' pick of the country which included virtually the entire Ndebele homeland, could not be considered for African use, even though some Native Commissioners were extremely reluctant to concede the point. But it was not quite as simple as that, for the Survey Department, responsible for assigning European land, and the Native Department, which demarcated the reserves, did not work in concert. The result was that most Native Commissioners had no idea of how much land had been granted to Europeans or where, since so much of it was lying unoccupied.[79] They wrote in to headquarters, but the Chief Native Commissioners were unable to enlighten them.[80] Often therefore they inadvertently included European farms within the reserve boundaries; the farms subsequently had to be excised and the reserve might be left quite inadequate.[81]

It must also be remembered that the creation of the reserves was intimately linked with the suppression of the Risings, especially in Mashonaland. Towards the end of hostilities the most urgent priorities facing the Native Commissioners were to get people to surrender, to disarm them, and then to settle them in the new reserves. As a general rule, 'rebels' were rounded up first, and then when the district seemed secure, 'neutrals' and 'collaborators' were attended to. One might logically expect that the 'collaborators' would have been signalled out for generous treatment, but nowhere in the written records is there any mentioned of a Native Commissioner specifically rewarding a chief for his 'loyalty' by assigning him a large reserve. In part this is accounted for by the fact that the settlement was clearly prejudiced by the amount of land alienated to Europeans before the Risings, and irrespective of the intricacies of Shona and Ndebele attitudes during the fighting such land could not be expropriated and made available for African use. On the other hand it is reasonable to surmise that some Native Commissioners—and most of them were actively involved in the fighting—may have decided, without mentioning the fact, to reward 'collaborators' so far as it was in their power to do so. In this category might be placed Chiefs Chirumanzu,[82] Chibi, Zimuto, Matibi, and Gutu, all of whom were rewarded for their 'loyalty' with subsidies in 1897,[83] and subsequently received generous treatment in the allocation of reserves. But whilst in some instances the 'rebels' were rounded up into small, condensed areas, and the 'loyalists' were left with the pick of the land, this was not always the case. In Mazoe, where the Rising involved nearly the whole district, Chief Chiweshe was the first to surrender and as a result found himself located on an extensive reserve named after him and rewarded with the nominal 'paramountcy'.[84] Similarly in Charter, the 'rebels' were situated on what became the Narira and Mangene Reserves, while 'collaborators' such as Gunguwo and Huchu were left stranded and subsequently had their land occupied by European farmers.[85] Another prominent 'loyalist', the Manyika chief Umtasa, who had greatly assisted the Company in 1893 and again in 1896, could not be helped, as nearly all his land had been expropriated before 1896. A subsequent N/C Umtali wondered 'whether there was ever such another disgraceful breach of faith in the whole history of the British Empire'.[86]

Thus it is difficult to detect any uniform pattern. Much depended on the accidents of alienation, the fortunes of war and the personal inclinations of the Native Commissioners. Nowhere is this better illustrated than at Marandellas, where 'pacification' took the form of clearing the road between Salisbury and Umtali and driving Africans away from their homes along the road into the neighbouring hills. When the Native Commissioner subsequently came to assign reserves, he did so in the areas into which Africans had been pushed, mistaking them for their traditional homes.[87]

In the light of such complexity, it is scarcely surprising that the quality and extent of the reserves should very greatly from district to district. These variations are illustrated in detail in Appendix I (see pp. 251–78). In Matabeleland, where land was generally more arid and thus had a smaller carrying capacity than in Mashonaland, the area of the 16 reserves chosen was estimated to be 7·7 million acres,[88] or a mere 17 per cent of the total area of the province (see map 3). Of this total, some 5·3 million acres comprised the remote, waterless and largely uninhabited Gwaai, Shangani, and Nata Reserves. As Milner confessed: 'The selection of the additional reserves has been a matter of no small difficulty owing to the fact that so large an amount of the best land in the country was, in the first days of the occupation, alienated to syndicates and private individuals.'[89]

Hence no reserve could be assigned in the Bulawayo District, and only a small one of under 5,000 acres in Umzingwane, where over half the

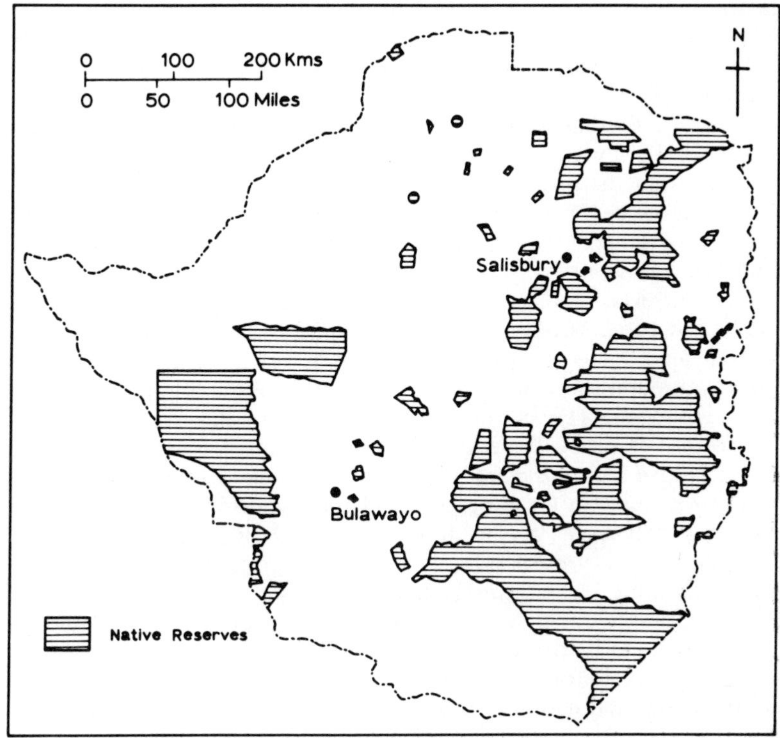

Map 3—Native Reserves, 1910 (*from Christopher 1971*).

district was in the hands of Willoughby's. Similarly, in Insiza and southern Bubi, the Native Commissioners were able to make only very limited and inadequate provision for Africans. The N/C Insiza's suggestion that the Company expropriate some European land was flatly rejected by Milton.[90] In Matobo a reserve was selected in the Matopos Hills by the first Native Commissioner, but his successor was unable to find it and it was eventually abandoned when found to contravene the peace terms issued at the end of the Rising.[91] This left the district without a reserve. The general situation in Matabeleland therefore was that practically the whole of the central *high veld* around Bulawayo was in European hands[92] and hence only grossly inadequate provision could be made for the Ndebele. The great bulk of the Matabeleland reserves lay in the dry Kalahari soils to the north and north-west of Bulawayo, which the Ndebele had never deigned to inhabit.

In Mashonaland, where the reserves totalled an estimated 17·1 million acres,[93] or 37 per cent of the total area of the province, the situation was a little better (see map 3). This was partly because much less African land had been taken up by Europeans, but an additional factor may have been a highly irregular circular from the CNC Mashonaland in August 1900 informing Native Commissioners that: 'It is to be clearly understood that after this no recommendation for the setting aside of any ground for a Native Reserve will be considered by [Milton]...so that adequate provision for all time should now be made.'[94] This was irregular because the Imperial authorities were insistent that the provision was *not* to be final, but the circular may have had the beneficial effect of persuading Native Commissioners to assign land generously, and there is evidence to this effect for the Mrewa and Victoria Districts.[95]

Even in Mashonaland, however, Resident Commissioner Clarke wrote, 'in some parts a difficulty in finding suitable land has been experienced...owing to the large portions of territory alienated to companies and individuals before the justice of making provision for natives had [met] the consideration which it has since received.'[96] The Chief Native Commissioner, H. M. Taberer, also admitted that 'in some cases Native Commissioners have been driven to select ground not altogether suitable for Reserves', and that while some reserves were 'unnecessarily large', 'this is mainly accounted for by the fact that they have had to select ground interspersed with granite and ground unfit for cultivation'.[97] This was certainly the case in Inyanga, where the Native Commissioner was forced to disregard the general injunction that the Shona be moved from easily defensible *kopjes*, and to assign reserves in precipitous, inaccessible, and badly watered country because all the good land had been taken up by Europeans.[98] In Victoria and Umtali, where land had also been extensively alienated, small scattered reserves were all that could be provided, the N/C Umtali observing that these would afford less danger in the event of another rising and would moreover facilitate the supply of labour.[99] The N/Cs Hartley, Makoni, Mazoe, and Salisbury all experienced great difficulty in selecting suitable reserves, since so much of the best land had been taken by Europeans. At the other extreme, however, in the remote and unhealthy districts on the borders of the country—Darwin and Mtoko in Mashonaland, Gwanda, Sebungwe, and Wankie in Matabeleland—where there had been no European penetration or settlement, it was not felt necessary to assign any reserves. This task was eventually undertaken by the Native Reserves Commission of 1914–15.

In the light of all this evidence, and there is further detail in Appendix I, it is not easy to agree with Richard Haw, speaking on behalf of the Rhodesian 'Ministry of Information', when he claims that the present poverty and desolation of the reserves 'is due to the way the land has been used', since 'there is no truth whatsoever in the allegation that Black areas comprise the *worst soils*'.[100]

Fortunately the full implications of the reserves settlement did not become apparent for a number of years; indeed, some Native Commissioners had no wish to disturb Africans by telling them that a division of the land had been made. In 1898 H. J. Taylor, the CNC Matabeleland, thought it unwise to mention the matter, as 'it would inevitably lead to a good deal of discontent amongst the natives, as they are much too primitive to understand the portioning out of land';[101] while the N/Cs Mazoe and Victoria refrained from pointing out the reserve boundaries until 1908 in order not to 'worry the minds of the natives prematurely'.[102] But such a fiction could only be maintained for a short period within the reserves, on unalienated land or in cases where European owners neither occupied their land nor charged Africans rent for living on it. As soon as landlords began to impose rent or labour agreements, Africans were only too aware that a land division had been made. This awareness was to spread rapidly after 1908, with the initiation of the Company's 'white agricultural policy', but for a few brief years there was a period of relative African prosperity which we shall now examine.

(iii) The Era of Peasant Prosperity

Despite all that had happened in the years 1890–6, peasant farmers in Rhodesia were able in the period 1896–1908 to seize the opportunities afforded by the opening of new markets, and to set off 'on the high road to prosperity'[103] in search of an agricultural security hitherto denied them by *shangwa*. The labour once employed in maintaining defensive positions against raiders could now be turned to agricultural production, while Shona manpower was no longer abducted for incorporation into the Ndebele state. Thus the Shona immediately began producing surplus crops[104] for sale to the Europeans, who numbered some 11,100 in 1901. Hence it proved possible, and obviously preferable, for the Shona to meet their tax commitments through the sale of foodstuffs and cattle rather than by becoming migrant labourers. Indeed, as Phimister has argued, such was the viability of the peasant sector at this time that mine wages were forced up from between 5/– and 10/– per month in 1896 to between 30/– and 80/– in 1903.[105] As Lawrence Vambe puts it: 'Now that my people were under foreign rule, they believed even more firmly than they had before that self-sufficiency in their own food supplies was essential to their limited freedom. As long as they grew enough food for themselves they were spared the humiliation of working for white men,'[106] white men who had, it should be remembered, so recently crushed the Shona Rising with appalling brutality. This conscious withholding of labour meant that Rhodesian employers were obliged to rely heavily on *chibaro* migrant labour from the north.

So we find that in 1903 African sales of grain and stock, some of which was exported, fetched about £350,000, while in the same year

African wage earnings amounted to only about £100,000 to £150,000. In other words, agricultural sales comprised some 70 per cent of all African cash earnings. An indication of the extent to which the Shona were responsible for this situation can be deduced from the fact that in 1902 only an estimated 13 per cent of able-bodied Shona men worked for three months for a white employer, compared to 48 per cent of the Ndebele; in the following year the figure was about 20 per cent for the Shona and about 50 per cent for the Ndebele.[107] The main reason for this difference was that the economy of the Ndebele had been shattered in the 1890s. Their cattle had been destroyed, their land expropriated, and their raiding brought to an end; hence they were obliged to become wage-earners far earlier than the Shona in order to meet the demands of both tax and rents. An additional factor was that wages tended to be higher in Matabeleland than in Mashonaland.[108]

Shona prosperity was made possible by a combination of factors. At this time many Shona were still living on the *high veld* within easy access of the main European markets and the railway line, the population was small and hence there was no pressure on the land.[109] In addition the opening of numerous small mines provided an increasing demand for food and beer for the mineworkers (mostly foreign migrants forced to come to Rhodesia by the lack of markets and employment opportunities at home) which the Shona were able to meet, and which resulted in increased prices for their produce—bags of maize fetching 30/– to 40/– at the turn of the century.[110] Also the number of African-owned cattle rose rapidly from an estimated 43,926 in 1901 to 195,837 in 1908, and many people found in the stock trade an easy way of meeting their financial obligations. Thus something of a minor agricultural revolution took place, mirroring exactly the earlier South African experience, with new crops such as market vegetables being grown as the demand arose. Hence, 'the Shona responded to the new dietary regulations for the mines introduced in 1907 by growing and marketing more beans and monkey nuts',[111] while the VaShawasha people, helped by the Jesuit fathers of Chisawasha Mission, were 'able to supply Salisbury with maize, cement, beef, timber, and a certain amount of wheat, barley, and grapes'.[112] Indeed, some Shona near Salisbury were at this time employing other Africans as wage labourers for 10/– per month, while many of those previously involved in the working of alluvial gold abandoned this 'in favour of meeting the more lucrative demands of an expanding produce market'.[113] In general, Native Commissioners displayed remarkably little enthusiasm for all this activity, largely because it reduced the labour supply,[114] but perhaps also because, like their counterparts in Nyasaland and elsewhere, they 'preferred the warlike noble savage to the passive unmanly farmers'.[115]

Even the doubling of the hut tax from 10/– to £1 in 1904,[116] though it meant that the African contribution to the revenue increased from

27 to 41 per cent, failed to curb this expansion.[117] This was certainly facilitated by the fact that the Shona faced no real competition as yet from European farmers. Arrighi estimates that in the 1903–4 season, European holdings 'accounted for approximately 5 per cent of the total acreage under cultivation and for less than 10 per cent of the total marketed output'.[118] Most European farmers found it far more profitable to trade in African produce than become producers themselves and, in the Marandellas District at least, they relied upon their tenants to grow sufficient maize to feed their 'foreign' labour force.[119] All this explains why the British South Africa Company and the white landlords, *bona fide* and absentee, were perfectly happy to allow the Shona to remain where they were, and why there was no concerted attempt to push them into the reserves.[120] After 1908, however, when Europeans began farming on a much larger scale, things began to change.

4 CONCLUSION

The much-needed Imperial awakening was a response both to the chronic maladministration of the Company and to the Shona and Ndebele Risings which so violently drew attention to these misdeeds. It managed to achieve a number of reforms, notably the creation of native reserves throughout the country and the posting of a Resident Commissioner to Salisbury; but it was not able, nor of course did it seek, radically to alter the economic and political basis on which Rhodesia had been created. Thus the reserves could be assigned only in areas left untouched by the whites, the large landowning companies were easily able to ward off the Company's attack on themselves. Any diminution in the Company's authority to govern was adequately compensated for by the emergence of the settlers as a potential political power. The threat of the white settlers, and in particular of the white farmers, was not yet menacing, and for a brief period many African peasants were able to bask in a certain degree of prosperity as they clung tenaciously to their economic independence. This was to be a short-lived phenomenon, however, and though Imperial intervention was able to modify, it could not eliminate either the past effects or the future implications of the age of the fortune-hunters.

NOTES

1. Cited in V. Stent, *A Personal Record of Some Incidents in the Life of Cecil Rhodes* (Bulawayo 1970), 67.
2. Minutes of the Company's meetings were henceforth submitted to the Colonial Office for examination.
3. C. Palley, *The Constitutional History and Law of Southern Rhodesia, 1888–1965* (Oxford 1966), 149 n. 3.

4. For an assessment of the role of the Resident Commissioner, see Palley, *Constitutional History*, 173–87.

5. Milner to Asquith, 18 November 1897. Cited in C. Headlam (Ed.), *The Milner Papers, South Africa, 1897–99, Vol. I* (London 1931), 178.

6. After M. E. Weale, N/C Chilimanzi, had been dismissed for 'cohabiting with native women', Resident Commissioner Clarke was told by Milner that 'the details of Native Administration will require the most careful watching for some time to come'. C.O. 417/258, Milner to Clarke, 10 October 1899.

7. The radical missionary Arthur Shearly Cripps wrote at the end of the Company period that: 'Southern Rhodesian natives have surely had much in past years to thank a succession of Imperial Representatives for, Resident Commissioners, to whom the first of their number, Sir Marshal Clarke, handed on a fine tradition.' A. S. Cripps, 'Native Rights under a new Government in Southern Rhodesia', *South African Quarterly*, **4**, 3, 1922, 6.

8. G. Sims, 'Paladin of Empire: Earl Grey and Rhodesia', *Central Africa Historical Association*, Local Series Pamphlet **26**, 1970.

9. As yet there exists no single study of the important Milton administration (1896–1914), though reputedly one is now being written. *Mbire*, **2**, 1973, 11.

10. Hist. MSS. MI 1/1/2, Milton to his wife, 25 September 1896.

11. Rhodes House, Oxford, Rhodes Papers, MSS. Afr. s. 77, Grey to Cawston, 26 May 1897.

12. M. C. Steele, 'The Foundations of a "Native" Policy in Southern Rhodesia, 1923–33', Ph.D. thesis, Simon Fraser University, 1972, 6. See also J. J. Taylor, 'The Native Affairs Department in Southern Rhodesia, 1894–1914', Ph.D. thesis, University of London, 1974. Stigger is at pains to show how the Company deliberately deceived the Colonial Office and succeeded in Matabeleland in continuing to employ in the Native Department a number of unpopular officials who had been recruited prior to the Ndebele Rising. P. Stigger, 'The Emergence of the Native Department in Matabeleland, 1893–1899', unpublished 1974, 27–36.

13. In Nyasaland for example district commissioners were almost constantly being moved around, and consequently were never really able to get in touch with the people. Compare this to the cases of W. E. Edwards, who was N/C Mrewa 1895–1931, and J. W. Posselt, who was N/C Charter 1902–35.

14. T. O. Ranger, *Revolt in Southern Rhodesia, 1896–7* (London 1967).

15. D. N. Beach, 'The Rising in South-Western Mashonaland, 1896–97', Ph.D. thesis, University of London, 1971.

16. C.O. 417/213, Milner to Martin, 24 August 1897; C.O. 417/392, Minutes by Grindle and Harris, 20 and 22 November 1904.

17. C.O. 417/168, Grey to Martin, 29 June 1896.

18. For the full correspondence, see C.O. 417/168–9.

19. C.O. 417/168, Grey to Martin, 29 June 1896. The High Commissioner's Proclamation actually stated 'not less than seven', but this was a misprint and should have read 'not more than seven'.

20. F. Wilson, 'Farming, 1866–1966', in M. Wilson and L. Thompson (Eds.), *The Oxford History of South Africa, Vol. II, South Africa 1870–1966* (London 1971), 117–18.

21. R. H. Palmer, 'Land in Zambia', in Palmer (Ed.), *Zambian Land and Labour Studies, Vol. 1*, National Archives of Zambia Occasional Paper 2 (Lusaka 1973), 56–66.

22. Nyasaland Protectorate, *Report of a Commission to Enquire into and Report upon Certain Matters Connected with the Occupation of Land in the Nyasaland Protectorate* (Zomba 1921), 5.

23. L 2/1/175, Memo by Taylor, 17 June 1904.

24. South Africa, *South Africa Native Affairs Commission, 1903–5, Vol. IV* (Cape Town 1905), Evidence of Sir M. Clarke, Resident Commissioner, 31 August 1904, 74. The CNC Matabeleland agreed with Clarke; he felt that: 'The object of the Native reserves is to provide land for those Natives who have been removed for not being prepared to enter

into contract as between landlords and tenant.' Evidence of H. J. Taylor, 8 September 1904, 154.

25. H. W. Fox, *Memorandum on Problems of Development and Policy* (London 1910), 22.

26. P. Mason, *The Birth of a Dilemma* (London 1958), 263.

27. Mason, *The Birth*, 264, 267–70, 313–15.

28. C. 9138, British South Africa Company, *Papers relating to the British South Africa Company: I. Southern Rhodesia Order in Council, dated 20th October 1898.* (London 1899), 61.

29. C.O. 417/209, Martin to Rosmead, 12 April 1897.

30. C.O. 417/213, Acting CNC Matabeleland to Milton, 24 July 1897.

31. C.O. 417/213, Martin to Milner, 23 August 1897, Minute by Graham, 21 February 1898.

32. Ironically, it was Milner himself who, as Colonial Secretary, approved the Southern Rhodesia Native Reserves Order in Council of 1920, which made the reserves permanent.

33. C.O. 417/213, Milner to Chamberlain, 31 December 1897, Chamberlain to Milner, 26 February 1898.

34. C.O. 417/320, Acting Administrator to Clarke, 5 December 1899 and 3 January 1900, Clarke to Milner, 8 January 1900.

35. EC 4/4/7, Executive Council Minute No. 674, 27 October 1902: EC 4/4/8, Executive Council Minute No. 703, 2 December 1902; C.O. 417/392, Clarke to Milner, 2 and 27 December 1902.

36. Thus in March 1903 Harding complained: 'It is time the boundaries of the reserves were settled.' C.O. 417/371, Minute by Harding, 21 March 1903.

37. C.O. 417/392, Minutes by Grindle and Harris, 20 and 21 September, and 22 November 1904.

38. C.O. 417/451, Chester-Master to Selborne, 8 January 1908.

39. C.O. 417/451, Crewe to Selborne, 11 July 1908.

40. Hist. MSS. MI 1/1/2, Milton to his wife, 25 September 1896.

41. In 1903 a Catholic missionary informed the Native Affairs Commission that: 'Such companies have grabbed already far too much land, and it is high time that a stop should be put to it. Such companies are the worst enemies of agriculture and the general development of the country. They promise any amount of things, but the execution therefore is delayed till the Greek Kalends.' *South African Native Affairs Commission, Vol. V*, Written reply by J. M. Ronchi, 1903, 361.

42. Initially, in 1899, the LegCo comprised the Administrator, the Resident Commissioner, 5 Company nominees and 4 elected settler members. In 1908 the settlers achieved a majority of 7 to 5, which was increased to 12 to 6 in 1914. In 1923 they achieved responsible self-government, and in 1965 they declared themselves independent.

43. Grey, who won a somewhat corrupt election in 1899, admitted his interests to the Native Affairs Commission. *South African Native Affairs Commission, Vol. IV*, Evidence of R. Grey, 31 August 1904, 61–72.

44. EC 4/2/2, Minutes of the Administrator's Council, 2 December 1896; Rhodes House, Oxford, Rhodes Papers, MSS. Afr. s. 228.1, Grey to Rhodes, 26 May 1897.

45. It is interesting to note that at much the same time the white planters of Nyasaland were winning a battle against Government attempts to force them to set aside some of the undeveloped land on their estates for the use of their African tenants.

46. A similar reform took place with regard to gold, for 'in 1903 all claims pegged before 1895 on which work had not begun were forfeited and thrown open to the public, and subsequent legislation required that registered claims be worked every year'. G. Kay, *Rhodesia: A Human Geography* (London 1970), 44.

47. L 2/2/93, Acting Director of Land Settlement to Secretary, Department of Administrator, 16 May 1914.

48. H. W. Fox, *Memorandum containing Notes and Information concerning Land Policy, with accompanying Papers and Maps* (London 1912), 31.

49. 'Report of the Surveyor General for the Two Years ending 31st March, 1900', in British South Africa Company, *Reports on the Administration of Rhodesia, 1898–1900* (London 1901), 175–6.

50. For Mphoeng and Raditladi, see Q. N. Parsons, 'Khama III, the Bamangwato, and the British, with Special Reference to 1895–1926', Ph.D. thesis, Edinburgh University, 1973, 117–20, 129–30, 168–9, 379–80.

51. J. M. Mackenzie, 'African Labour in the Chartered Company Period', *Rhodesian History*, **1**, 1970, 43–4.

52. EC 4/4/9, Executive Council Minute No. 822, 6 April 1903.

53. The 1898 Order in Council stipulated a theoretically colour-blind franchise but, as in the Cape, there were property, income, and literacy qualifications which barred all but a tiny handful of Africans from getting onto the voters' roll. These qualifications were raised periodically in order to 'maintain standards'.

54. L 2/1/175, Acting C/C Bulawayo to C/C Bulawayo, 25 May 1904, Memo by C/C Bulawayo, 4 June 1904, Memo by Taylor, 17 June 1904, Atherstone to Newton, 27 June 1904.

55. M. P. K. Sorrenson, *Origins of European Settlement in Kenya* (Nairobi 1968), 167–8, 224–5.

56. In 1909 a group of 23 Karanga from the Dutch Reformed Church's Morgenster Mission applied for land in Victoria; in 1914, 17 Sotho applied for land, also in Victoria; and in the same year the Sotho chief Moroka asked for 100,000 acres in Rhodesia for himself and his 40,000 followers, who were scattered about the Transvaal and the Orange Free State.

57. For example, the CNC Mashonaland in his 1906 Report mentioned that 'sundry natives of the more enlightened type, some of whom were Mashonas, made enquiries about buying land'. *Report of the Chief Native Commissioner Mashonaland for the Year ended 31st March, 1906* (Salisbury 1906), 4.

58. Ranger, *Revolt*, 268–310.

59. D.O. 63/3, Memo by Taylor, February 1927.

60. Grey and Milton did lease for five years—the cost of outright purchase proving too great—the farms Insangu (33,000 acres) in Bubi District, and De Beers (200,000 acres) in Insiza/Belingwe, which were used as temporary reserves but which therefore afforded only temporary security.

61. J. G. McDonald, *Rhodes—A Life* (London 1927), 270.

62. L. H. Gann, *A History of Southern Rhodesia* (London 1965), 133.

63. S 235/445, Firm of Bulawayo lawyers to CNC, 13 March 1947. I am indebted to Keith Rennie for this reference.

64. S 1542/N2, Report of the Insiza Native Board Meeting, 27 March 1931.

65. S 1542/N2, Report of the Umzingwane Native Board Meeting, 18 May 1933. The local N/C commented that: 'The Natives appear to have convinced themselves that Mr. Rhodes did make them a promise about a Reserve in this District, though they cannot state definitely what it was.' S 1542/N2, N/C Umzingwane to S/N Bulawayo, 27 May 1931.

66. NB 6/4/5, Report of the N/C Insiza for the month August 1903.

67. NB 6/4/2, Report of the Acting Assistant N/C Gwelo on a patrol, 6 April 1898.

68. RC 3/7/14, Milton to Chester-Master, 17 December 1907.

69. *Report of the Chief Native Commissioner Mashonaland for the year 1909* (Salisbury 1910), 8.

70. R. Hodder-Williams, 'The Development of Social, Economic and Political Attitudes in a European Community, 1890–1968', draft thesis, 178.

71. The N/Cs Lomagundi, Makoni, Marandellas, Melsetter, Mrewa, Ndanga, Umtali, and Victoria all mention in their early reports that they encouraged this movement in certain instances, notably when they felt that white farmers were being unreasonable.

72. D. O. 119/586, Report of the N/C Victoria for the quarter ending June 1900.

73. T. O. Ranger, *The Agricultural History of Zambia*, Historical Association of

Zambia Pamphlet No. 1, (Lusaka 1971), 14; Hist. MSS. ED 6/1/1, Reminiscences of 'Wiri' Edwards, 102.

74. N 3/24/11, N/C Hartley to CNC Mashonaland, 7 July 1900; L 2/2/117/10, N/C Lower Gwelo to CNC Matabeleland, 20 May 1899; N 3/24/21, Acting N/C Mrewa to CNC Mashonaland, 29 January 1898; *African* (*South*) *659*, Acting N/C Mrewa to CNC Mashonaland, 21 May 1901.

75. The CNC Mashonaland informed his deputy that 'it is not permissible to have a Native Reserve on a Gold Belt'. N 3/24/11, CNC Mashonaland to Assistant CNC Mashonaland, 12 March 1900.

76. The N/C Makoni revealed that 'Mr. Milton told me that it was not desirable to make a Native Reserve on the railway line'. N 3/24/16, N/C Makoni to CNC Mashonaland, 2 December 1899. The railways were built remarkably quickly, to serve the interests of the mining industry. Bulawayo was linked to South Africa in 1897, Salisbury to Beira in 1899, Salisbury to Bulawayo in 1902, and Bulawayo to Victoria Falls in 1904. A. H. Croxton, *Railways of Rhodesia* (Newton Abbot 1973).

77. P. S. Garlake, 'The Mashona Rebellion East of Salisbury', *Rhodesiana*, **14**, 1966, 10.

78. British South Africa Company, *Reports, 1898–1900*, 175–6. The actual figure given (converted from morgen) was 15,762,364 acres, but the accuracy implied is quite spurious.

79. A similar situation appears to have obtained in Kenya, where 'no one has any idea of what land is available for survey' and the administration had 'only the haziest ideas' about the location of reserves. Sorrenson, *Origins*, 183.

80. The N/C Umtali asked his chief to 'please inform me if there is any ground available for native reserve ... It is impossible for me by looking at the country to tell whether ground is vacant or not, from what I know the whole country is pegged off as farms or for large companies'. The CNC commented that 'it has been impossible to find out with any accuracy what ground has been alienated or to find beacons of Farms and Concessions granted'. N 3/24/32, N/C Umtali to CNC Mashonaland, 28 January 1898; N 3/24/1/1, CNC Mashonaland to Under Secretary, 18 March 1898.

81. Instances of this kind occurred in at least six districts: Charter, Salisbury, Umtali, and Victoria in Mashonaland; and Belingwe and Umzingwane in Matabeleland.

82. The situation here was somewhat complicated by the fact that N/C Weale had married one of the chief's daughters.

83. D. N. Beach, 'The Politics of Collaboration: South Mashonaland, 1896–7', University of Rhodesia, Salisbury, Department of History, Henderson Seminar No. 9, 1969, 9.

84. C. G. Chivanda, 'The Mashona Rebellion in Oral Tradition: Mazoe District', University College of Rhodesia, Department of History, undergraduate seminar paper, 1966, 13–14.

85. D. N. Beach, 'Afrikaner and Shona Settlement in the Enkeldoorn Area, 1890–1900', *Zambezia*, **1**, 2, 1970, 31; Beach, 'Politics of Collaboration', 30.

86. S 1542/L4, N/C Umtali to CNC, 29 September 1938.

87. R. Hodder-Williams, 'Marandellas and the Mashona Rebellion', *Rhodesiana*, **16**, 1967, 51.

88. The spuriously accurate figure given was 7,751,160 acres.

89. C.O. 417/213, Milner to Chamberlain, 31 December 1897.

90. NB 6/1/2, Report of the N/C Insiza for the year 1898–9.

91. NBE 1/1/1, N/C Matobo to CNC Matabeleland, 31 July 1898; C.O. 417/213, Martin to Milner, 18 September 1897.

92. Even the Government surveyors, Fletcher and Espin, complained in 1900 that more farms could not be laid out, 'with a few brushes of colour. We have often pointed out the difficulty of obtaining suitable ground in Matabeleland where such large tracts of the best land have been granted to companies'. L 2/2/86, Fletcher and Espin to Secretary, Department of Administrator, 10 May 1900.

93. The spuriously accurate figure given was 17,138,560 acres.

94. N 4/1/1, CNC Mashonaland to all N/Cs, Mashonaland, 26 August 1900.

95. ZAD 3/1/1, Evidence of W. Edwards and J. A. Halliday to Native Reserves Commission, 5 June and 11 August 1914.

96. C.O. 417/392, Clarke to Milner, 2 December 1902.

97. N 3/24/1/1, CNC Mashonaland to Under Secretary, 18 March 1898.

98. N 3/24/12, N/C Inyanga to CNC Mashonaland, 12 October 1900.

99. NUA 2/1/3, Report of the N/C Umtali for the half-year ending March 1900.

100. Rhodesia Information Service, *Land Apportionment in Rhodesia* (Salisbury 1965), 8.

101. C.O. 417/320, Memo by CNC Matabeleland, 22 July 1898.

102. ZAD 3/1/1, N/C Mazoe to Secretary, Native Reserves Commission, 29 May 1915.

103. British South Africa Company, *Reports, 1898–1900*, 199.

104. In 1903, the missionary A. S. Cripps noted that Shona farmers would 'produce in good seasons a great surplus of grain for trading'. *South African Native Affairs Commission, Vol. V*, written reply by A. S. Cripps, 1903, 320.

105. I. R. Phimister, 'Peasant Production and Underdevelopment in Southern Rhodesia, 1890–1914', *African Affairs*, **73,** 291, 1974, 221. See also G. Arrighi, 'Labour Supplies in Historical Perspective: A Study of the Proletarianization of the African Peasantry in Rhodesia', *Journal of Development Studies*, **6,** 1970, 228 n. 14.

106. L. Vambe, *An Ill-Fated People* (London 1972), 176. Even the BSA Company, noting that the acreage under cultivation in Mashonaland in 1898–9 was estimated to be 542,700 compared to 236,186 the previous year, observed: 'It is obvious that the natives now plant crops for sale, and are not content, as formerly, to grow merely for their own consumption.' British South Africa Company, *Reports, 1899–1900*, 179.

107. Arrighi, 'Labour Supplies', 229 n. 30 and 31.

108. C. van Onselen, *Chibaro: African Mine Labour in Southern Rhodesia, 1900–1933* (London 1976), 228.

109. In 1903 the N/C Lomagundi noted that 'the native by having a sufficient area of land to raise more than sufficient crops for his own consumption, absolutely free of all rent or tax on it, is in the position of an independent landed class'; while in the same year the N/C Makoni observed that 'at present the Natives living in these Reserves cultivate as much ground as they please, the products of which are in excess of their consumption and the large remaining surplus they sell to the traders in order to meet their Hut Tax and by this mode of living the average Mashona does not require to look for work'. N 3/6/3, N/Cs Lomagundi and Makoni to CNC Mashonaland, November 1903.

110. M. G. B. Rooney, 'European Agriculture in the History of Rhodesia, 1890–1907', M.A. thesis, University of South Africa, 1968, 116.

111. J. M. Mackenzie, 'African Labour in South Central Africa, 1890–1914 and Nineteenth Century Colonial Labour Theory', Ph.D. thesis, University of British Columbia, 1969, 208. 'Between 1890 and 1912 much, if not most, of the fresh produce requirements of Rhodesian mines was supplied by the competitive local black peasantry.' van Onselen, *Chibaro*, 42.

112. Vambe, *An Ill-Fated People*, 149. Mission stations not infrequently acted as stimulants to agricultural innovation.

113. I. R. Phimister, 'Alluvial Gold Mining and Trade in Nineteenth-Century South Central Africa', *Journal of African History*, **15,** 1974. 454.

114. 'The natives today are cultivating twice the amount they did when we came to the country', wrote 'Wiri' Edwards in 1906, 'and so long as the land is unlimited and they have a market for their produce, will the labour supply suffer.' In 1898 the N/C Malema welcomed a swarm of locusts as 'not an unmitigated evil, for a really abundant harvest of kaffir corn and mealies would probably have the effect of reducing the number of Native labourers 50 per cent'. N 9/4/19, Report of the N/C Mrewa for the month June 1906; NB 6/4/2, Report of the N/C Malema for the month November 1898.

115. M. L. Chanock, 'The Political Economy of Independent Agriculture in Colonial

Malawi: The Great War to the Great Depression', *Journal of Social Science*, **1**, 1972, 117.

116. 'At present the paltry sum of 10/– per hut is so easily earned it will never induce them to work', wrote the N/C Makoni in 1903. N 9/1/8, Report of the N/C Makoni for the year ending March 1903. The Company had wanted the tax increased to £2, while some white employers thought £4 would be a more suitable amount, but the Resident Commissioner vetoed these proposals.

117. Hut tax receipts rose as follows: 1897–8, £35,638; 1898–9, £73,122; 1901–2, £92,415; 1904–5, £176,538. The £200,000 level was reached in 1909–10, £300,000 in 1925–6, and £400,000 in 1937–8.

118. Arrighi, 'Labour Supplies', 209.

119. Hodder-Williams, 'The Development', 178.

120. The N/C Victoria noted in 1899 that: 'This district is very much depended on for grain and if the natives were shifted into Reserves from farms whenever the farmers were unreasonable the supply would be greatly interfered with.' N 9/4/4, Report of the N/C Victoria for the month July 1899.

CHAPTER 4

The Beginnings of the Squeeze 1908–14

As the white population increases ... the squeezing-out process is inevitable, and it was for this reason that the reserves were created.

Administrator's Secretary, 1909.[1]

1 BACKGROUND

In South Africa, it was the mineral revolution which ultimately led to the impoverishment of the African peasantry. In Rhodesia, paradoxically, it was the absence of such a revolution which had much the same effect. In 1907 a party of British South Africa Company Directors came to Rhodesia,[2] toured the country, and decided that the time had come to put an end to the myth of the 'Second Rand'. The myth had persisted for so long partly because mineral exploitation had been severely hindered by the Risings of 1896–7 and by the South African War of 1899–1902, which had cut Rhodesia's rail links to the south.[3] The end of that war was followed by a brief mining boom, but this collapsed in the financial crisis of 1903–4. The Company then made tentative enquiries into land settlement schemes elsewhere in the British Empire, and set up its own Land Settlement Committee in 1905 before sending out its Directors two years later. The Directors, no doubt influenced by contemporary Imperial policies in Kenya, concluded that it was essential to diversify the economy and that the best way of doing this was to encourage European farming, thereby promoting greater economic self-sufficiency, cutting the import bill, and raising the value of land and providing more traffic for the railway, both of which at the time were owned by the Company. This 'white agricultural policy', as it was called which began in 1908, was ultimately to affect radically the position of Africans on the land.

In pursuance of this new policy, the Company launched an attack on the native reserves in the years 1908–14, with the intention of recovering all the best land and making it available for European settlement. The attack met with opposition, however, and the Company began to think in terms of a reserves commission which might achieve the same result and at the same time legalize the Jamesonian legacy.

Imperial responses were conditioned, inevitably, by the wider South African economic and political situation. Having won the war, the British proceeded magnanimously to lose the peace to the Afrikaners and to sanction the creation of the Union of South Africa in 1910. Thereafter, it was always a major objective of Imperial policy to maintain a 'moderate' Afrikaner government in Pretoria, loyal to the British Empire. There is nothing new about neo-colonialism! It was confidently expected that Rhodesia would join the Union, perhaps in 1914, when the Company's charter was due for review, and Imperial attitudes towards land policies were very much conditioned by this belief.

The settlers, whose political power was steadily growing, began to make their presence felt. They challenged the Company's claim to the ownership of the unalienated land, they were suspicious of the Company's motives in attacking the reserves; they also claimed that land prices 'fluctuated continually' and were fixed 'apparently by the after-breakfast mood of some official in London Wall'.[4] More important, as the number of white farmers grew, so they came into conflict and competition with the many successful African farmers, and, with the help of the Company, they began the long process of proletarianizing the peasantry.

2 POLICY

(i) The White Agricultural Policy

As an immediate consequence of the directors' tour of 1907, a number of far-reaching changes were introduced in an attempt to promote the growth and expansion of European farming. To begin with, an Estates Department was set up in 1908 designed specifically to promote European settlement and deal with all applications for land, while an information office under a Superintendent of Emigration was opened in London with a branch in Glasgow, and two agents were sent to South Africa to publicize Rhodesia at the leading agricultural shows there. The Estates Department 'possessed a fairly numerous staff, including an engineer, a citrus adviser and land inspectors'.[5] The type of immigrants it sought were people, '... endowed with capital and experienced in farming on the African *high veld*. In addition they had to be loyal to the British connection.'[6]

Also in 1908 the Department of Agriculture was reorganized and a first Director of Agriculture appointed. He was Dr. E. A. Nobbs, a trained scientist from the Cape—previous officials had been amateurs—and he was responsible for stimulating a great deal of agricultural research much of which was published in the pages of the *Rhodesia Agricultural Journal*. A number of specialists were appointed to the

Department, including a botanist, an entomologist, a chemist, an agriculturist, an irrigation engineer, and a tobacco expert. An experimental station and farm were opened near Salisbury, and a bevy of visiting experts were encouraged to come and offer their advice. The Department was thus in a position to place a wide range of extension facilities at the disposal of the new European farmer, and in 1910 it took over the grading of maize for export, a job previously undertaken by railway officials. Some idea of the extended scope of the Department may be gauged from the fact that its annual average expenditure rose from £10,065 in the years 1903–4 to 1908–9, to £22,476 in the period 1909–10 to 1913–14.

The Company itself began to develop an interest in tobacco, citrus, and in ranching. It used its Central Farms, near Bulawayo, Gwelo, Marandellas, Sinoia, and Umtali, to familiarize new immigrants from Britain, who had to possess a minimum of £700 capital, with the problems of farming on the Rhodesian *high veld.* A Land Bank was set up in 1912 with a share capital of £250,000, to make credit facilities 'available for persons of European descent only'.[7] The Bank gave loans of up to £2,000 for the purchase of farms, livestock, and agricultural equipment, and for improvements such as fencing and irrigation works, etc. The loans had to be repaid at 6 per cent interest within ten years. The Bank was of crucial importance in helping new European farmers to establish themselves on the land. Its success led white farmers elsewhere (notably in Kenya where one was not established until 1930)[8] to demand something comparable. Such facilities were not available to African farmers in Rhodesia until 1945.

In addition, the minimum price of ranching land was reduced, until 1912, to about 8½d. per acre, while agricultural land was reduced to 3/9d. This compares with the 1904 average prices of 34/4d. in the Orange Free State, 33/– in the Cape, 28/6d. in the Transvaal, and 25/– in Natal,[9] while land along the Northern Rhodesian line of rail was fetching between 3d. and 8d. per acre at this time.[10] Also a much simpler form of land title was issued, rebates of between 20 and 30 per cent on the purchase price were granted in the event of positive improvements being made to the land, a concession claimed in practice by an 'infinitesimal' number of farmers;[11] in addition, the Mines and Minerals Ordinance was revised so as to restrict the privileges of prospectors on occupied farms,[12]—an interesting comment on the state of the mining industry.

The Company also decided in 1907 to draw a distinction for the first time between its administrative and its purely commercial revenue and expenditure. Land was placed on the commercial side, to the intense displeasure of the settlers, who asserted that the Company owned the land only in its adminstrative capacity. The matter was eventually submitted to the Privy Council for arbitration in 1914 (see chapter 6, pp. 133–5). Also in 1914, as a result of settler parliamentary criticism the previous year, the Company introduced a Land Settlement Ordinance which would have created a board administered jointly by the Company and the settlers, with compulsory power of purchasing unoccupied land within 25 miles of the railway line for resale to immigrants, and powers of taxing undeveloped land in proportion to its distance from the railway. It was estimated at this time that only 8·4 million of the 33 million acres situated within 25 miles of the railway remained unsold, but a very high proportion of this lay in the remote and inhospitable Wankie District along the Victoria Falls railway; there was little available on the *high veld.* Fortunately for the absentee owners, the Ordinance was dropped when the Company refused to admit that its adoption would not prejudice the settlers' claim to the ownership of the unalienated land in the case then being heard by the Privy Council.[13]

Such were the manifestations of the new white agricultural policy; its effects will be examined presently.

(ii) The Attack on the Reserves

In order to promote European settlement, the new Estates Department clearly needed land. But as a result of Jameson's earlier generosity[14] and the assignment of native reserves throughout the country, it soon discovered that there was very little suitable land near the railway which it could offer to incoming settlers. There were two possible solutions to this problem: to attack the absentee landlords or the native reserves. Since a compromise with the landlords had been arrived at only with great difficulty in 1903, it was clearly easier, and a good deal more politic, to attack the reserves.

Though colonial administrators were often in the habit of seeking 'final solutions' to problems which defied finality, it was clear to everyone at the time that the reserves settlement of 1902 was far from immutable. Indeed, the Colonial Office's subsequent approval in 1908 was given strictly on the understanding that the reserves were provisional and were open to further consideration. The reasons are fairly obvious. Topographical knowledge of Rhodesia was in its infancy in 1902, and hence many reserve 'boundaries' were subsequently found to be 'faulty, vague or impossible to locate',[15] while many of the estimated areas of the reserves later proved equally inaccurate. Gradually, as more white farms were occupied and surveyed, it became possible to determine some of the reserve boundaries more accurately; to the delight of the Estates Department it was frequently found that the guesses of 1902—for they were no more than that—had underestimated the areas of many reserves. The Surveyor-General, W. J. Atherstone, subsequently a member of the 1914–15 Native Reserves Commission and the 1925 Land Commission, wrote a lengthy memorandum in August 1908, in which he compiled a list of such reserves, and came to the conclusion that those in Mashonaland were 'extremely excessive' and that many of them should be reduced.[16] The point was taken up the following year by F. W. A. Taylor, an official of the Estates Department, who reiterated that many of the reserves were far in excess of what had originally been intended and that there was now only a limited amount of land available for incoming settlers. He therefore proposed that his Department, in conjunction with the Native Department, should define the reserves more accurately and 'thoroughly inspect, locate and report on any land considered suitable for settlement and make definite proposals for new boundaries of these Reserves so as to exclude from them such land as is recommended for farming purposes.'[17]

The Native Department was prepared to consider amendments. At a conference of its senior officials in 1909, it was agreed that some reserves were excessive, others were insufficient, and hence 'a careful re-adjustment' was needed.[18] Nevertheless, as the CNC Mashonaland pointed out, while some reserves might appear excessive on paper, in reality 'owing to the nature of the country, it is often necessary to include large tracts which are entirely useless to anyone',[19] a view with which Administrator Milton was in full accord.[20] Native Commissioners were therefore requested to study the requirements of their districts and to suggest possible readjustments.

The Estates Department made no bones about the kind of adjustments it wanted. C. D. Wise, the Director of Land Settlement, believed that reserves should be reduced where they were situated on the routes of projected branch railway lines, and pressed for the exchange of all 'red and black soil which the natives never work, for a lighter class of soil'.[21] The Company approached the Colonial Office on the subject, and was told that all proposals should go through the Resident Commissioner. He in turn suggested that equality of area should be the basis of any exchange, but this the Company rejected, arguing that each case should be judged on its merits, a view upheld by the Colonial Office. Hence in 1910, Wilson Fox, the Company's General Manager, instructed Milton, Wise, and P. S. Inskipp the Commercial Representative, 'to put your heads together and make an attack in force upon the existing conditions'.[22]

This 'attack in force', though it succeeded in reducing the reserves by some half a million acres by 1914, did not in fact yield the results anticipated by the Estates Department. Details of the numerous exchanges of land are to be found in Appendix I (see pp. 252–78), from which it appears that the only potentially injurious reduction was to the Chikwanda Reserve, Gutu District, but this was approved by the Resident Commissioner after a personal inspection; the largest single reduction, over 800,000 acres, occurred in the notorious Gwaai Reserve, Nyamandhlovu District, and the population of the surrendered area numbered only twelve.

Much of the credit for repulsing the Company's attack must be given to the two British Resident Commissioners, Fair and Burns-Begg, and to the Native Commissioners of Mashonaland. Both Resident Commissioners, on taking up office, were told to give 'careful attention' to the reserves question,[23] and this they did, personally inspecting in all cases the areas involved in any proposed major exchanges of land. They were thus able to prevent the Estates Department pushing through proposals which were contrary to African interests. In this role as protectors of the reserves, as in their earlier one of preventers of blatant forced labour, the Resident Commissioners revealed the very real value of an Imperial presence in Salisbury.

No less important were the Native Commissioners, especially those in Mashonaland, where the Estates Department most wished to cut down the reserves. The Native Commissioners were prepared to allow very considerable reductions to reserves which were not needed, but they were not prepared to sanction exchanges which they considered blatantly prejudicial to the people's welfare. Thus in Chilimanzi, where hundreds of people had recently moved into the Serima Reserve to avoid paying rent, the N/C was strongly critical of a proposal that the whole reserve be surrendered: 'Because there are a few thousand acres of good ground there is no reason why the whole reserve should be thrown open and the natives turned out of their homes, where they have been living ever since we conquered the country.'[24] In a similar situation in Hartley, the N/C believed that 'if Reserves were to be further cut down ... it would be breaking faith' with Africans to whom he had guaranteed security of tenure.[25]

Such determined opposition invoked the wrath of the Company's Commercial Representative, P. S. Inskipp, who complained bitterly to the London Office that 'nearly every case in which difficulty has arisen has occurred in Mashonaland, and I regret to say that I do not consider that the Native Department of that province shows any disposition to co-operate with the Commercial Branch'.[26] Similarly, Atherstone bemoaned the fact that 'it is extremely difficult to reduce present Reserves even when they are doubtless in excess of requirements ... it appears difficult to get the Native Department to propose any reduction in any instance'.[27] Interestingly, there existed in Kenya at precisely the same time 'a smouldering quarrel between the Land Office, anxious to obtain land for settlement, and the provincial administration, anxious to protect African rights to land'.[28]

The failure of the Company's attack produced a search for alternative solutions. Thus in 1911 Wise and Inskipp, complaining of slow and difficult progress, suggested that a reserves commission be set up comprising a representative of the Estates and Native Departments, with Atherstone, who was known to favour a reduction of the reserves, as a 'neutral' chairman.[29] But the idea was, for the moment, rejected as being 'highly detrimental to European settlement and the general interests of the country';[30] indeed Milton was warned 'not to agree to any final settlement which will for all time to come prevent European settlement in areas which are suitable for white occupation'.[31]

The Imperial authorities were also at this time opposed to the idea of finality and wished to persevere with the existing elastic system in which all amendments to the reserves were subject to Imperial scrutiny, and the Company was under an obligation to provide land for Africans according to their needs.[32] On the other hand, they were concerned at the number of proposed changes the Company was putting forward since this was 'tinkering with a question which ought to be dealt with as a whole and because it is likely to have a most irritating effect on the natives'.[33] They were also worried that the role of the reserves was apparently changing with Africans being shunted into them as a result of the expansion of European farming, a certain amount of railway construction, the imposition of grazing fees, and the rapidly increasing numbers of African cattle.[34]

By 1914, however, a number of political considerations combined to convince the British Government of the desirability of a final settlement of the reserves question. In that year the Company's twenty-five-year-old charter was up for renewal, and the settler majority in the Legislative Council was increased from two to six seats—an event which, as the Colonial Office acknowledged, 'must inevitably result in some diminution of the control of the Imperial Government over the internal affairs of the territory'.[35] It seemed clear that the Company's administration was coming to an end and that in all probability Rhodesia would join the Union of South Africa, whose constitution contained a clause explicitly specifying that possibility. It was felt that a settlement was essential before such a change transpired, since 'afterwards the Imperial Government will have no control'. Moreover, the new settler-elected members would probably have 'scant sympathy' for the reserves[36] and have to be bought off, and induced to accept a commission by being allowed to contest the Company's claim to the ownership of the unalienated land in the Privy Council.[37]

By degrees, and as the attack on the reserves failed to harvest the expected dividends, the Company too began to favour a final settlement. In 1913 a director, Rochfort Maguire, following consultations with High Commissioner Gladstone, Resident Commissioner Burns-Begg, and the settler leader Charles Coghlan, felt that: 'We should do better by consenting to a general commission subject to satisfactory composition of commission and terms of reference. Do not consider that in any other way we have any chance of reclaiming areas set aside for native reserves, but not required.'[38] Later in the same year another director, Dougal Malcolm, after discussions with Gladstone, proclaimed that the Company was prepared to accept a commission provided it was empowered to make a final settlement which would relieve the Company of any further obligation to provide reserves. Malcolm enquired whether there would be any objection if the commission were to recommend an overall reduction of the reserves, and Gladstone, on his own initiative, thought there would not be provided the whole scheme was to African advantage.[39] This concession was clearly the decisive factor, and the Company went on to win important victories relating to the composition and terms of reference of the commission (see chapter 5, pp. 104–7).

Thus a protracted sequence of correspondence and discussion between Imperial and Company officials came to an end in June 1914, when the Native Reserves Commission set about the task of producing a final settlement of the reserves. Essentially it was the Company's frustrations and the Colonial Office's fears which drove them both to support such a final settlement. The Company, having failed in its attack on the reserves, perceived in the proposed commission the opportunity to renew its attack; while the Colonial Office, though alive to the advantages of the powers it retained under the existing flexible system, was conscious that these powers would diminish as the political power of the settlers increased and as Rhodesia moved towards union with South Africa. Ironically, not long after the Native Reserves Commission began its work, the First World War broke out and Rhodesia's political future was 'frozen' for the duration of hostilities. Finally, it should be noted that the two sides looked to the 1914 Commission to provide mutually exclusive recommendations: the Company wanted the best land taken out of the reserves and made available for new settlers, while the Colonial Office wanted adequate land for future requirements bearing in mind that Africans were increasingly being squeezed into the reserves.

(iii) The *Rationale* of the Reserves

At the same time that Imperial and Company officials were contemplating the suitability of the reserves and the possibility of reaching a final settlement, another discussion was going on regarding their very purpose. Initially, as we have seen in the previous chapter, the reserves had been created in the immediate aftermath of the Risings of 1896–7, but it was not intended that they should be permanent. In the decade preceding the First World War, Rhodesia was slowly recovering from its earlier upheavals, but the country's political and economic future remained largely undetermined. The pattern of white settlement varied greatly. In areas such as central Matabeleland and Melsetter, white farmers were comparatively thick on the ground; while in the remote Gwanda, Mtoko, and Wankie Districts they were non-existent and it had therefore not been thought necessary to demarcate any reserves before 1914, and the Darwin and Sebungwe reserves had yet to be defined with any degree of accuracy. Thus one finds that in 1915 only an estimated 55 per cent of the African population lived in the 20·5 million acres of reserves; in Mashonaland the proportion was 65 per cent and in Matabeleland only 36 per cent. The remainder lived either on the 22·4 million acres which had been alienated to Europeans by 1913, or on the 47·8 million acres which remained unalienated.

In the circumstances, it was virtually impossible to evolve a coherent, country-wide land policy, and there existed a very wide divergence of opinion on the relative merits of African settlement within and outside the reserves. Policy was therefore not dictated from above, but was evolved locally in response to particular circumstances such as the degree of white penetration and the attitudes of European farmers, the relative amount and nature of the land reserved for Africans and Europeans, and sometimes the personal idiosyncrasies of Native Commissioners.

On the whole the Imperial authorities tended to favour the retention of adequate reserves as a sanctuary for those being evicted from European farms, and in order to protect 'tribal society' and build up some form of local self-government. 'An increasing body of natives divorced from the land is incompatible with this policy', wrote one official.[40] The Company, on the other hand, took a very different view, one which was later shared by the Native Reserves Commission. It argued that reserves were for those who could not rapidly be assimilated into the new conditions, and consequently where the tribal way of life could still be maintained. But it did not feel responsible for providing land for every unborn African since European civilization was inevitably bringing about the disintegration of the tribal system; hence agriculture would cease to be the sole means of livelihood, and the need for reserves would diminish rather than increase, as Africans began to play an integral role in a de-segregated economy.[41] This was the voice of international capitalism, which had yet to perceive the advantages of Southern African racial prejudices.

As for the settlers and the farmers in particular, they generally believed that large reserves encouraged idleness and that land should only be provided for those whose labour was not required, and then only in areas which could be of no possible use for European settlement.[42] Among the Company's local officials, however, there existed a divergence of views. Those in the Estates and Land Settlement Departments tended, like the farmers, to feel that all Africans whose labour was not needed should be sent packing into the reserves. Thus Atherstone failed 'to see any use of native tenants on a private farm over and above the privilege the owner of such farm has of obtaining a certain amount of labour from among them'.[43] Native Commissioners, on the other hand, often encouraged Africans to remain on, or even move onto, European farms in the hope that they would learn something from the white farmers. W. S. Taberer, the CNC Mashonaland, was a fervent believer in this approach. 'If every reserve were cut down to one half it would be the best thing that could happen' he wrote, 'get them out of the reserves—throw them in contact with civilization and progress, and you will make useful citizens of them.'[44] The Administrator, Milton, was also in favour 'of encouraging natives to live on farms ... and not to provide Reserves in convenient localities'.[45]

A wide diversity of approach is thus discernible which reflects the fact that while European farming was increasing in scale it had not as yet triumphed over African agriculture. Also discernible are the seeds of the great segregation debate which was to dominate the following decade.

(iv) Outside the Reserves

By 1908 it had become apparent that the position of Africans on both alienated and unalienated land was in need of revision. The law regulating African settlement on European farms, the High Commissioner's Proclamation of 1896, had been an emergency post-Risings piece of legislation. Twelve years later, European farmers were charging Africans rents varying between 10/– and 40/– with often an additional 10/– for each wife after the first. 'Rack-renting' was acknowledged to have been one of the major causes of the 1906 Bambatha Rebellion in Zululand,[46] and the Company was particularly concerned about the situation in Matabeleland, where absentee landlords were earning some £30,000 a year by indulging in what was known locally as 'kaffir farming', 'an inelegant phrase that nevertheless conveys accurately the source of non-productive white land-owner profits'.[47] They lived off their tenants' rents rather than by the sweat of their brows. The practice, which was widespread in Southern Africa, was disliked by Native Commissioners on the grounds that it was immoral, and by *bona fide* white farmers on the grounds that it locked up both land and labour which could be put to better use.[48] It was a delegation of the latter which in 1907 successfully persuaded Milton and the visiting British South Africa Company Directors to introduce a locations ordinance, modelled once again on Cape legislation, with a view to limiting the numbers of Africans allowed on European farms and penalizing the absentee landlords. The result was the Private Locations Ordinance of 1908 whose implementation was delayed until 1910 as a result of agitation from absentee landlords, who felt that it was 'totally uncalled for in the conditions existing in the country under which the native enjoys unexampled happiness and prosperity'.[49]

The Ordinance stipulated that all agreements with tenants should be written rather than verbal and witnessed by a Native Commissioner; that owners who were occupying their land should take out a licence of 1/– per annum for each adult male on their farm, whereas absentee landlords should pay 5/– and that there should be a maximum of 40 adult males permitted on each farm of 3,175 acres. At the insistence of the Native Department, the draft Ordinance had contained clauses guaranteeing African tenants sufficient land and covering all kinds of agreements, but opposition from the farming community meant that by the time the Ordinance had passed through the Legislative Council, the first clause had been eliminated and labour agreements were exempted, to the relief of the white farmers of Melsetter whose tenants worked for three months a year without pay.[50]

The desire to increase the labour supply was undoubtedly one of the main motives behind the passing of the Private Locations Ordinance, though it could be disguised, for the benefit of Imperial officials, as an attack upon absentee landlordism. A far more blatant attempt to procure labour, however, was the Company's imposition of a rent on unalienated land, a rent which went straight into its commercial pocket.

The Company had been urged to take this step in 1906 on the grounds that 'it might have the effect of sending labour on to the farms, where labour was short',[51] and it decided to take the plunge in 1908 citing the 1884 Natal Squatters Rent Law as a precedent. In discussion, Milton was in favour of adopting the Cape rental of 10/–, but the CNC Matabeleland and the London Office argued that the Natal rate of £1 should be enforced. Milton was told to use his discretion in collecting the rent in the more remote districts, 'though it should at the same time be your object to extend the area of collection as fast as can prudently be done'.[52] In Matabeleland, where 64 per cent of the African population lived outside the reserves and was thus used to paying rents or offering labour, no difficulty was anticipated in connection with the new rent, but in Mashonaland wholesale movements into the reserves, and even into neighbouring Mozambique, were predicted. The CNC Mashonaland was asked whether, in the light of these reports, he wished to recommend any exemptions. He replied that if it were simply desired to raise revenue a sliding scale would be appropriate, but if it were the intention to clear Africans off the land, 'the whole Native Department condemns the measure out of hand'. The Department had not been consulted and had no option 'but to acquiesce in what it considers a most unwise and unfair proposition. There are not a few Native Commissioners who go so far as to predict the very gravest trouble'. Marshall Hole, Milton's secretary, sourly informed the CNC that 'it does not appear that you were directly asked to express an opinion',[53] and his objections were brushed aside.

The rent was first imposed in 1909, when £9,682 was collected, only £3,619 of it in Mashonaland. There were no Imperial objections, doubtless because this was a sphere in which the British could exercise no control unless they decided to contest the Company's claim to ownership of the unalienated land. But, as one official observed, 'it seems hardly worth while to do so at present'.[54]

3 ACTUALITY

(i) White Farmers, Black Peasants

The white agricultural policy was in many ways a success. In the years 1908–14 over $5\frac{1}{2}$ million acres of land were sold, and the 1911 census revealed a total of 1,324 European farmers compared to only 545 in 1904 (see table II), while the number of occupied farms rose from 301 in 1904 to 2,042 in 1914, when 183,407 acres were estimated to be under crops. By 1912, according to van Onselen, 'commercial agriculture was sufficiently profitable to draw capital previously employed in mining', while 'after 1912 most of the mines' food requirements were met by European commercial agriculture'.[55] For the most part, the new European farmers concentrated on the production of maize and tobacco, and on cattle ranching.

Initially the Europeans obtained maize seeds from African farmers, and soon they were growing maize throughout much of Mashonaland, 'with some success, but in a primitive and extensive fashion, so that the European yields were little better than those of the African peasant farmers'.[56] In particular it was the 'Gold Belt' areas, which were first made available to white farmers in 1903, which were opened up for maize production. It was initially grown, by African labour rather than machinery, to feed African labourers at the mines, but it began to be exported in quantity for the first time in 1909. Production rose dramatically from 45,815 (203 lb) bags in 1903–4 to about 180,000 bags in 1906–7 to 634,133 bags in 1913–14. Exports, mostly to Britain, rose from 11,442 (200 lb) bags in 1909 to 202,105 bags in 1914 (see table III), and some indication of the extent to which it 'caught on' can be gauged from the fact that an estimated 78 per cent of European land under cultivation in 1924 was devoted to maize.

TABLE II

Estimated Number of European Farmers, 1904–65

1904	545	1931	2,582
1907	772	1941	3,169
1911	1,324	1951	5,094
1921	2,355	1965	5,700

TABLE III

Production, Exports, and Yields of European-grown Maize, 1900–65

Year	*Production (203 lb bags)*	*Exports (200 lb bags)*	*Yield (bags per acre)*
1899–1900	c. 17,000	n.a.	n.a.
1903–04	45,815	n.a.	n.a.
1906–07	c. 180,000	n.a.	n.a.
1908–09	n.a.	11,442	n.a.
1909–10	n.a.	19,555	n.a.
1910–11	393,166	23,378	n.a.
1911–12	n.a.	6,796	n.a.
1912–13	n.a.	38,963	n.a.
1913–14	634,133	202,105	3·93
1914–15	914,926	346,855	5·47
1915–16	680,285	51,259	3·88
1916–17	938,130	222,218	4·62
1917–18	591,722	214,257	3·08
1918–19	889,969	333,001	5·13
1919–20	1,120,548	488,665	6·45
1920–21	1,220,768	346,556	6·55
1921–22	662,636	32,556	3·64
1922–23	1,505,580	789,411	6·80
1923–24	1,080,084	313,585	4·66
1924–25	1,068,904	383,338	4·47
1925–26	1,393,654	434,592	5·81
1926–27	1,659,597	547,156	6·20
1927–28	1,268,100	597,834	4·29
1928–29	1,826,345	582,675	5·61
1929–30	1,917,252	745,010	6·04
1930–31	1,436,644	636,194	5·25
1931–32	1,882,856	1,136,140	7·44
1932–33	1,156,321	644,251	4·66
1933–34	1,728,065	333,603	7·01
1934–35	1,269,185	311,822	4·76
1935–36	1,985,848	934,086	7·45
1936–37	2,039,341	1,426,355	7·35
1937–38	1,432,003	396,336	5·18
1938–39	1,209,818	43,238	4·55
1939–40	1,625,292	387,550	6·49
1943–44	1,673,459	246,539	6·85
1946–47	885,030	3,370	3·51
1947–48	1,912,005	70	5·91
1954–55	2,734,920	nil	7·51
1956–57	3,777,000	2,520,000	10·20
1960–61	5,951,600	3,810,000	14·60
1964–65	5,201,000	50,000	12·00

Tobacco, which was ultimately to develop into 'the mainstay of European farming and a major support of the Rhodesian economy', was, like maize, widely grown by Africans before the European occupation. It had the attraction of offering a quick return for capital invested—a necessity if new immigrants were to be attracted to Rhodesia—and of being best grown in the previously neglected sandy soils so that 'the Company would now be able to sell many farms which had hitherto attracted few buyers'.[57] The British South Africa Company did a great deal to stimulate its production. It appointed a tobacco expert, G. M. Odlum, to the Department of Agriculture and sent him off to study tobacco growing in America, Turkey, and Greece, whence he returned with fourteen Greeks, who were to assist in the development of Turkish tobacco.[58] European farmers began to grow the crop avidly, especially in Mashonaland, and production rose swiftly from 132,310 lb in 1909–10 to about 2,240,000 lb in 1912–13. The following year, when 3,061,750 lb were grown (see table IV), 'over-production brought chaos to the industry and for several years it floundered'.[59]

TABLE IV

Production of European-grown Tobacco, 1903–65

Year	*lb*	*Year*	*lb*
1903–04	147,355	1928–29	7,042,464
1906–07	166,505	1929–30	5,844,203
1909–10	132,310	1930–31	8,644,390
1910–11	c. 450,000	1931–32	15,026,202
1911–12	c. 1,000,000	1932–33	14,170,642
1912–13	c. 2,240,000	1933–34	26,792,092
1913–14	3,061,750	1934–35	21,205,924
1914–15	426,423	1935–36	22,401,707
1915–16	637,261	1936–37	22,048,804
1916–17	910,684	1937–38	26,709,747
1917–18	620,171	1938–39	23,442,092
1918–19	1,467,612	1939–40	35,701,124
1919–20	2,947,627		
1920–21	3,746,982	1941–42	49,061,281
1921–22	3,182,259	1943–44	34,464,449
1922–23	2,810,781	1949–50	107,017,869
1923–24	3,878,460	1955–56	171,671,368
1924–25	2,405,940	1960–61	233,351,177
1925–26	5,659,809	1962–63	194,782,358
1926–27	19,264,532	1963–64	323,835,833
1927–28	24,943,044	1964–65	245,988,593

Cattle ranching, which began to expand over much of the Matabeleland *high veld* also owed its origin to African initiative, though in this case the Europeans simply stole the bulk of the Ndebele cattle after the war of 1893 and subsequently added to this haul by acquiring much of the herd looted from Mpezeni's Ngoni in Northern Rhodesia in 1899.[60] The 'indigenous' cattle were, according to a visiting professor from Edinburgh University, 'remarkable for their hardiness and ability to keep their flesh during the long dry season when pasturage is poor, but are very small in carcase'.[61] This was confirmed in the drought of 1912, when, as the CNC Mashonaland noted, 'the superiority of the condition of the native stock, as compared with the better breed animals owned by Europeans, was most marked'. The local cattle were in fact upgraded by crossing with bulls imported from Northern Rhodesia, Nyasaland, and South Africa, which helped to add weight and quality to the existing durability.[62] Some 33,000 head of cattle were imported in the years 1909–13, and the number of European-owned cattle rose sharply from 38,611 in 1907 to 341,878 in 1914. Experts came from Texas, and a number of ranching companies began operating on a large scale for, as the handbook for prospective settlers put it, 'while 15,000 acres is taken as the minimum area suitable for ranching, opportunities exist for the establishment of large ranching concerns (involving 50,000 acres and upwards) for those possessed of the necessary means'.[63]

All this activity inevitably gave rise to conflict and competition between European farmers[64] and the Shona and Ndebele. In the previous chapter we have seen how the Shona in particular were quick to seize the new opportunities afforded, and to opt out of the labour market by growing a sufficient surplus to meet their tax and other commitments. But European maize production posed an obvious threat to African peasant farmers, and European tobacco was grown predominantly on the sandy soils which the Shona had long favoured.[65] Indeed, in 1908 the CNC Matabeleland noted of new settlers: 'In selecting their land they have naturally been guided by the number of natives located thereon, whose knowledge of the productive powers of the soil must necessarily be the best guide.'[66] Similarly, as the number of African-owned cattle more than doubled—from 195,837 in 1908 to 406,180 in 1914—this led to tremendous competition for grazing lands with the Europeans, whose own cattle were increasing even more rapidly and whose number exceeded the number of African cattle for the first time in 1919 (see table V). This competition was especially fierce in Matabeleland where the land was drier and the European farms larger than in Mashonaland. Thus Europeans began to challenge Africans for markets,[67] for cattle, and for land—beginning what Marshall Hole aptly called 'the squeezing-out process'.[68]

Prior to this rapid expansion of European farming, white landowners had very little reason to turn Africans off their land since they could

TABLE V
Estimated Cattle Holdings, 1901–73

Year	*African*	*European*
1901	44,000	12,000
1907	164,000	39,000
1911	330,000	164,000
1916	492,000	469,000
1921	854,000	905,000
1931	1,628,000	954,000
1941	1,769,000	851,000
1951	1,810,000	1,155,000
1961	1,988,000	1,586,000
1971	2,786,000	2,709,000
1973	3,037,000	2,573,000

extract from them crops, rents, or labour, as desired, and because African farmers were playing such a vital role in food production. But by 1914 the situation had begun to change. Because European agriculture was labour- rather than capital-intensive,[69] and because 'the sight of white men, and even more so white women, performing heavy, unskilled manual labour is one that is generally repugnant to most Rhodesians and South Africans',[70] the white farmers needed black labour. Here they came into competition with the mines which were also labour-intensive, and which could generally afford to pay higher wages.[71] The demand for labour indeed grew very rapidly. 'In 1905, it was calculated that Southern Rhodesia needed no more than 25,000 labourers all told', writes Philip Mason, but 'by 1910, the mines alone wanted 39,000 and the farmers another 23,000.'[72] The white farmers needed large supplies of seasonal labour—at precisely the time when local Africans needed to tend to their own crops. They thus found themselves in much the same position as white farmers elsewhere in Africa, heavily reliant on migrant labour from depressed areas and demanding a reduction of African land-holdings and a tax mechanism which would effectively compel local Africans to work on their farms.[73] This was not going to be easy, for the Shona 'developed an almost universal anti-farmer mentality which considered that a Shona . . . had sunk very low, socially and economically, if he worked for a white farmer'.[74] The situation was much the same in the Eastern Province of Northern Rhodesia, where the Ngoni preferred to seek work in Southern Rhodesia rather than on the local farms, even in years when local wages were high. But in areas such as central Matabeleland, Melsetter, and the Shire Highlands of Nyasaland, where virtually all the good land was in European hands, the farmers found things much easier. The Ndebele, for example, were 'so determined to stick to their old haunts or places they like, that they will agree to almost anything (within reason) rather than leave'.[75]

In response to the widespread refusal of local Africans to work, and in order to reduce the competitiveness of African farmers and cattle-owners, the European farmers began to impose high rents and other burdens to evict Africans from their farms and push them into the reserves, which were situated further away from the main markets.[76] Thus began the first steps in the 'proletarianization of the African peasantry'.

(ii) The Movement into the Reserves

By 1908, at the time of the beginnings of the squeeze, the general tendency in Mashonaland was 'to leave the farms as soon as they become occupied, and move into the reserves',[77] while in Matabeleland, where the reserves were less ample and far less desirable, the people preferred to remain on European land and make the best terms they could. At various times in the next six years attempts were made to force the people of both provinces to seek shelter in the reserves.

The Private Locations Ordinance of 1908, for example, was thought likely to involve the movement into the reserves of 1,335 Africans in nine districts of Mashonaland, and 199 in two districts of Matabeleland, as these numbers were in excess of the permitted 40 adult males per farm.[78] In practice many more than this actually moved, especially in the Belingwe, Bubi, Bulawayo, Matobo, and Umzingwane Districts in the years 1910–11. This was because absentee landlords got round the 5/– per adult male licence fee they were obliged to pay for their tenants by the simple expedient of increasing their rents. In Matobo they were doubled, and elsewhere increases of between 50 and 100 per cent were reported, thus underlying the almost universal difficulty of legislating between landlord and tenant.[79]

The Company's imposition of a rent on unalienated land in 1909, so strongly criticized by the CNC Mashonaland, almost immediately caused 1,800 Africans to move into the reserves in the Charter District; while in Fort Victoria: 'Paramount Chief Bere ... was much upset at the idea of his Tribe being broken up. Practically all his natives who live on unalienated land are leaving the District.'[80] In Melsetter, where the unalienated land was particularly precious to Africans because of the extensive area of land taken up by Europeans and the total inadequacy of the reserves, the rent caused

> great dissatisfaction and in some cases distress. Within the last year practically all natives on whom the tax would fall have transferred their quarters to native reserves or alienated land. The tax is extremely unpopular and the

natives are distressed at having to give up their old homes, occupied by their ancestors from time immemorial, and by themselves for twenty years under the whiteman's rule, rent free.[81]

Movement into the reserves continued in 1910. In Gutu it was described as 'enormous', and the N/C complained that it 'has entailed a lot of extra work ... besides badly disfiguring my registers',[82] while in Lomagundi it was complicated by the fact that the reserves had not been properly surveyed so that the N/C could not be certain of settling displaced Africans within their boundaries.[83]

The Company followed up its rent with a dog tax of 5/– in 1912, which was bitterly resented, partly because dogs were widely used to keep down vermin, and partly because 'when dogs were first registered the natives were informed that no tax was being imposed'.[84]

Also in 1912, a number of ranching companies in Matabeleland decided to subject their tenants to grazing fees on top of the normal rents, an innovation which 'has given rise to a great deal of dissatisfaction'.[85] The move was widely condemned. CNC Taylor noted that: 'The natives will naturally ask, is there no finality to these impositions?', while Marshall Hole commented bluntly: 'These Companies seem determined to exact their pound of flesh.'[86] Native Commissioners wrote gloomy reports about this latest demand. Africans were complaining that they had been encouraged to buy cattle by the administration and now they were in effect being taxed for doing so, and many said they would have to leave; 7,429 people, together with some 11,000 head of cattle, were expected to move into the Belingwe, Gwaai, Lower Gwelo, Que Que, and Shangani Reserves. In Bubi, the announcement was greeted 'with a storm of protest and angry feelings', and the people complained eloquently that the landowners 'will be taking money from the flies in our kraals next; better be dead than pay such demands'.[87] News of the grazing fees caused 'Lulu' Harcourt, the Colonial Secretary, to record his 'disapproval and apprehension' and questions were asked in the Commons, but the Company pointed out that Africans always had the option of moving into a reserve and hence there was no scheme, as existed in Northern Rhodesia, for compensating people who were moved off land required by Europeans.[88] This information at least helped to convince the Colonial Office that adequate reserves were the only real means of safeguarding African interests.[89]

Despite the raising of Imperial eyebrows, the harassment in Matabeleland continued. In 1912, when an outbreak of east coast fever imposed restrictions on the movement of cattle, some landowners seized the opportunity to raise their rents; while others, rather than pay for the erection of dipping tanks ordered African cattle-owners to quit, which was an impossible demand at such a time. Others again, in 1913, refused to allow Africans who had been evicted from neighbouring farms to move cattle across their land, so that the Africans were obliged to sell for whatever they were offered. In the same year, some of the companies agreed to amend their grazing fees after their tenants had all given notice, but in most cases the tenants decided to leave anyway 'as they could not understand such a fast-and-loose policy'.[90] In 1914, the Compulsory Dipping Ordinance was passed, which 'enabled compulsory dipping to be applied in any area where this was the wish of the majority of farmers'.[91] African farmers, whose wishes were not consulted, often had to pay dipping fees of 1/– or 2/– per head of cattle per annum, and by 1923 three-quarters of all African cattle were being compulsorily dipped. Finally in 1914, some of the larger landowning companies in Matabeleland were contemplating a further increase in rent, 'but decided that owing to the political situation [the First World War] this was an inopportune time for such increase'.[92]

4 CONCLUSION

The evidence presented to the Native Reserves Commission of 1914–15 bears eloquent testimony to the effects of the great squeeze. In the Matobo District, for example, with its large numbers of African cattle, the N/C reported a net decrease in population of 7,500 for the years 1908–14, which he attributed directly to European pressures,[93] while movements off both alienated and unalienated land were especially numerous in the Insiza and Nyamandhlovu Districts of Matabeleland, and in the Mashonaland Districts of Charter and Lomagundi. It is small wonder that land grievances in Matabeleland were soon to be given coherent and overt expression in the Ndebele National Home Movement, and that Chief Maromo of Charter complained:

> My people are scattering in all directions on account of our land being cut up into farms, there is not room for us on the Reserve. We value and appreciate what the Government has done for us especially in liberating us from the Matabele rule but, we feel the Government has saddled us with an equally hard yoke and that is the partition of our land into farms for living on which we are compelled to pay rent.[94]

The squeeze was clearly being felt. Between them, the British South Africa Company and the white landowners had demonstrated their power and ability to pressurize the African peasantry, with the intention of persuading the Imperial authorities to agree to a 'final solution' after their earlier attack on the reserves had been repulsed. 'The whole native question and policy hinges more and more on the Reserves each year', wrote the S/N Gwelo in 1910,[95] as the squeeze was getting under way. It was therefore particularly unfortunate, as CNC Taylor pointed out two years later, that 'when the Reserves were originally selected the water supplies were quite adequate, but owing to the repeated droughts during the past ten years the flow of all the rivers and streams has steadily diminished'.[96] Thus, while in 1904 Atherstone had confidently predicted that the reserves could carry a population of at least $4\frac{1}{2}$ million and Milton had believed that they would suffice for another 50 years,[97] serious doubts were being cast on these assumptions by 1914, as Native Commissioners in Matabeleland in particular began to complain of the difficulty of locating displaced Africans in the reserves. Such was the situation confronting the Native Reserves Commission when it assembled in 1914. It was just one year after the Natives Land Act had proclaimed that 'segregation' was to be the official land policy of the Union of South Africa.

NOTES

1. A 3/15/11, Hole to Milton, 26 November 1909.
2. They came to Rhodesia partly in response to settler complaints that the Company was favouring the miners against the farmers unduly, and that land settlement was being discouraged by the high price of land. In addition, following his visit to Rhodesia in 1906, High Commissioner Selborne had urged the Company to set up a committee of investigation, so that the mineral and agricultural resources of the country be exploited as fully and as quickly as possible. M. G. B. Rooney, 'European Agriculture in the History of Rhodesia, 1890–1907', M.A. thesis, University of South Africa, 1968, 65.
3. Phimister makes the point that by 1894–5 Rhodes, at least, was under no illusion about Rhodesia's mineral potential, and that the Jameson Raid and the other political disturbances which followed 'were in a number of respects a direct consequence of the failure of the "Second Rand" to materialize between the Limpopo and the Zambezi'. I. R. Phimister, 'Rhodes, Rhodesia and the Rand', *Journal of Southern African Studies*, **1**, 1974, 75.
4. E. T. Jollie, *The Real Rhodesia* (London 1924), 56. The BSA Company's headquarters were in London Wall, a street in the City of London.
5. V. W. Hiller (Ed.), *A Guide to the Public Records of Southern Rhodesia under the Regime of the British South Africa Company, 1890–1923* (Cape Town 1956), 224.
6. R. Hodder-Williams, 'Afrikaners in Rhodesia: A Partial Portrait', *African Social Research*, **18**, 1974, 616.
7. S 138/21, Manager, Land Bank, to CNC, 3 September 1926.
8. R. M. A. van Zwanenberg with A. King, *An Economic History of Kenya and Uganda 1800–1970* (Dar es Salaam 1975), 209, 288–9; R. M. A. van Zwanenberg, *Colonial Capitalism and Labour in Kenya 1919–1939* (Dar es Salaam 1975), 20–6.
9. R. Hodder-Williams, 'The British South Africa Company in Marandellas: Some Extra-institutional Constraints on Government', *Rhodesian History*, **2**, 1971, 56 n. 85.
10. R. H. Palmer, 'Land in Zambia', in Palmer (Ed.), *Zambian Land and Labour Studies, Vol. 1*, National Archives of Zambia Occasional Paper 2 (Lusaka 1973), 57.
11. Department of Lands, Memorandum on Land Settlement Policy, 1925, 9.
12. P. F. Hone, *Southern Rhodesia* (London 1909), 290–7.
13. Southern Rhodesia, *Legislative Council Debates*, 8 October 1914, 788–9.
14. Jameson came to repent of his earlier actions. As one of the Company Directors who toured Rhodesia in 1907, he told a questioner: 'As regards these concessions—the Company have to a certain extent locked up the country, and I must confess that in those early days I was principally responsible for a great many of them. ... I may tell you that the Chartered Company are more sick of them than anybody else.' Hone, *Southern Rhodesia*, 187.

15. A 3/18/39/3, Milton to London Office, 10 May 1913.
16. ZAD 3/2/1, Atherstone to Secretary for Mines, 17 August 1908.
17. L 2/2/117/1, F. W. A. Taylor to Wise, Director of Land Settlement, 20 July 1909.
18. L 2/2/117/1, CNC Mashonaland to all N/Cs Mashonaland, 24 March 1909.
19. L 2/2/117/1, CNC Mashonaland to Wise, 16 November 1909.
20. Milton observed that: 'Large portions of some of the reserve areas are totally unsuitable for occupation by Europeans or natives, either because of the absence of water, or because of their mountainous or rugged nature.' A 3/18/39/3, Milton to London Office, 10 May 1913.
21. L 2/2/117/1, Memo by Wise, 4 March 1910.
22. A 1/5/8, Fox to Milton, 29 April 1910. Later in the year, Milton was told that reserves which were in excess of the original estimates, 'will have to be dealt with at no distant date by way of surrender to the Company's Estate of all such portions as are not actually needed for native purposes'. A 3/18/39/2, London Office to Milton, 17 December 1910.
23. RC 3/7/14, Selborne to Fair, 11 August 1908; RC 3/3/23, Gladstone to Burns-Begg, 12 April 1911.
24. L 2/2/117/40, Acting N/C Chilimanzi to S/N Victoria, 22 September 1911.
25. L 2/2/117/24, Acting N/C Hartley to CNC Mashonaland, 26 April 1909.
26. LB 2/1/14/2, P. S. Inskipp to London Office, 28 December 1912.
27. L 2/2/117/29, Atherstone to Hole, 12 July 1911.
28. M. P. K. Sorrenson, *Origins of European Settlement in Kenya* (Nairobi 1968), 183.
29. L 2/2/117/29, Wise to P. S. Inskipp, 29 March 1911; LB 2/1/14/2, P. S. Inskipp to London Office, 22 April 1911.
30. A 3/18/39/14, Meeting of Maguire, Birchenough, Milton and Fox, 31 July 1911. The idea had also been proposed both by the South African Native Affairs Commission of 1903–5 and by the Company's Native Affairs Committee of Enquiry of 1910–11.
31. A 1/5/8, Fox to Milton, 29 April 1910.
32. C. O. 417/514, Minute by Lambert, 12 December 1912.
33. RC 3/3/29, Burns-Begg to Gladstone, 13 February 1912.
34. RC 3/8/8, Burns-Begg to Gladstone, 1 April 1913; C.O. 417/523, Minute by Just, 24 June 1913.
35. C.O. 417/550, Colonial Office to Secretary to Treasury, 11 February 1914. The elected members' majority over the Company's nominees was extended from 7–5 to 12–6.
36. C.O. 417/550, Minutes by Tait and Lambert, 23 and 24 January 1914.
37. C.O. 417/539, Minute by Lambert, 7 April 1914.
38. LB 2/1/14/2, Maguire to (?) Wise, 14 February 1913.
39. C.O. 417/526, Gladstone to Harcourt, 13 November 1913.
40. C.O. 417/534, Minute by Anderson, 11 August 1913. See also C.O. 417/526, Minute by Vernon, 22 December 1913.
41. C.O. 417/534, Company to Colonial Office, 30 July 1913.
42. In Kenya too the settlers were anxious to cut down the reserves and so enhance the flow of labour. L. Woolf, *Empire and Commerce in Africa* (New York 1968), 343–51.
43. L 2/1/175, Atherstone to Newton, 27 June 1904.
44. *Report of the Chief Native Commissioner Mashonaland for the year ended 31st March, 1906* (Salisbury 1906), 4. C. L. Carbutt, who later became Chief Native Commissioner (1930–5), told the 1903–5 South African Native Affairs Commission: 'I consider that all reserves should be done away with, and the Natives forced to acquire and reside on land on the same terms as Europeans ... the labour difficulty ... is in a very great measure, if not entirely, due to the system of setting aside Native reserves. This places the Native on a plane entirely independent of the economic conditions which govern the lives and industry of the European population of the country, and permit of his living an indolent life in luxury, where many a poor white has the greatest difficulty in keeping body and soul together.' South Africa, *South African Native Affairs Commission, 1903–5, Vol. V* (Cape Town 1905), Written reply of C. L. Carbutt, 1903, 314.
45. T 2/29/64/12, Minute by Milton, 3 August 1914.

46. See S. Marks, *Reluctant Rebellion* (Oxford 1970).

47. C. Bundy, 'The Emergence and Decline of a South African Peasantry', *African Affairs*, **71,** 285, 1972, 375.

48. In South Africa: 'The unpopularity of "kaffir farming" amongst whites who were not receiving rent in this manner lay in the fact that it deprived them of labour.' F. Wilson, 'Farming, 1866–1966', in M. Wilson and L. Thompson (Eds.), *The Oxford History of South Africa, Vol. II, South Africa 1870–1966* (London 1971), 129.

49. A 3/21/71, Secretary, Rhodesia Chamber of Mines, to Secretary, Department of Administrator, 15 June 1908.

50. J. K. Rennie, 'Christianity, Colonialism and the Origins of Nationalism among the Ndau of Southern Rhodesia, 1890–1935', Ph.D. thesis, Northwestern University, 1973, 187–92.

51. *Legislative Council Debates*, 22 May 1906, 27. A rent had also been recommended by the South African Native Affairs Commission and the Company's 1906 Native Labour Enquiry Committee.

52. A 3/15/16, London Office to Milton, 21 March 1908. This is reminiscent of Harry Johnston's 1894 policy in Nyasaland: 'As we extend the scope of our Administration more directly over the Protectorate, so no doubt we shall be able, acting with prudence and gentleness, to extend the taxable area.' F.O. 2/66, Johnston to Rosebery, 22 January 1894. Cited in R. H. Palmer, 'Johnston and Jameson: A Comparative Study in the Imposition of Colonial Rule', in B. Pachai (Ed.), *The Early History of Malawi* (London 1972), 305.

53. A 3/15/16, CNC Mashonaland to Hole, 23 December 1908, Hole to CNC Mashonaland, 16 January 1909.

54. C.O. 417/448, Minute by Grindle, 14 November 1907.

55. C. van Onselen, *Chibaro: African Mine Labour in Southern Rhodesia, 1900–1933* (London 1976), 41–2.

56. F. Clements and E. Harben, *Leaf of Gold: The Story of Rhodesian Tobacco* (London 1962), 51.

57. G. Kay, *Rhodesia: A Human Geography* (London 1970), 113; Hodder-Williams, 'The British South Africa Company', 51.

58. In connection with the Greeks, Odlum cabled Wise: 'Kindly request that farmers and others treat them with consideration, for they are not quite Barbarians, many of them being very nice people. None of them speak any language other than Greek, but they have books and will soon learn.' Hodder-Williams, 'The British South Africa Company', 52.

59. Kay, *Rhodesia*, 46.

60. As the offical handbook for prospective settlers nicely observed, the large number of African cattle existing in 1890 'was reduced to a small fraction' by 'lung-sickness, rinderpest and war', adding that 'the great bulk of our European-owned cattle is derived from native breeds'. Southern Rhodesia, *Handbook for the Use of Prospective Settlers on the Land* (London and Ipswich 1924), 30.

61. H. Weinmann, *Agricultural Research and Development in Southern Rhodesia, 1890–1923*, University of Rhodesia, Department of Agriculture Occasional Paper 4 (Salisbury 1972), 108.

62. *Report of the Chief Native Commissioner Mashonaland for the year 1912* (Salisbury 1913), 3. One white Rhodesian rancher recalled: 'My scheme was to start with native stock, acclimatized to local conditions, and cross them with fairly decent bulls; and later to cross the progeny with first-class Aberdeen-Angus beasts. It was a slow way of beginning, but the only sound one. By the third or fourth generation the herds would be fully graded up to type, yet retain the indigenous stamina; and the grazing of their forebears would "tame" the land into fit conditions to carry good stuff.' W. Robertson, *Rhodesian Rancher* (London and Glasgow 1935), 13.

63. Southern Rhodesia, *Handbook 1924*, 14.

64. Gann and Duignan acknowledge that: 'The frontier farmer's racial outlook was

usually of the harshest ... The pioneering period saw a great deal of cruelty, for on the farms and in the mining camps the white boss was usually a law unto himself. Insults and beatings went unpunished; manslaughter or even murder earned derisory penalties. White juries were notoriously unwilling to convict whites for crimes committed against blacks.' L. H. Gann and P. Duignan, 'Changing patterns of a White Elite: Rhodesian and Other Settlers', in Gann and Duignan (Eds.), *Colonialism in Africa, 1870–1960, Vol. 2. The History and Politics of Colonialism 1914–1960* (Cambridge 1970), 108.

65. R. H. Palmer, 'Red Soils in Rhodesia', *African Social Research*, **10,** 1970, 747–58.

66. NB 6/4/9, Report of the CNC Matabeleland for the month September 1908.

67. B. A. Kosmin, 'The Inyoka Tobacco Industry of the Shangwe People: A Case Study of the Displacement of a Pre-Colonial Economy in Southern Rhodesia, 1898–1938', *African Social Research*, **17,** 1974, 554–77; I. R. Phimister, 'Peasant Production and Underdevelopment in Southern Rhodesia, 1890–1914', *African Affairs*, **73,** 291, 1974, 217–28.

68. A 3/15/11, Hole to Milton, 26 November 1909.

69. Hodder-Williams notes that: 'The survey of farmers in the Marandellas District carried out by Company officials in 1914 makes abundantly clear the poverty of capital assets. A single wagon and a couple of ploughs, normally only single disc ones, represents the average; a maize shelter, some oxen and a few milking cows, tack for the oxen and a collection of small tools made up the inventory. This meant that most of the cultivation was done by hand.' R. Hodder-Williams, 'The Development of Social, Economic and Political Attitudes in a European Community, 1890–1968' draft thesis, 177.

70. L. H. Gann, *The Birth of a Plural Society* (Manchester 1968), 141.

71. For mining industry, see van Onselen, *Chibaro*; I. R. Phimister, 'History of Mining in Southern Rhodesia to 1953', Ph.D. thesis, University of Rhodesia, Salisbury, 1975.

72. P. Mason, *The Birth of a Dilemma* (London 1958), 225. For two sharply differing discussions of the labour question at this time, see J. M. Mackenzie, 'African Labour in the Chartered Company Period', *Rhodesian History*, **1,** 1970, 43–58; C. van Onselen, 'Black Workers in Central African Industry: A Critical Essay on the Historiography and Sociology of Rhodesia', *Journal of Southern African Studies*, **1,** 1975, 228–46.

73. In Nyasaland between 1901–21, Africans who did not work one month in the year for a white employer were taxed at double the rate of those who did, a measure introduced at the insistence of the white planters of the Shire Highlands, who paid very low wages.

In Matabeleland in 1912, the Rhodesian Landowners' and Farmers' Association passed a resolution pointing out that, 'the present system of exploiting natives squatting on private lands for an annual rental per head is the principal cause of the labour trouble', and demanding that the Private Locations Ordinance be amended so that all African tenants should show that they were 'contributing towards the economic development of the State by working for an employer for at least six months in every year'. *Bulawayo Chronicle*, 2 February 1912.

74. L. Vambe, *An Ill-Fated People* (London 1972), 219.

75. A 3/21/53, N/C Bulalima-Mangwe to CNC Matabeleland, 21 September 1906.

76. One white farmer acknowledged that the reserves 'did not offer the same facilities for getting rich rapidly that much private land offered. They were mostly so situate that grain would have a smaller value, and the opportunities for selling beer—a very important source of income—would be much curtailed'. *Bulawayo Chronicle*, 2 February 1912.

77. *Report of the Chief Native Commissioner Mashonaland for the year 1909* (Salisbury 1910), 8.

78. A 3/21/71, CNCs Matabeleland and Mashonaland to Hole, 5 and 22 October 1908.

79. The problem of African tenants on European estates in the Shire Highlands bedevilled the history of Nyasaland, where the Government was forced to recognize that 'we can never in practice compel a landlord to put up with large numbers of tenants whom he does not want', and that 'however good a law we may seem to devise a native tenant's position will always be to some extent precarious if we antagonise his landlord'. National Archives of Malawi, S 1/835/20, Minute 2 by C. H. Wade, 3 August 1920; S 1/698/30, Minute 27 by C. H. Wade, 31 October 1930.

80. L 2/2/117/46, S/N Victoria to CNC Mashonaland, 10 December 1908.

81. N 9/1/2, Report of the Acting N/C Melsetter for the year 1909.

82. N 9/4/23, Report of the N/C Gutu for the month April 1910.

83. N 9/4/23, Report of the Acting N/C Lomagundi for the month June 1910. This was a widespread problem, since so many boundaries were ill-defined. Hence some people who were really living on reserves paid rent to the Company by mistake, while others who thought they had settled inside the reserves subsequently found that they had not.

84. N 3/6/1, Acting N/C Ndanga to S/N Victoria, 15 July 1911. The dog tax had been recommended by the 1910–11 Native Affairs Committee of Enquiry. Vambe describes an unsuccessful attempt by his people to evade it. Vambe, *An Ill-Fated People*, 15–20.

85. *Report of the Chief Native Commissioner Matabeleland for the year 1912* (Salisbury 1913), 1.

86. A 3/15/12, CNC Matabeleland to F. W. Inskipp, 1 August 1912, Memo by Hole, August 1912.

87. A 3/15/12, N/C Bubi to CNC Matabeleland, 13 November 1912.

88. C.O. 417/520, Minute by Harcourt, 7 December 1912; 55 H.C. DEB. 5s., 10 and 23 July 1913, cols. 571–2, 2027; A 3/15/12, Newton to Burns-Begg, 8 October 1913. In Northern Rhodesia Africans were entitled to receive £1 to £2 per hut, plus 10/– for each cultivated acre, but even so in 1913 Chief Mapanza was complaining: 'We are tired of moving from one place to another. We are tired of being accused of grass burning and being made to pay for the damage done to crops and grazing lands ... the whiteman is always giving us trouble.' Meeting of Secretary for Native Affairs with Native Chiefs at Mapanza, 14 October 1913.

89. C.O. 417/526, Minutes by Vernon and Anderson, 22 and 27 December 1913.

90. N 9/1/16, Report of the N/C Bubi for the year 1913.

91. Weinmann, *Agricultural Research*, 111.

92. N 9/1/17, Report of the N/C Gwelo for the year 1914.

93. ZAD 3/1/1, Evidence of N/C Matobo to Native Reserves Commission, 8 July 1914.

94. ZAD 3/2/2, N/C Charter to Secretary, Native Reserves Commission, 15 November 1915.

95. LB 2/1/14/7, S/N Gwelo to CNC Matabeleland, 29 December 1910.

96. A 3/18/39/2, CNC Matabeleland to Hole, 4 April 1912.

97. L 2/2/117/8, Atherstone to Newton, 26 January 1904, Milton to Newton, 29 January 1904.

CHAPTER 5

The Native Reserves Commission 1914–15

As the area in question, which is practically a conglomeration of kopjes with very small cultivable valleys in between, is infested with baboons and is only traversable by pack animals, I see no objection [to making it a native reserve].

Acting Director of Land Settlement, 1915.[1]

1 BACKGROUND

The Native Reserves Commission travelled about Rhodesia during the dry seasons of 1914 and 1915, issuing a report at the end of each year.[2] It suggested numerous alterations to the existing 20,491,151 acres of reserves, but on aggregate it proposed that an estimated 5,610,595 acres be added and 6,673,055 acres deducted, giving a net reduction of 1,062,460 acres.[3] After some deliberation the Imperial Government approved the proposed alterations in February 1917, but vociferous opposition to the Commission's findings delayed the promulgation of the necessary Order in Council until November 1920.

Commissions of enquiry generally fall into one of three categories: those which genuinely seek answers to complex questions and hence are manned by experts; those designed as a public relations exercise by governments which have already made up their minds and hence are packed with nonentities—men who can be relied upon to produce the right answer; and finally, those commissions whose basic task is to remove a controversial issue from the heat of public debate quietly, and very slowly de-fuse it, which are usually comprised of civil servants. In the case of the Rhodesian Native Reserves Commission, elements of the second and third categories are clearly apparent, for not only were the personnel and the terms of reference highly favourable to the British South Africa Company, but something of a conspiracy of silence surrounded both the Commission and the subsequent debate on its work.

Also apparent is the unmistakably South African focus of the Commission. The administrative experience of all its members was confined to Southern Africa; many of the unspoken assumptions in the report are clearly of white South African origin, while all the comparative tables refer only to countries to the south of Rhodesia.

The Commission was to comprise three members—two of them, including the chairman, to be appointed by the Imperial Government, and the third by the Company. In fact the choice of personnel made it virtually certain that the eventual report would be acceptable to the Company. The High Commissioner for South Africa, the influential Lord Gladstone, was responsible in name and in reality for the appointment of the Commission. Acting on his own initiative, he offered the job of chairman to Robert Coryndon, as he was unable to spare the more suitable Herbert Sloley, an acknowledged 'native expert'.[4] In view of the fact that Coryndon had been a Company employee in North-Western Rhodesia until as recently as 1907, the Colonial Office was somewhat taken aback. Even the pro-Company Henry Lambert felt constrained to suggest that they should at least pay Coryndon's expenses, so as 'not to allow it to be said that the whole Commission was the Company's affair'. Sir Percy Anderson, the permanent under-secretary, went even further: 'Our Commissioner should not be a man who has been in the service of the Company and he must be paid by us. We shall have to defend his work in Parliament and must have a man like Caesar's wife ought to have been.' Gladstone was therefore informed that the Chairman must be someone 'who is beyond suspicion of any bias in the Company's favour',[5] but he had already approached Coryndon without waiting for formal approval and rather than create embarrassment the Colonial Office dropped its objections.[6] When the appointment was subsequently criticized, a discreet veil was drawn and the Colonial Office stoutly defended Gladstone's initiative.

Coryndon was indeed an unfortunate choice. He was, as Lewis Gann acknowledges, 'a "Company man" by personal experience and sympathy'.[7] He was one of the hand-picked 'Rhodes' Apostles',[8] joined the Pioneer Column of 1890, fought in the war of 1893 and the Risings of 1896, and was private secretary to Rhodes during the Jameson Raid enquiry. He was then sent to Lealui to become the first Resident of Barotseland in 1897,[9] and was the Company's Administrator of North-Western Rhodesia from 1900–7. He then left the service of the Company, though, as he wrote at the time: 'I am still and shall always remain a staunch champion of Rhodesia and the Company.'[10] He subsequently became Resident Commissioner for Swaziland (1907–16), and Basutoland (1916–17), before attaining a knighthood and the Governorship of Uganda (1917–22) and Kenya (1922–5), where he died in office.

Coryndon was 'essentially an open-air man with a keen affection for horses, dogs and guns'.[11] He was very much a part of the fortune-hunting scene of the 1890s, and indeed described himself as one of a band of 'keen glorious adventurers'.[12] Not surprisingly, as Marshall Hole recalled, he shared the 'Colonial prejudices ... of the early Rhodesian pioneer ... and had been inclined to dogmatize, as most of us did, on the relations between whites and natives'.[13] Though Hole suggests that Coryndon subsequently outgrew these prejudices, in North-Western Rhodesia he 'could not abide the "cheekiness" and "arrogance" of "so-called educated natives"',[14] he deliberately misled and threatened Lewanika into granting land concessions to the Company, and he allowed his subordinates to perpetrate a number of abuses which forced the Colonial Office to wonder subsequently 'how far Mr. Coryndon, who was in charge while these things were being done, is to be trusted in Swaziland'.[15] In Swaziland, he was in fact responsible for a 'final' land settlement which ratified the alienation of nearly two-thirds of the country to Europeans, while on his departure from Basutoland in 1917 the local African newspaper, *Mochochonono*, wrote: 'Mr. Coryndon was very unpopular... an unsympathetic ruler – an autocrat ... the bold truth is the Basuto are not at all sorry that Mr. Coryndon is leaving them.'[16] In Uganda, in contrast to his predecessors, he openly espoused the interests of the white planters;[17] while at the height of the constitutional crisis in Kenya, he reassured the hysterical settlers with the comment: 'Gentlemen, you may remember that I am South African born.'[18]

The second member of the Commission, the Company's nominee, was an equally unfortunate choice. The Company ignored a fairly broad hint from the Colonial Office that it should appoint a senior member of the Native Department[19]—it was primarily concerned after all with attacking rather than defending the reserves—and chose at first its Treasurer, Francis Newton.[20] This was not an unreasonable appointment, though Newton was one of those Imperial officials cognisant of the Jameson Raid who had remained silent and been temporarily banished to the Caribbean for his pains. He was the owner of five farms, totalling 21,547 acres of land.[21] But within a month of the Commission beginning its work, Newton was recalled to his administrative duties in Salisbury. He was replaced by the Surveyor-General, W. J. Atherstone.[22] The Colonial Office raised no objection to Atherstone's appointment as alternate member, which was a little surprising considering that he was on record as favouring the reduction of the reserves.[23] and had privately advocated their diminution by 4 million acres.[24] In 1912 he had bought 19,385 acres bordering a native reserve in the Marandellas District, though he did not begin to develop the land until 1944.[25] In a manner reminiscent of the Jameson era, Atherstone joined the Commission before Imperial approval of his appointment had been received.[26]

As the third member Gladstone appointed his former military secretary, Major Edward Garraway, who (like Lindsell, the Imperial nominee to the 1894 Land Commission) had been a participant in the Jameson Raid. He had served as a doctor in the British Bechuanaland Police from 1892–1901, and like Coryndon, had seen action in Rhodesia in the war of 1893 and the Risings of 1896. He had been employed briefly by the Company in 1895.[27] Though 'not a man of brilliant ability', Garraway appears to have been appointed because: 'He knows the natives thoroughly and gets on with them. He can talk Kaffir.' But, the Colonial Office noted, 'even tender hearted Lord Gladstone found Garraway so unless he had him retired'.[28] All four commissioners thus shared a common Southern African background.

The Company achieved a victory not only in the choice of commissioners but also with regard to the terms of reference. The Colonial Office had originally suggested an enquiry into the adequacy of each reserve, but the Company argued, successfully, that the Commission should be empowered to regroup the reserves, which were dotted about rather haphazardly, as this would allow new reserves to be created, 'thus getting free corresponding areas, which are now native reserves, for other purposes'.[29]

While the Commission went about its business, behind the scenes the old battle raged between the Native Department and the Land Settlement (formerly Estates) Department. The latter, under its energetic Acting Director, Frank W. Inskipp, naturally saw in the Commission the chance to realize the ambitions which had earlier been thwarted by the Resident Commissioners and the Native Commissioners. The Land Settlement Department was very thorough; it drew up a schedule showing which reserves now exceeded the areas estimated in 1902, and land inspectors were sent out to examine such land and other areas which Inskipp hoped he might persuade the Commission to reduce. These reports were then forwarded, with recommendations, to the Commission before it visited the areas in question. Not content with this, Inskipp also put forward counter-proposals to those Native Department recommendations of which he disapproved, and here he was greatly assisted by the Company's directive that the Native Department should keep the Commercial Representative informed in advance of all recommendations it wished to submit to the Commission. The attack on the reserves was clearly being renewed with a vengeance.

2 POLICY

(i) The Report

The Native Reserves Commission began its work on 4 June 1914, issued an interim report on 29 November, and then went into recess. It reconvened on 1 May 1915, concluded its fieldwork on 11 November, and issued its final report on 16 December. The commissioners inspected Matabeleland and southern Mashonaland in 1914, and the remainder of Mashonaland in 1915, travelling 5,404 miles by train, 3,492 miles by mule wagon or on horseback, and 1,549 miles by car.

The Commission found 104 reserves in existence, varying in size from under 5,000 to over 3 million acres, and totalling in all some 20,491,151 acres. The African population was estimated to be 732,153, of whom 405,376, or about 55 per cent, were living in the reserves. This gave an average of 50·5 acres per head, or 28 acres if the whole population were to live in the reserves. The comparable figures for the rest of Southern Africa were as follows:

Territory	*Acres per head of population now living in reserves*	*Acres per head of total population*
Cape	11·0	8·3
Natal	14·7	6·6
Transvaal	4·2	1·5
Orange Free State	2·3	0·5
Basutoland	16·4	16·4
Swaziland	19·0	14·7
Bechuanaland	484·0	459·0

The recent increase of European settlement, the Commission admitted, had stimulated the need for a more accurate definition of the reserves, 'with the object of drawing a clear division between land available for Europeans and that set aside for natives'. Moreover, it had often been found that 'land has been assigned to natives which is quite unsuitable for their purposes, though desirable from a European point of view, while land eminently fitted to carry a native population, and actually inhabited by natives, has been left open'.[30] Unfortunately, at no point did the Commission state its criteria for assessing whether land was suitable for Africans or for Europeans.

The Report commented on the squeezing out process of recent years, which, it said, Africans had learnt to accept with equanimity, while the commissioners were gratified to find so little conflict of interest over land between black and white, and such an absence of hostility. These were convenient and comforting assumptions, but they overlooked, for example, the storm of protest and angry feelings at the introduction of grazing fees in 1912.

The Report adopted, almost word for word, the Company view that reserves were for those who could not immediately be assimilated into European conditions, and it therefore dismissed as absurd and extreme the notion that every unborn African had 'an indefeasible right to land', since in that case the whole country would eventually be needed as a reserve.[31] Instead, as education broke down the tribal system, the need for reserves would diminish.[32] Indeed, the commissioners assumed that the capacity of Africans to make good use of their land would keep pace with their rising population. Hence an adequate allocation in 1915 would also suffice fifty years later![33]

In general, the Commission preferred medium-sized reserves distributed throughout the country to small reserves in the settled districts and very large ones elsewhere, but because 'vested interests limit our choice so much', it was 'not possible to secure this object as completely as we would have wished'.[34] Thus it was unable to increase the size of some of the small reserves near the main centres because of the existence of 5,002 surveyed farms, 2,082 of which were occupied. The Commission did not contemplate the possibility of expropriating Europeans, and thus, in effect, it ratified the work of the Jamesonian era.

The Commission believed that the existing reserves were more than sufficient for present and future needs. The proportion of waste land in them was held to be no larger than in the mountainous Basutoland and Swaziland, or the waterless Bechuanaland, and if 'much good land has been occupied by whites, there is much good land remaining to the native population'. Because the Chief Native Commissioner had probably underestimated the size of the African population, the commissioners had made their recommendations 'on a rather more generous scale than would otherwise have been the case'.[35] No attempt was made to arrive at a suitable fixed acreage per head of population because of very great regional diversity; instead, the reserves of each district were studied as a whole. Though they recommended that the reserves be reduced by 1 million acres to an estimated 19,428,621 acres, this still left 26·5 acres per head of the entire population, and it was probable that between 15 and 20 per cent of the population would always live outside the reserves.

With regard to the areas which were being taken from the reserves, the commissioners suggested that Africans could either remain on the land and pay rent, or else they could move to another reserve, which would be no hardship provided the reserves were sufficient and suitable. Fortunately there were believed to be few cases where Native Commissioners, having in the past encouraged Africans to settle on land, would now have to tell them to leave. Europeans should not, the Report added, occupy land or impose rents in the remote and thinly populated surrendered reserves for at least two years; in the more populated areas the time limit should be four years.

Very few members of the public came forward to give evidence to the Commission, largely on account of the First World War, and in its most quoted passage it said:

> We did not, as a rule, examine native chiefs unless there was some point to be elucidated or some definite information to be gained ... We felt that we might do more harm than good by questioning the natives upon a matter of which they were very likely to misunderstand the real scope.[36]

Finally, like its Northern Rhodesian counterparts of the 1920s, the Commission made a number of optimistic recommendations concerning the more efficient use of the reserves. The reserve boundaries should be clearly beaconed and water supplies and adequate roads provided where necessary. It was premature—European agriculture had not yet advanced sufficiently—for agricultural schools or model farms, but Native Commissioners should encourage the use of better methods and Africans might be employed as agricultural demonstrators. Education was the greatest single factor in improving the use and occupation of the land, but there was no royal road to progress.

(ii) The Report under Examination and Attack, 1915–20

(*a*) *The Imperial Authorities*

Despite appearances to the contrary, the Commission was an Imperial one, and its recommendations had to be approved by the British Government before they could become law. The most important factor involved was, to quote the terms of reference, 'that Native Reserves should be finally assigned and demarcated, and that thereafter there should be no further assignment'.[37] Clearly, therefore, the subject deserved the most careful attention. Unfortunately the First World War, and the campaign against the Germans in East Africa, was consuming the attention of Imperial officials in South Africa and in London. Given the recognition that 'it is impossible for us sitting in this [Colonial] Office to offer any useful criticism',[38] London was more than ever dependent on the advice of its local officials.

The Resident Commissioner at the time (1915–18) was Herbert Stanley, who had been secretary to High Commissioner Gladstone (1910–15), and was subsequently to become Imperial Secretary (1918–24), Governor of Northern Rhodesia (1924–7), High Commissioner for South Africa (1931–5), and Governor of Southern Rhodesia (1935–42). Again, the choice was not a happy one. Stanley was an avowed champion of settler interests. He was on intimate terms with South African cabinet ministers, and had been appointed Resident Commissioner in preference to the 'native expert' Sloley, because the Colonial Office wanted 'someone who will keep in touch with white opinion without intruding himself'.[39] In the 1920s, he was the driving force behind the quite unnecessary creation of native reserves in Northern Rhodesia, where he also reorganized the Civil Service along South African lines, with all junior posts along the line of rail being reserved for Europeans, and advocated a Central African federation which would have made possible 'an immediate large extension of self-government ... for the unofficial European communities of Northern Rhodesia and Nyasaland'.[40] On retirement he settled in Cape Town.

Stanley was however responsible for the one decisive piece of Imperial intervention—the creation of 1·7 million acres of 'reserve' reserves. He was acting as host to Coryndon and Garraway while the Report was being drafted, and when all the adding and subtracting had been done, the net reduction of the reserves was going to be 2,778,860 acres, a conclusion which clearly would have pleased the Company.

Coryndon showed Stanley the relevant portions of the draft. Stanley recalled:

> I told him *sans phrase*, that I regarded so large a surrender as impolitic, in my judgement it would shock sentiment at home, and though I did not know what view the High Commissioner and Secretary of State might take I doubted very much whether it would be favourable. In any case my opinion, if an expression of it should be invited by His Excellency, would be strongly adverse. Coryndon was not pleased and we had a long (though amicable) wrangle, in which he figured as the champion of right and justice and I as a Machiavellian manipulator. Finally, however, he came round to the view that it was useless to kick against the prick, and the suggestion of a compromise by the creation of reserve Reserves emerged. I encouraged the idea and urged him to make the additions approximately equivalent in acreage to the area which would otherwise have been surrendered. The ultimate result fell short of that ideal, but Coryndon assured me that he had gone as far as he could go conscientiously, and Garraway was satisfied that any further extension could not reasonably have been justified.[41]

This last minute piece of Imperial intervention resulted in an extra 1·7 million acres being added to the reserves, so that the overall reduction changed from 2·7 to 1 million acres—a reduction which, it was hoped, would cause less of a scandal than the Commission's original intent.

Unfortunately this was the extent of Imperial intervention, and Stanley had neither the time nor the inclination to examine for himself any of the areas proposed for exchange, as Resident Commissioners had always done in the past. Had he done so, he might conceivably have withheld his approval. The general, and no doubt realistic, view however was that there was no real alternative between outright acceptance or rejection of the Report, and rejection would inevitably involve the expenditure of more time and money. One needs to remember too that at this time the British Government was by no means hostile to European settlement; it had encouraged white farmers to go to Kenya, and was about to do the same in Tanganyika. The British believed, in general, that settlers promoted economic development and produced export crops more efficiently than African peasant farmers, while there were obvious political and strategic advantages to be gained from planting white settlers as liberally as possible throughout Africa.

The Imperial authorities were also greatly influenced by the Commission's claim, bogus as it turned out, that its recommendations were generally acceptable to the Native Department, while some officials persisted in believing that 'the inevitable tendency is for natives to come out of the Reserves and to work under European conditions'.[42] Buxton, the High Commissioner, and Tait, at the Colonial Office, suggested that a further million acres of reserves should be assigned for possible future use in order to balance gains and losses, but the idea was rejected because it was feared that the Company would in any event contest the 'reserve' reserves, and that it was difficult to justify a proposal 'which is admittedly put forward on grounds of sentiment rather than of practical necessity or advantage'.[43] Hence, despite the possibility of 'exposing ourselves to attack from sentimentalists and negrophilists',[44] the Colonial Office decided in February 1917 to accept the Coryndon Report,[45] and, following pressure in the House of Commons,[46] to publish it in October.

(*b*) *The Critics*

It was not until November 1920 however that an Order in Council, revoking Article 81 of the 1898 Order and making a purportedly final settlement of the reserves, could be issued. The reason for the delay was the emergence of a vociferous campaign of opposition to the Commission's findings, conducted largely by two 'sentimentalists and negrophilists', John Harris and Arthur Shearly Cripps.

Harris was Organising Secretary of the Anti-Slavery and Aborigines' Protection Society (APS), and a dedicated critic of the Company. He had visited Rhodesia in 1914 to collect evidence for the presentation of the African case in the land question then before the Privy Council (see chapter 6, see pp. 133–5), hoping to get affidavits from African chiefs saying that the land really belonged to them. Not surprisingly, the Rhodesian administration reacted strongly; Harris was 'shadowed' by detectives, forbidden to enter the reserves, and was eventually sent home.[47] No doubt stimulated by the experience, Harris made use of every means of protest at his disposal; he wrote to newspapers and journals, had questions asked in the Commons,[48] engaged the Colonial Office in voluminous correspondence,[49] thus confirming Lambert's opinion of the APS as 'a parcel of busybodies',[50] and finally published his book, *The Chartered Millions* in 1920 which received vitriolic reviews in the Rhodesian press.

Arthur Shearly Cripps was a remarkable Anglican poet-missionary, who had lived since 1901 near the Afrikaner centre of Enkeldoorn in the Charter District. He had read history at Oxford, and had been strongly influenced by peasant protests against the Enclosure Acts. He had become a member of the Land Restoration League which wanted the land returned to the 'Commonweal of England', and it was because he believed that he was seeing history repeating itself in Rhodesia that he became such a passionate champion of the rights of African peasants in the reserves.[51] He believed in living as Africans lived, in poverty, a life-style which did not endear him to the administration,[52] and he is remembered today, by Africans, as a saint. Cripps first assailed Drummond Chaplin (who succeeded Milton as the Company's Administrator in 1914) and High Commissioner Buxton with criticisms of the Commission, but when this had no effect he came to England in 1920, burst into print,[53] and embarked on 'much mischief [and] agitating among all sorts of people and amongst others the Archbishop of Canterbury'.[54]

Much of the Harris/Cripps criticism was concerned with the fact that the total area of the reserves had been reduced, and little was made of the more significant point that in general good land had been taken out of the reserves and much poorer land substituted in lieu. The APS issued a memorandum containing all their criticisms, which resulted in the Colonial Office being inundated with missionary protests. One official thought the whole agitation 'quite spurious',[55] while another observed urbanely that 'these good people are evidently ignorant of the most elementary facts of the case'.[56] It was just as well for the Colonial Office that the critics did not have access to information which would have made their case far more damning.

The British Government was also confronted with protests from the Ndebele National Home Movement, led by Nyamanda, Lobengula's eldest son (see chapter 6, pp. 151–3). Nyamanda and his cousin, Madhloli Kumalo, claimed in petitions and interviews with Company and Imperial officials, that instead of the reserves being reduced they should have been increased as they were mostly situated in unhealthy districts and were often dry and uninhabitable. Both had been evicted from European farms several times and had no wish to move to the waterless Gwaai or Shangani. They were informed by Buxton, however, that the Commission's findings were no longer open to argument and that outside the reserves Africans would have to make the best terms they could with the white farmers.[57]

Local European pressures were slightly more successful, for though the Colonial Office at first believed 'we cannot safely start revising the Commission's decisions',[58] it was forced to do so following effective protests by Cripps and two other missionaries, Lloyd and Upcher, in the cases of the Sabi, Chiduku, and Inyanga North reserves, in the Charter, Makoni, and Inyanga Districts; while the Company agreed, in response to Native Department recommendations, to assign more land later in the Wankie District.[59] Details of these amendments are to be found in Appendix I (see pp. 251–78).

(c) *The Native Reserves Order in Council*

In the discussions prior to the promulgation of the Native Reserves Order in Council of 1920, Taylor, the Chief Native Commissioner, Douglas-Jones, the Resident Commissioner, and Buxton, the High Commissioner, all suggested that a loophole be left open to permit further exchanges of land which were in the African interest.[60] The Colonial Office flatly rejected the proposal, recalling that it had persuaded the Company to agree to the Commission on the understanding that it would be empowered to make a final settlement, and it feared that such a loophole would only produce a renewed attack on the reserves from the settlers. The proposal did at least draw attention to a defect in the draft Order, which appeared to be more concerned with relieving the Company of its obligations than with securing African rights. It was therefore decided, following the Northern Nigerian example, to vest the reserves in the High Commissioner,[61] so that the Order would be 'a kind of charter for the native', thus helping the Colonial Office against pressure from the settlers on the one hand, and the APS on the other.[62]

The question of Rhodesia's political future influenced the final drafting of the Order in Council, as it had the appointment of the Native Reserves Commission in 1913–14. Rhodesia was either about to join the Union of South Africa or become a self-governing colony. Buxton acknowledged that in either event it would be impossible to safeguard African interests as effectively as in the High Commission Territories, and that 'some stipulations might perhaps be insisted on by Crown in granting responsible government but this might not be practicable in the event of entry of Union'.[63] But even in the former case, as he later admitted, such stipulations could not be 'other than illusory'.[64] Lambert at the Colonial Office agreed. 'We shall have to trust the Resp. Government to work the system handed over to them fairly', he wrote, 'and it will not be easy to do more than to secure that the natives are well protected when handed over.'[65] Hence the vesting of the reserves in the High Commissioner.

Finally on 9 November 1920 the Southern Rhodesia Order in Council 1920 received the royal assent. This 'charter for the native' revoked Article 81 of the 1898 Order, with its obligation on the Company to assign sufficient and suitable land 'from time to time', and purported to make a final assignment of the reserves. There were to be no compulsory removals from surrendered reserves before 14 February 1922.[66] Thus a royal seal was placed upon the work of the Native Reserves Commission and upon the earlier work of Dr. Jameson.

3 ACTUALITY: AN APPRAISAL

Sir Robert Coryndon died in office as Governor of Kenya in 1925, and the Duke of York, later King George VI, hastily returned to Nairobi to take charge of the funeral arrangements. Coryndon's widow later wrote seeking memorials from some of her husband's former colleagues for a biography which she planned, but unfortunately never completed. One reply, from Garraway, a fellow commissioner, claimed that the Report of the Native Reserves Commission was 'a memorial of his zeal and energy, and has gone far to make the Native Policy of Rhodesia, the successful administration which it is today'.[67] Such a charitable assessment has found few supporters outside the ranks of British South Africa Company employees.

Before the Report was even signed it had been criticized by Stanley (as we have seen) and subsequently Buxton, Tait, and Stanley all took exception to the reduction of the reserves by 1 million acres, while the opposition to some of its recommendations forced the Colonial Office to agree to amendments. These contemporary criticisms have been amply justified by subsequent appraisals. Even writers not noted for their hostility towards Rhodesian administrations, such as Gann, Duignan, and Hanna, have had harsh things to say about the Commission. Gann pointed out, as already noted, that Coryndon was 'a "Company man" by personal experience and sympathy', and that the Commission's recommendations 'were influenced to a considerable extent by pressure from the Company's own Lands Department'.[68] Duignan commented that if Africans got some good land, 'it was by accident or because no excuse could be found to move them'.[69] Hanna noted the Commission's belief that a significant proportion of Africans would always live outside the reserves, and stated that 'on any other assumption its estimate of native requirements would have been grossly inadequate'.[70] Other writers have been equally critical.[71] To assess the validity of such criticisms it is necessary now to examine the way in which the Commission went about its task.

Coryndon was typically a man of firm opinions, and one of these was that the reserves should be cut down. In a letter written from the Salisbury Club before the Commission had even begun its fieldwork, he asked the Chief Native Commissioner to 'indicate the points where you think farmers may have some reasonable claim to portions of native reserves adjoining their farms; *if any*,[72] places where the native areas might be extended'.[73] He had also decided, as early as July 1914, that medium sized reserves of 200,000–300,000 acres scattered evenly throughout the country, were preferable to the existing situation in Matabeleland of practically no reserves at all in the centre and huge reserves in the outer districts.[74] On this assumption he went on to argue that although 'it may not be possible at this stage to do much towards creating Reserves' in central Matabeleland, yet 'something might be done' to cut down the large outer reserves, while small reserves should be abolished wherever possible.[75] CNC Taylor pointed out that many small reserves in Matabeleland had been occupied only recently, as Africans had been turned off European farms. They had asked for security, had even helped to beacon the boundaries in some cases, and should not be disturbed again without good reason. Milton commented that to 'take 50 farms of 3,000 m. in that region [central Matabeleland] for native Reserves would be impolitic and even impossible ... without resorting to expropriation'. Instead Africans should work on European farms.[76] Thus the large reserves were reduced and the large farms left untouched; African land was expropriated, European land was not.

In the previous chapter the Company's unsuccessful attack on the reserves and its decision to agree to the Commission in the hope of renewing this attack have been described. It was therefore not surprising that in March 1914, before the Commission began its work, the Commercial Representative, Percy S. Inskipp, informed the Director of Land Settlement, Charles Wise, that he required a schedule showing the acreage of the reserves as approved in 1902, and that:

> In cases where the areas shown on the maps exceed the area approved by the Executive Council, a description of the land should be given, more particularly that portion which the Company would propose to take back. A description of the land is also desired where the number of natives would seem to warrant a reduction in the area of any reserve.[77]

Hence land inspectors, some qualified, others merely 'old residents' or 'reliable', were sent out into those reserves which the Land Settlement Department considered it had a good chance of persuading the Commission to reduce.[78] Their reports were sent to Frank W. Inskipp, the Assistant (later Acting) Director of Land Settlement, who then submitted recommendations to the Commission covering both land which he wished taken out of the reserves and land which the Native Department wished to add to them. He was helped in the latter respect by a directive from the London Office that 'the Board is anxious that the Commercial Representative should be kept regularly informed in advance by the Native Department of any recommendations which that Department considers it necessary to bring before the Commission'.[79] The information was then passed to Frank Inskipp, who submitted counter-proposals if he felt that the Native Department was threatening European interests. The Land Settlement Department was thus placed in a position of very real advantage.

Frank Inskipp's first letter to the Commission, in July 1914, is most revealing. He began by quoting figures from the 1903–5 South African Native Affairs Commission, which showed that at that time the Rhodesian reserves allowed 94 acres per head of population, compared to 16·5 acres for the rest of Southern Africa, excluding Bechuanaland. Thus, he deduced, the reserves could be 'considerably reduced', as they were 'vastly in excess' of requirements, although this was not realized until recently when they were found to be 'out of all proportion' to the land remaining for European settlement. Because the land had been approved by the Secretary of State, 'it was not possible to take any steps to rectify the matter until the appointment of the present Commission afforded an opportunity of reopening the question'. With increasing

European settlement, 'this locking up of large areas of unutilised land has now become seriously felt, and settlement more particularly in areas adjacent to centres and the Railways,[80] is being greatly retarded'. His Department had sent inspectors into the reserves, and he thought it a good idea to send their reports to the Commission before it visited the areas concerned. He wished to suggest right away that the Chibi and Matibi Reserves, Chibi District, be reduced by 3·8 million acres, as they were 'more susceptible to reduction than any other Reserves, *one or two of which*[81] it will be proposed should be enlarged'. Further proposals would follow.[82] Inskipp was thanked for his trouble and informed that: 'It would be a great advantage to the Commissioners if similar statements could be furnished in respect of the other Reserves as they are visited.'[83] They were.

These Land Settlement Department reports exhibit a marked degree of cynicism. For example, here is Inskipp expressing his approval of a proposed new reserve in the Matopos: 'As the area in question, which is practically a conglomeration of *kopjes* with very small cultivable valleys in between, is infested with baboons and is only traversable by pack animals, I see no objection to this.'[84] A similar degree of magnanimity was displayed towards the proposed Umtasa North Reserve:

> I understand that the greater part of this land applied for consists of a steep gorge with the Hondi river flowing through it and that this portion at least is quite unsuitable for European occupation. Further that natives are thickly scattered throughout the area and that the climate is intensely hot and probably malarious. In view of these facts and of the remoteness of the land from market and railway, I suggest that there is no objection to its reservation.[85]

Comments in a similar vein were passed about the proposed additions to the Zwimba Reserve—'mountainous, and the few small patches of cultivable land arc very difficult of access'; and the Ndanga Reserve—'very mountainous ... very low and unhealthy'. The existing Muwushu Reserve was said to be 'useless for anything else but natives', and the proposed Wankie Reserve was 'most exceptionally poor'. On the other hand, Inskipp was warned not to advocate the abolition of the Soshwe Reserve, 'as the farmers in the vicinity are dependent upon it for their labour supply'. In Gwanda the proposed new reserve was valued at 9/– per morgen, and Inskipp was moved to enquire 'whether there is any other area, of about the same size in the same neighbourhood, which is of poorer quality' which could be chosen instead.[86] There was.

It is abundantly clear, therefore, that the claims of European settlement were pressed for all they were worth and a good deal more, and one must now ask how the Commission responded to such claims. Fortunately, A. H. Holland, the Commission's secretary in 1915, who two years later was rewarded with a free farm of 3,175 acres from the surrendered Gwebi Reserve,[87] kept a diary which (though marred by a chronic lack of punctuation) helps provide the answer to this question.

Holland's diary reveals an unmistakable similarity of approach between the Commission and Frank Inskipp. Msana Reserve, which was reduced by half, 'would make ideal farming country', Holland noted, 'as there is plenty of water and rich red soil also a good class of sand soil'. Kunzwi Reserve, reduced by two-thirds, was 'excellent for grazing and well watered ... [with] rich red chocolate soil ... it was ideal farming land'. The Chiweshe Reserve 'is the best I have so far inspected there is excellent black rich soil in all the valleys which are numerous it is fairly well watered and heavily timbered the black soil is too heavy for the present primitive native method of cultivation but would make ideal European farms if it was not so far from the Railway'. Thus Chiweshe was reprieved. Finally, Holland remarked of the Bushu Reserve: 'The reason why we are anxious to do away with this Reserve is because the soil is exceptionally rich and better for European than native cultivation and also because it is so near the Railway and big mining centre.'[88] But both Chief Bushu and the N/C Mazoe asked for the reserve to be retained, and in the absence of any counter-proposal from Inskipp, the Commission was obliged to agree.

One must assume that Holland's thinking was shared by the commissioners since he would surely have mentioned the fact had this not been the case. It therefore appears that the unstated criterion on which the Commission considered land to be suitable for Europeans but unsuitable for Africans was, quite simply, rich red soil. There was still some slight justification for holding such a view, though the Commission expressly stated in its Report that it had not placed too much importance on the Shona tendency to neglect the red soils, as this was not a permanent feature and all types of soil would eventually be used. Indeed, in 1912 the Resident Commissioner had pointed out that the soils argument no longer held the same validity, since Africans who owned ploughs were beginning to make use of the heavy red soil while Europeans found the light sandy soils ideal for tobacco growing,[89] and Holland himself noted that 'an increasing number of natives are now beginning to use ploughs and are accordingly cultivating heavier soils in the *vleis*'.[90] This being the case, it was surely most inappropriate for a Commission, appointed to make a final assignment of land to cover all future needs, to extract from the reserves the choicest areas of red soils merely because they were not at that time being extensively utilised by Africans.

Commissions are obviously greatly dependent on the amount and type of evidence submitted to them. We have seen how thoroughly the Land Settlement Department presented its case. But, largely as a result of the First World War, the list of witnesses who appeared before the Commission was exceedingly thin: 33 Native Department officials, 48 chiefs and headmen, 12 white farmers, 7 missionaries, the Director of

Land Settlement, the Commercial Representative, the Medical Director, a civil commissioner, a ranching manager, a land inspector, and a surveyor. In addition, 3 farmers' associations, a missionary, and a Native Commissioner submitted written evidence.

Particularly regrettable was the inertia of the missionaries on a subject which so profoundly affected African welfare. Archdeacon Etheridge was reported as saying at the 1920 Missionary Conference that many missionaries 'did not realise the importance of giving evidence ... they had only themselves to blame. Personally he had circularised all the missionaries of the English Church asking them to give evidence in writing. By no means did all of them comply with his request'.[91] This was no doubt because, as John White (Cripps' friend and ally) recalled:

> The minds of many men were turned to very important and tragic events. The Commission commenced in 1914, and I think that many people felt that it was a wrong time, and if the Central Powers [i.e. Germany and Austria-Hungary] had come out best anything that happened in connection with the Commission would have been of very little service indeed.[92]

Many awoke to their responsibilities after the Report had been approved and published, and they did manage to secure a few amendments, but by then it was really too late.

The Native Commissioners were in a difficult position. Some had gone off to the various theatres of war, leaving inexperienced men, unfamiliar with the district, in their place. Their recommendations were first vetted by Inskipp and then often ignored by the Commission. Marshall Hole, who was secretary to the Commission during 1914, asserted in response to APS criticisms, that it was the evidence of the Native Commissioners which had 'supplied the backbone of the Commission's recommendations, in no single instance was the advice given by them disregarded'.[93] Hole's claim is an important one, since Imperial acceptance of the Report was largely based on the Commission's assertion that its recommendations were generally acceptable to the Native Department. The claim is demonstrably false, however, and this is illustrated fully in Appendix I (see pp. 251–78), which contains a district by district analysis of the recommendations of Inskipp and the Native Department, and of the Commission's final proposals.

In fact Native Commissioners remained in complete ignorance of the detailed proposals until the Report received Imperial assent in February 1917. When they finally saw the Report, many of them expressed shock and amazement. 'Wiri' Edwards, who had been N/C Mrewa since 1895, complained bitterly that:

> There has been such a complete destruction of the Mangwendi Reserve that I cannot help thinking some mistake has been made in drawing up the boundaries ... This part of the Reserve is thickly populated, the taxation amounting to £900. There are over 3,000 head of native cattle, and two dipping

> tanks have been erected and paid for by the natives there ... the announcement will come as a thunderbolt to them and cause very grave dissatisfaction, but until I hear further I do not intend to mention the matter to them.[94]

Edwards' colleague, J. W. Posselt, N/C Charter since 1902, was even more damning. He remarked,

> I was under the impression that one of the objects of the Commission was to ascertain the requirements of the natives, but at no time during the touring of the Reserves did I detect any anxiety on their part to increase the area of any of the Reserves. Is this then the matter of rejoicing for shareholders in having secured an additional million acres of land?[95]

Equally seriously, H. M. G. Jackson, the S/N Bulawayo, who had served in the Native Department since 1895 and who later became Chief Native Commissioner, revealed that:

> The Commission attributed to me views which I had never uttered, in regard both to the Semokwe and the Gwanda Reserves. I told the Chairman of the Commission that I had no knowledge of either area and that I had seen neither. He assured me that they were both tracts of very good land and that the only drawback was want of water. My acquiescence was not necessary, was not sought and was certainly not given. I have seen proofs of no evidence attributed to me and cannot understand how I came to be credited with such views.[96]

What Jackson had said was that the Matabeleland reserves should not be reduced as this would shake the people's confidence in the Government.[97] In all, at least eight Native Commissioners were highly critical of the Commission's recommendations.

The Commission was also contemptuous of African evidence. In its Report it brazenly admitted that it 'might do more harm than good by questioning the natives upon a matter of which they were very likely to misunderstand the real scope'.[98] Moreover, A. H. Holland, secretary during 1915, recalled that when Africans were questioned, and when Coryndon disagreed with them

> he went to infinite trouble to give them the reasons why he disagreed; and the natives invariably appeared to acknowledge the justice of his remarks and, in many cases, stated, at the end of our interviews, that they were quite satisfied to leave the question of the boundaries of their particular reserve in the hands of the Commission.[99]

Such magnanimity is scarcely credible.

The Commission claimed that the Land Settlement Department had 'shown itself to be candid and reasonable' and had made 'no attempt to influence the Commission in favour of the white settler as against the native'. It promptly contradicted itself by saying that: 'Whatever influence has been brought to bear in favour of the settler has been balanced by the influence of the Missions and the Native Department on behalf of native interests.'[100] The analysis contained in Appendix I (see pp. 251–78) reveals quite clearly the fraudulence of this claim and suggests that the Land Settlement Department had every reason to feel satisfied with the Commission. And indeed it did. In December 1915, Frank Inskipp wrote that the Commissioners had 'shown a willingness to meet the view of this Department wherever possible'.[101] A week later, he commented on the land which was to be added to the reserves:

> It is disappointing that it has been found necessary to recommend the assignment of so much new land; at the same time the greater part of the land recommended *is of inferior quality and therefore more suited for native than for European occupation*;[102] further it is hoped that the native reserve land to be returned to the Company will prove of greater extent and superior quality to that for which application has been made.[103]

This letter reveals both Inskipp's satisfaction with the Commission's work and just how closely he worked with Coryndon, for these comments were made a week before the Report had even been signed and five days before the High Commissioner, whose Commission it was, was informed of its findings.

Inskipp had every reason to feel satisfied. Of the 5,610,595 acres added to the reserves, 1,716,400 acres were the last-minute 'reserve' reserves insisted on by Stanley: the fly-ridden Omay, the waterless Gwaai, and the remote Chimanda and Chiswiti. In addition, 14 entirely new reserves totalling some 3,082,075 acres, were created. Of these, Inyanga North, Sebungwe, Semokwe, Matopo, and Umtasa North were considered to be quite useless by the local Native Commissioners; Gwanda, Mtoko, and Wankie were extremely poor and also back debts, since they were created in districts where the lack of European pressure had hitherto made the provision of reserves unnecessary; Mzarabani was simply part of the rearrangement in Darwin where the reserves had previously not been defined with any accuracy; Urungwe had already been agreed to in a pre-1914 exchange and was merely defined properly; and Ndanga East was chosen by Inskipp after he had rejected the first choice on the grounds that it contained good agricultural land. Thus 11 of the 14 new reserves, or 2,821,014 of the total of 3,082,075 acres, were either extremely poor land, or back debts, or both. Moreover in Matabeleland, where the shortage of land was most acute, the original proposals would have resulted in a loss of 387,674 acres, and only the belated provision of the useless Gwaai and Omay 'reserve' reserves turned this into a net gain of 872,826 acres. The only new reserve in central Matabeleland was the Matopo, and that was only traversable by pack animals (see table VI).

TABLE VI

Recommendations of the Native Reserves Commission, 1914–15

(i) Mashonaland

District	*Area of District (acres)*	*Area of Old Reserves*	*Area of Proposed Reserves*	*Percentage of Population on Old Reserves*
Charter	3,322,480	1,736,777	1,444,977	75
Chibi	7,532,800	4,168,271	1,410,106	61
Chilimanzi	1,210,880	347,672	286,855	74
Darwin	3,240,320	904,183	1,191,967	75
Gutu	1,644,800	711,066	638,956	76
Hartley	4,259,840	567,001	508,172	97
Inyanga	1,726,720	135,686	252,596	13
Lomagundi	9,600,000	412,086	887,274	25
Makoni	2,321,280	595,310	530,650	86
Marandellas	1,566,080	448,431	395,131	95
Mazoe	1,710,080	288,553	320,199	75
Melsetter	2,064,000	477,354	426,769	62
Mrewa	1,717,120	1,444,269	1,170,284	99
Mtoko	1,866,240	nil	520,880	nil
Ndanga	4,125,440	863,336	1,258,446	73
Salisbury	1,479,040	612,203	469,381	84
Umtali	1,649,920	593,018	572,197	34
Victoria	1,290,249	254,028	339,118	54
Totals for Mashonaland	52,327,289	14,559,244	12,623,958	65

On the other hand, it might be argued, as the Company did at the time in response to APS attacks,[104] that much of the 6,673,055 acres taken from the reserves was of equally dubious value, since reductions from Matibi, Gwaai, and Shangani accounted for 4,084,502 acres of this total. But this overlooks the fact that Matibi was said to be 'highly suitable for ranching',[105] and that the central part, comprising 1·8 million of the total reduction of 2·6 million acres, subsequently formed part of the Company's 2·5 million acre Nuanetsi Ranch. It also ignores the fact that of the uninhabited 877,867 acres originally taken from Gwaai, 600,000 acres were promptly returned in the shape of a 'reserve' reserve. The half a million acres taken from Shangani were no doubt useless—

TABLE VI (contd.)
Recommendations of the Native Reserves Commission, 1914–15
(ii) Matabeleland

District	*Area of District (acres)*	*Area of Old Reserves*	*Area of Proposed Reserves*	*Percentage of Population on Old Reserves*
Belingwe	2,850,560	1,182,362	1,106,452	80
Bubi	4,595,840	1,665,923	1,120,638	42
Bulalima-Mangwe	4,325,120	1,102,205	1,254,412	58
Bulawayo	350,000	nil	nil	nil
Gwanda	5,079,040	nil	225,411	nil
Gwelo	4,433,280	121,107	177,017	26
Insiza	1,920,000	64,321	64,321	5
Matobo	1,138,560	51,431	176,010	44
Nyamandhlovu	2,782,080	1,377,867	1,100,000	21
Sebungwe	9,719,680	203,187	1,099,487	nil
Selukwe	992,640	158,740	158,740	46
Umzingwane	602,880	4,764	4,764	1
Wankie	6,960,000	nil	317,481	nil
Totals for Matabeleland	45,749,680	5,931,907	6,804,733	36
Totals for Southern Rhodesia	98,076,969	20,491,151	19,428,691	55

they were subsequently returned to Africans as a Native Purchase Area in 1931—but of the 2,588,553 acres of other reductions a high proportion, including some 400,000 acres lying within 20 miles of the railway line, had been personally selected by Inskipp's team of land inspectors as being highly suitable for European farms or ranches; while Holland's diary reveals that the search for good red soil from the reserves was not altogether in vain. Indeed, within five years of the 1920 Order in Council, over 2 million acres of former reserves had been bought; 1·8 million acres by the Company for its Nuanetsi Ranch, and 256,141 acres, in nine different districts, by private individuals. The attack on the reserves was at last reaping dividends.

4 CONCLUSION

The Native Reserves Commission sat at a time when the world to which it belonged was tearing itself to pieces on the battlefields of Europe. The commissioners were all men of an age which had assumed that ordered progress, along lines laid down by high Victorian principles, was inevitable. They were, as Lewis Gann remarks with pride, 'not afraid to make what a later generation has called ethnocentric value-judgements, and did not beat about the bush'.[106] Perhaps therefore it is not surprising that so many of their confident predictions for the future, which must certainly have influenced their recommendations, were to prove utterly unfounded. Very little conflict of interests between white and black was envisaged by the commissioners; 'tribalism' was thought to be on its way out together with extensive and unproductive methods of farming, non-commercial attitudes to cattle, and the attachment to ancestral lands; the provision of water supplies would transform the carrying capacity of the reserves; the population increase would be slow and would not outstrip the more intensive utilization of land; and in general, the inestimable benefits of European civilization would be bestowed upon eager African recipients.

Alas for such prognostications! The next decade in fact witnessed increasing conflict between the races and consequent demands for segregation, a policy which Coryndon personally considered 'futile and even dangerous'[107] and for which his Commission had provided a very inadequate basis.[108] Africans did not on the whole adopt more intensive methods of farming since they were in the process of being pushed away from easy access to markets; water supplies did not produce miracles and the Matabeleland reserves in particular began increasingly to dry up; the cattle market was shortly to collapse, and hence propaganda directed at encouraging voluntary de-stocking fell on deaf ears; the population increased far beyond European expectations; and Africans did not lose their attachment to their ancestral lands, nor indeed their resentment of Europeans who had not only usurped so much of this land, but were also in the process of pushing more and more Africans into those reserves which Coryndon had left.

Thus the optimism of the Commission appeared curiously misplaced to a somewhat more chastened and introspective post-war generation. As early as March 1920, before the Native Reserves Order in Council had even been passed, the Company's Administrator, Drummond Chaplin, acknowledged that: 'It appears certain that some of the reserves as defined by the Native Reserves Commission will not be large enough to accommodate all the natives who might naturally be expected to live in such reserves.' In some cases, such as Selukwe, the reserves were already congested; while in others they would not be able to carry the numbers of people and livestock likely to be moved off European land in the future. Consequently, 'considerable numbers of natives will eventually be unable to remain where they are, or to find accommodation in the neighbouring reserves'.[109] This exactly mirrored the thinking of the missionary John White, who wrote in the same year to John Harris of the APS that: 'The Natives know now that the choice land of the country has been appropriated by the white people and that they have been driven into the least desirable parts of the country.'[110]

The Native Reserves Commission thus attacked on two fronts. It cut down many of the reserves within easy access of the main markets and therefore intensified the squeeze on the African peasantry; while it also reduced some of the larger reserves in the outlying districts, in what was clearly an attempt to curb 'idleness' and overcome the reluctance of Rhodesian Africans to seek wage-labour within the country.

NOTES

1. T 2/29/64/12, F. W. Inskipp to P. S. Inskipp, 23 February 1915.
2. Both the Interim and the Final Report were published in Cd. 8674, Southern Rhodesia, *Papers relating to the Southern Rhodesia Native Reserves Commission, 1915* (London 1917).
3. Not 6 million as claimed by Leys and Bull. C. Leys, *European Politics in Southern Rhodesia* (Oxford 1959), 9-10; T. Bull (Ed.), *Rhodesian Perspective* (London 1967), 25.
4. C.O. 417/526, Gladstone to Harcourt, 19 November 1913. Chanock notes that: 'Gladstone had stipulated earlier that the Imperial Government's representative should "carry weight with the European residents as well as with the natives," and no doubt remembered Maguire's stigmatising Sloley as a "negrophilist".' Maguire was a leading director of the BSA Company. M. L. Chanock, 'British Policy in Central Africa, 1908–26', Ph.D. thesis, Cambridge University, 1968, 147.
5. C.O. 417/550, Minutes by Lambert and Anderson, 24 and 26 January 1914, Harcourt to Gladstone, 31 January 1914.
6. Tait minuted: 'I suppose Lord Gladstone has also sounded Major Garraway—otherwise Mr. Coryndon might have taken his place as the neutral member of the Commission and someone quite independent might have been selected as Chairman.' C.O. 417/538, Minute by Tait, 19 February 1914.
7. L. H. Gann, 'The Southern Rhodesian Land Apportionment Act, 1930: An Essay in Trusteeship', National Archives of Rhodesia and Nyasaland, *Occasional Paper 1*, 1963, 75.
8. The 'Apostles' were a group of twelve young men recruited by Rhodes in 1889, given £10 and a new outfit, and despatched to Mafeking as 'the advance guard of an army of settlers'. H. M. Hole, *Old Rhodesian Days* (London 1928), 9.
9. His diary at this time contains entries such as the following. 'Tried the 3 prisoners sent down ... for stealing and at their confessions I tied them up and flogged them.' 'Got men up and choked them off for insubordination.' 'Sent Elias ... to tell Namoyamba about absence of boys [as carriers] and to threaten what would happen as last resort.' 'Pressed two boys then went to Sianyamia's and caught two delinquents, thrashed them and then pressed three more. Frightened all natives about here.' University of Zambia Library, Coryndon Diary, 5, 6 and 8 May 1899, 8 August 1902.
10. University of Zambia Library, Coryndon Pension Papers, Coryndon to H. W. Fox, 26 November 1907.
11. Rhodes House, Oxford, Coryndon Papers, MSS. Afr. s. 633 10/1, Memoir by H. M. Hole, 14 September 1926, fol. 38.

12. Hist. MSS. GI 1/1/1, Coryndon to Giese, 27 November 1907.

13. Rhodes House, Oxford, Coryndon Papers, MSS. Afr. s. 633 10/1, Memoir by H. M. Hole, 14 September 1926, fol. 54.

14. G. L. Caplan, *The Elites of Barotseland, 1878–1969* (London 1970), 79.

15. C.O. 417/467, Minute by Lambert, 10 January 1910. For Coryndon in Swaziland, see Q. N. Parsons and R. H. Palmer, 'The Roots of Rural Poverty: Historical Background', in Palmer and Parsons (Eds.), *The Roots of Rural Poverty in Central and Southern Africa* (London 1977), 17.

16. University of Zambia Library, Coryndon Newspaper Cuttings, *Mochochonono* (The Comet), Basutoland, 12 December 1917.

17. V. Harlow and E. M. Chilver (Eds.), *History of East Africa, Vol. II* (Oxford 1965), 424; E. A. Brett, *Colonialism and Underdevelopment in East Africa* (London 1973), 179.

18. E. Huxley, *White Man's Country: Lord Delamere and the Making of Kenya, Vol. II* (London 1935), 156. In 1924, on the occasion of the visit of the Duke and Duchess of York to Kenya, the London *Daily Sketch* noted proudly that 'Sir Robert has been known to administer a sound thrashing with his own hands to a "hard case" when more official methods were useless'. University of Zambia Library, Coryndon Newspaper Cuttings, *Daily Sketch*, 21 November 1924.

19. Cd. 8674, Colonial Office to Company, 8 April 1914, 2.

20. F. J. (later Sir Francis) Newton had served as A.D.C. and private secretary to High Commissioner Robinson (1880–9) and in the administration of British Bechuanaland and the Bechuanaland Protectorate (1888–97). He had also been appointed by the Imperial Government to enquire into the 'Victoria Incident' which had preceded the Matabele War of 1893. After being banished to British Honduras and Barbados for his complicity in the Jameson Raid, he returned to Rhodesia where the BSA Company appointed him Treasurer of its administration, a post he held until 1919. Disappointed at not being made Administrator when Milton retired in 1914, Newton subsequently lent his support to the settler movement for responsible Government, and became Colonial Secretary (Minister of Internal Affairs) (1923–4) in the first settler cabinet, and finally ended an eventful career as Southern Rhodesia's first High Commissioner in London (1924–30). On retirement he settled in Salisbury.

21. Hist. MSS. AT 1/2/1/6, Memorandum on Land Settlement Policy, 1926.

22. W. J. Atherstone served first in the Transvaal and the Cape before joining the Surveyor-General's office in Rhodesia in 1898. He became Surveyor-General (1903–31) and was a member of both the Native Reserves Commission (1914–15) and the Land Commission (1925). On retirement he served as a member of the Native Land Board (1931–46).

23. ZAD 3/2/1, Atherstone to Secretary for Mines, 17 August 1908. This letter had appeared as Appendix II to the *Report of the Native Affairs Committee of Enquiry, 1910–11* (Salisbury 1911), 57–9.

24. RC 3/3/23, Note by Atherstone, 4 January 1911.

25. R. Hodder-Williams, 'The British South Africa Company in Marandellas: Some Extra-institutional Constraints on Government', *Rhodesian History*, **2**, 1971, 47, 48 n. 39.

26. ZAD 2/1/1, Newton to Coryndon, 8 July 1914.

27. E. C. F. (later Sir Edward) Garraway was a member of the South African Constabulary (1901–8), became Military Secretary to High Commissioner Gladstone (1910–13), Resident Commissioner for Bechuanaland (1916–17) and Basutoland (1917–26), before retiring to Ireland.

28. Colonial Office minutes cited in Chanock, 'British Policy', 147.

29. C.O. 417/539, Malcolm to Lambert, 26 March 1914.

30. Cd. 8674, 9.

31. As early as 1900 the Company's Chief Secretary had derided as 'impossible ... the hypothesis that land is to be provided for every native who is born during all time'. N 3/24/28, Chief Secretary to CNC Mashonaland, 5 December 1900.

32. Commenting on an earlier expression of this view in 1913, Anderson, at the

Colonial Office, had noted that: 'The Company approach the question from an entirely different point of view from that of H.M.G. Education and civilization of the native appear to them to mean an increasing number of natives working for Europeans as wage earners. Our idea is to develop and improve the native tribal organization so that they may more and more govern themselves and manage their own affairs. An increasing body of natives divorced from the land is incompatible with this policy.' C.O. 417/534, Minute by Anderson, 11 August 1913.

33. The Commission estimated that the African population would double itself in thirty-seven years, while Chief Native Commissioner Taylor thought eighty years would be nearer the mark. In fact it has quintupled in fifty years.

34. Cd. 8674, 23, 27.

35. Cd. 8674, 18, 20.

36. Cd. 8674, 14. The radical missionary, A. S. Cripps, commented: 'Such a statement does not flatter unduly any hope that the Commissioners faced fairly and squarely what was quite conceivably an important part of their duty—the eliciting of tribal points of view.' A. S. Cripps, *The Sabi Reserve* (Oxford 1920), 52. In Northern Rhodesia in 1913, the Secretary for Native Affairs made a point of collecting African evidence on the question of native reserves in the Southern Province, a procedure repeated by the three reserves commissions which sat in the territory during the 1920s.

37. Cd. 8674, 15.

38. C.O. 417/578, Minute by Batterbee, 19 December 1916.

39. C.O. 417/531, Minute by Lambert, 9 February 1914.

40. C.O. 795/40, Memo by Stanley, 12 March 1931. I am indebted to Ian Henderson for this reference. Marilyn Jones notes that: 'Stanley informed the Colonial Office that he was opposed to the implementation of the Tanganyika land ordinances in Northern Rhodesia. It permitted settlers to stay on the land "only on sufferance". The Rhodesian concept he contended was more relevant to Northern Rhodesia, and it would ensure that intending settlers could be sure of being able to make a permanent home there. Amery commented: "This is an interesting example of the South African view to which Sir Stanley is naturally inclined."' M. Y. Jones, 'The Politics of White Agrarian Settlement in Northern Rhodesia, 1898–1928', M. A. thesis, University of Sussex, 1974, 72 n. 1.

41. C.O. 417/578, Stanley to Rodwell, 20 October 1916.

42. The official added: 'I am confirmed in this opinion by all that I have learnt of the East African and West African land systems.' C.O. 417/578, Minute by Batterbee, 19 December 1916. Batterbee's colleague Lambert took the very forthright view that: 'The idea that the native has an inalienable right to vegetate in reserves while the white man has to work does not seem to me to be either just or even good for the native. It is far better that he should come under gradual economic pressure—either he will then have to go out and work or he will have to farm less wastefully than he does at present.' C.O. 417/578, Minute by Lambert, 24 December 1916.

43. C.O. 417/578, Long to Buxton, 1 February 1917.

44. C.O. 417/578, Minute by Batterbee, 19 December 1916.

45. Cd. 8674, Colonial Office to Company, 1 February 1917, 67–8.

46. 96 H.C. DEB. 5s., 18 July 1917, col 329; 2 August 1917, cols. 2257–9; 97 H.C. DEB. 5s., 9 August 1917, cols. 550–1, 15 August 1917, col. 1133.

47. 'Harris does not understand the natives' opined the S/N Bulawayo, while Milton confessed he could not see 'how or why he can be arrested *before* he commits any offence'. A 3/15/10, S/N Bulawayo to CNC, 23 November 1914, Milton to Tredgold, 14 December 1914. See also R. Whitehead, 'The Aborigines' Protection Society and White Settlers in Rhodesia, 1889–1930', University of London, Institute of Commonwealth Studies, *Collected Seminar Papers of The Societies of Southern Africa in the 19th and 20th Centuries, Vol. 3* (London 1973), 99–101.

48. One questioner asked: 'Is the object of the reduction of these reserves to deprive the natives of the land and to provide cheap labour to the Rhodesian and other companies?' 96 H.C. DEB. 5s., 2 August 1917, cols. 2258–9.

49. Some of this was published in Cmd.547, Southern Rhodesia, *Correspondence with the Anti-Slavery and Aborigines Protection Society relating to the Native Reserves in Southern Rhodesia* (London 1920). Marshall Hole vigorously defended the Company against APS attacks: H. M. Hole, 'Rhodesian Natives and the Land', *Ways and Means*, **6,** 1920, 18–25.

50. C.O. 417/555, Minute by Lambert, 3 December 1914.

51. D. V. Steere, *God's Irregular: Arthur Shearly Cripps* (London 1973); M. C. Steele, '"With Hope Unconquered and Unconquerable...": Arthur Shearly Cripps, 1869–1952', in T. O. Ranger and J. Weller (Eds.), *Themes in the Christian History of Central Africa* (London 1975), 152–74; A. S. Cripps, *An Africa for Africans* (London 1927). He had also been influenced by Olive Schreiner's book, *Trooper Peter Halket of Mashonaland* (London 1897), which was a searing indictment of the Company's behaviour.

Cripps was not, as Mlambo claims, the brother of Sir Stafford Cripps, though according to the present Lord Parmoor 'he may have been a distant cousin to whom our family records do not extend'. E. Mlambo, *Rhodesia: The Struggle for a Birthright* (London 1972), 41 n. 10; Steere, *God's Irregular*, 2.

52. Drummond Chaplin, who succeeded Milton as Administrator in 1914, commented after a tour of Cripps' mission: 'It was a pleasant change to visit the Hope Fountain Mission near Bulawayo the following week and see some really civilising work being done.' A 3/20/3, Chaplin to Buxton, 5 August 1920.

53. Cripps, *The Sabi Reserve*; A. S. Cripps, 'The Reserves Commission in Southern Rhodesia', *Contemporary Review*, **118,** 1920, 553–6.

54. Hist. MSS. CH 8/2/2/6, Gell to Chaplin, 6 May 1920.

55. C.O. 417/633, Minute by Tait, 22 July 1919.

56. C.O. 417/634, Minute by Lambert, 22 March 1919.

57. C.O. 417/641, Note of proceedings at an interview granted by the High Commissioner, 18 August 1920.

58. C.O. 417/606, Minute by Lambert, 31 October 1918.

59. A number of other, very minor, boundary alterations were made to the Bushu, Lower Gwelo, Madziwa, Makoni, Semokwe, and Wedza Reserves, but in no case were African interests prejudiced.

60. C.O. 417/636, Douglas-Jones to Buxton, 13 March 1920, Buxton to Milner, 30 March 1920; A 3/20/3, CNC to Secretary, Department of Administrator, 23 June 1920.

61. In Bechuanaland and Swaziland only Crown Land was vested in the High Commissioner, but in these territories the native reserves were owned by Africans, which was not the case in Southern Rhodesia. Native reserves in Northern Rhodesia (1928–9) and native trust lands in Nyasaland (1936) and Northern Rhodesia (1947) were all vested in the Secretary of State for the Colonies, rather than the High Commissioner, in an endeavour to provide maximum safeguards for Africans in the event of any future political union with Southern Rhodesia.

62. C.O. 417/636, Minute by Fiddes, 21 April 1920.

63. C.O. 417/637, Buxton to Milner, 4 May 1920.

64. C.O. 417/678, Buxton to Connaught, 9 May 1922.

65. C.O. 417/637, Minute by Lambert, 11 May 1920.

66. Cmd.1042, Native Reserves in Southern Rhodesia, *Despatch to the High Commissioner for South Africa transmitting the Order of His Majesty in Council of the 9th November, 1920* (London 1920).

67. Rhodes House, Oxford, Coryndon Papers, MSS. Afr. s. 633, 10/1, Memoir by E. C. F. Garraway, 1926, fol. 77.

68. Gann, 'The Southern Rhodesia Land Apportionment Act', 75; L. H. Gann, *A History of Southern Rhodesia* (London 1965), 188.

69. P. J. Duignan, 'Native Policy in Southern Rhodesia, 1890–1923', Ph.D. thesis, Stanford University, 1961, 210–11.

70. A. J. Hanna, *The Story of the Rhodesias and Nyasaland* (London 1960), 183.

71. See, for example, B. N. Floyd, 'Land Apportionment in Southern Rhodesia',

Geographical Review, **52**, 1962, 575; R. McGregor, 'Native Segregation in Southern Rhodesia', Ph.D. thesis, University of London, 1940, 90–3; P. S. Hassing, 'The Christian Missions and the British Expansion in Southern Rhodesia, 1888–1923', Ph.D. thesis, The American University, 1960, 246–58.

72. Author's emphasis.

73. T 2/29/64/12, Coryndon to CNC, May 1914.

74. In support of this proposal he cited the following arguments: '(1) They would be much easier to supervise and to control than areas of from five to ten times the size; (2) tribalism, with all its objectionable and retrogressive features, would be more effectively broken up; (3) material progress and education of the natives would be more rapid and thorough if they were kept in closer touch with the surrounding white population; (4) the labour supply would be more evenly distributed and more rapidly developed by closer contact with the demand; (5) the tendency to segregation which is, I believe, a futile and even dangerous principle in native administration, would be avoided; (6) it will allow of a more equitable division of the various types of country and soil to the different requirements of the native and the white settler; and (7) the areas would still be sufficiently large to allow the natives to retain their feeling of independence and ownership.' T 2/29/64/12, Coryndon to Newton, 23 July 1914.

75. T 2/29/64/12, Coryndon to Newton, 23 July 1914.

76. T 2/29/64/12, Memo by CNC, July 1914, Minute by Milton, 3 August 1914.

77. LB 2/1/15, Wise to F. W. Inskipp, 16 March 1914.

78. C.O. 417/551, P. S. Inskipp to London Office, 25 March 1914.

79. A 3/18/39/4, London Office to Chaplin, 11 December 1914.

80. The Company's directors 'pointed out to Mr. Coryndon that should good agricultural land, suitable for occupation by Europeans, be found to occur in the vicinity of any of the proposed [branch railway] routes it would be to the interest of the community that it should be reserved for white settlement'. L 2/2/121, London Office to Acting Commercial Representative, 19 June 1915.

81. Author's emphasis.

82. T 2/29/64/12, F. W. Inskipp to Secretary, Native Reserves Commission, 10 July 1914.

83. ZAD 2/2/1, Secretary, Native Reserves Commission, to F. W. Inskipp, 12 August 1914.

84. T 2/29/64/12, F. W. Inskipp to P. S. Inskipp, 23 February 1915.

85. LB 2/1/16, Report by F. W. Inskipp, 22 July 1915.

86. L 2/2/122, Land Inspector Howell to F. W. Inskipp, 28 August 1915; L 2/2/117/9, Land Inspector Jenkinson to F. W. Inskipp, 19 May, 1914; S 3/1/3, Land Inspector English to F. W. Inskipp, 30 May 1914; LB 2/1/16, F. W. Inskipp to P. S. Inskipp, 4 November 1915; L 2/2/121, Land Inspector Jenkinson to F. W. Inskipp, 1 June 1915; L 2/2/121, F. W. Inskipp to Land Inspector Boyes, 15 January 1915.

87. L 2/2/117/7, F. W. Inskipp to CNC, 24 August 1922.

88. Hist. MSS. HO 7/2/1, Holland's Diary, 21 and 23 May, 2 and 10 November 1915, 4, 8, 99–100, 104.

89. C.O. 417/514, Douglas-Jones to Rodwell, 18 September 1912.

90. Hist MSS. HO 7/2/1, Holland's Diary, 25 June 1915, 29.

91. *Proceedings of the Southern Rhodesia Missionary Conference 1920* (Salisbury 1920), 17.

92. ZAH 1/1/1, Evidence of J. White to Land Commission, 10 March 1925, 204.

93. A 3/18/39/5, Memo by Hole, 7 January 1920.

94. A 3/3/20/2, N/C Mrewa to S/N Salisbury, 18 June 1917.

95. A 3/3/20/2, N/C Charter to S/N Salisbury, June 1917. He subsequently told the 1925 Land Commission that the Company had failed to provide adequate reserves throughout the country, and suggested that 'if ... a position has now arisen to provide more land, then every effort should be brought to bear and meet this demand, preferably in setting aside more ground as Reserves or for exclusive native use'. ZAH 2/1/1, N/C Charter to Secretary, Land Commission, 20 March 1925.

96. N 3/24/9, S/N Bulawayo to CNC, 26 July 1919. The Commission claimed (Cd. 8674, 56, 58) that Jackson had approved of the new Gwanda and Semokwe reserves.

97. ZAD 3/1/1, Evidence of H. M. G. Jackson to Native Reserves Commission, 9 July 1914.

98. Cd. 8674, 14.

99. Rhodes House, Oxford, Coryndon Papers, MSS. Afr. s. 633, 10/1, Memoir by A. H. Holland, 2 December 1926, fol. 60.

100. Cd. 8674, 21.

101. LB 2/1/16, Report by F. W. Inskipp, 2 December 1915.

102. Author's emphasis.

103. LB 2/1/16, Report by F. W. Inskipp, 9 December 1915.

104. In 1917 Inskipp wrote that: 'The bulk of the surrendered land is remotely situated and in many places of such poor quality as to be even unsuited for ranching; e.g. the half million acres surrendered from the Shangani Reserve: on the other hand the land added to the Reserves is on the whole more accessible and of better quality.' This apparent remarkable change of mind on Inskipp's part is nullified however when he continues: 'I would venture to suggest that a copy of this minute be forwarded to the London Office in view of the adverse comments which are being passed in the House of Commons.' LB 2/1/17, F. W. Inskipp to Acting Commercial Representative, 2 November 1917.

105. L 2/2/117/9, Land Inspector Jenkinson to F. W. Inskipp, 19 May 1914.

106. Gann, *Southern Rhodesia*, 188.

107. T 2/29/64/12, Coryndon to Newton, 23 July 1914.

108. Lord Buxton, High Commissioner at the time, expressed the view, during a House of Lords debate on the Report of the 1925 Land Commission, that 'the Coryndon Commission originally did dot about small reserves in rather too large numbers'. 64 H.L. DEB. 5s., 23 June 1926, col. 556.

109. A 12/1/16, Memo by Chaplin, 25 March 1920.

110. Rhodes House, Oxford, APS Papers, G163, White to Harris, 2 August 1920.

CHAPTER 6

The Drive to Segregation 1915–25

The objects of our native policy ... [are to secure] *the development of the native in such a way that he will come as little as possible in conflict or competition with the white man socially, economically and politically.*

Editor, Native Affairs Department Annual, 1923.[1]

1 BACKGROUND

The decade 1915–25 witnessed profound changes in Europe. In the course of the most destructive war in the continent's history, the old Habsburg, Romanov, and Ottoman Empires collapsed in ruin, and the forces of nationalism, communism, and fascism vied with each other to fill the vacuum which had been left. The old order was disappearing.

In Africa although the former German colonies were duly parcelled out among the victorious allies, the First World War did bring about a certain loss of European self-confidence. After the major European powers had exhibited their lust for destruction so blatantly, it was no longer quite so easy to believe in *la mission civilisatrice* in Africa and Asia, or to bask in the comfortable Victorian assumptions of cultural superiority which had so recently been voiced in Rhodesia by the Native Reserves Commission. One result of this was a growing recognition that there might after all be something of value in African societies, and hence the somewhat contagious spread of 'indirect rule' policies in British colonies in the 1920s and 1930s. Ironically, white attempts to preserve 'the tribal way of life' clashed diametrically, as they had done earlier in South Africa, with the aspirations of the rising African elites towards 'Westernization' and more modern forms of political association.

In Rhodesia, where the majority of Europeans stolidly declined to share in the general mood of introspection, the decade witnessed important political changes which were to sow the seeds of the UDI crisis of the 1960s. In 1922 the tiny and almost exclusively European electorate rejected the opportunity of becoming the fifth province of the Union of South Africa, as Rhodes had always envisaged, and voted instead by a majority of 8,774 to 5,989 for responsible Government. Thus the era of Company rule came to an end, and on 1 October 1923 Southern Rhodesia, with its estimated 35,900 Europeans and 890,000 Africans, became a 'self-governing colony'.[2] This meant that effective political power had passed into the hands of the white settlers, for the Rhodesian Civil Service and armed forces were responsible to Salisbury and not, as in other colonies, to London. Moreover, the new Southern Rhodesian Government was responsible to an all-white Legislative Assembly and, every five years at least, to an overwhelmingly white electorate, with all that this implied in the realm of 'native policy'.

It is true that a number of safeguards, similar to those imposed in the post-Risings Order in Council of 1898, were written into the 1923 Constitution by the Colonial Office to prevent the passing of discriminatory legislation without Imperial assent. But the last Resident Commissioner left in 1923, to be replaced by a Governor, whose powers were much less than those of his autocratic counterparts in more orthodox colonies. The first incumbent, Sir John Chancellor (1923–8) grew increasingly frustrated at his lack of real power and by 1926 was complaining: 'It is a humiliating position to be in, Governor of a tin-pot self-governing Colony like this ... now that the new constitution of S. Rhodesia is in working order, the Governor has become a "passenger".'[3] Indeed the Imperial authorities became increasingly spectators of the Rhodesian scene, armed with the powers of veto but not of initiation, and hence unable to check the growing political and economic dominance of the settlers.

In 1915–25 European agriculture expanded rapidly and came to assume an increasingly important position in the Rhodesian economy. By 1921 it contained the largest single group of white income-earners in the country. The settlers in fact greatly enhanced their economic position in this period whilst simultaneously achieving political control, and they were able to mount a further, and increasingly successful, attack upon the African peasantry in order to safeguard their position. A very important part of this attack was the demand for segregation of land-ownership, which was to culminate in the Land Apportionment Act of 1930. This chapter will be much concerned with the segregation debate and the related movement of Africans into the reserves; for the moment it is sufficient to note that both these phenomena were part of an overall economic and political struggle for dominance in which the settlers aspired to command the heights and articulate African opinion looked in vain to the British Government for protection.

2 POLICY

(i) Introduction

During the decade 1915–25 the dilemma which at one time or another confronts all colonial regimes, began to make itself apparent in

Rhodesia, when administrators for the first time addressed themselves to the question which has haunted all their successors: what was to be done with the Africans? Hitherto, Africans had been considered so backward that hardly anyone had bothered to ask the question. Early officials concentrated on instilling 'the dignity of labour' to the extent that they frowned upon African commercial farming. But as a new skilled elite emerged and began to buy land, use ploughs, read newspapers, and even mount a slight challenge to the established order by forming political associations, the question naturally arose of how to channel this advance; and in particular how to channel it so that Africans would not come into social, economic, or political competition with Europeans. The solution which occurred to most people was that of segregation.

Despite the constitutional change which took place in 1923, the day-to-day administration of African affairs changed remarkably little. The same Native Commissioners continued to hold office, and the Native Department itself continued to enjoy a greater degree of autonomy than any other since, following the South African precedent and at British insistence, the Premier (late Prime Minister) was also made Minister of Native Affairs. Sir Charles Coghlan, Premier from 1923–7, was very much involved in railway matters and had comparatively little time to devote to African affairs, thus allowing the Native Department to go its own way.[4]

(ii) The Privy Council Land Case

One of the most important factors determining land policy at this time was the 1918 Privy Council judgement on the ownership of the land. The problem of who owned the unalienated land of Southern Rhodesia dated back to 1891 when the Company had acquired the Lippert Concession. The Imperial Government approved the Concession and made no attempt at the time to contest the Company's assumption of ownership. But from 1902 onwards this assumption was challenged by the settlers who, with an eye to the future, argued that the Company could only own the land in its administrative capacity and that when it ceased to administer the territory ownership should pass into the hands of the new Government. The Colonial Office declined to settle the issue in 1908, but in 1914 it agreed to submit the question to the Judicial Committee of the Privy Council.[5] It did so because of the imminent revision of the Company's charter, the growing political power of the settlers, and the fear of settler opposition to the appointment of the Native Reserves Commission.

The Council's decision was delayed by the war until 1918,[6] by which time there were four contestants: the Company, the settlers, the

Africans, and the Crown. The African case was sponsored by the Aborigines' Protection Society following John Harris' abortive trip to Rhodesia in 1914, while the Colonial Office's belated decision to enter the case came as a complete shock to the Company.[7] The shock must have been even greater when judgement was pronounced on 29 July 1918, and the Crown was declared to be the rightful owner. The decision appears to have been arrived at by a process of elimination. The Privy Council declared that the Lippert Concession was valueless as a title deed since the Company had never paid Lobengula his 'annual *douceur*', and that the Company did not acquire the land by right of conquest in 1893 since conquest was only valid in the name of the Crown. The African case was summarily dismissed on the grounds that the Ndebele sovereignty, and with it all African rights to land, had been broken up and replaced by a new, 'and, as their Lordships do not doubt, a better' system, as defined by the 1894 Order in Council. After displaying a degree of ethnocentricity reminiscent of the Native Reserves Commission, the Privy Councillors concluded that 'whoever now owns the unalienated lands, the natives do not'. Finally, the settlers were unable to prove that the Crown had already disposed of its rights of ownership in favour of some future government. Ownership was accordingly vested in the Crown.[8]

The Privy Council also concluded that the Company, in compensation for its loss of ownership, was entitled to be reimbursed by the Crown for all its past expenses incurred in administering Southern Rhodesia, calculated at £4·4 million down to 1918. For as long as the Company continued to govern, however, it was entitled to sell land and pocket the money in part-liquidation of this debt. Eventually ownership of the land, except for the native reserves and all public works and buildings, was confirmed by the Crown on the new Southern Rhodesian Government at a cost to the settlers of £2 million, the Crown paying only the £1¾ million still outstanding to the Company.

The effect of the Privy Council judgement was to bring administration virtually to a standstill. At one blow the Company was deprived of what it had always regarded as one of its major commercial assets and, as it had yet to pay a dividend, it decided to concentrate squarely on its shareholders' interests and to spend no more money on administration than was absolutely essential. This was serious enough, but because the sale of land was the only way in which it could recoup its administrative expenses, the Company was forced to sell land at the maximum price possible. This in effect retarded European settlement, prevented the creation of more reserves in districts where they were badly needed, and made it impossible to assign land for individual purchase by Africans or to allow the revenue from mission and trading sites in the reserves to be used to develop the reserves. As Drummond Chaplin, the Company's Administrator, explained:

> [We] cannot possibly ... afford to reserve land in the old liberal way for administrative purposes, still less to assign large areas free of charge or on easy terms for native use or for European settlement. In other words, under existing conditions the Crown Land[9] cannot be, as it ought to be, at the disposal of the Administration to be sold, leased or used for the benefit of the community. The Company is compelled to get the last penny it can out of the land, and the people are consequently deprived of facilities to which under ordinary circumstances they would be fairly entitled.[10]

The effects of this situation were nowhere more keenly felt than in the debate on segregation.

(iii) The Segregation Debate

(*a*) *Introduction*

The key to the segregation debate was the law, dating back to 1894, which proclaimed that 'a native may acquire, hold, encumber and dispose of land on the same conditions as a person who is not a native'. As has been shown in chapter 3 the Company managed to prevent the law becoming effective by the simple expedient of refusing to sell land to Africans—and indeed to Indians[11]—and most European farmers did the same. The result was that by 1925 only 14 farms, totalling 46,966 acres, had been sold to Africans, mostly at inflated prices.[12] A detailed list of these farms is to be found in Appendix II (see pp. 279–82).

Naturally, very few Africans were in a position to afford freehold farms, whether they were encouraged to buy or not, and half of those who managed to obtain farms were black South Africans. Thus 'Article 43', as the law became known,[13] was in itself of very little concern to the mass of the population. Yet its ultimate effect, in the shape of the Land Apportionment Act of 1930, was to touch everyone.

'Segregation' was a useful word precisely because it meant different things to different people. It was demanded during the decade 1915–25, with very different intent, at farmers' meetings, parliamentary sessions, missionary conferences, and in the pages of the Chief Native Commissioner's annual reports. The debate was however principally concerned with land ownership since, as R. A. Fletcher, one of Rhodesia's most influential farmers and subsequently a Minister of Agriculture, pointed out in 1910: 'wholesale segregation of natives was an impossible proposition, because it would affect the labour supply and labour was essential for the development of the country.'[14] In other words, Africans were not to be moved *en bloc* into 'African areas' because their labour was required on the white farms; rather they were to be allowed to buy land only in certain prescribed areas.

The impetus towards segregation of landownership or 'possessory segregation' as it was called came, not surprisingly, from South Africa and in particular from Natal, where Theophilus Shepstone with the full backing of the Colonial Office had made the Native Department a state within the state and had erected a segregationist framework which later became something of a model for Rhodesia and the rest of South Africa.[15] The model was carried a stage further when Milner's post-war South African Native Affairs Commission of 1903–5 (which included one Rhodesian representative and whose terms of reference covered Rhodesia) reported that 'wherever Europeans are living, repugnance is shown to the invasion of their neighbourhood by Natives for residential purposes'. Moreover, the presence of African farms in European areas 'cannot fail to accentuate feelings of race prejudice and animosity, with unhappy results. It will be far more difficult to preserve the absolutely necessary political and social distinctions if the growth of a mixed rural population of land-owners is not discouraged'. The Commission therefore recommended: '(1) That purchase by Natives should in future be limited to certain areas to be defined by legislative enactment. (2) That purchase of land which may lead to tribal, communal or collective possession or occupation by Natives should not be permitted.'[16] These observations and recommendations, which were implemented in the 1913 Natives Land Act, were shared by most white Rhodesians and were in fact endorsed by the Company's own Native Affairs Committee of Enquiry of 1910–11.[17]

The basic driving force behind the movement to segregation—and it is worth emphasizing in view of the complexity of motivating factors—was the intense hatred displayed by the overwhelming majority of European farmers at the idea of Africans buying land in their midst. European farmers were opposed to the emergence of an African land-owning class of commercial farmers for two basic reasons. In the first place they objected to Africans as neighbours. As labourers or rent-paying tenants they were of course welcome, for they were beholden to the European farmer and could be evicted by him at will; but as landowners they would have to be treated (legally at any rate) as equals, and this was something which would cut right across Southern African racial prejudices.[18] Perhaps more important, if Africans 'invaded' the European farming areas they would, by and large, be tilling the better soils and have equal access to markets, and hence be in a strong position to compete with European farmers. Indeed the white farmers were afraid that as the African earning capacity increased, so more and more Africans would be in a position to buy land and they wanted the law changed before this could happen.[19]

It was this fear and prejudice which was the decisive factor; had the call for segregation been voiced by Native Commissioners and missionaries alone, against the wishes of the white farmers, the Land Apportionment Act would never have reached the statute book.[20] Ranger is therefore quite mistaken when he argues that it was essentially the support of Cripps, White, and the APS which was the decisive factor; he has paid insufficient attention to 'European voices'.[21] It was only the recognition that an open land market would inevitably increase racial friction that led people such as Taylor, the Chief Native Commissioner, and Cripps, the radical missionary, to come round in support of some form of segregation. In addition, there were conflicting fears for the future[22] which helped to bring about a convergence of opposites. Though Africans had managed to buy very little land on the open market, many white farmers were convinced that this would soon change and hence they were worried by the future potential of Article 43. On the other hand, missionaries, Native Commissioners and Africans themselves tended to fear that past patterns would continue, and that Europeans would eventually buy up all the remaining good land before Africans were able to compete effectively. Pressures for a change in the law were thus applied from diverse quarters, and each of the main pressure groups will now be examined in turn.

(*b*) *The European Farmers*

The most powerful group demanding segregation was undoubtedly the European farmers. This is not surprising since by 1921 they comprised by far the largest single section—24·54 per cent, of white income-earners.[23] As the great majority of white Rhodesians envisaged retiring onto a farm,[24] questions such as 'possessory segregation' naturally aroused a wide interest among the European public. As the political power of the settlers grew, so almost by definition did that of the farmers. In 1930, 13 of the 30 members of the Legislative Assembly were, or had been, farmers,[25] while all Rhodesian Prime Ministers (with the exception of the first, Coghlan, who was a lawyer) and the majority of cabinet ministers have been farmers.[26] The Rhodesia Agricultural Union, which by 1918 had 46 affiliated associations and a membership of 1,200, held annual congresses which were well attended by Government ministers and whose resolutions carried considerable weight.[27] Thus, when the Land Commission of 1925 presented its report on segregation, it did so to a government and a parliament in which the voice of the white farmer was strongly represented.

White farmers were almost unanimously opposed to an open land market,[28] though they were in some confusion over what was to replace Article 43. The majority clearly felt that no compensation was called for, but the more astute gradually came to realize that the Imperial Government would not agree to amend the law unless separate areas were assigned in which Africans were allowed to purchase land. They tended to get extremely agitated on the very few occasions when Africans did manage to buy land from private owners. In 1908, R. A. Fletcher, at the time Chairman of the Bulawayo-based Rhodesian Landowners' and Farmers' Association, and later President of the Rhodesia Agricultural Union (1910–14) and Minister of Agriculture (1928–32), complained that it was 'not the proper thing',[29] and he moved a resolution in the Legislative Council calling for a prohibition on the sale of land to Africans pending the determination of a uniform South African policy. He argued that they should accept the views of the South African Native Affairs Commission, and observed that when Africans bought land, the white owners of adjoining farms inevitably suffered. Moreover: 'The natives in this country are still savages, and there was not a native in Rhodesia who knew anything of the responsibility of the landowner.' Fletcher was afraid of a situation arising comparable to that in Natal, 'where whole tracts of land were occupied by natives and the white settler driven away'. Newton replied however that the Company could not undertake the serious task of seeking an amendment to the existing law, and the motion was withdrawn.[30] But Fletcher's Association was clearly not happy with the situation, for in the following year it informed the Company that the law was 'a danger and a menace' which should be withdrawn until the African was 'considerably advanced in civilization'.[31] The Chamber of Mines and the Rhodesia Native Labour Bureau, on the other hand, were prepared to accept that Africans should be able to buy land, but only in limited amounts in specified areas provided that the land was beneficially occupied and not rented to others and that communal tenure was prohibited.[32]

Farming opinion continued to be aroused whenever Africans bought farms. In 1911, when a third farm in the Fort Victoria area passed into African hands, a protest meeting was called and a resolution passed demanding the repeal of the law,[33] while in 1916 when a European was trying to sub-divide his farm near Bulawayo and sell parts of it to Africans, H. M. Heyman, representing the predominantly rural Gwelo constituency and once a member of the 1894 Land Commission (see chapter 2), introduced a motion calling for legislation to deal with the matter. Once again the South African Commission was invoked—it was pointed out that the value of adjoining farms would depreciate, that African owners would no longer be under the control of the Native Department, and that future European settlement would be adversely affected. Two members, John McChlery, who had led a somewhat farcical 'populist' movement in 1912,[34] and Lionel Cripps, thought that Africans might be allowed to buy land within defined areas. The motion was duly passed[35] and was reinforced by one from the Rhodesia Agricultural Union deprecating such sales as 'a menace to the white Settler'.[36] Chaplin however refused to take any action while the Report of the Native Reserves Commission was still under consideration.

The farmers tried yet again in 1921, after Madhloli Kumalo, a nephew of Lobengula, bought a farm in Nyamandhlovu. The Rhodesia Agricultural Union demanded legislation making it impossible for Europeans to sell to Africans; and Fletcher, who had introduced the 1908 motion, moved a resolution in the Legislative Council drawing attention to the Chief Native Commissioner's Report for 1920, and suggesting that the Company inform the Colonial Secretary of the serious consequences which would result from any delay in amending the law. 'It was becoming a matter of common knowledge that probably there was a good field for exploitation in the selling of land to natives', Fletcher suggested. He acknowledged that it was impossible to prevent Africans buying land outside the reserves, 'however much it was against the grain of a good many European settlers', and that the important thing to do was to limit it to defined areas. Friction was reported from districts in which Africans had bought farms, and it was generally agreed that it was about time the rot was stopped. The resolution was passed,[37] but once again Chaplin refused to endorse it, particularly in the light of the Privy Council judgement.

The settlers, including Fletcher, brought their case to London at the end of 1921, however, and during discussions at the Colonial Office on the issue of responsible government, they once again admitted their fear that Africans would begin buying more land in the future. The Colonial Office stonewalled, but eventually agreed that if after responsible government was granted an impartial enquiry revealed the need to amend the law, then it might be amended.

Thus the agitation of the European farmers finally began to make headway when it dropped its demand for a total ban on African landownership and concentrated instead on a separate purchase areas policy, as advocated by the Chief Native Commissioner and supported by the missionaries. The farmers had acquired respectable allies.

(c) *The Native Department*

The Native Department, having won its spurs by its spirited defence of the reserves against the attacks of the Estates Department[38] (see chapter 4), took the view that the desire for individual ownership was progressive that it 'generally presupposes thrift and industry',[39] while giving Africans 'a real interest in the country and our Government and practically insures their loyalty for all time'.[40] Such views were shared by the Kenya provincial administration, which believed that 'individual freehold title was the highest form of evolution in land tenure',[41] though the notion of a landed bulwark against the masses did not obtain wide acceptance in Colonial Office ideology until the advent of nationalism in the 1950s.

Whilst most Rhodesian Native Commissioners were agreed that the desire for individual tenure should be encouraged, the major problem was where precisely it should find expression. At first it was believed that room might be found in some of the existing reserves,[42] but after the Native Reserves Commission had completed its work, and in the face of the continuing movement of people off European land and into the reserves, it was recognized that they were not capable of housing such an experiment. By 1915 H. J. Taylor, the Chief Native Commissioner, had acknowledged the fact that African purchase of land on the open market was producing strong European resentment, and that in the circumstances it would be better for this to be confined to designated areas.[43] By 1920, in the face of a growing shortage of land in parts of Matabeleland, it was felt that the designated areas should adjoin the reserves so that the progressiveness of individual owners could influence the communal farmers of the reserves. The N/Cs Gwanda and Insiza were complaining that the reserves could not accommodate all those likely to be evicted from European farms in the future, and that Europeans were applying for land next to the reserves which ought to be earmarked for African purchase.[44] The matter was raised at a departmental conference in 1920, the S/N Gwelo stressing the urgent need to assign unalienated land for African purchase, especially in districts where the reserves were inadequate.[45] It was stressed that land should be offered for sale at moderate prices, since in Gwanda Africans were being offered land at 13/– per morgen which was inferior to that being offered Europeans at 5/– per morgen.[46]

Taylor, who was to become a member of the 1925 Land Commission, spelt out the position clearly in his annual report for 1920, which influenced settlers, missionaries and Imperial officials alike. He noted that more farms were being bought by Africans:

> In the interests of all it is not desirable that natives should acquire land indiscriminately, owing to the inevitable friction which will arise with their European neighbours. It is advisable, therefore, to reserve land contiguous to existing reserves for individual purchase or lease by them.

African aspirations in this direction were legitimate, Taylor argued, and any attempt to restrict them would be foolish.[47]

Thus the Native Department's thinking, and that of Taylor in particular, evolved from the recognition of European colour prejudice, and the desire to encourage African individual tenure despite this. The difficulty of course would be to find sufficient areas of suitable land to offer Africans as purchase areas. Taylor's colleagues at Gwanda and Insiza supported him for more immediate reasons however—they were short of land and a purchase areas policy held out the prospect of getting more.

(*d*) *The Missionaries*

Missionary attitudes tended to follow closely those of Taylor and the Native Department. At first the missionaries also envisaged individual tenure being introduced into the reserves,[48] but subsequently they backed Taylor's idea of separate areas bordering the reserves, partly as compensation for losses suffered at the hands of the Native Reserves Commission. Repenting of their apathy at the time of the Commission, the missionaries, with the radical Cripps and his friend John White[49] in the vanguard and supported by the APS, launched a vigorous campaign in favour of Taylor's scheme both in Rhodesia and in England.[50] They demanded early action because of the increasing number of post-war settlers who were taking up land, but they stressed that Article 43 should not be surrendered 'except on terms of a fair partition of all un-alienated land', and Cripps in particular was anxious that segregation should be accompanied by a really liberal land policy as he wished to avoid the cruel and fraudulent fiasco which had occurred in South Africa.[51] Naturally, the missionaries' concept of fairness and liberality would differ radically from that of the white farmers.

The basic reason why the missionaries came to support and champion a policy of possessory segregation was best expressed by John White in 1923. 'Against such a racial division in the past I have protested in principle', he wrote to John Harris of the APS. 'I could not see the justice of it. My views have undergone a change. The right of natives to purchase land anywhere means that they purchase nowhere. The practical difficulties seem insurmountable. If the Government would set apart a fair proportion of land, suitable for native cultivation, and cede it to them on reasonable terms, I for one would be prepared to agree to the conditions they wish to impose, viz. that the natives be excluded from the white areas.'[52] Cripps similarly believed that: 'Failing the working of God's own miracles of grace amongst our European population, it is only too likely that the sort of friction which our Chief Native Commissioner sees as an imminent danger will multiply itself amongst us before many years be out.'[53] Thus it was the existence of 'this strong racial prejudice',[54] coupled with the fact that Africans were effectively being prevented from buying land on the open market and a fear that (as in South Africa) they would end up with very little land, which caused the missionaries to follow in the footsteps of the white farmers.[55]

(*e*) *The African Associations*

African voices also participated in the segregation debate, though not as articulately as after 1925 when the Land Commission's hearing of evidence effectively publicized the whole issue. In the early 1920s, however, overt African political activity in Rhodesia was naturally preoccupied with the inadequacies of the reserves and the problems bequeathed by the Native Reserves Commission. This was especially true of the Ndebele royalist movement under Nyamanda and Madhloli (which is discussed later in this chapter, see pp. 151–3). Nevertheless, many of the very small group of Africans who had succeeded in buying farms played prominent roles in the African associations which emerged in

Rhodesia (as elsewhere in Central and East Africa) in the 1920s,[56] and it was only natural that they should address themselves to the question of possessory segregation. They tended to find themselves in much the same dilemma as the missionaries.

A meeting of the Registered Native Voters—it cannot have been a large meeting—at Gwelo in January 1923 pointed out that Africans had been unable to buy land from the Company in the past, and expressed the vain hope that under the new Government there would be no such restrictions. It also resolved to form the Rhodesian Bantu Voters' Association (RBVA).[57] In May 1924, J. T. Bammings, Secretary of the Rhodesian Native Association, submitted a memorandum asking for 'the allocation of plots of land for purchase by Individual natives';[58] a call which was reinforced in July by a request from the RBVA for the assignment of unalienated land adjoining the reserves, which Africans could buy at fair and reasonable prices with ample time being given to purchasers.[59] The RBVA's Mfengu president, Garner Sojini, who went to see Chief Native Commissioner Taylor about the question was told of the appointment of the Land Commission, and 'expressed his appreciation of the interest that the Government was taking in this matter'.[60] The S/N Bulawayo took a somewhat uncharitable view of the RBVA's interest, however, asserting that its leaders had read about the question in the newspapers, and had included it 'in their propaganda and they will probably later claim the credit of having obtained concessions for the masses'.[61] They did.[62]

On the whole, it would be true to say that the leaders of the African associations, like the missionaries, were prepared to go along with a policy of possessory segregation purely as a means of getting more land. Thus, as in South Africa, segregation gained the support of widely differing sections of society. It was championed, as Cripps put it, both by 'those who are genuinely keen on native development, like our Chief Native Commissioner', and by 'quasi-repressionists, apprehensive that clause 43 might prove eventually to be, in its working, not a mere pious recommendation or aspiration, but a living and expansive reality'.[63]

(*f*) *The Company Response*

The Company's traditional policy had always been to refuse both African applications for land and European requests to change the law. In 1915, however, the newly arrived Drummond Chaplin felt it desirable to reach a definite policy, rather than allow the matter to drift, as had happened with serious consequences in South Africa where there was very little land left for African purchase.[64] But Chaplin's colleagues preferred to maintain the *status quo*, and it was not until 1920 in response to the situation in Gwanda where Europeans were applying for land adjoining the already overcrowded reserve, that he wrote to London asking that Africans be given the first option of buying the land.[65] However, the Privy Council judgement meant that the Company was obliged to sell land at the highest price it could get, and Chaplin was accordingly informed that the Company could not deal with the land 'except on the strictest business lines' disregarding questions of public policy, and thus Africans could not be permitted to buy land in Gwanda to the exclusion of Europeans.[66] In effect therefore, the Company dropped out of the debate, which then became one between the settlers and the Imperial authorities.

(g) *The Imperial Response*

The Imperial response was one of extreme caution, as illustrated by the comment of one Colonial Office official in 1913 that: 'H.M.G. must not be committed to a policy of segregation ... except as following in the wake of S. African opinion later on.' This set the tone of Imperial deliberations, though there was a gradual movement in favour of some form of segregation. In 1913 the Colonial Office rejected Gladstone's proposal that the question be included in the Native Reserves Commission's terms of reference,[67] though by 1916 Stanley acknowledged that there were 'valid objections to the indiscriminate intermixture of European and native landowners', and that a case for altering the existing law could probably be established though the matter was not urgent.[68] In 1920 Buxton, under pressure from Cripps, took much the same line observing that it was not in the interests of either race for African farms to be indiscriminately interspersed among European ones, and that while nothing should be done without careful consideration, provided Africans were given sufficient land, segregation 'might be not undesirable, and it may anyhow in the end prove inevitable'.[69]

The Colonial Office preferred to await developments rather than take the initiative. In 1921 a settler delegation arrived in London to discuss future constitutional arrangements and took the opportunity to press the issue. They urged that Taylor's separate land purchase areas policy be adopted, and they admitted that they were afraid that Africans would soon begin to exercise their right to buy land more effectively than in the past. Henry Lambert, assistant under-secretary at the Colonial Office, observed that while nothing could be done as long as the Company retained its administration, their case had missionary backing. However, the Secretary of State could not agree to amend the law as:

> It is of too long standing, it has been too much quoted by us to Aborigines Protection and other Societies, it is too essential a point of principle. What he might do, since the point of the Elected Members is a real one, is to promise them that if after Responsible Government has come into force full and impartial enquiry shows the need for some amendment of the clause, he will agree to amend.

The last clause was significantly rephrased in the official despatch to read 'he would be prepared to consider an amendment', which left the Imperial Government free to reject the findings of any subsequent enquiry.[70]

Thus the ultimate decision, as with the reserves question, was entrusted to a commission. By the time the Land Commission began its work in 1925, possessory segregation had become the prevailing orthodoxy, and the only real point at issue was the nature of the compensation to be offered to Africans for the withdrawal of a right which they had effectively been barred from exercising.

(iv) The Native Department and the Reserves

Though the Native Department was much preoccupied with the segregation issue in the years 1915–25, the Report of the Native Reserves Commission, and the increasing number of Africans being yearly evicted from European farms and forced to move into the reserves, caused many Native Commissioners to rethink their whole attitude towards the land question. In the past they had tended to regard African settlement on European farms as something progressive and to be encouraged. But in the face of the prevailing attitudes of white farmers they gradually came to look upon the reserves as havens of rest where Africans could live relatively free from European exactions, and where they might be able to develop 'along their own lines'. Thus we find Taylor, the Chief Native Commissioner who in 1904 had looked on reserves as 'only a temporary makeshift' which involved 'the negation of all progress',[71] writing in 1922 that: 'In the interests of the natives it is highly desirable that the movement to the Reserves should be encouraged.' He had arrived at this conclusion because the chiefs were in favour of the movement into the reserves as the tribal system could be maintained more easily than when the people were scattered over farms, while the reserves also offered greater scope for mission work and for industrial schools.[72]

This belated desire to bolster the tribal system came at a time when there were numerous references to its decline. In 1915 the N/C Matobo observed, 'every day it becomes more evident that we will have to deal with the natives individually and not collectively',[73] while Taylor himself wrote that the chiefs would soon 'cease to be recognised as a medium of the Government' and that 'the time is not far distant when the tribal system will cease to perform a useful function'.[74] What to put in its place? 'We have the lesson of India before our eyes', wrote the clear-sighted N/C Belingwe, 'sufficient surely to make us think twice before entertaining the idea of imposing on these people ideas of democracy alien to their very nature.'[75] The most popular solution was the South African one of native councils for which provision had been made in the 1923 Constitution, because: 'As a vent for the psychological necessity of the native to express himself politically, native councils founded on and developed from the existing system are far preferable to any exotic political growth not based upon an interest in the soil.'[76] Encouraging Africans to move into the reserves thus became for many Native Commissioners a means by which to slow down the break-up of the tribal system and to hinder the growth of potentially hostile political movements. As the S/N Gwelo put it: 'If there exists a political situation it is in connection with the land question, and the cause of discontent will disappear as soon as the natives are settled in the Reserves.'[77]

3 ACTUALITY

(i) White Farmers, Black Peasants

The decade of the segregation debate witnessed a further expansion of European farming and a not unconnected dramatic decline in African agriculture. Though European production fell during the First World War when many farmers were away on active service,[78] there was a post-war boom as new settlers arrived and an increase in mining activity created a larger internal market for agricultural commodities. Then came the recession of 1921–3, caused by a combination of external and local factors which hit Africans far harder than Europeans, but this was followed by a period of renewed expansion as the new settler Government of 1923 did all it could to encourage the further development of European agriculture.

Thus the average annual expenditure of the Department of Agriculture rose from £33,468 in the years 1918–19 to 1922–3 to £75,636 in the period 1923–4 to 1928–9 (see table VII). The number of European farmers increased from 1,324 in 1911 to 2,355 in 1921, while altogether some $8\frac{1}{2}$ million acres were alienated to Europeans in the period 1915–25, which brought the total European area up to just over 31 million acres, or a third of the entire country. This was sometimes very striking, as at Lomagundi in 1920 when the Native Commissioner reported that 'land has been taken up in all directions and the European population has practically doubled itself'.[79] The price of land rose to an average of 7/– per acre in 1920, and some of the absentee landlords took advantage of this and began to subdivide their huge estates and to sell off parts to the new immigrants. Finally, the new Government greatly increased the amount of money devoted to road building and maintenance in the major white farming areas, in an endeavour to expand the existing infrastructure.

European agriculture continued to be dominated by maize, tobacco,

TABLE VII

Expenditure of the Department of Agriculture on European Farming, 1904–51

Year	*Expenditure* (£)
1903–04 to 1908–09	10,065 (average)
1909–10 to 1913–14	22,476 (average)
1914–15 to 1917–18	18,436 (average)
1918–19 to 1922–23	33,468 (average)
1923–24 to 1928–29	75,636 (average)
1929–30	131,795
1930–31	263,306
1931–32	211,296
1933–34	203,364
1945–46	404,669
1946–47	677,379
1947–48	1,012,354
1948–49	929,237
1949–50	1,196,943
1950–51	1,675,373

and cattle during this period, with exports being facilitated by low railway rates made possible by the shipment of substantial quantities of Katanga copper to Beira by the Rhodesian railways. Maize production fluctuated a good deal, rising from 914,926 (203 lb) bags in 1914–15 to a peak of 1,505,580 bags in 1922–3 and then falling to 1,068,904 bags in 1924–5. Maize exports rose from 346,855 (200 lb) bags in 1915 to a peak of 774, 449 bags in 1923, and then dropped to 383,338 bags in 1925. After the collapse of tobacco through overproduction in 1913–14, the industry slowly recovered and production rose from 426,423 lb in 1914–15 to a record 5,659,809 lb in 1925–6. The number of European-owned cattle continued to rise sharply, from 394,856 in 1915 to 1,006,086 in 1925, while African-owned cattle increased similarly from 445,795 to 1,095,841 in the same period. This dramatic twofold increase naturally intensified the racial competition for grazing lands. An export market was opened up to Johannesburg in 1916 and cattle exports rose from 12,928 in that year to 72,738 in 1926, by which time Southern Rhodesia was exporting to South Africa, the Belgian Congo, Mozambique, Britain, Germany, and Northern Rhodesia, with South Africa taking some 80 per cent of the total.

Thus European farming emerged from its pioneer period to a position in which it was firmly established as a central sector of the Rhodesian economy with its members occupying strategic positions in government and parliament. W. M. Leggate, for example, who was the colony's first

Minister of Agriculture and Lands (1923–5) and then became Minister of Internal Affairs (1925–33),[80] had once been President of the Rhodesia Agricultural Union (1919–20), as indeed had R. A. Fletcher, the Minister of Agriculture (1928–32). As might be expected, this increasing success gave rise to a good deal of aggression towards Africans living on European land. The British High Commissioner for South Africa, Athlone, who visited Rhodesia in 1926, noted that the great majority of European farmers demanded excessive grazing fees and 'made considerable profit out of the unfortunate natives'. He observed that as dipping was compulsory, 'the temptation to make exorbitant profits in this way must be difficult to resist'.[81]

Relations were particularly bad in the Insiza District between Bulawayo and Gwelo. In 1918 the local Native Commissioner remarked that: 'The eagerness of some land owners to make a profit out of the [Compulsory Dipping] Ordinance—either by charging high dipping fees or by increasing the rent charges to cover the cost of constructing tanks, has left a very bad impression on the natives.' The following year he mentioned the case of one farmer who 'captured 70 head of native cattle ... trespassing on his farm[82] (not on cultivated land) and charged the owners of the cattle an ox value at £5 and £4 in cash'. The N/C commented: 'When farmers descend to such contemptible methods of enriching themselves at the expense of ignorant natives, it is not surprising if the natives do retaliate by burning farms out, but unfortunately decent farmers suffer in the process of retaliation, as when once a grass fire is started there is no saying where it will end.'[83] Sinoia, to the north-west of Salisbury, was little better, and following a series of violent speeches by local farmers on the labour problem, Coghlan informed Governor Chancellor in 1927 that he 'would not advise the Secretary of State to remove from the constitution the present restrictions regarding control of native affairs, so long as the Colony contained a number of hotheads like the Sinoia farmers, who were unfit to be trusted to give the natives fair treatment'.[84] Rhodesia continued to contain many white hotheads, and in the light of all this evidence it is scarcely surprising that most Africans should feel that 'the white Rhodesian farmer ... represented the worst in European racial feelings ... he was harsh, domineering, unfair, inhuman and took the law into his own hands when dealing with Africans, some of whom felt that they were placed in the same class as the cattle or even lower'.[85]

It is against such a background of racial hostility that one needs to look at the impoverishment of the African peasantry in Rhodesia. The remarkable prosperity enjoyed by many Shona farmers in the early years of the century was brought to an end by a combination of factors. Primarily, African farmers faced the full blast of competition from heavily subsidized European farmers while simultaneously being pushed away from easy access to markets, a process greatly facilitated by the work of the Native Reserves Commission. In addition, Africans were confronted with an ever-increasing number of costly dues—taxes, rents, dipping and grazing fees etc.—at a time when their own appetite for consumer goods was on the increase. The end result was that when they were no longer able to sustain themselves and purchase their requirements from the sale of their agricultural produce, they would be forced to become wage-labourers.

It was inevitable that European and African farmers would come into open conflict, and the conflict would probably have occurred earlier than it did but for the intervention of the First World War which led many Europeans to abandon their farms and presented Africans with an opportunity to sell maize and cattle at rising prices. This situation lasted until 1920. Then came the slump of 1921–3, which, in Arrighi's words, 'radically altered the position of the African peasantry in the structure of the Rhodesian economy'. In 1920, Africans sold some 198,000 bags of maize at 10/– per bag; in 1921 they sold 43,600 bags at 5/–, a drop in earnings from about £100,000 to under £10,000. Similarly, in 1919 they sold some 20,000 head of cattle at £7 to £8 each, while in 1922 they sold practically none.[86] On top of all this, prices were rising fast. Between 1914 and 1920 the cost of ten types of goods widely purchased by Africans rose on average by 165 per cent, while African wages went up by only 13 per cent in the same period.[87]

Thus Africans were forced out onto the labour market, and many employers, especially the farmers, took advantage of the situation to reduce wages, to as low as 5/– in some districts. Many tenants could no longer afford to pay the rents and other fees demanded by their landlords, and since the price of maize and cattle had fallen so low there was far less incentive to remain close to the main markets. Thus Africans increasingly moved into the reserves, and 'once the migration had taken place, the future ability of Africans who had migrated to obtain their cash requirements through the sale of produce was, of course, jeopardized'.[88] This was because of the greater cost, and difficulty of marketing their produce from the native reserves,[89] which by now were beginning to show distinct signs of overcrowding.

(ii) The Movement into the Reserves

'I begin to wonder how much longer the process of squeezing the native out can go on', observed A. C. Jennings (the man responsible for developing water supplies in the reserves) to the Land Commission of 1925.[90] Jennings was speaking specifically of the period 1915–25, and some idea of the scale of this squeeze can be gauged from the following estimates of the African population made by the Native Reserves and Land Commissions:

	1915	*1925*
Within the reserves	405,376	516,335
Outside the reserves	326,777	297,612
Total	732,153	813,947

Thus, while the total African population was estimated to have risen by 11 per cent during the decade, the number living within the reserves increased by 27 per cent while the number outside showed a decrease of 9 per cent. In round figures, more than 60,000 people must have moved into the reserves in these ten years. (See also table VIII for the remarkably static number of Africans living on European farms.) It was little wonder, therefore, that the Chief Native Commissioner spoke of 'a continual stream of natives moving from private farms and unalienated land',[91] and that the annual reports of Native Commissioners during this period abound with references to 'a considerable exodus', 'a steady drift' and the like, with sometimes as many as three or four thousand people moving into the reserves in one district alone during the course of a year.[92] Movements on such a scale would have been inconceivable in Nyasaland where the Government was terrified whenever European planters in the Shire Highlands threatened to evict a few hundred tenants, and where Africans continued to challange the legality of the Europeans' claim to the land. But in Rhodesia the white farmers were in a far stronger position, and memories of the savage suppression of the 1896–7 Risings precluded the possibility of overt resistance.

TABLE VIII

Estimated African Population on Alienated European Farms, 1913–61

1913	153,000	1941	158,000
1926	159,000	1951	182,000
1931	180,000	1961	169,000

Many of those who moved were among the 48,000 who found themselves living on the 6·7 million acres excised from the reserves by the Coryndon Commission.[93] In 1917 they were informed of the Commission's recommendations, the Chief Native Commissioner being present when large numbers were involved. It was not intended that all should move; they had the option of staying and paying rent or agreeing terms with new owners. A quick census in 1918 in fact revealed that some 17,616 people were reluctant to move, most especially in 'the old traditional areas' in Salisbury, and at Ndanga, where 'the graves of their ancestors are on the reverted land'.[94] It was Company policy, however, to induce a gradual 'voluntary' movement, and by May some 5,514 had moved, and a further 3,000 had moved in Mrewa by March 1921, the APS being informed that such movements were by no means uncommon among African societies. But many people chose to remain on their ancestral lands, and the refusal of Chief Charumbila and some 4,000 of his people to vacate the surrendered Mlinya Reserve in Victoria District, for which there were many European applicants, called forth the wrath of the peppery S/N Victoria, C. L. Carbutt. 'I suggest that I be authorised to warn him that he will be ejected by force if necessary', Carbutt wrote to the Chief Native Commissioner, adding (in words reminiscent of the recent Tangwena affair) that 'it will probably be necessary to turn the people out of their huts with their chattels and then burn the huts, before they move'.[95] It was found, however, following a High Court decision, that the powers of Native Commissioners to order the removal of Africans to reserves were somewhat deficient. The deficiency was promptly remedied by the passing of the Native Regulations Act of 1924.[96]

An additional factor inducing movement into the reserves was the rent on unalienated land,[97] though it was not enforced universally and many Native Commissioners continued to oppose it as they had when it was first introduced in 1909. In 1917 the Chief Native Commissioner noted that there was widespread reluctance to pay the rent following a succession of bad seasons, the introduction of compulsory dipping in many areas, abnormal economic conditions resulting from the war, and the fact that no action had been taken in the past against defaulters.[98] Notwithstanding this situation the Company, especially after the Privy Council judgement, continued to press for as much rent as it could get,[99] even in 1922 at Inyanga where there had been a severe famine and there was no room in the reserves. Here 'the natives felt that the B.S.A. Coy. in its land policy was merely exacting the last pound of flesh', a policy of passive resistance was adopted and the Native Commissioner was only able to collect less than £300 per annum compared to £1,000 before.[100] By March 1924, following the slump of 1921–3 and a serious drought, the amount outstanding over the whole country was £18,608 and the matter was referred to the Cabinet, which by a majority of three to two decided to persevere with the rent but write off all arrears. Coghlan saw no objection if the rent led to an increased movement into the reserves, as this would help the Government's policy of 'sane segregation', though Moffat, who was to succeed him in 1927, pointed out that many reserves were getting overcrowded and that some Native Commissioners would be only too glad for Africans to remain where they were. He also felt that: 'For us, the Government, after having conquered the country and taken it away from them to, as a Government, charge them rent for living on their old homes does seem to me to be rather "rubbing it in."'[101] Nevertheless the rent was 'rubbed in', continuing to be a useful, if diminishing, source of revenue,[102] and a means of driving more and more Africans into those reserves which were still capable of accommodating them.

Indeed the very scale of this movement into the reserves confronted the administration with the choice of either providing more reserves in order to cope with the influx, or of attempting to increase the carrying capacity of the existing reserves by providing wells and boreholes and by encouraging more intensive methods of cultivation. The latter alternative clearly held the greater appeal for the white electorate, and so began the 'development of the reserves' (which will be discussed in chapter 8, see pp. 201–205), but there were emergency situations in Inyanga, Mtoko, Victoria, and Wankie, which led to the creation of additional reserves in these four districts in 1924. Unfortunately, as Appendix I (see pp. 264–76) reveals, the land selected was of very poor quality.

(iii) The Ndebele National Home Movement

'We are witnessing the genesis of nationalism to-day in the native race', wrote the N/C Makoni in 1923,[103] at a time when the first stirrings of movements of 'exotic political growth'[104] were beginning to trouble the administration. It is abundantly clear that by about 1920 the land question, coupled with the attitude of the white farmers, had become a source of major grievance. The situation was particularly critical in Matabeleland where, as Governor Chancellor confessed, 'there is undoubtedly cause for complaint'.[105] To be turned off a farm in central Matabeleland often entailed a trek of 50 to a 100 miles to the nearest reserve which was usually deficient in water supplies; many Ndebele whose homes were on the *high veld* succumbed to malaria when they moved to the lower, fever-stricken areas.[106] It was in such circumstances that the Ndebele National Home Movement was born. According to Ranger, this was 'in some ways the first "modern" political movement in Southern Rhodesia',[107] and it is also significant as an early, and unsuccessful, attempt by black Rhodesians to enlist the support of the British Government.

The movement was led by Nyamanda, the eldest son of Lobengula, and his cousin, Madhloli Kumalo. Both had been evicted several times from European farms, and they gained considerable local support in their attempts to restore the Ndebele monarchy and to secure a National Home where all the Ndebele might settle and be free from the exactions of the white farmers.

In March 1919 Nyamanda sent a petition to George V 'which is in some ways a landmark in Rhodesian African political history'.[108] Nyamanda stated that the Ndebele had 'no piece of land of their own', that they were scattered about on farms . . . parcelled out to white settlers, and are practically created a nomadic people living in this scattered condition under a veiled form of slavery, they not being allowed individually to cross from one farm to another, or from place to place except under a system of permit or Pass, and are practically forced to do labour on these private farms as a condition of their occupying land in Matabeleland.

He called for Imperial control over African administration, the restoration of the Ndebele monarchy, and the return of the unalienated land to the Lobengula family since 'the right of conquest ... is now repudiated by the civilized world'.[109] The petition was brushed aside by the Imperial authorities who considered it largely the work of leaders of the Ethiopian Church in South Africa with whom Nyamanda was in contact. Chief Native Commissioner Taylor on the other hand believed that Nyamanda should be given some land, only to have this rejected because of the Company's difficulties following the Privy Council judgement.[110]

Nyamanda then endeavoured to travel south to present his grievances to High Commissioner Buxton, but was not allowed to go. Instead he went around collecting money from the Ndebele in order to buy land, and he harked back to Rhodes' broken promise of 1896. He obtained an interview with Chaplin in April 1920 and repeated his requests, only to be told that the acquisition of a large tract of land was out of the question. Madhloli then took up the running; he travelled to Cape Town and petitioned the departing Buxton in August 1920, complaining that the reserves were dry and unhealthy and that the Ndebele were being evicted from European farms. He pointed out 'the dire necessity of finding suitable land for our occupation ... to appease the existing discontent between the people and the Rhodesian Government'.[111] Madhloli was granted an interview with Buxton, who informed him that the findings of the Coryndon Commission were no longer open to discussion, and that outside the reserves the Ndebele would have to make the best terms they could with the white farmers.[112]

Despite these setbacks the campaign continued into 1921, when Prince Arthur of Connaught, the new High Commissioner, came to Rhodesia and addressed the Ndebele in the Matopos Hills, twenty-five years after the famous Rhodes *indabas* of 1896. He duly delivered what he thought was a final 'no' to the request for a restoration of the monarchy, and although he had not personally seen the reserves he blandly assured the assembly that they had been carefully selected, were 'wide and fertile', and with few exceptions contained good supplies of water.[113] The following day, 13 August 1921, saw 'the final effort of the National Home movement'.[114] Nyamanda was granted an interview with Connaught. He handed in another petition calling for the exchange of Gwaai and Shangani for 'more salubrious land of equal dimensions' and 'one large composite Reserve or Native Territory of the size adequate enough to meet the needs of present and future population ... under the chieftainship of the acknowledged son of the late Lobengula'.[115] Once again the petition was brushed aside, the Imperial authorities agreeing with Chaplin that while Nyamanda 'has at present acquired a certain amount of popularity by voicing a popular cry for more land', there was little doubt that 'the natives are at present being unduly exploited by Nyamanda'.[116] This can scarcely have been the case, for at the end of 1922 the N/C Umzingwane was reporting that: 'The agitation for a Head of the Matabele Nation appears to have died down, but the land question and dipping fees are subjects much discussed.'[117]

The new Governor, Chancellor, adopted a rather more positive approach to Ndebele land grievances than Chaplin had done. He consulted with H. M. G. Jackson, the Assistant Chief Native Commissioner and a former S/N Bulawayo, who felt that the Ndebele had been badly treated and who tried to persuade some of them to move out to the Belingwe District in south-east Matabeleland. One chief went with some of his followers, but soon returned after encountering hostility from Shona residents in the area. Chancellor asked if there was any other way of relieving the situation, and Jackson suggested a possible move to the Sabi Reserve in the Charter District of Mashonaland which contained patches of the red soils favoured by the Ndebele. Chancellor persuaded Coghlan to agree to the idea,[118] and a few Ndebele families moved to the Sabi in 1925. That such a scheme could have been propounded is itself eloquent testimony to the land problem in Matabeleland.

4 CONCLUSION

Thus the decade 1915–25 was one in which Africans were brought face to face with the realities of European rule, and with the full implications of the wholesale alienation of the 1890s and the expansion of European agriculture. As one Colonial Office official observed: 'I fear that a good deal of the natives' grievances is the inevitable result of the white population—there is I suppose no country where there is a white settled population in which that population has not insisted on having the best land for itself—and got it.'[119] This was clearly the case in central Matabeleland, where the Ndebele bitterly resented being pushed into distant and inhospitable reserves by aggressive white farmers who, as one Minister of Agriculture had the grace to admit, 'have ever so much more land than they ... can profitably make use of'.[120] In Mashonaland, many peope were also evicted from white farms while others moved into the reserves because they could literally no longer afford to remain on European or Crown Land. Faced with this situation, the Native Department began to talk optimistically about promoting local self-government in the reserves and stemming the disintegration of the tribal system. The land problem was largely instrumental in the birth of 'modern' African politics, in the form of the Ndebele Home Movement and other associations, which are discussed in the next two chapters. Nyamanda tried to appeal to the Imperial authorities for help, but like the nationalist leaders of a later generation, he was told that the British Government had no intention of intervening in the internal affairs of Rhodesia. Such was the situation in 1925, when the Land Commission was established to enquire into the much debated question of segregation.

NOTES

1. N. H. Wilson, 'The Development of Native Reserves', *NADA*, **1**, 1923, 88.
2. The electorate totalled 18,810, of whom only about 60 were Africans. See M. A. G. Davies, *Incorporation in the Union of South Africa or Self-Government: Southern Rhodesia's Choice, 1922* (Pretoria 1965); J. D. Fage, 'The Achievement of Self-Government in Southern Rhodesia, 1898–1923', Ph.D. thesis, Cambridge University, 1949.
3. Rhodes House, Oxford, Chancellor Papers, MSS. Brit. Emp. s. 284, 9/1, Chancellor to Thompson, 23 October 1926, fol. 466–7.
4. M. C. Steele, 'The Foundations of a "Native" Policy in Southern Rhodesia, 1923–33', Ph.D. thesis, Simon Fraser University, 1972, 27–9.
5. Cd. 7509, Southern Rhodesia, *Papers relating to a Reference to the Judicial Committee of the Privy Council on the Question of the Ownership of Land in Southern Rhodesia* (London 1914).
6. This lengthy delay persuaded the Colonial Office to seek a quick settlement with the Company in Northern Rhodesia, with the result that the BSA Company's mineral rights, which later became so enormously profitable, were not subjected to searching legal analysis.
7. Malcolm wrote of the Imperial decision: 'I can't believe they can get the Court to say that without annexing or expressing any kind of intention to act as owners of the land they nevertheless became owners in '93, and have been so since. Since Mons. Jourdain discovered that he had been talking prose all his life without knowing it, there has been nothing quite like it.' Hist. MSS. Ch 8/2/2/11, Malcolm to Chaplin, 19 March 1915.
8. Special Reference as to the Ownership of the Unalienated Land in Southern Rhodesia, *Report of the Lords of the Judicial Committee of the Privy Council, delivered on the 29th July, 1918* (London 1918), 16–21. The Council believed: 'It would be idle to ignore the fact that, between the subjects of Her Majesty Queen Victoria and those of this native monarch, [Lobengula] whose sovereignty she was pleased to recognise, there was in all juridical conceptions a great gulf fixed, which it would, perhaps, be only fanciful to span ... Some tribes are so low in the scale of social organisation that their usages and conceptions of rights and duties are not to be reconciled with the institutions or the legal ideas of civilised society. Such a gulf cannot be bridged. It would be idle to impute to such people some shadow of the rights known to our law, and then to transmute it into the substance of transferable rights of property as we know them.' *Report ... of the Privy Council*, 3, 17.
9. At about this time, the term 'Crown Land' came into common usage to describe what had previously been termed 'unalienated land'.
10. Hist. MSS. Ch 8/2/2/13, Chaplin to Milner, 6 May 1920.
11. For example, the S/N Bulawayo believed that 'loyalty and an outlook in conformity with our general ideals' could not be expected of Asians, while the N/C Bulalima-Mangwe was worried that Asian landowners might cohabit with African women, and Coghlan

warned the British Indian Association in Salisbury that they 'would be better advised to leave the matter alone rather than raise possible trouble'. A 3/18/39/5, S/N Bulawayo to CNC, 2 November 1922; S 246/433, N/C Bulalima-Mangwe to S/N Bulawayo, 25 June 1923, Notes of an Interview between the Premier and the Colonial Secretary with Representatives of the British Indian Association, 12 December 1924.

12. This figure is compiled on the basis of two, slightly differing, 'schedules of land owned by natives, 1925' in files S 96 and Hist. MSS. AT 1/2/1/10. Compare this with Nyasaland, where by the same year Africans had bought 4,383 acres in freehold and had leased 1,180 acres, and with Natal, where by 1907 there were 1,548 registered African landowners holding 191,466 acres. Native Archives of Malawi, S 1/1332/25, Lands Officer, List of Native Tenants on Crown Land and Native Owners of Freehold Land, 15 August 1925; D. Welsh, *The Roots of Segregation* (Cape Town 1971), 199–200.

13. Article 43 of the Southern Rhodesia Constitution Letters Patent 1923. It had previously been Article 83 of the Southern Rhodesia Order in Council 1898, and Article 33 of the Matabeleland Order in Council 1894.

14. *Bulawayo Chronicle*, 7 October 1910.

15. Welsh, *Roots of Segregation*; D. Welsh, 'The Cultural Dimension of Apartheid', *African Affairs*, **71**, 282, 1972, 35–53.

16. South Africa, *South African Native Affairs Commission, 1903–5, Vol. I* (Cape Town 1905), 34–5.

17. Southern Rhodesia, *Report of the Native Affairs Committee of Enquiry, 1910–11* (Salisbury 1911), 10. This Committee recommended that Africans should not be allowed to buy land outside the reserves for the present.

18. 'Segregation is necessary because fundamental race difference exists; and herein lies the core of the matter', wrote Sybil Bowker in 1920. S. Bowker, 'A Scheme for Segregation Areas', *Contemporary Review*, **117**, 1920, 548.

19. In Natal, writes Welsh, 'it is clear that the colonists favoured segregationist ideas not because Africans were "barbarous", "primitive", or "savage" but because a significant group of Africans no longer conformed to these stereotypes and claimed admission into the upper caste'. Welsh, *Roots of Segregation*, 321.

20. A fact conveniently overlooked by Gann in his attempt to depict the Act as a work of Imperial trusteeship. L. H. Gann, 'The Southern Rhodesian Land Apportionment Act, 1930: An Essay in Trusteeship', National Archives of Rhodesia and Nyasaland, *Occasional Paper 1*, 1963, 71–91.

21. T. O. Ranger, *The African Voice in Southern Rhodesia* (Nairobi 1970), 117, 172–3. In a recent work Eshmael Mlambo has followed Ranger in exaggerating the influence of the philanthropic lobby on Rhodesian affairs. It would be exceedingly difficult to demonstrate his belief that the APS really 'played ... a major part in improving the ... plight' of black Rhodesians. E. Mlambo, *Rhodesia: The Struggle for a Birthright* (London 1972), 30.

22. Richard Gray writes that: 'For the majority of Europeans who supported segregation, fear was the most widespread and compelling factor ... It was not simply the threat of economic competition, or even of political infiltration; it was a combination of these factors together with the shadow of miscegenation and the presence of a vast mass of people across a cultural gulf which seemed unbridgeable.' R. Gray, *The Two Nations* (London 1960), 19.

23. The 1921 census revealed the following distribution of income earners:

Occupational Groups	*Income Earners*	*Per Cent*
Agriculture	3,626	24·54
Commerce	2,481	16·79
Public Services	2,150	14·55
Mining	1,897	12·84
Railways	1,637	11·08

Occupational Groups	*Income Earners*	*Per Cent*
Industries	1,492	10·10
Commercial Services	740	5·01
Professions	655	4·43
Independent means	98	0·66
	14,776	100·00

24. 'Farmers dominated European society: they were well organized and powerfully represented in the Southern Rhodesian legislature. Farmers also had numerous allies in other white social strata, for many businessmen, civil servants, professional people and even ordinary workmen would invest their savings in land as a speculation, allowing the investor to benefit from rising real estate values, or as a saving for eventual retirement.' L. H. Gann and P. Duignan, 'Changing Patterns of a White Elite: Rhodesian and Other Settlers', in Gann and Duignan (Eds.), *Colonialism in Africa, 1870–1960, Vol. 2: The History and Politics of Colonialism 1914–1960* (Cambridge 1970), 110.

25. Steele, 'Native Policy', 35.

26. Mlambo, *Rhodesia*, 20, 41 n. 1.

27. D. J. Murray, *The Governmental System in Southern Rhodesia* (Oxford 1970), 63.

28. Only two of the 110 white farmers interviewed by the Land Commission in 1925 were genuinely in favour of an open land market (see chapter 7, p. 180).

29. *Bulawayo Chronicle*, 12 June 1908.

30. Southern Rhodesia, *Legislative Council Debates*, 1 July 1908, 151–3.

31. *Bulawayo Chronicle*, 5 October 1909. The Land Commission echoed this view when it stated that 'until the Native has advanced very much further on the paths of civilisation, it is better that the points of contact ... between the two races should be reduced'. Southern Rhodesia, *Report of the Land Commission, 1925* (Salisbury 1926), 5.

32. *Bulawayo Chronicle*, 22 October 1909.

33. *Rhodesia Herald*, 7 July 1911.

34. I. Henderson, 'White Populism in Southern Rhodesia', *Comparative Studies in Society and History*, **14,** 1972, 387–99.

35. *Legislative Council Debates*, 10 May 1916, 282–92.

36. N 3/16/9, Resolution of the Rhodesia Agricultural Union, 12 August 1916.

37. *Legislative Council Debates*, 18 May 1921, 763–74.

38. John Harris, in the course of his tirade against the Company, made the comment, which may have been sincere or merely 'tactical', that 'there are few territories under the dominion of Great Britain where natives have greater or more merited confidence in their Native Commissioners than in Rhodesia'. J. H. Harris, *The Chartered Millions* (London 1920), 222.

39. NUA 5/1/1, Report by Conference of S/Ns, 16 October 1909.

40. N 3/16/9, N/C Inyanga to S/N Umtali, 29 May 1914. The Attorney-General, Tredgold, took the view that: 'As a broad principle we should encourage individual holding of land. The landowner is a more settled member of the community than before he achieved that position. He has something very definite to lose which cannot easily be replaced... The landowner has alway been a steadying influence when too radical changes are proposed. He is less likely than others to join in the extreme steps of rebellion.' N 3/16/9, Note by Tredgold, 22 February 1915.

41. M. P. K. Sorrenson, *Origins of European Settlement in Kenya* (Nairobi 1968), 178.

42. NUA 5/1/1, Report by Conference of S/Ns, 16 October 1909; *Report of the Chief Native Commissioner for the year 1913* (Salisbury 1914), 1–2.

43. A 3/15/11, CNC to Chaplin, 9 March 1915.

44. A 12/1/16, Memo by Chaplin, 25 March 1920; N 3/24/4, N/C Insiza to S/N Gwelo, 2 August 1920, S/N Gwelo to CNC, 31 August 1920.

45. S 138/37, Minutes of Conference of N/Cs, 31 August and 1 September 1920.

46. N 3/24/4, N/C Gwanda to S/N Bulawayo, 26 August 1920.

47. *Report of the Chief Native Commissioner for the year 1920* (Salisbury 1921), 1–2.

48. *Proceedings of the Southern Rhodesia Missionary Conference 1913* (Salisbury 1913), 6, 28; *Missionary Conference 1920*, 19–24; *The Times*, 9 March 1920; C.O. 417/637, Stanley to Lambert, 9 June 1920; C.O. 417/656, Archbishop of Canterbury to Milner, 13 August 1920.

49. See C. F. Andrews, *John White of Mashonaland* (London 1935).

50. 143 H.C. DEB. 5s., 21 June 1921, Cols. 1126–7; C.O. 417/675, Cripps to Churchill, 17 August 1921, White and Burnet to Churchill, 15 October 1921, APS to Colonial Office, 6 June, 29 August and 23 November 1921; *Missionary Conference 1922*, 7–8, 23; 145 H.C. DEB. 5s., 20 June 1922, cols. 1023–4; N 3/16/9, White to Devonshire, 19 January 1923, Fuller to N/C Melsetter, 2 February 1923, Cripps to Devonshire, 12 March 1923; C.O. 767/1, Cripps and White to Ormsby-Gore, 1 October 1923, APS to Coghlan, 7 November 1923; C.O. 767/3, APS to Colonial Office, 11 March 1924; *Missionary Conferenc 1924*, 8, 27–8; A. S. Cripps, 'Native Rhodesia's Now or Never', *South African Quarterly*, **5**, 1923, 6–9; A. S. Cripps, 'Native Rhodesia's Now or Never' (revised), *NADA*, **1**, 1923, 44–51; A. S. Cripps, 'A Difficult and Delicate Operation', *NADA*, **2**, 1924, 98–106; C. C. Fuller, 'Notes on (a) Education and (b) Land', *NADA*, **1**, 1923, 28–9; T. J. Jones (Ed.), *Education in East Africa* (New York 1924), 234.

51. *Missionary Conference 1924*, 8, 27.

52. Rhodes House, Oxford, APS Papers, G166, White to Harris, 3 December 1923.

53. Cripps, 'Native Rhodesia's Now or Never', 46.

54. Rhodes House, Oxford, APS Papers, G166, White to Harris, 2 January 1923.

55. Thus in 1924 Cripps could write enthusiastically that 'a policy of areas for native land-purchase has, to its lasting credit, been propounded by our Colony's Government'. Cripps, 'A Difficult and Delicate Operation', 100.

56. The records of these associations have been deligently studied by a plethora of scholars seeking the roots of nationalism, though it could be argued that some of them at least, by acting as a safety valve, were of rather greater assistance to colonial administrators than to the African masses in whose name they claimed to speak.

57. S 138/18, S/N Gwelo to CNC, 24 January 1923.

58. S 138/18, Secretary, Rhodesian Native Association, to CNC, May 1924.

59. S 138/18, President, RBVA, to Chancellor, 25 July 1924.

60. S 138/18, CNC to Secretary to Premier, 22 September 1924.

61. S 138/18, S/N Bulawayo to CNC, 10 September 1924.

62. Ranger, *African Voice*, 110.

63. Cripps, 'Native Rhodesia's Now or Never', 48. When Cripps submitted evidence to the 1925 Land Commission, he recalled that C. T. Loram, in the course of a lecture in Salisbury in 1922, had mentioned that the 1913 South African Natives Land Act 'was backed by friends and enemies of the natives. This support by both sides was dangerous'. ZAH 1/1/4, Evidence of A. S. Cripps to Land Commission, 23 September 1925, 1670.

64. A 3/15/11, Memo by Chaplin, 3 February 1915.

65. C.O. 417/671, Chaplin to Malcolm, 22 December 1920.

66. Hist. MSS. CH 8/2/2/11, Malcolm to Chaplin, 19 May 1921.

67. C.O. 417/526, Minute by Tait, 10 December 1913, Harcourt to Gladstone, 19 December 1913.

68. C.O. 417/578, Stanley to Buxton, 19 October 1916.

69. C.O. 417/638, Buxton to Milner, 29 June 1920.

70. C.O. 417/674, Minute by Lambert, 21 October 1921, Churchill to Connaught, 22 December 1921.

71. L 2/1/175, Memo by Taylor, CNC Matabeleland, 17 June 1904.

72. A 3/18/39/24, CNC to Secretary, Department of Administrator, 27 April 1922.

73. N 9/1/18, Report of the N/C Matobo for the year 1915.

74. *Report of the Chief Native Commissioner for the year 1918* (Salisbury 1919), 13; *Report of the Chief Native Commissioner for the year 1915* (Salisbury 1916), 2.

75. 9/1/26, Report of the N/C Belingwe for the year 1923.

76. N. H. Wilson, 'Native Political Movements in Southern Rhodesia', *NADA*, **1**, 1923, 19.

77. N 9/1/23, Report of the Acting S/N Gwelo for the year 1920.

78. An estimated 64 per cent of European men between the ages of 15 and 44 were away on military service, with the result that many farms were temporarily abandoned.

79. N 9/1/23, Report of the N/C Lomagundi for the year 1920.

80. The original designation of this post was the rather confusing one of 'Colonial Secretary'.

81. D.O. 9/3, Athlone to Amery, 15 October 1926. The following year, the N/C Umtali cited the case of a white farmer who had built a dipping tank for his tenants' cattle in 1918, charged 3/6d. per head per annum compared to 1/– in the reserves, and 'today he owns 200 head, all of which he got from the natives for fees, with the exception of 18 head'. F 35/26(5), N/C Umtali to CNC, 1 February 1927.

82. In 1914 the N/C Bulalima-Mangwe wrote that: 'The excessive fining of natives for trespass is a common practice in this District, and a source of considerable revenue to many of the white inhabitants ... It seems that natives are afraid of many people here, and are very chary of bringing cases against white people, however much their rights are infringed ... Much of the trouble arising from alleged trespass is due to the fact that landowners do not take any steps to demarcate their boundaries, so that neither natives, nor anyone else knows where they are. It is thus possible for unscrupulous persons to make a living out of the trespass laws, and instead of their being a protection, they become an instrument of extortion.' Such behaviour was clearly still prevalent in 1925, for the CNC noted that 'quite a number of cases have occurred in which Natives have been victimized by bogus land-owners'; the S/N Victoria asserted 'I am afraid it cannot be denied, that Europeans, of a certain type, endeavour to exploit their native neighbours and take advantage of their ignorance'; and the President of the Rhodesia Agricultural Union admitted that many white farmers made handsome profits from continuous impounding of African cattle and charging fines of £1 per head, citing one case of an impounding farmer who sold his farm at a 50 per cent profit, bought the farm next door, and continued impounding. N 3/7/2, N/C Bulalima-Mangwe to CNC, 14 January and 11 February 1914; S 653, CNC to Fuller, 9 November 1925; ZAH 2/1/1, S/N Victoria to CNC, 27 February 1925; ZAH 1/1/4, Evidence of H. G. M. Huntley to Land Commission, 2 June 1925, 1384–6.

83. N 9/1/21, Report of the N/C Insiza for the year 1918; N 9/4/37, Report of the N/C Insiza for the month September 1919. One white farmer from Umtali lost 70 head of cattle in a grass fire started by an African neighbour. ZAH 1/1/3, Evidence of D. Barry to Land Commission, 16 April 1925, 1005–13.

84. D.O. 63/3, Chancellor to Amery, 1 April 1927.

85. L. Vambe, *An Ill-Fated People* (London 1972), 219.

86. G. Arrighi, 'Labour Supplies in Historical Perspective: A Study of the Proletarianization of the African Peasantry in Rhodesia', *Journal of Development Studies*, **6**, 1970, 216. In Gwanda, where Africans owned some 30–40,000 head of cattle, this was 'their principal source of income, hence their chief means of paying rent and taxes, and for purchasing supplies'. L 2/2/122, N/C Gwanda to S/N Bulawayo, 22 July 1919.

87. *Report of the Chief Native Commissioner for the year 1920* (Salisbury 1921), 5.

88. Arrighi, 'Labour Supplies', 217.

89. Arrighi notes that: 'It was generally recognized that grain crops could not bear the cost of more than 15 miles of ox-wagon transport when railway costs were to be added.' Arrighi, 'Labour Supplies', 215.

90. ZAH 1/1/1, Evidence of A. C. Jennings to Land Commission, 2 March 1925, 12.

91. N 3/24/36, CNC to Secretary, Department of Administrator, 22 March 1923.

92. Some of the larger figures cited include: 1917 Nyamandhlovu 2,940; 1920 Charter 3,000, Mrewa 3,000, Darwin 2,000, Gwelo 2,000, Bulalima-Mangwe 1,200; 1921 Selukwe 4,000; 1922 Darwin 2,000; 1924 Bubi 2,400; 1925 Bulalima-Mangwe 2,560, Mazoe 1,000.

93. There were an estimated 42,100 living on the 5·7 million acres added to the reserves

by the Coryndon Commission. N 3/24/1/4, CNC to Secretary, Department of Administrator, 11 October 1917.

94. A 3/18/39/23, CNC to Secretary, Department of Administrator, 6 December 1918, Acting S/N Salisbury to CNC, October 1918, N/C Ndanga to S/N Victoria, 6 October 1918.

95. S 1561/33, S/N Victoria to CNC, 29 May 1924. Similarly in Nyasaland, the P/C Northern Province informed the Resident Chinteche: 'I approve of your demolishing the ... Huts of adult male defaulters who are physically fit ... Huts of women whose husbands are in Rhodesia and have not paid the hut tax ... When huts are destroyed in a village you or the Assistant Resident must be present at the village ... the simplest way of destroying a hut is to have it demolished with poles by your machillamen. If you burn and a wind gets up other huts are apt to catch fire.' National Archives of Malawi, S 1/312/21, P/C Northern Province to Resident Chinteche, 11 February 1926.

96. Southern Rhodesia, *Legislative Assembly Debates*, **1**, 16 June 1924, cols. 192–4.

97. At first village headmen were responsible for its collection, but by 1918 they were found to be 'fast losing control over the members of their Kraals as a result of civilization', and thereafter each individual was made responsible for paying his rent. A 3/15/16, CNC to Secretary, Department of Administrator, 5 January 1918.

98. N 3/16/6, CNC to Accountant, Commercial Branch, 9 August 1917.

99. Mlambo is wrong when he says that it was discontinued after the Privy Council decision. Mlambo, *Rhodesia*, 16.

100. S 138/12, N/C Inyanga to CNC, 17 April 1926.

101. S138/12, Clerk, Lands Department, to Atherstone, 1 July 1924, Secretary to Premier to Acting Secretary, Minister of Agriculture, 6 October 1925, Coghlan to Secretary to Premier, 31 March 1925, Minute by Moffat, 4 April 1925.

102. The amount collected dropped from £6,598 in 1915 to £2,305 in 1925.

103. N 9/1/26, Report of the N/C Makoni for the year 1923.

104. Wilson, 'Native Political Movements', 19.

105. C.O. 767/2, Chancellor to Thomas, 24 September 1924.

106. ZAH 1/1/4, Evidence of C. Bullock to Land Commission, 17 June 1925, 1407–13.

107. Ranger, *African Voice*, 70.

108. Ranger, *African Voice*, 72.

109. C.O. 417/617, The Petition of Nyamanda ... to the King, 10 March 1919.

110. Hist. MSS. CH 8/2/2/6, Chaplin to Gell, 8 April 1920.

111. C.O. 417/641, Madhloli etc., Farewell to the High Commissioner, 12 August 1920.

112. C.O. 417/641, Note of Proceedings at an Interview granted by ... the High Commissioner, 18 August 1920.

113. C.O. 417/663, Speech made by ... the High Commissioner .... in the Matopos, 12 August 1921.

114. Ranger, *African Voice*, 84.

115. C.O. 417/663, Address ... by Nyamanda etc., 13 August 1921.

116. C.O. 417/663, Chaplin to Douglas-Jones, 28 September and 11 October 1921.

117. N 9/1/25, Report of the N/C Umzingwane for the year 1922.

118. C.O. 767/2, Chancellor to Thomas, 24 September 1924.

119. C.O. 417/559, Minute by Lambert, 8 May 1915.

120. Hist. MSS. NE 1/1/2, Downie to Newton, 2 November 1925.

CHAPTER 7

The Land Commission 1925

Measures that appear wise and generous to-day may ... in future years become harsh and oppressive.

Governor of Southern Rhodesia, 1926.[1]

1 BACKGROUND

The Morris Carter Land Commission, the most renowned of all Rhodesian commissions of enquiry, was appointed in January 1925, completed its work by the end of that year, and reported in favour of a policy of separate land purchase areas for Africans and Europeans. It recommended that an estimated 6,851,876 acres of the unalienated land be assigned to Africans as Native Purchase Areas; that 17,423,815 acres be reserved for future purchase by Europeans; and that 17,793,300 acres, in remote and tsetse-ridden areas, be left unassigned.[2] The Report was then subjected to close scrutiny by the Rhodesian and British Governments and, after a protracted period of negotiation, the Land Apportionment Act, embodying the greater part of the Land Commission's recommendations, was passed in 1930 and brought into effect the following year.

Unlike the Native Reserves Commission, which had reported to the British High Commissioner for South Africa, the Land Commission was appointed by the Southern Rhodesian Government. It was not therefore an Imperial commission, though Imperial approval would be needed before any change in the existing law could be brought about. At this juncture the Rhodesian Government played its cards with consummate skill.

In August 1924, Coghlan, the first Rhodesian Premier, informed Governor Chancellor that he intended to appoint Taylor (as chairman) and Atherstone to the proposed commission; and he asked the Imperial Government to appoint the third member since he doubted, not without reason, whether a commission composed entirely of Rhodesians would be considered impartial.[3] A few weeks later he went even further, and proposed that the Imperial nominee should be the chairman,[4] anticipating that this would increase the chances of securing eventual Imperial approval of the Report. Davis, at the Colonial Office, showed that this judgement was not misplaced when he minuted that although the appointment of an Imperial chairman would not commit the Colonial Office to approval: 'We do not wish to have a Report presented to us which we have to reject and if we could find a good Chairman, there would be less likelihood of this happening.' An additional argument was that if the Imperial nominee was not chairman, Taylor would have to act in that capacity and he was the most important advocate of a change in the law. It was then agreed that neither government should be bound to accept the Commission's Report, and that the Colonial Office should give no instructions to the chairman, as this might involve committing themselves to a change in the law, whereas the Commission should be as impartial as possible. It was further agreed that the chairman should be someone quite unconnected with Southern Africa, and of all the names put forward by the various African departments of the Colonial Office, it was decided to appoint Sir William Morris Carter, formerly Chief Justice of Uganda and recently retired from the same post in Tanganyika, who had the advantage of being available.[5]

The choice of personnel made the Commission's acceptance of segregation virtually inevitable. H. J. Taylor, the Chief Native Commissioner, who was something of a lordly, inflexible patrician, had for years advocated a policy of assigning land adjoining the reserves for purchase by Africans, recognizing that European farmers were strongly averse to Africans buying in their midst. Despite some Imperial misgivings when he was appointed the first Chief Native Commissioner for the whole country in 1913,[6] Taylor had come to earn the respect of the British Government—he was given a knighthood in 1926—and his advocacy of segregation had influenced missionaries and Imperial officials alike. He was, however, a committed party, and this had been a major factor in persuading the Colonial Office to nominate Carter as chairman.

The choice of W. J. Atherstone, now Director of the Department of Lands, was even more surprising in view of the controversy which had arisen following his appointment as alternate member of the Native Reserves Commission of 1914–15. Not unnaturally, the choice drew protests from Harris and Cripps, the main critics of the Coryndon Commission, and from the Southern Rhodesia Missionary Conference.[7] Coghlan defended the appointment by saying that he had first consulted Taylor who had approved the choice,[8] but it was scarcely to be expected that Taylor would 'veto' a fellow departmental head. Chancellor took the rather strange view that although 'Atherstone has adopted an anti-native attitude in regard to the land question ... his presence on the Commission is not open to objection'.[9] Atherstone's sympathies lay naturally with the European farmers who had been demanding segregation for a decade and more, and on his own admission he felt entitled 'to fully weigh the interests of European settlement' on the Commission.[10] He also took delight in testing the knowledge of African witnesses to show that many of them underestimated the extent of an acre and hence overestimated their own requirements.

Though Morris Carter, the Imperial chairman, had no previous connections with Southern Africa, this made little difference for he had already earned a reputation, in both Uganda and Tanganyika, for favouring the development of European plantations and for exhibiting no reluctance to curtail African lands.[11] As a direct result of his efforts in Rhodesia, he subsequently headed the Kenya Land Commission of 1932–3, which barred Africans from acquiring land rights in the 'White Highlands'.[12] Carter proved to be a somewhat impatient and overbearing chairman who was often guilty of browbeating witnesses, especially those whose views conflicted with his own.

The 1924 Missionary Conference and John Harris of the APS both requested that a missionary representative be appointed to the Commission—Cripps optimistically proposed John White[13]—but this was smoothly turned down on the grounds that it 'would not in any way enhance the value of the Commission with the public in Rhodesia—rather the contrary', and that the missionary case could more usefully be put in supplying evidence to the Commission.[14] A similar argument had been adduced when the BSA Company had declined to appoint a Native Department official to the Native Reserves Commission.

The missionary initiative did at least have the effect of causing Coghlan to wonder whether it was worth while setting up the Commission, since its recommendations could hardly be acceptable both to his own electorate and to 'philanthropic bodies'. Chancellor refused to take such a gloomy view, however, and he pointed out that the dangerous example of South Africa was well understood in Rhodesia.[15] Hence he had approved a directive of January 1924, from Leggate, the Minister of Agriculture, to the effect that land adjoining the reserves which might be needed for African purchase areas should not be sold to Europeans, otherwise, Leggate argued

> We may find ourselves in the same position as in the Union where a policy of segregation has been decided upon but, owing to public antagonism no lands have been set aside which natives can purchase under individual tenure—a one-sided arrangement which caused native unrest and suspicion.[16]

The white Rhodesians thus realized, even at this early stage, the tactical advantages to be gained by presenting themselves in a rather more 'liberal' light than their kith and kin in South Africa.

As though to emphasize the inevitability of the Commission's findings, the original terms of reference proposed by the Rhodesian Government had assumed that an amendment to the existing law was necessary, and all that was required was for the Commission to demarcate separate areas.[17] The High Commissioner, Athlone, pointed out, however, that the Commission's first task should be to ascertain whether an amendment was in fact necessary.[18]

The Colonial Office believed that the Commission would be able to do little more than indicate certain general areas in which rights to land might be restricted, if it were found that segregation was desirable, since 'Experience in Union subsequent to passing of Native Land Act 1913 would seem to show that actual delimitation of native and non-native areas may be a matter which will require prolonged investigation if any degree of finality is desired'. Chancellor, when pressing the revised terms of reference on a reluctant Coghlan, also pointed out that the Commission could not possibly deal with the whole country since there were vast unsettled areas in the low-lying Zambezi and Limpopo valleys and in the tsetse fly zones.[19] The Land Commission, however, declined to play such a limited role. A few days after its first public session, it had a circular issued to Native Commissioners asking them to suggest suitable areas in their districts for purchase by Africans and Europeans and to regard the matter as 'extremely urgent'. In the following month they were asked 'to inspect personally, where feasible, the areas in question'—always a good idea—and to report on soil characteristics and consult with chiefs 'and any intelligent natives' with regard to the suitability of such areas from an African point of view.[20] Native Commissioners were thus given very little time indeed in which to consider their recommendations for African purchase areas.

On this occasion, despite the fact that European farmers were afforded every opportunity to make their views known to the Commission, there was no *éminence grise* working behind the scenes, as Frank Inskipp had done with the Native Reserves Commission. But there was no need, for by 1925 the Europeans had acquired some 31 million acres of land, about one-third of the entire country, and this left Native Commissioners to scrape the barrel in their search for African purchase areas. Moreover the Report itself would be submitted to the Rhodesian Government and its recommendations debated in the Rhodesian Parliament. Had the Commission proposed an attack upon European interests or recommended the expropriation of European land on a large scale, its Report would clearly have ended up as waste paper. Settler political power was thus a very real constraint which the Commission had to take into account.

2 POLICY

(i) The Report

The Land Commission was appointed on 8 January 1925. It took evidence between 2 March and 21 October and issued its Report on 10

November. It thus completed its work in one year compared to the two years taken by the Native Reserves Commission. It travelled 7,108 miles, 1,467 by rail and 5,641 by car, and it visited every district except for the fly-ridden Sebungwe in the north-west. Evidence was collected from 234 Europeans and some 1,753 Africans,[21] the later constituting 'the most important single source for the African voice, or for African voices, in Southern Rhodesia in the 1920s'.[22]

Not surprisingly, in the light of the segregation debate described in the previous chapter, the Commission came to the conclusion that 'an overwhelming majority of those who understand the question are in favour of the existing law being amended'. Moreover, it was claimed, this was no mere passing phase of local opinion since many eminent writers, such as Basil Mathews, Lord Lugard, J. H. Oldham, Professor Gregory and E. H. Brookes, had come to support segregation in the light of deteriorating race relations in the world and the possibility of future 'wars of extermination'. However desirable it was that the two races should live side by side, this was not practicable, and 'until the Native had advanced very much further on the paths of civilisation, it is better that the points of contact ... should be reduced'.[23] Racial prejudices could not be ignored and could be overcome more easily if the opportunities for friction were reduced to the minimum compatible with the co-operation necessary for developing the country's resources. It would be easier for progressive Africans to acquire land if separate purchase areas were assigned, since in the past they had been unable to purchase from government and had had to pay inflated prices to private owners. The Commission's enquiries had indeed made many Africans aware for the first time of their right to buy land, and if nothing were done there would be considerable dissatisfaction and discontent.

The Commission then examined the practicability of assigning separate areas. It found that over 43 million acres were still unalienated and while much of this was unsuitable, sufficient good land remained for a policy of separate areas to be practicable and in this respect Rhodesia was more fortunate than South Africa. But the problem would become more difficult each year and should therefore be tackled at once. The Legislative Assembly would need to show 'a determination to do justice' in providing a fair proportion of land for Africans since: 'It will be only natural that a fair and equitable apportionment of land in the Colony will seem to many Europeans a generous and perhaps over-generous provision for the Native.'[24] The widest diversity of opinion existed on the amount which should be assigned to Africans; some considered that the reserves alone were more than sufficient, others that they should be given 60 per cent of the available unalienated land. Most Europeans thought less than a quarter should be given, Native Commissioners favoured between a quarter and a half, while most Africans and missionaries believed the land should be divided equally. No one suggested large-scale expropriation of Europeans, though some advocated the provision of large compact African areas.

The Commission noted that advocates of the African cause were reluctant to surrender his potential right to own all the land in the country, and did not wish to do anything to benefit the current generation at the expense of posterity. It believed, however, that they overestimated the value of the existing right, for while Europeans had acquired some 31 million acres, Africans had only managed to buy 45,000 acres, and although many had been unaware of their right, the majority did not possess the means to acquire large areas. Their purchasing power would doubtless increase, but it would be many years before they could compete on equal terms with Europeans, who would in the meantime acquire all the best land if nothing was done. On the other hand, many Europeans were unaware of the African right to buy anywhere, and of the need, if this were withdrawn, to secure a real *quid pro quo.* They also did not appreciate the extent to which Africans were certain to buy land in the future, and they were afraid that the creation of large African purchase areas would prejudice future European settlement. But such fears were unfounded for vast unalienated areas were calling out for settlement, many white farms were of excessive size, and there were still large unoccupied blocks of land held by companies and syndicates.

Having ascertained that it was both expedient and practicable to assign separate areas, the Commission turned its attention to how this might best be effected. It decided first not to assign some 17,793,300 acres, mostly infested by tsetse fly, comprising nearly the whole of the Sebungwe, and parts of the Chibi, Darwin, Gwanda, Hartley, Lomagundi, Nyamandhlovu, and Wankie Districts. This Unassigned Area could be used later to minimize the effects of any miscalculations which the Commission might make.

The method of apportioning the remaining land was then considered. A division of the country into two was rejected as being impracticable because the reserves could not be tampered with, it would involve wholesale movements of Africans, would prevent their learning from Europeans, and would damage the labour supply. The creation of one or two large African areas was also rejected as it would involve heavy expropriation costs. Thus:

> The policy which we recommend is, on the one hand, to leave existing European interests as far as possible undisturbed, and to make available for acquisition by Europeans all possible land in what are predominantly white areas, while, on the other hand, providing suitable land for private acquisition by Natives in or near to the districts in which they are at present residing, in sufficient quantity to satisfy their present and their future needs ... these

Native areas should, wherever possible, adjoin the existing Native Reserves so as to form with them compact Native areas.[25]

Such a policy would provide a potential source of conveniently placed labour for the Europeans, and it would allow Africans close proximity to the roads used by neighbouring Europeans and the opportunity to study European methods of agriculture, and also to give an example to Africans in the reserves. It would moreover lead to the earlier introduction of native councils and would simplify African administration.

In every case except one, the Commission found it possible to attach the new areas, called Native Purchase Areas (NPAs), to the reserves, the result being to reduce the separate blocks of African land from 51 to 44. In central Matabeleland, Victoria, and Melsetter, however, it was not found possible to assign NPAs near to the large African populations living on European farms and provision could only be made for them in adjacent districts.

The Commission recommended a total of 6,851,876 acres of NPAs, which, with the reserves, would bring the total African area up to 28,933,362 acres; while on the other hand, some 17,423,815 acres were added to the European area which then totalled 48,605,898 acres.[26] It was estimated that the NPAs would have to provide for 250,000 Africans, so that a family unit of $3\frac{1}{2}$ would be allowed an average 106 acres and sufficient grazing for $5\frac{1}{2}$ head of large stock. Communal tenure should not be permitted in the NPAs, and the purchase price should be the same as that charged to Europeans. The minimum size of a holding should be 8–10 acres, and only in exceptional circumstances should Africans be allowed to own more than 1,000 acres in freehold. A Native Land Board should be set up to supervise the purchasing of the land and the general development of the Native Purchase Area. Africans already living in the NPA should be allowed to remain until the land was sold, alien Africans should not be allowed to buy land until they had worked in Rhodesia for at least five years, and townships should be established in the NPAs for the benefit of retired urban workers.

The Commission then made its most radical recommendations. It considered that 'the general aim should be to cause Natives as far as possible to move from European to the Native Purchase Areas or to the Reserves'.[27] 'Kaffir-farming' would thus be brought to an end. There was little difficulty in Mashonaland where the majority of the population lived in the African areas, and the rest could easily move there. Thus all Mashonaland rent agreements should cease within three years of the implementation of a separate areas policy. Melsetter was an exception, and the proposed Native Land Board should give the situation there further study. In central Matabeleland,[28] however, the bulk of the population lived on farms, and those paying rent should be allowed to remain for the rest of their lives, but no new rent agreements should be made. Elsewhere in Matabeleland, existing agreements should continue for six years as the situation was not quite as simple as in Mashonaland.

Labour agreements were of course a very different matter as they formed an important factor in the labour supply of the white farming community, and hence they should remain unaltered as should agreements which imposed no burden. Africans on unalienated European land should be encouraged to move, but should be allowed to stay on payment of rent until the land was sold, though no new permits to stay should be given.

In the towns, separate areas should be provided where African traders could open shops, and there should also be residential suburbs for the African professional men of the future. Africans should be allowed to build their own houses and there should be uniformity in municipal regulations. Locations were not sufficient, however; there should also be village settlements where families could cultivate small pieces of land and be free from the evil influences of town life.

(ii) The Report under Examination and Attack, 1926–31

(*a*) *Introduction*

It had taken five years for the Native Reserves Commission's proposals to be implemented, and a similar period elapsed before the bulk of the Land Commission's recommendations became law. The intervening period was again taken up with prolonged correspondence between Rhodesian and Imperial authorities, with various pressure groups such as the APS, the missionaries, and the African political associations attempting to influence the eventual outcome. The delay was particularly unfortunate, for whereas in 1928 'natives were anxious to buy and had plenty of money to give',[29] by 1931 when the Land Apportionment Act was finally implemented this was no longer the case for the Depression had 'hit the native hard'.[30] As with the segregation debate in the previous chapter, each of the various interest groups will be examined in turn.

(*b*) *The Rhodesian Authorities*

Before the Report of the Land Commission could become law it required the approval of both the Rhodesian and the British Government. Notwithstanding the comment by Ethel Tawse Jollie, widow of Colquhoun and the Empire's first lady parliamentarian, that 'it required considerable altruism on the part of a body of settlers and farmers to accept a holus-bolus partition of their country',[31] approval in Rhodesia was a comparative formality and Coghlan's Government had little trouble in persuading the country of the desirability of adopting the Report. A number of farmers' associations, it is true, complained about the creation of Native Purchase Areas in their particular district, but such complaints were brushed aside on the grounds that the Commission had considered the interests of the country as a whole, and that to approve one such amendment would lead to a flood of similar applications.[32] On the three occasions when the Report was debated in the Legislative Assembly, there was little serious opposition. Governor Chancellor, a strong advocate of the scheme, who greatly helped the Rhodesian Government by commending it to the African Society in London in 1926 and again in 1929,[33] agreed to speak to the leaders of the two opposition parties, Montagu and Johnson. He obtained from them an assurance that they would not treat the subject as a party issue and would do their best to secure its smooth passage.[34] The only real opposition came, after the 1928 election, from Davies of the Labour Party,[35] and Danziger, an errant member of the ruling Rhodesia Party, who both favoured a more rigorous form of segregation as the only means of preventing the white working class being submerged by the tide of advancing Africans. The Rhodesian Government therefore enjoyed a fairly smooth political ride, and the main causes of delay were beyond its control: the death of Coghlan in 1927, the intervention of a general election in 1928, the tardiness of Imperial deliberations, faulty Imperial legal advice on one occasion, and the election of a Labour Government in Britain in 1929.

It is important to recognize that the Rhodesian Government was in the enviable position of being able to employ two conflicting sets of arguments in support of the Commission's proposals. To its own *back veld* voters it argued that Europeans were gaining 'all white' zones and a very large extension to the European area; to the Imperial Government and the various critics it pointed out that Africans were getting some 7½ million acres[36] of land which they would not otherwise have been capable of acquiring, which was more than they would need for many years, and was far more generous than the allocation to blacks in South Africa. In addition, there were some 18 million acres left over to redress any possible miscalculations. The practice of saying one thing in Salisbury and something quite different in London was later developed to a fine art by Godfrey Huggins.

It should also be borne in mind that the Rhodesia Party of Coghlan (1923–7) and Moffat (1927–33) did not envisage the Land Apportionment Act as a first step towards a subsequent policy of complete segregation. This was something adopted by Huggins (1933–53) and his United Party in the wake of the Great Depression and the ensuing fear of African competition. Both Coghlan and Moffat genuinely believed that the limited segregation they were seeking was essentially 'liberal' in nature.

In 1926 Coghlan was immediately 'very favourably impressed' with the Land Commission's Report, but saw no point in opening discussions in Rhodesia until he could get some idea of the likely Imperial response.[37] In June 1926 he was in London with two of his ministers, discussing railway matters, when he took the opportunity to raise the subject with the Dominions Office, which had just taken over the handling of Rhodesia's affairs from the Colonial Office. Coghlan was clearly afraid of a negative Imperial response, but both the general tone of a short debate in the House of Lords and the discussions with the Dominions Office were encouraging. At a meeting in July, Amery, the Dominions Secretary, informed him that the broad lines of the Report were acceptable, but that detailed consideration would have to be reserved for a later stage.[38] It was agreed that Coghlan would introduce a resolution in the Legislative Assembly seeking general approval of the Report, following which he would submit a detailed scheme for Imperial scrutiny prior to introducing a Bill in the Assembly.[39]

Armed with this limited Imperial blessing and with Chancellor's assurance that the opposition leaders would keep the debate out of party politics and on a high plane,[40] Coghlan introduced his motion, calling for general approval of the Report (with the exception of the Neutral Areas) in May 1927.[41] Though inclined at times to be somewhat intolerant and petulant in debate, Coghlan on this occasion controlled himself and the debate went smoothly. He commended this 'very excellent report upon which we hope to be able to found ... a white future'. Rhodesia was

> essentially a country where the white man has come and desires to stay, and he can only be certain of doing that if he has certain portions of the country made his exclusively ... Only in this way can I see salvation for the future of the country. We must have social segregation at least.

He went on to stress that the indiscriminate African right to purchase land was an evil that needed to be remedied while there was still time, since it was 'an incubus which sooner or later may mean ruin to the country'.[42] Taylor had assured him that the NPAs would suffice for at least forty years[43] and therefore: 'I am satisfied that we are doing more than fair justice to the native. We are treating the native generously.'[44] The only serious opposition was voiced by Gilfillan, a man 'well known for holding archaic ideas in regard to the relations between the white and black races',[45] who voiced the fear of the white farmers of Melsetter that giving more land to Africans might affect the labour supply, as 'it is only the landless men who are the labourers'; as much as possible should be secured for the Europeans since 'this country was acquired to make room for the surplus population of the Empire'.[46] Protests were made concerning the proposed NPAs: in Hartley—too near the railway; Salisbury—only 20 miles from the town; and south Melsetter—the last land remaining for European settlement. But Coghlan refused to consider such amendments. His speech and the whole debate—as was the case with the 1929 and 1930 debates—were considered most satisfactory by the Dominions Office.[47]

Later in 1927, Amery visited Rhodesia and stressed the importance of implementing the Report without delay, though differences of opinion arose in connection with the Unassigned Area. However within a fortnight Coghlan was dead. He was succeeded, despite the misgivings of Chancellor,[48] by Howard Unwin Moffat, son of the missionary politician John Smith Moffat, and grandson of Robert Moffat, confidant of Mzilikazi. Moffat was 'a man of transparent honesty and high character' who took his obligations to Africans seriously.[49] He was even a member of the APS and had corresponded with the Society during the years preceding the granting of responsible government. It was not until February and March of 1928 that Moffat was able to forward a draft Order in Council (later replaced by a Bill) and the schedules of the various categories of land to London. He asked optimistically for an early reply in view of his forthcoming general election, but the reply eventually arrived the day before parliament opened and the matter was held over for a further year.

The Rhodesia Party duly won the election of September 1928, though the quality of Members of the Legislative Assembly apparently did not improve.[50] In February 1929 Moffat submitted his draft Land Apportionment Bill to London, which was generally approved, and the Bill was then formally debated in the Rhodesian Legislative Assembly in April, May, and June.[51] Again the debate went relatively easily for the Government. Moffat reiterated that the prime motive behind the policy had been 'to deal with the immediate evil ... of the native buying land in among the European farmers', and he asserted that a very fair provision had been made for Africans for a considerable time to come. The two opposing arguments (so useful to Moffat) were brought out in the debate: Huggins and Bertin claimed that it was the Europeans who were being asked to give up more since very few Africans as yet wanted individual tenure; O'Keeffe was afraid that Africans were getting richer and 'if we do not put him where he ought to be, he will be purchasing land all over the country'.[52] The only real opposition came from Danziger and Davies, who both advocated total segregation with Africans banished to Wankie or, better still, to Bechuanaland, in order to preserve white civilization. The Bill was opposed by the three Labour members and Danziger, out of a House of 30, and finally passed on 10 June 1929.

This however was just two days after the election of Ramsay MacDonald's Labour Government in Britain, and the Rhodesians were consequently obliged to enter a series of fresh negotiations. Moffat grew somewhat restive at the delay. In July he even contemplated resigning if the Bill was not approved, saying 'we must fight the matter out to the end ... otherwise we must hand over our Native Policy to the Imperial Government'. He recognized that the Labour Party could not ignore its left wing, 'but the Secretary of State has got to face the music, or else there is going to be trouble'. Eventually Newton, now Rhodesian High Commissioner in London, managed to convince Lord Passfield (formerly Sidney Webb), of the sincerity of Moffat's aims,[53] but a further blow fell in October when the Law Officers of the Crown reported, with a classical turn of phrase, that the Land Apportionment Bill was repugnant to Article 43, was void *ab initio* and could not be validated *ex post facto.*[54]

This necessitated an amendment to Article 43, carried out on 26 March 1930, followed by a re-submission of the Bill to the Rhodesian Parliament. The debate was naturally much speedier than in the previous year, though the Bill was still opposed by the same members as before.[55] Davies cited examples from South Africa and India to illustrate his belief that the white working class was in imminent danger of submersion beneath the black advance; Moffat asserted that, on the contrary, the Bill would prevent such conflict and indeed the need for repressive legislation. In this respect he was clearly mistaken. The Bill was duly passed on 12 May 1930 and approved by a British Order in Council of 28 July, and the Land Apportionment Act (No. 30) of 1930 was finally brought into effect on April Fool's Day, 1931.

(c) *The Imperial Authorities*

It was not a very difficult task for the Rhodesians to obtain Imperial approval of the Report. The Colonial Office had appointed Morris Carter as chairman in the expectation that this would make rejection less likely,[56] while in 1925 Rhodesia was placed under the newly-constituted Dominions Office[57] which also dealt with the older dominions and the Irish Free State. The new Office was regarded as little more than a post office by Colonial Office officials,[58] and though the details of the land apportionment scheme were subjected to very close scrutiny, they were none the less examined by men who were dealing with the problems of established white governments and who were thus inherently more favourably disposed towards the Rhodesian Government than the Colonial Office might have been. Also it would be erroneous to assume from recent Anglo-Rhodesian constitutional disputes that there was at this time any fundamental difference of approach or principle between the two governments. When Amery visited Rhodesia in 1927 he was favourably impressed with the country, its government and its administration of Africans,[59] and though at one point Moffat contemplated resigning if the Bill were not passed, neither side was anxious to cause embarrassment to the other. Thus when Moffat felt obliged to protest officially at suggestions that his Government might not enact the legislation in the spirit intended, he asked the

Governor to write privately and inform the Dominions Office that he regretted having to take this step. Similarly, the Dominions Office suggested in 1927 that the draft Rhodesian proposals be submitted privately in order that 'we can thus avoid any suggestion of differences of opinion' becoming public,[60] no doubt as a defensive mechanism against possible APS criticisms.

The initial Imperial response, from High Commissioner Athlone and from Parkinson at the Dominions Office, was that the Commission had made out an adequate case for amending the law. This view was never subsequently challenged, and attention thereafter tended to concentrate on details rather than on principles. Athlone, for example, noted that no NPAs had been assigned near the main centres, which were precisely where Africans would be able to farm most successfully. He felt the price of land should be reduced for African purchasers, and he believed the proposed abolition of rent agreements impracticable, 'unwise and unnecessary'.[61] Notwithstanding such criticisms, the general tenor was clearly favourable as witnessed in the 1926 House of Lords debate,[62] when Lord Olivier, a prominent figure on the left of the Labour Party and author of *The Anatomy of African Misery*, described the Report as 'the most broadminded and liberal document that I have seen emanate from any official source with regard to Southern Rhodesia on the land question';[63] a view which was endorsed by Lord Buxton, the former High Commissioner to South Africa.

The definitive minute on the whole question was written in July 1926 by Sir Charles Davis, the first permanent under-secretary at the Dominions Office and an old college friend of Amery's. Davis wrote:

> No one can argue as an abstract proposition that the proposed distribution ... is inherently just and reasonable. But the Report having been published must be regarded generally as representing the maximum which public opinion in Southern Rhodesia would be prepared to concede to the natives, and the question is whether the natives will be better served by the proposed distribution than by maintaining the status quo.

It was not, in all honesty, an easy question to answer in 1926; but Davis believed that time would run against Africans as it had done in South Africa, and that on an open market they would not be able to acquire anything like the 7 million acres now allotted to them. 'There seems, therefore, no alternative before His Majesty's Government but to express general approval of the Report', though there was a mass of detail to which they could not be committed in advance.[64]

The principal points of detail which preoccupied Imperial officials (who were aware that 'we are legislating for what may well be the indefinite future, and therefore need ... to take all the more care', [65]) were that the terms of purchase should be made as easy as possible so that Africans would effectively be able to buy land; that when Africans were moved off European land everything possible should be done to mitigate hardship; and that at least half of the Unassigned Area should be guaranteed to Africans, since, as Amery put it, 'the pro-native section and even a number of responsible people' were afraid that unless this was done, they would end up getting none of the land.[66] The Dominions Office in fact made very little headway with these proposals. Moffat insisted, apparently as a matter of principle, that Africans should pay exactly the same as Europeans and pointed out that both could buy from the Government more cheaply than from private owners. Assurances were given, which were not subsequently kept, that Africans living in the NPA would not be asked to move until the land was sold, that those who were moved off European land could be resettled in unalienated parts of the NPA; and that 'the Government have no idea of moving any Natives from Crown Land'. Finally, no mathematical division of the Unassigned Area was guaranteed, but alienations there were not to take place without the consent of the High Commissioner who would be able to appoint a commission or call for reports from the Native Land Board on the question.[67]

Not even the arrival of the Labour Government with Lord Passfield as Dominions Secretary and its warning to the Rhodesians that this meant 'not merely a change of persons but a change of principles',[68] could upset what by now was virtually an agreed measure. One of the permanent officials, Tait, immediately prepared a detailed minute for the benefit of the new incumbents, informing them that the scheme 'has been generally regarded as making generous provision for the Natives, and there seems little doubt that it should be brought into effect'. He warned that their powers were purely negative, and that they could enforce no alternative other than that of leaving matters as they stood.[69] This was indeed, and has remained, the crux of the 'Rhodesian problem'; the British could only veto, they could not initiate. Though Ponsonby, the new parliamentary under-secretary, was at first 'very wary of the Permanent Official standing ready with a piece of blotting paper to blot the signature of approval',[70] he soon became convinced of the soundness of Tait's advice. After interviews with Taylor (now living in retirement in Britain) and Newton, and a close examination of the map, he had come to believe that the Bill had been framed with careful regard for African interests; that its rejection would be welcomed by some Europeans who considered that it went too far; that Africans would stand a better chance of buying land than under the existing system, and that while segregation was objectionable in principle, in practice it worked in the long term to the benefit of Africans in a country such as Rhodesia, where Europeans were settled in considerable numbers.[71]

Thus the Act which finally emerged in 1930 was very much an agreed measure, though as Moffat correctly predicted: 'The carrying out honestly and fairly of ... such legislation must depend ultimately on the *bona fides* ... of the Government of the Colony.'[72]

(*d*) *The APS and the Missionaries*

The campaign launched by the APS and the missionaries against the findings of the Land Commission was less sustained and effective than their earlier struggle against the Report of the Native Reserves Commission. A major reason for this of course was that they had already accepted Taylor's idea of separate purchase areas in principle, and had warmly welcomed the appointment of the Land Commission.[73] Thus, as Olivier pointed out to Harris in 1929: 'We are heavily handicapped by the general advocacy of segregation by most of our friends in Southern Rhodesia.'[74] Both Cripps[75] and White believed, not without a certain anguish of mind,[76] that in Rhodesian conditions, segregation, coupled with a liberal allocation of land, was the best that they could hope to achieve. But neither they, nor indeed the APS, believed that the Land Commission's recommendations had been particularly liberal; indeed, the APS called the proposed division 'a monstrously disproportionate proposition'.[77] All of them resolved to challenge its findings, although, as in the case of the Imperial authorities, criticisms were confined to particulars rather than principles.

The land apportionment scheme, rather like the Anglo-Rhodesian settlement proposals of 1971, was a complex package deal which placed white spokesmen for African interests, such as White and Cripps, in an acute dilemma. Was it better to continue with the existing system under which Africans had been able to buy so little land but would no doubt buy more in future, or should they accept segregation and the 7 million acres of NPAs? It was a question which was no easier for the missionaries to answer than it had been for the Imperial Government. Eventually they came to accept the Land Apportionment Act. And here one must take issue with Ranger, for just as he has exaggerated the influence which White and the APS had upon the setting up of the Land Commission, so too he has exaggerated the extent of their opposition to its proposals and he does not mention their ultimate acquiescence.

It is true that there was a good deal of missionary criticism on points of detail, and much of this was voiced at the 1926 and 1928 Missionary Conferences which Cripps and White, who chaired them, were attempting with some success to turn into a political forum in which they could speak out on behalf of 'this large dumb proletariat'.[78] In 1926 they both felt that the Report as it stood was unsatisfactory and they urged the Conference to negotiate for amendments. Instead, the Conference, fearing attacks on the Report from the white farmers, expressed its 'very hearty appreciation' of the Commission's work and approved the Report, subject to half the Unassigned Area being granted to Africans and the other half to Europeans. Two years later, the Conference congratulated the Legislative Assembly for passing its 1927 resolution and rejoiced that a Bill was on its way. It also recommended that native village settlements be definitely assigned in the Bill, rather than be left to the doubtful goodwill of the municipalities.[79] Individual missionaries raised points which concerned them: Cripps argued that communal tenure should be permitted in the NPAs,[80] which ought to be larger and in more compact blocks;[81] White noted that the NPAs adjoined the reserves and would therefore be in the same granite areas, while the European area was being extended where the soil was known to be considerably richer, a view shared by Hardaker;[82] Cotton was concerned, with good reason, about the future of Africans living in the European area.[83]

The main energies of the missionaries were, however, expended in a desperate attempt to ensure that at least half of the 17·8 million acres of the Unassigned Area be guaranteed to Africans, even if this meant guaranteeing the other half to Europeans. They doubted, with some justification, whether the Rhodesian Government would assign the land fairly.[84] Opposition on this point persisted right down to 1930[85] when White, though regretting that they had been unable to obtain the assurance they had sought, admitted that: 'To have the assurance that the matter of the future assignment of the land does not rest with the local legislature, but with the High Commissioner, is a great thing accomplished.' The APS too regarded this outcome as 'not, on the whole, unsatisfactory', and Harris and White were both agreed that 'if the Bill was lost altogether, it would be of disservice to the native people'.[86] In the event the missionary fears proved groundless, for virtually the whole of the useless Unassigned Area was eventually given to Africans, thus helping to make the land apportionment map a little more respectable.

If the Rhodesian protagonists concentrated their attention on the Missionary Conference, the APS and its allies in Britain were most vocal in the period immediately following the election of the Labour Government in 1929. Passfield and Ponsonby were quickly put under pressure: firstly, in the Commons, where the Bill was said (quite erroneously) to embody 'an entirely new principle in Empire legislation, in differentiating between whites and blacks';[87] and secondly, in the columns of *The Manchester Guardian* where, in a spate of adverse comment, the Bill was described as a 'Slave-State policy' which would produce 'a landless, homeless, legally controlled proletariat of workers'—an editorial called upon Passfield to veto this 'specious Land Law'.[88] Passfield and Ponsonby were eventually won over by the arguments of Newton and the permanent officials at the Dominions Office. Leggate, the minister responsible for internal affairs, was sent to London in November 1929 to convert the unofficial opponents of the Bill. Making skilful use of the arguments that the African right to purchase land anywhere had in the past proved 'a paper right ... a barren right' and that they were now being offered 7 million acres but might eventually require more than half of the Unassigned Area, Leggate eventually convinced Harris, the two Buxtons of the APS,[89] and the formidable C. P. Scott, Editor of *The Manchester Guardian.* He completed a successful visit by informing the Empire Parliamentary Association that the Bill was the finest piece of legislation passed in the interests of Africans since the settlers had taken over the Government in 1923. He subsequently informed the APS, in words that do not quite bear the ring of truth: 'Had you been successful in your opposition ... you would certainly have earned the lasting ill-will of the natives of this country.'[90]

(*e*) *The African Associations*

In Rhodesia (as in most other parts of East and Central Africa) a number of African associations sprang up in the 1920s as a small, educated, Christian elite emerged to challenge some of the cruder assumptions of their colonial rulers. These associations are discussed more fully in the next chapter; their leaders, however, were prominent among the African witnesses who appeared before the Land Commission. They tended to share the missionaries' general endorsement of the principle of territorial segregation and were also generally hostile to the proposed division, feeling that the land should have been divided into equal areas for Africans and Europeans. Like the APS and the missionaries they were unable to mount a serious campaign of opposition, although there were attempts to unite the various associations, as happened in Nyasaland and Tanganyika, thereby strengthening their bargaining powers.[91] The attempts were not successful, however, and in the absence of any strong unity it was not difficult for the administration to play off one association against another—Shona against Ndebele, emergent capitalist against peasant, and young against old. As the S/N Bulawayo put it: 'It seems to me that the more of these Societies there are the better, for their jealousy of each other and lack of unanimity is a source of weakness to all of them.'[92]

One of these pressure groups was the Native Welfare Association which was based in Gwelo with an entirely Christian leadership. The Association managed briefly, by utilizing the land issue, to bring together the local, urban-based, educated elite and the Shona chiefs from surrounding rural areas. At a meeting in 1926, it stated its belief that the evidence given by Africans to the Commission had favoured an equal distribution of land, and hence it 'could not agree with the Report' and asked for a new commission.[93] The following year it asserted, with much justice and a first-hand knowledge denied to the Imperial authorities, that the NPAs were 'quite dry and very infertile and ... far too small'. It also raised the matter of 'the unsatisfactory position with regard to native squatters',[94] a matter which its general secretary, A. M. Zigode (the child of a Shona–Mfengu marriage), again brought to the Government's attention in 1930, pointing out that when squatters were moved off farms there was nowhere for them to go. Zigode requested and was sent a copy of the Land Apportionment Act.[95] CNC Taylor, himself a member of the Land Commission, conceded that the resolutions passed were 'illustrative of the difficulties which attend consideration of the Lands Commission Report in so far as Matabeleland is affected'. The local official at Gwelo took a rather more orthodox line however, and banned some of the Association's leaders from holding further meetings.[96]

The Mfengu-led Rhodesian Bantu Voters' Association (RBVA), meeting in Bulawayo in 1926, also argued in favour of an equal division of land[97] as advocated by Africans and missionaries to the Commission.[98] At a meeting in 1929 it was decided unanimously to oppose the Bill since it 'does not show any security for the native land' and was contrary to the African evidence that the land should be divided equally. Masoja Ndhlovu, a leading member of the militant Industrial and Commercial Workers' Union (ICU), was present at this meeting and aired his views forcefully: 'Let us tell the Government that this Bill is wrong. Our people have been driven to lands where they cannot live, our cattle die for the want of water ... Let us tell the Government that the Bill is no good, it is all for the white man.' Arguing in much the same vein as Danziger in the Legislative Assembly, Ndhlovu continued: 'Rhodesia is big, let them cut the land in half and let us live on the one side and the white man on the other, if they cannot do this they should at least give us a place for Reserves where there is water.'[99] The following year, at a meeting of the ICU, Ndhlovu must have alarmed the C.I.D. spies present when he proclaimed: 'Let us get into a hell of a row over this Land Apportionment Bill, we don't know where the land is, it may be in the Kalahari Desert ... I am going to fight for our freedom—the whiteman must give us land. We are the original people of Africa.'[100]

There were, however, other, and much quieter, African voices to be heard in the 1920s. The predominantly Shona and Government-approved[101] Native Welfare Association urged the administration in 1929 to pass the Bill 'regardless to the many petitions and criticisms already made by Farmers Assocations' about certain of the NPAs. Such petitioners, the Association claimed, 'should humbly limit themselves in speech and writing... strictly to what they know and avoid dangerous generalizations until they have mastered their facts and figures, for the natives are quite sensitive on questions of injustice'.[102] A similar voice was heard in 1927, when a group of 'advanced natives'—landowners, traders and artisans—told Amery that the Commission deserved 'great praise beyond measure', adding that: 'The Land Purchase Areas set for us has imbued every Native heart with great Ambition and Expectation. We are all eagerly awaiting the day when we shall be called upon to take up land.'[103]

This diversity of opinion is a clear indication of the degree of social differentiation which had taken place by the 1920s, and which was equally apparent in the African evidence submitted to the Land Commission. The main concern of the vast majority of peasant farmers in the reserves was the need for more land, and when they learnt that an extension of the reserves did not lie within the Commission's terms of reference they were obviously bitterly disappointed. But there was a very small class of incipient capitalists (some local and some South African), which had managed to make money and was able to buy farms, to whom the questions pondered by the Commission were of immediate relevance and many of this class were quite prepared to accept segregation as a precondition for the provision of Native Purchase Areas. There was also something of a generation-gap, especially in north-eastern Mashonaland, where the African evidence clearly revealed that while many young people aspired to own their own farms and become large-scale commercial farmers, this was something quite beyond the expectations of the older generation.[104]

3 ACTUALITY: AN APPRAISAL

In the event, the Land Apportionment Act has turned out to be the most contentious piece of legislation ever passed by a Rhodesian Government. Since 1950 it has occupied a prominent place in political debate, and indeed the promise to repeal it was largely responsible for the fall of the United Federal Party Government at the 1962 election. Since UDI, it and its successor, the 1969 Land Tenure Act, has been a major bone of contention in the various Anglo-Rhodesian negotiations over the independence issue. For the whites in Rhodesia the Act has become something of a *Magna Carta*, guaranteeing the preservation of their way of life against encroachment from the black hordes, whereas for Africans the Act is seen as blatantly discriminatory and palpably unjust. On both sides the issue has become emotionally charged, defying all attempts at rational analysis.

Once the Land Apportionment Act finally found its way onto the statute book in 1930, there was surprisingly little subsequent discussion of its merits. There was a brief controversy between W. M. Macmillan, then of Witwatersrand University, and R. D. Gilchrist, a Rhodesian member of parliament who was soon to become a cabinet minister, about the feasibility of moving so many Africans from the European areas;[105] and another between Lucy Mair and Ethel Tawse Jollie on whether the Land Commission had acted principally in the interests of Europeans.[106] The first really critical studies were not written until the early 1940s. Sir Keith Hancock argued that 'it may be doubted whether the Commission made an excessive demand upon the sense of justice of the European community', as the whites, already well endowed, got more land, while the NPAs were 'scattered in such a manner as to keep European employers in close touch with supplies of labour'.[107] Roy McGregor, in a valuable thesis, commented critically on the decision to leave vested interests untouched, the nature of the NPAs, the proposed movements of population, and the overall feasibility of segregation.[108] Criticism naturally mounted after the Second World War when segregation was no longer fashionable, and in time was voiced even by four Rhodesian commissions of enquiry.[109] To what extent is this criticism valid?

The Land Commission's *modus operandi* was certainly not as suspect as that of the Native Reserves Commission. But it was confronted with the reality of the vested interests that had grown up in the 35 years since the European occupation, and it sat moreover in the midst of a tobacco boom when there was a strong settler demand for land near the line of rail. Obviously influenced by this boom, the commissioners followed Chancellor's suggestion of assigning to Europeans 'the settled areas on the high plateaux and to Natives certain areas adjacent to their reserves',[110] and they appear to have accepted Coghlan's view that Africans did not want or need land near the railway line,[111] for they wrote to the General Manager of Rhodesia Railways enquiring into projected future extensions as these would have 'an important bearing on the question of European and Native land areas'.[112] Such an assumption belied the earlier positive African response to the market, and indeed one of the professed aims of the Native Purchase Areas, namely the encouragement and growth of a prosperous and contented class of African commercial farmers. The assumption does however fit neatly into the series of attacks launched upon the competitiveness of African agriculture ever since 1908.

The commissioners may also be criticized for not examining the NPAs they selected with sufficient care, an oversight which was to give rise to serious problems in later years. Whereas the Native Reserves Commission had spent two years at work and had travelled one third of its mileage on horseback or by mule wagon in areas were roads were bad or non-existent, the Land Commission completed its work within a year and did no such rough travelling. Moreover, the Native Commissioners, who were asked to recommend possible NPAs, were given very little time in which to make a considered judgement.

It has already been shown that the personnel of the Commission was clearly predisposed towards segregation, and this emerges very strongly from the manner in which evidence was collected. In general, all witnesses who were in favour of segregation were given a polite hearing and asked to propound their views, while those who opposed this policy were immediately confronted with hostile questions which frequently caused them to change their minds.[113] This was particularly true of African witnesses, for the majority of whom the inadequacy of the reserves was of far more consequence than the merits or otherwise of separate areas. If all other arguments failed, the Commissioners made great play with the notion that if the existing law remained, Europeans would buy up all the remaining land. This may have appeared likely in 1925 before the tobacco slump and the Great Depression but one can, with the wisdom of hindsight, question its validity; moreover it ignored the fact that many Europeans, Coghlan and Moffat included, were convinced (and somewhat alarmed) that before long Africans would indeed begin to exercise their right much more effectively than hitherto.

In view of the Commission's bias, it is not surprising that such an overwhelming majority of witnesses went on record as favouring the principle of segregation, a principle which the Rhodesia Agricultural Union considered 'so widely acknowledged that it has come to be regarded as almost axiomatic'.[114] Indeed many Europeans and Africans were surprised to learn of the existence of Article 43.[115] 'By what right does the native demand to buy land?' asked one Salisbury farmer,[116] while after a month of taking evidence the Commission felt obliged to ask Native Commissioners to inform Africans of their right to buy anywhere, so that they could contemplate the matter before giving evidence[117]—and before it was taken away from them.

Of the 234 Europeans who gave evidence, only 10 admitted being opposed to the principle of segregation.[118] Of the 110 white farmers and landowners interviewed,[119] only two, a Canadian and a former Native Commissioner, were genuinely opposed to the idea.[120] In no case did a farming association recommend land for a Native Purchase Area in its district, one farmer even suggesting that the NPAs be situated in Northern Rhodesia,[121] while the Rhodesia Agricultural Union considered that the very maximum which should be assigned was one million acres provided that none of it was required for European settlement. As one Marandellas farmer admitted: 'It is difficult for a farmer to take any unbiased view as to what is best for himself from the farmers point of view or best for the natives ... or the country in general.'[122]

The African evidence to the Commission has been analysed in some depth by Richard Gray and Terence Ranger.[123] What neither mentions, however, is that only 7 of the 1,753 African witnesses came out firmly against the principle of segregation.[124] This does not of course imply that the majority of Africans positively welcomed the notion; for the majority in fact the question was at best academic and they expressed no opinion; others were browbeaten into acceptance by pressure from the Commission; while others gave the idea at best only half-hearted support. For all, it would be fair to say, the amount of land to be given was of far greater significance than the pros and cons of segregation.

Grievances over land were frequently expressed to the Commission. Many witnesses complained at having constantly been moved off European farms, and some who had managed to buy land explained that they had done so simply as a defence against further evictions. The evidence also reveals that land purchase was well beyond the means of the great majority of the people, who were far more concerned with conditions in the reserves. There were numerous requests for an enlargement of the reserves,[125] but the Commission replied that this did not fall within its terms of reference. The missionary Cripps promptly protested that the Commissioners should not therefore be allowed to take evidence, as they had been doing, on the possibility of introducing individual tenure in the reserves. Chancellor, after a brief wrangle with Carter and Coghlan, upheld Cripps' protest as he had no desire to 'raise controversial questions which it was desirable to avoid'.[126]

Appendix I (see pp. 251–78) contains a district by district analysis of the proposals of Native Commissioners to the Land Commission; the recommendations of the Commission; the subsequent amendments made by Taylor and Atherstone in 1926–9 when it was decided to abandon the proposed one million acres of Neutral Areas and replace them with an additional half million acres of NPAs; and the eventual, though by no means final, assignments made in the Land Apportionment Act of 1930.

This analysis clearly vindicates the view expressed in 1935 by A. C. Jennings, a member of the Native Land Board set up under the Act to administer the NPA, that 'the availability of Crown Land became almost the determining factor in delimiting the Native [Purchase] Area'.[127] By 1925 the Europeans had acquired 31 million acres of land, the native reserves totalled $21\frac{1}{2}$ million acres, and a further 18 million acres were quite unsuitable for assigning to anyone because of the tsetse fly and other problems. Native Commissioners were therefore obliged to make their choice from the remaining 25 million acres which had not hitherto been acquired by the land-hungry Europeans. They were thus forced once again to scrape the barrel, as they had done when selecting the original reserves at the turn of the century. Thirteen of the thirty-two Native Commissioners specifically mentioned that they found it difficult or impossible to select suitable purchase areas, as so much of the best land had been alienated in the past.[128] Others undoubtedly faced the same problem but thought it too obvious to deserve mention. A typical response came from the N/C Nyamandhlovu, who 'had to take into consideration the fact that the best part of the land has already been taken up by Europeans';[129] while Taylor and Atherstone, in their selection of the additional half million acres of NPAs in 1926–9, made 'every endeavour ... to confine the selection of these

TABLE IX

Recommendations of the Land Commission, 1925
(i) Mashonaland

District	*Native Reserves (acres)*	*Native Purchase Areas*	*Unassigned Area*	*European Area*	*European Area as Percentage of District*
Bikita	662,000	99,900	nil	1,049,940	58
Charter	1,878,340	42,183	nil	1,264,117	40
Chibi	1,409,300	108,175	1,783,000	3,328,005	50
Chilimanzi	301,500	80,951	nil	782,349	67
Darwin	1,219,700	1,024,600	51,000	782,460	25
Gutu	834,000	234,581	nil	642,779	38
Hartley	402,500	97,421	340,000	3,149,839	79
Inyanga	446,290	171,545	nil	1,035,925	63
Lomagundi	901,000	237,838	4,216,000	5,054,762	49
Makoni	600,500	196,795	nil	1,424,785	64
Marandellas	428,500	109,562	nil	1,023,538	65
Mazoe	244,000	4,115	nil	1,487,565	86
Melsetter	436,200	582,840	nil	927,200	48
Mrewa	1,122,000	40,300	nil	469,700	29
Mtoko	696,800	316,500	nil	815,180	45
Ndanga	864,000	nil	nil	993,280	53
Salisbury	454,506	6,773	nil	1,035,041	69
Umtali	558,300	155,423	nil	871,557	55
Victoria	356,000	148,177	nil	1,349,903	73
Totals for Mashona-land	13,815,456	3,657,679	6,390,000	27,487,925	54

areas to Crown Lands but owing to such land not being available in sufficient quantities, it was found impossible to do so'.[130] It is also interesting to note that, as in the case of the Coryndon Commission, the Carter Commission's original assignment of land to Africans was one million acres short of its final proposal; in 1915 the 'reserve' reserves had been added at the instigation of Resident Commissioner Stanley, while in 1925 it was Morris Carter himself who had the perspicacity to see that a mere $5\frac{1}{2}$ million acres of Native Purchase Areas would not be politically acceptable to the Imperial authorities.[131]

Of the 7,464,566 acres of Native Purchase Areas assigned in the Land Apportionment Act, some 4 million acres comprised five large, remote,

TABLE IX (*contd.*)

Recommendations of the Land Commission, 1925
(ii) Matabeleland

District	*Native Reserves (acres)*	*Native Purchase Area*	*Unassigned Area*	*European Area*	*European Area as Percentage of District*
Belingwe	1,088,700	168,300	nil	867,800	41
Bubi	1,511,569	1,201,950	nil	1,861,841	41
Bulalima-Mangwe	1,344,000	581,408	nil	2,162,272	53
Bulawayo	nil	nil	nil	344,960	100
Gwanda	231,500	1,318,281	278,600	4,250,979	70
Gwelo	184,300	330,554	nil	3,452,506	87
Insiza	67,600	212,560	nil	1,522,720	84
Matobo	179,000	7,259	nil	940,141	83
Nyamandhlovu	1,126,000	26,900	270,000	1,391,180	49
Sebungwe	1,446,687	nil	6,568,700	250,213	3
Selukwe	150,000	48,215	nil	731,065	79
Umzingwane	4,765	nil	nil	637,795	99
Wankie	445,400	nil	4,286,000	3,383,800	42
Totals for Matabeleland	7,779,521	3,895,427	11,403,300	21,797,272	49
Totals for Southern Rhodesia	21,594,957	7,553,106	17,793,300	49,285,197	51

low-lying, and in some cases tsetse-infested areas in Darwin, Melsetter, Bubi, Bulalima-Mangwe, and Gwanda, and indeed over half of the NPA lay along the borders of the country (see table IX and map 4). This land, writes John Ford, 'was, for the most part, carefully sited within the *Grenzwildnis* [no-man's lands] and therefore was virtually useless'.[132] A glance at map 4 reveals the paucity of the provision in central Matabeleland in particular and within reasonable access of markets generally. It is therefore not altogether surprising that as early as 1928 the S/N Bulawayo reported that 'very little of the land allocated for Native Purchase on the North side of the Railway Line in Matabeleland is of any use for the purpose' as the vast bulk was either waterless

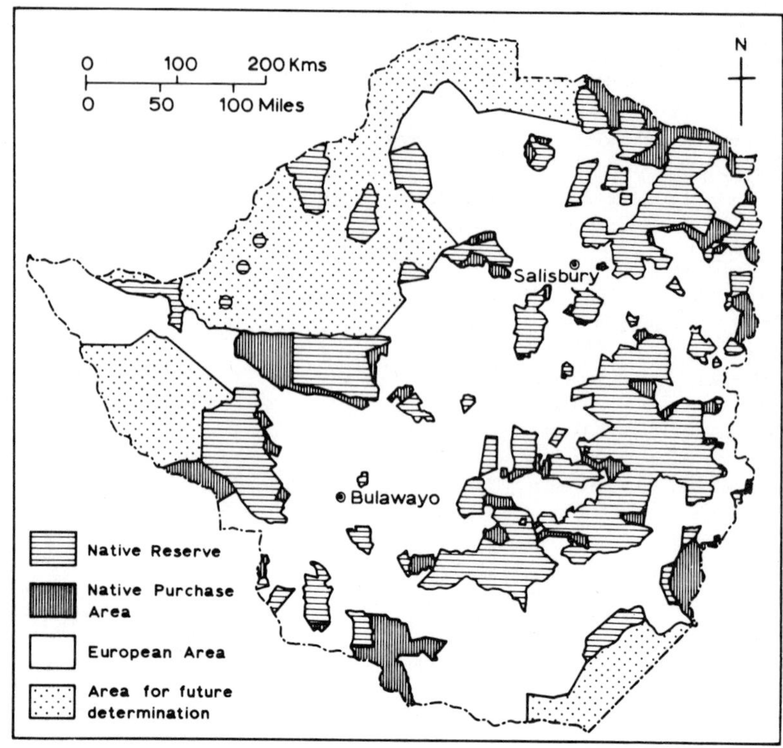

Map 4—Land Apportionment, 1930 (*from Christopher 1971*).

or in the teak forest belt, and that 'every native to whom they have been offered has declined to live on them'.[133] This of course confirms the views expressed by some of the African associations; and even the Native Land Board which administered the NPAs, confessed that in many of them 'there is an entire absence of natural streams and surface supplies of water'.[134] Very soon Moffat and Huggins, who were chiefly responsible for implementing the Act during the 1930s, found good reason to criticize the Commission. In 1932 Moffat was surprised at the meagreness of the provision in Matabeleland, and he admitted that at the time the Act was passed he was 'under the impression ... that there would be no further adjustments of land required; but that is not the case'.[135] Four years later, Huggins condemned the Commission for following the mistakes of the Coryndon Commission 'in not paying sufficient attention to the quality of land and the availability of water'.[136] One could argue however, that had it done so, its recommendations would inevitably have involved the extensive expropriation of land which would have been politically unacceptable to the white electorate. Finally, by 1943 the Rhodesian Government had come to admit, at least privately, that some 4,727,000 acres of the NPAs were 'generally unsuitable for division into small holdings'.[137] This was clearly not the kind of *quid pro quo* which African and missionary witnesses had in mind when they agreed to the abandonment of Article 43.

'A great deal of nonsense is talked about the necessity of preserving land for European occupation,' wrote Ethel Tawse Jollie in 1924, 'for there are many regions where white settlement will never take place, and there is plenty of land for both black and white if it is properly utilized. At present many white farmers would be better off with less land and more improvements.'[138] There was much truth in this contention, as a post-Depression committee acknowledged when it said that one of the major problems of the agricultural industry was that most white land holdings were 'heavily mortgaged and greatly in excess of what the farmer can productively use'.[139] This being the case, in marked contrast to the desperate shortage of African land in many areas, it was surely inappropriate for the Land Commission to extend the European Area from 31 to 48 million acres. Far too much European land, some 7½ million acres in 1926 (over 6 million of it within 35 miles of the railway) lay unoccupied and wholly undeveloped. Even Atherstone observed:

> It can scarcely be considered good policy to place settlers into more and more remote and unfavourable situations while there are extensive areas of suitable land conveniently situated in respect of the principal centres and railways already alienated but undeveloped and unoccupied by Europeans.[140]

White Rhodesians had in fact obtained all the land they were ever likely to need by 1925, since although European agriculture expanded dramatically in the next forty years[141] the actual area of European land

TABLE X

Land Apportionment, 1900–70 (millions of acres)

	1900	*1913*	*1925*	*1930*	*1960*	*1968*	*1970*
Native Reserves	24·9	24·9	21·6	21·6	21·0	40·1	39·9
Native Purchase Area				7·5	8·1	4·3	3·7
Special Native Area					12·9		
European Land (alienated)	15·8	22·4	31·2				
European Area (alienated and unalienated)				49·1	48·1	35·7	44·9

rose from 31·2 million acres in 1925 to only 35·7 million acres by 1968, before being increased again for purely political reasons (see table X). Almost all development, with the exception of the Sabi-Limpopo *low veld*, has taken place in areas which were already part of the European Area in 1925. One cannot therefore accept Lewis Gann's claim that Europeans would 'certainly have done better to leave land apportionment to the impersonal operation of the market which would have worked entirely in their favour'.[142] Certainly R. A. Fletcher, Rhodesia's Minister of Agriculture and Lands in 1929, would not have agreed. He acknowledged that:

> suitable Crown Land is very limited, being for the greater part either the 'tags and ends' left out in the early 'pegging' of the country, or geographically and climatically practically impossible at the present stage of the country's development ... A glance at the map will show that the habitable part of Southern Rhodesia has either been alienated or ear-marked as Native Reserves. ... A more detailed examination of the District Maps on which Crown Land, alleged to be suitable and available for settlement, has been demarked only brings home more strikingly the paucity of the Government resources in this connection.[143]

In other words, the Europeans had already taken the best of the country, and the Land Commission, instead of increasing what was already an excessive slice of the cake,[144] would have been better advised in drawing the settlers' attention to greater development of the land they already possessed in such abundance.

4 CONCLUSION

One must conclude by agreeing with Hancock that the Carter Commission's findings did not make excessive demands on the generosity of white Rhodesia. When the Land Apportionment Act was finally passed in 1930, the country's 48,000 Europeans (of whom only 11,000 were settled on the land),[145] were given on average 1,000 acres per head of population. Their share of the land was greater than that of the one million still predominantly rural Africans who had only 29 acres per head in 14 of the 19 districts of Mashonaland and in 10 of the 13 Matabeleland districts. In addition to getting the lion's share of the land, in quality even more than in quantity, the Europeans also obtained the segregation they had been demanding for so long; while the continuing legacy of the Jameson era ensured that the land selected for the Native Purchase Areas offered only minimal opportunity to the emerging African middle class. One ICU speaker told his Bulawayo audience in 1930: 'The Premier says that there will be land for the natives. That is because the Government has heard us knocking at the door.'[146] The Government had indeed heard the knocking, but had taken pains to open the door the merest fraction.[147]

On the whole, the Report of the Land Commission is a more tolerant, 'liberal' document than the earlier Coryndon Report. Carter and his colleagues, perhaps unconsciously reflecting the views of a chastened post-war generation, were no longer certain of the inevitable triumph of European values; these now had to be safeguarded and protected by 'segregation'. Times change. Segregation, which appeared a positive belief to many in the 1920s and 1930s, was seen as hopelessly reactionary by another post-war generation, especially as it came to be firmly associated with the 'white south' of Africa and the United States of America. But in recent years the pendulum has swung again, and many black Americans have come to see segregation as a means of preserving their cultural identity against the pervasive pressures of white America. Clearly therefore it is more instructive to examine the reality, rather than the theory, of segregation. And in Rhodesia the reality was that as a result of the Land Apportionment Act, the Europeans established a position of economic and political dominance which they were determined to defend at all costs against Africans who now had less and less opportunity of competing with them on anything approaching equal terms. Segregation in Rhodesia spelt separateness but not equality.

NOTES

1. J. R. Chancellor, 'Southern Rhodesia and its Problems', *Journal of the African Society*, **26,** 101, 1926, 3.
2. Southern Rhodesia, *Report of the Land Commission, 1925* (Salisbury 1926), 20.
3. C.O. 767/2, Chancellor to Thomas, 14 August 1924.
4. C.O. 767/2, Chancellor to Thomas, 1 September 1924.
5. C.O. 417/705, Minutes by Davis and Parkinson, 13 and 16 September 1924.
6. The Resident Commissioner, Burns-Begg, recalling that Taylor had been in charge of the Matabeleland Native Department at a time when forced labour had flourished before the Rising of 1896, commented: 'He has, I will confess, scarcely the ability that I should like to see in the head of the Native Department but he is keen, energetic and hard-working and is, in my opinion, a better official than Mr. Taberer [the CNC Mashonaland].' C.O. 417/524, Burns-Begg to Gladstone, 24 May, 1913.
7. Rhodes House, Oxford, APS Papers, G166, Harris to Cripps, 6 January 1925.
8. Hist. MSS. NE 1/1/1, Coghlan to Newton, 9 March 1925.
9. Cited in M. C. Steele, 'The Foundations of a "Native" Policy in Southern Rhodesia, 1923–33', Ph.D thesis, Simon Fraser University, 1972, 436.
10. F48/L5, Atherstone to Secretary, Department of Agriculture, 30 October 1927.
11. In Uganda Morris Carter had chaired a committee (1911–21) which had recommended that about 80 per cent of the land in Ankole, Bunyoro, Busoga, and Toro could be alienated without damage to African interests. V. Harlow and E. M. Chilver (Eds.), *History of East Africa, Vol II* (Oxford 1965), 477–9; E. A. Brett, *Colonialism and Underdevelopment in East Africa* (London 1973), 219.
12. In 1927 the Kenyan Department of Agriculture wrote to its Rhodesian counterpart

asking for 'your advice regarding the "exclusively White area" proposals and how it is thought such areas can be maintained ... in conditions which are much the same as ours'. Hist. MSS. AT 1/2/1/6, Deputy Director of Agriculture, Kenya, to Secretary, Department of Agriculture, Southern Rhodesia, 4 March 1927.

13. Rhodes House, Oxford, APS Papers, G166, Harris to Cripps, 6 January 1925.

14. Hist. MSS. NE 1/1/1, Newton to Coghlan, 12 February 1925.

15. C.O. 767/2, Chancellor to Thomas, 13 October 1924.

16. F35/2(1), Leggate to Coghlan, 21 January 1924.

17. C.O. 767/3, Minute by Tait, 4 November 1924.

18. C.O. 417/705, Athlone to Amery, 12 November 1924.

19. C.O. 767/3, Amery to Chancellor, 28 November 1924, Chancellor to Amery, 15 December 1924.

20. S 348, CNC to all S/Ns and N/Cs Salisbury Division, 10 March and 3 April 1925.

21. *Land Commission*, 2.

22. T. O. Ranger, *The African Voice in Southern Rhodesia* (Nairobi 1970), 111.

23. *Land Commission*, 4–5.

24. *Land Commission*, 7.

25. *Land Commission*, 12.

26. Carter and Taylor also proposed Neutral Areas of 1,099,870 acres in which either race could own land. Atherstone dissented from this proposal, the idea was subsequently abandoned, and the alternative of adding a further half million acres to the NPA was adopted.

27. *Land Commission*, 33.

28. In the Bulawayo, Umzingwane, Bubi, Nyamandhlovu, Matobo and Insiza Districts, and in parts of Selukwe, Gwelo, Bulalima-Mangwe, and Gwanda.

29. Rhodes House, Oxford, Chancellor Papers, MSS. Brit. Emp. s. 284, 7/5, Notes by Chancellor, 5 February 1928, fol.93.

30. One observer wrote in 1935: 'Unfortunately the depression in agriculture and in the price of cattle has hit the native hard, as it has the European farmer, and although many applications for land are received, the number who have actually taken up land is not as large as it would have been in 1923–24.' E. T. Jollie, 'Native Administration in Southern Rhodesia', *Journal of the Royal Society of Arts*, **83,** 1935, 980.

31. Jollie, 'Native Administration', 980. See also her valuable book, one of the best settler critiques of the Company: *The Real Rhodesia* (London 1924).

32. F 48/L5, Atherstone to Secretary, Department of Agriculture, 3 October 1927.

33. In 1926 he told his audience that he hoped the Report would soon be implemented, that no time should be lost if they were to avoid the difficulties facing South Africa, and that while 'some measure of segregation of the natives is necessary for the comfort and happiness of Europeans and natives alike', absolute segregation 'would be at once impracticable and disastrous'. Chancellor, 'Southern Rhodesia', 3, 4. See also J. R. Chancellor, 'Progress and Development of Southern Rhodesia', *Journal of the African Society*, **28,** 110, 1929, 149–54.

34. D.O. 63/3, Chancellor to Amery, 1 April 1927.

35. 'The Labour Party in Rhodesia', Chancellor noted with approval, 'did not exist to make strikes, but to prevent them'. D.O. 63/5, Chancellor to Amery, 10 April 1928.

36. The NPAs were increased from 6·8 to 7·4 million acres in size after it was decided to abandon the one million acres of Neutral Areas proposed by Carter and Taylor (see note 26).

37. Rhodes House, Oxford, Chancellor Papers, MSS. Brit. Emp. s. 284, 8/3, Coghlan to Chancellor, 8 March and 2 May 1926, fol. 52–3, 70.

38. D.O. 63/2, Note of a discussion between Amery and Coghlan, 30 July 1926.

39. D.O. 63/2, Minute by Davis, 29 July 1926.

40. D.O. 63/3, Chancellor to Amery, 1 April 1927. Coghlan informed Chancellor that: 'If the opposition made this a party question, which in my opinion they are quite capable of doing ... I would rather drop the whole thing since continuity of policy is essential

in this matter.' Rhodes House, Oxford, Chancellor Papers, MSS. Brit. Emp. s. 284, 8/3, Coghlan to Chancellor, 14 April 1927, fol. 105.

41. Southern Rhodesia, *Legislative Assembly Debates*, **6**, 5 May 1927, cols. 93–114; 12 May 1927, cols. 318–32; 13 May 1927, cols. 333–71; 31 May 1927, cols. 1010–22; 17 June 1927, cols. 1623–74; 20 June 1927, cols. 1676–90.

42. *Legislative Assembly Debates*, **6**, 5 May 1927, cols. 97, 99, 101.

43. S 924/G1/1, CNC to Secretary to Premier, 3 May 1927. This estimate was no more accurate than his 1915 opinion that the African population would take eighty years to double in size.

44. *Legislative Assembly Debates*, **6**, 5 May 1927, col. 108. On much the same lines, D. M. Stanley, a lawyer from Melsetter, told the Commission: 'Camouflage it as we will, conquest, peaceful penetration, or by invitation, the fact remains that we have dispossessed the native of his land, and much that he holds dear. Now for the sake of our honour, we must treat them as generously as possible, compatible with our retaining our supremacy. The part is poor morality but sound common sense.' ZAH 2/1/1, Written statement by D. M. Stanley to Land Commission, 1925.

45. D.O. 63/3, Chancellor to Amery, 7 July 1927.

46. *Legislative Assembly Debates*, **6**, 12 May 1927, cols. 330, 328.

47. D.O. 63/4, Minute by Davis, 16 July 1927.

48. Chancellor had suggested that Bisset, the Senior Judge recently imported from the Cape be made Premier, but this was flatly rejected by the Rhodesian Cabinet and the suggestion had the effect of cooling relations between the new Government and Chancellor, who subsequently found that ministers 'were a good deal more difficult to deal with than they used to be'. D.O. 63/5, Chancellor to Amery, 10 April 1928; Rhodes House, Oxford, Chancellor Papers, MSS. Brit. Emp. s. 284, 9/1, Chancellor to Thompson, 16 March 1928, fol. 720. See R. W. Baldock, 'Sir John Chancellor and the Moffat Succession', *Rhodesian History*, **3**, 1972, 41–52.

49. Chancellor added that Moffat: '... has the advantage of the traditions associated with his name in connection with the treatment of natives. But he is virtually without the qualities of a leader. Uneducated, with a very slow moving mind, unreceptive of ideas, almost inarticulate as a speaker, and very undistinguished in personality.' Rhodes House, Oxford, Chancellor Papers, MSS. Brit. Emp. s. 284, 9/1, Chancellor to Thompson, 3 September 1927, fol. 580.

50. Moffat confessed that 'we have some very poor members'. Governor Rodwell agreed. He hoped that at the next election 'at least half-a-dozen seats in the Assembly will be filled by better men than the present incumbents'. He mentioned four particularly useless members, and added 'there are several others who would not be missed'. Hist. MSS. NE 1/1/7, Moffat to Newton, 14 June 1930; D.O. 35/370, Rodwell to Thomas, 9 March 1932.

51. *Legislative Assembly Debates*, **8**, 23 April 1929, col. 15; 25 April 1929, cols. 71–95; 14 May 1929, cols. 750–72; 23 May 1929, cols. 1112–28; 27 May 1929, cols. 1165–1226; 28 May 1929, cols. 1229–38; 29 May 1929, cols. 1311–62; 30 May 1929, cols. 1363–1402; 31 May 1929, cols. 1457–68; 6 June 1929, cols. 1713–14; 10 June 1929, col. 1781.

52. *Legislative Assembly Debates*, **8**, 28 May 1929, col. 1233; 27 May 1929, col. 1166.

53. Hist. MSS. NE 1/1/7, Moffat to Newton, 15 July and 2 August 1926, Newton to Moffat, 24 July 1929.

54. D.O. 63/6, Law Officers of the Crown to Passfield, 14 October 1929.

55. *Legislative Assembly Debates*, **9**, 29 April 1930, col. 1379; 2 May 1930, cols. 1613–28; 8 May 1930, cols 1866–74; 9 May 1930, cols, 1915–16; 12 May 1930. col. 1939.

56. C.O. 417/705, Minute by Davis, 16 September 1924.

57. This was very much the brainchild of Leo Amery, who, on becoming Colonial Secretary in November 1924, 'stipulated that I should be allowed to create a new and entirely separate office to deal with the Dominions'. L. S. Amery, *My Political Life, Vol. II* (London 1953), 335.

58. C. Parkinson, *The Colonial Office from within* (London 1945), 96.

59. D.O. 63/4, Amery to Ormsby-Gore, 21 August 1927; Amery, *My Political Life*, 406.

60. D.O. 63/6, Rodwell to Harding, 4 February 1929; D.O. 63/4, Minute by Davis, 16 July 1927.

61. D.O. 9/2, Athlone to Amery, 7 May 1926. The Dominions Office agreed that the proposals 'cannot be regarded as inherent in the scheme'. D.O. 63/2, Note of a discussion between Davis, Harding, Tait and Parkinson, 4 January 1927.

62. 64 H.L. DEB. 5s., 23 June 1926, cols. 542–64.

63. 64 H.L. DEB. 5s., 23 June 1926, col. 544.

64. D.O. 63/2, Minute by Davis, 29 July 1926.

65. D.O. 63/6, Minute by Wiseman, 5 April 1929.

66. S 480/129, Rough notes of a Meeting of Ministers with Colonel Amery, 15 August 1927.

67. D.O. 63/6, Memos by Moffat and H. M. G. Jackson, February 1929.

68. D.O. 63/6, Minute by Ponsonby, 18 July 1929.

69. D.O. 63/6, Minute by Tait, 15 June 1929.

70. Hist. MSS. NE 1/1/7, Newton to Moffat, 11 July 1929.

71. D.O. 63/6, Minute by Ponsonby, 18 July 1929.

72. D.O. 63/6, Memo by Moffat, February 1929.

73. Harris, writing as Secretary of the APS, asked Newton 'to intimate privately to Sir Chârles Coghlan how very much we appreciate the decision of the Southern Rhodesia Government to appoint this Commission'. S 235/361, Harris to Newton, 10 February 1925.

74. Rhodes House, Oxford, APS Papers, G168, Olivier to Harris, 13 July 1929.

75. In his book *An Africa for Africans*, published in 1927, Cripps claimed that: 'Natives in the Charter District of Mashonaland, which has been my home for many years desire Segregation Areas (away from Europeans' Farms and Estates) ... as a means to further Native Self-Determination and Native Self-Development', adding that 'the policy of Segregation Areas is worth trying as a remedy for grave and complex maladies'. Subsequently Cripps came to change his mind, and in 1950 shortly before his death, he had a typewritten statement inserted in the last six copies of the book, which read: 'When I wrote this book, which was published in 1927, I was willing to approve of Segregation for Africans and Europeans—if Africans should be given a fair share of the land in the Colony. But afterwards I did not consider that Africans, in my opinion, were given a fair share in the Southern Rhodesian Scheme of Land Apportionment, and lost my faith in Segregation for Southern Rhodesia. I am thankful for Segregation as planned by the Morris Carter Commission for opening the way for Africans to purchase plots of land but I do not believe that Segregation is a righteous policy for a British Colony. Can it be a right policy for Christian people? Certainly not! A. S. Cripps.' A. S. Cripps, *An Africa for Africans* (London 1927), 67–8, 197; D. V. Steere, *God's Irregular: Arthur Shearly Cripps* (London 1973), 119–20.

76. Cripps wrote of: 'The extraordinary solemn responsibility that rests upon those who wish the Natives well at this crisis in our Colony's history. Clause 43 has huge potentialities as to the future, if insignificant effectiveness at the present moment of time.' Ranger confirms that 'men like John White, indeed, bore a heavy and terrifying responsibility in this matter'. Cripps, *Africa for Africans*, 195; Ranger, *African Voice*, 116.

77. APS to Amery, 7 June 1926, cited in D.O. 63/2, Minute by Parkinson, 7 December 1926. In 1927 Cripps wrote that 'the Native Land-Purchaser does not appear to me to be getting his fair quid pro quo under the Commission's recommendations', a view which he had no cause to alter in later years. Cripps, *Africa for Africans*, 177.

78. J. White, 'The *Rationale* of the Missionary Conference of Southern Rhodesia', *NADA*, **2,** 1924, 68. The Mayor of Salisbury, J. H. Smit, later a cabinet minister under Huggins, refused to open the 1928 Conference because of his hostility to White's views.

79. *Proceedings of the Southern Rhodesia Missionary Conference 1926* (Salisbury 1926),

9–10; *Missionary Conference 1928*, 5–6, 33. Municipalities were not legally obliged to assign Native Village Settlements until 1945.

80. A. S. Cripps, 'African Land Tenure', *NADA*, **4**, 1926, 96–101. For a reply, see C. L. Carbutt, 'Communal Land Tenure', *NADA*, **5**, 1927, 42–5.

81. Cripps, *Africa for Africans*, 197.

82. *Missionary Conference 1926*, 37; *Missionary Conference 1928*, 30.

83. *Rhodesia Herald*, 20 August 1926; *Manchester Guardian*, 2 July 1929.

84. One Matabeleland farmers' association, for example, wanted two-thirds of the area given to Europeans. *Bulawayo Chronicle*, 4 September 1926.

85. *Missionary Conference 1930*, 18; Rhodes House, Oxford, APS Papers, G168, Harris to Leggate, 6 January 1930; D.O. 35/354, APS to Passfield, 2 May 1930.

86. Rhodes House, Oxford, APS Papers, G168, White to Harris, 17 August 1930, APS to Leggate, 4 June 1930, Harris to White, 28 February 1930.

87. 229 H.C. DEB. 5s., 10 July 1929, col. 866.

88. *Manchester Guardian*, 17 and 19 June 1929.

89. His arguments about the Unassigned Area did not, for a while, convince the APS.

90. Hist. MSS. MO 13/1/1, Interview between Leggate, Harris and T. F. Buxton, 19 November 1929, fol. 203–5, Leggate to C. P. Scott, 19 November 1929, fol. 206–11, Leggate to Moffat, 22 November 1929, fol. 212–13; W. M. Leggate, 'Southern Rhodesia: Some Problems of Native Development and Trade', Address to the *Empire Parliamentary Association*, 27 November 1929, 6–7; Rhodes House, Oxford, APS Papers, G168, Leggate to APS, 25 March 1930.

91. Ranger, *African Voice*, 183–6.

92. S 138/18, S/N Bulawayo to CNC, 30 November 1929.

93. S 138/18, Acting S/N Gwelo to S/N Bulawayo, 19 July 1926.

94. S 138/18, Secretary, Southern Rhodesia Native Welfare Association, to Secretary to Premier, 28 March 1927.

95. S 138/21, Zigode to Secretary to Premier, 27 May 1930.

96. S 138/18, CNC to Secretary to Premier, 27 April, 1927 N/C Gwelo to S/N Bulawayo, 30 July 1927.

97. It is stretching the imagination somewhat to suggest that this meeting 'flared out in resolutions repudiating and condemning the Carter findings and recommendations'. Ranger, *African Voice*, 174. Perhaps this is one of those occasions when 'it is at times hard to discern where the African voice begins and where the off-stage directions of the author end'. Review by Sholto Cross in *Transafrican Journal of History*, **2**, 1, 1972, 131.

98. The Acting S/N Bulawayo considered this suggestion regarding the evidence as 'interesting, but I am not aware that it is correct or that it can be of any consequence, if it is'. S 138/18, Acting S/N Bulawayo to CNC, 16 June 1926.

99. S 138/18, Detective Watt to Chief Superintendent, C.I.D. Bulawayo, 14 July 1929.

100. S 138/267, Detective Maybrook to Chief Superintendant, C.I.D. Bulawayo, 5 May 1930.

101. 'Assuming that some such organisation [as the Rhodesian Native Association] is inevitable', wrote H. S. Keigwin, Director of Native Development, 'it might be well to have at its head a man [J. S. Mokwile] whose movements we can control, whose mind we can to some extent inform, and whose influence is likely to be for moderation, or at least a respect for those in authority'. S 138/10, Director of Native Development to CNC, 1 July 1924.

102. Hist. MSS. MA 15/1/1, Resolutions of the Executive Committee of the Southern Rhodesia Native Association, 1929.

103. D.O. 63/3, Address by advanced natives to Amery, August 1927.

104. ZAH 1/1/4, Evidence to Land Commission at Darwin, Concession and Mtoko, 17, 20 and 28 July 1925, 1424–7, 1436–8, 1453–5.

105. W. M. Macmillan, 'The Development of Africa: Impressions from Rhodesia', *Political Quarterly*, **3**, 1932, 552–69; R. D. Gilchrist, 'Rhodesia's Place in the Native Problem', *Journal of the African Society*, **32**, 126, 1933, 135–9; W. M. Macmillan, 'Southern

Rhodesia and the Development of Africa', *Journal of the African Society*, **32**, 128, 1933, 294–8.

106. L. P. Mair, *Native Policies in Africa* (London 1936), 66–75; E. T. Jollie, 'Southern Rhodesia's Native Policy', *United Empire*, **28**, 1937, 336–41.

107. W. K. Hancock, *Survey of British Commonwealth Affairs, Vol. II*, Part 2 (London 1942), 104.

108. R. McGregor, 'Native Segregation in Southern Rhodesia', Ph.D. thesis, University of London, 1940, 106–21.

109. Southern Rhodesia, *Report of the Urban African Affairs Commission, 1958* (Salisbury 1958), 25; Southern Rhodesia, *Second Report of the Select Committee on Resettlement of Natives* (Salisbury 1960), 27; Rhodesia, *Report by the Constitutional Council on the Land Apportionment Act, 1941* (Salisbury 1964), 17; Rhodesia, *Report of the Commission of Inquiry into Racial Discrimination 1976* (Salisbury 1976), 9.

110. C.O. 767/4, Chancellor to Amery, 11 April and 13 May 1925.

111. *Legislative Assembly Debates*, **3**, 21 May 1925, col. 734.

112. Projected routes at this time included Sinoia–Kafue, Wankie–Walvis Bay, West Nicholson–Messina, Umvuma–Odzi, Fort Victoria–Messina, Bromley–Umvuma, and Umvuma–Portuguese border. S. 235/361, Secretary, Land Commission, to General Manager, Beira and Mashonaland and Rhodesia Railways, 20 February 1925, Acting General Manager, Beira and Mashonaland and Rhodesia Railways, to Secretary, Land Commission, 6 March 1925.

113. At Fort Victoria, for example, the landowner John Hongwe and his friends, who initially took the view that the existing system should continue so that they could learn from European farmers, were persuaded to change their minds after the matter had been 'carefully explained'. ZAH 1/1/4, Evidence of John Hongwe and others to Land Commission, 5 September 1925, 1612–13.

114. ZAH 2/1/1, Secretary, Rhodesia Agricultural Union, to Secretary, Land Commission, 27 July 1925.

115. One African landowner told the Commission that the people 'are afraid to go and ask for the land, because they were told that natives could not buy any land'. ZAH 1/1/2, Evidence of Maya to Land Commission, 28 March 1925, 615.

116. ZAH 1/1/1, Evidence of H. D. Rawson to Land Commission, 6 March 1925, 191.

117. S 235/361, Secretary, Land Commission, to CNC, 1 April 1925.

118. Two of these ten were Anglican missionaries at St. Augustine's, Penhalonga, near Umtali. Baker believed it was too late in the day for segregation and warned of the dangers of land hunger creating a revolutionary peasantry, while Cotton commented on how the 1913 Natives Land Act had embittered race relations in South Africa, and suggested that segregation was impracticable because of the need for African labour and that no European capital or skills would be invested in any Native Purchase Area, and spoke of the need for a loyal contented African peasantry and for a band of patriotic English agriculturists free from racial prejudice. ZAH 1/1/3, Evidence of R. H. Baker and W. A. Cotton to Land Commission, 16 and 17 April 1925, 982–94, 1075–82.

119. Twenty-one white farmers gave evidence as representatives of 14 different farmers' associations. The figure of 234 Europeans and 110 white farmers are my own, rather than the Commission's incorrect figures of 233 and 85.

120. A number of white farmers from the Chipinga area of Melsetter opposed segregation because they were afraid that the Sabi Valley, with its rich agricultural potential, would be declared a NPA.

121. ZAH 1/1/4, Evidence of W. B. Cumming to Land Commission, 8 June 1925, 1389–91.

122. ZAH 1/1/3, Evidence of R. I. Keys to Land Commission, 21 April 1925, 1199.

123. R. Gray, *The Two Nations* (London 1960), 14–31; Ranger, *African Voice*, 110–37.

124. One of the seven, an Ndebele trader, told the Commission: 'I think that we natives ought to make it our duty, if the law says that we have the right to buy land anywhere,

to be as near to the white people and the white farmers, so that we can have some education from the white people. We require some education as regards agriculture from the farmers. If we are neighbours of the white farmers we can then learn how to develop the soil.' ZAH 1/1/2, Evidence of S. Mazwi to Land Commission, 28 March 1925, 608.

125. The Government medical officer for Marandellas, who had often travelled through the reserves, endorsed African criticisms pointing out that 'there are enormous tracts of land which are absolutely useless from an agricultural point of view ... The acreage of the reserves seems very large, but the portion of arable land in them is indeed extremely small'. One African witness noted perceptively: 'As far as the Reserves are concerned they are a matter of disappointment to us in so far as the soil is poor and some of them have no water, and I feel that if separate areas were set aside for purely native purchase the same thing may happen in regard to those areas as has happened in regard to the Reserves.' ZAH 1/1/3, Evidence of T. D. McLaren to Land Commission, 21 April 1925, 1147–8; ZAH 1/1/1, Evidence of N. Sinyanga to Land Commission, 24 March 1925, 486.

126. S 235/361, Cripps to Chancellor, 18 April 1925; C.O. 767/4, Chancellor to Amery, 13 May 1925.

127. A. C. Jennings, 'Land Apportionment in Southern Rhodesia', *Journal of the Royal African Society*, **34**, 136, 1935, 306.

128. The N/Cs Charter, Hartley, Marandellas, Mazoe, Ndanga, Salisbury, Bulawayo, Gwelo, Insiza, Matobo, Nyamandhlovu, Selukwe and Umzingwane.

129. ZAH 1/1/2, Evidence of N/C Nyamandhlovu to Land Commission, 28 March 1925, 577.

130. S 924/G1/1, CNC to Secretary to Premier, 3 May 1927.

131. Atherstone recalled that: 'When we first started on our labours of compiling a report the Chairman proposed that we should not consider any question of a proportion of land as between the races, but that in our selection of land for the natives we should be guided wholly by the evidence we had collected. To this both Sir Herbert Taylor and I expressed absolute agreement. We thereupon went through the evidence and made our full selections in accordance therewith ... After the areas had been plotted on the maps and their extents ascertained, which took some days, the Chairman was disappointed at the result and stated that it did not give the proportion of land which he anticipated and which he thought would be equitable. We thereupon re-examined the evidence and made a further selection which is embodied in our unanimous recommendations in the report—adding something over a million acres to our first selection. This I certainly considered to be a final selection of land; and consequently I was considerably surprised when the Chairman one morning informed me he proposed to add to the areas and to discuss in this connection the question of neutral areas with Sir Herbert Taylor—a discussion carried on apart from myself.' S924/G1/1, Atherstone to Fynn, Treasurer, 23 February 1927.

132. J. Ford, *The Role of the Trypanosomiases in African Ecology* (Oxford 1971), 350.

133. S 138/21, S/N Bulawayo to CNC, 18 June and 21 August 1928.

134. *Report of the Native Land Board for the year ending 31st March, 1935* (Salisbury 1935), 6.

135. *Legislative Assembly Debates*, **12,** 3 May 1932, cols. 1480, 1487.

136. *Legislative Assembly Debates*, **16,** 28 May 1936, col. 2427.

137. D.O. 35/1169, Baring to Machtig, 9 June 1943; D.O. 35/1167, Baring to Machtig, 5 October 1943.

138. Jollie, *The Real Rhodesia*, 279.

139. Southern Rhodesia, *Report of the Committee of Enquiry into the Economic Position of the Agricultural Industry of Southern Rhodesia* (Salisbury 1934), 25. Twenty-two years later, another committee reported that 'large tracts of land in the Colony are either undeveloped or under-developed'. 'Report of the Select Committee on the Development of Unimproved Land', in Southern Rhodesia, *Votes and Proceedings of the Legislative Assembly*, 1956, 110.

140. *Report of the Director, Department of Lands and Surveyor General for the year 1926* (Salisbury 1927), 5. The Rhodesian Government passed a very mild Land Tax Act in 1928, but it was not enforced until 1931.

141. M. Yudelman, *Africans on the Land* (Cambridge, Mass. 1964), 90.

142. L. H. Gann, 'The Southern Rhodesian Land Apportionment Act, 1930: An essay in Trusteeship', National Archives of Rhodesia and Nyasaland, *Occasional Paper 1*, 1963, 86.

143. F 35/2 (14), Memo by Fletcher, 8 April 1929.

144. Even a representative of the Marandellas North Farmers' Association admitted that 'the white population ... does not need anything like the 21 million acres which has been acquired'. ZAH 1/1/3, Evidence of T. D. McLaren to Land Commission, 21 April 1925, 1148, McLaren was being conservative, the real figure should have been 31 million acres.

145. Jennings, 'Land Apportionment', 310.

146. S 138/267, Detective Jackson to Chief Superintendent, C.I.D. Bulawayo, 11 May 1930.

147. A botanist in the Department of Agriculture told the Commission that 'only exceptionally qualified natives ... should be exempted from native law and allowed to buy land. I think that the qualifications should be extremely high, so that while you do not shut the door to a native either purchasing land or in other ways becoming equal to a white man, you make the doorway very narrow'. ZAH 1/1/1, Evidence of F. Eyles to Land Commission, 19 March 1925, 410.

CHAPTER 8

The Fear of Competition 1926–36

We are going too fast in the development of the native.

Chief Native Commissioner, 1933.[1]

1 BACKGROUND

The prolonged negotiations preceding the passing of the Land Apportionment Act in 1930, the subsequent unavailing attempts to implement the Act fully, and the development work designed to increase the carrying capacity of the reserves were the main issues of land policy in the decade following the Report of the Land Commission. The decade, which saw Salisbury linked to London by air transport and telephone,[2] was also marked by increasing, and at times hysterical, European fears of African competition which were intensified when the world Depression hit Rhodesia in 1920–1. The Depression, which drove many white farmers off the land in Kenya, Nyasaland, and Northern Rhodesia, threatened the political and economic hegemony of the white Southern Rhodesian farmers and workers, and produced a series of demands for total segregation and non-competition between black and white which the new Huggins[3] Government attempted to meet through its Industrial Conciliation and Maize Control Amendment Acts of 1934. In the 1920s, many theorists had been concerned with the problem of how best to channel African advancement; in the 1930s, serious attention was devoted to the best way of stopping it altogether.

Thus we find Huggins, who became Prime Minister in 1933, and C. L. Carbutt, the Chief Native Commissioner (1930–6), contemplating the possibility of packing all 'advanced natives' off to Northern Rhodesia, so that Southern Rhodesia 'would be freed of the embarrassing necessity to consider native interests'.[4] A number of attempts were also made to remove the very small number of African voters from the franchise,[5] while Huggins pressed hard for the abolition of Imperial control over discriminatory legislation. Carbutt, whose conservatism may have been congenital,[6] but was more probably a reflection of the times, was an out-and-out segregationist whose 'brain drain' proposal elicited from Downing Street the response: 'Colonel Carbutt is Chief Native

Commissioner and not as one might think one of the wilder kind of European farmers.'[7]

This was a decade therefore when Europeans began to move decisively towards South African policies, when legislation protecting Europeans was introduced: when Carbutt could warn that 'we are going too fast in the development of the native';[8] when Harold Jowitt, the dynamic Director of Native Development who continually poured scorn on those Europeans who were afraid of African competition and was thus regarded as a 'fanatic' by Huggins[9] was forced to pack his bags for Uganda; and when the Dominions Office became aware of 'the profound difference between the attitude towards natives of the heads of the Native Depts of Northern and Southern Rhodesia'.[10]

The Dominions Office observed this trend in Rhodesian affairs with a certain stoic resignation. It had long accepted that the granting of responsible government would inevitably entail a considerable diminution of Imperial control. No longer was it possible to take the initiative, as had happened with the establishment of native reserves after 1896 and with the decision in 1913 to appoint a reserves commission. The British now possessed the power to veto but not the ability to initiate. Moreover, once approval had been given in principle to legislation such as the Land Apportionment and Industrial Conciliation Acts, it proved impossible to raise matters of principle again when such acts were amended in later years.[11] Nevertheless, the power to refuse assent to discriminatory legislation or to possible amendments to the reserved clauses in the constitution was a real and meaningful one, the exercise of which sometimes irritated Rhodesian governments. A number of amendments were made to the land apportionment scheme as a result of Imperial suggestions, and the first Rhodesian draft was rejected in 1928 because it was 'virtually a request for a blank cheque'.[12] In addition, several bills designed to 'scotch native agitators'[13] were turned down, and only when the Rhodesian Government began to frame its security legislation in non-discriminatory terms did the Dominions Office give its consent, although it found it 'impossible to be enthusiastic about this form of legislation'.[14] Similarly, the Huggins–Carbutt scheme was rejected on the grounds that no British government could contemplate a situation in which Africans in any colony would have no hope of advancement, and that any Rhodesian policy which was less liberal than that of South Africa would be very badly received.[15] More important still, the Dominions Office opposed any attempt to remove Africans from the franchise as being 'open to serious political objections',[16] and while yielding on a number of minor points stood firm in resisting Huggins' attempt to do away with the reserved clauses in the consititution.[17] Rhodesia was thus left to cope as best it could with the manifold problems of African advancement.

2 POLICY

(i) Introduction

Land policies grew increasingly divorced from reality during the years 1926–36. What was supposed to happen in theory began to conflict more and more with conditions as they existed on the land, where Native Commissioners were being confronted with problems of growing magnitude. In particular it became more apparent each year that the African areas were simply not capable of absorbing the population movements envisaged under the Land Apportionment Act. In this respect Southern Rhodesia was following identically the South African experience, and soon foolhardy administrators in Northern Rhodesia were to repeat the same mistake.[18] In Southern Rhodesia a great deal of effort was devoted to the so-called 'development of the reserves' in an endeavour to increase their carrying capacity, and hence meet the demands of the European farmers and the Land Apportionment Act that Africans should continue to be squeezed out of the European Area. Such a policy, which has remained constant up to the present day, inevitably produced a great deal of suffering and bitterness, as will be shown towards the end of this chapter when the 'African Voice'[19] is examined. The earlier parts of the chapter are concerned with the Native Purchase Area, the development of the reserves and the squeeze outside them, and with the ongoing relations between white farmers and black peasants.

(ii) The Native Purchase Area

The most positive aspect of the Land Apportionment Act was the creation of $7\frac{1}{2}$ million acres of Native Purchase Areas (NPAs) wherein would emerge, it was hoped, a wealthy, contented and conservative group of African middle class farmers who would act as a buffer against revolution from below and would, the Land Commission hoped, 'contribute towards the prosperity of the country by the production of exportable products'.[20]

Indeed such were the expectations aroused by the Land Commission's taking of evidence that in the years 1926–8 there were some 150 written applications for land in the proposed NPAs in Bulalima-Mangwe, Gwanda, Insiza, and Melsetter, while addition verbal requests were made to the N/C Selukwe and the S/N Victoria. The Government's initial reaction was to do nothing until the Commission's Report had been finally approved and converted into legislation. In September 1927, however, H. J. Taylor, still Chief Native Commissioner and a former member of the Land Commission, proposed the setting up of a provisional Native Land Board in order to deal with outstanding applications. Moffat approved the idea, provided there were 'no objections... by members of the House or by any of the European communities to the sale of these blocks of land'.[21] A provisional Board was duly set up in February 1928, but it had a short and unhappy life. The problems of actually dividing the NPAs up into individual holdings proved much greater than anticipated, there were legal and financial difficulties, shortages of staff and the inevitable quarrels with the 'European' Lands Department over spheres of influence. As a result, the Board went into liquidation in 1929.

The S/N Bulawayo cast light on the failure of the Board, and at the same time provided a gloomy warning for the future when he reported in August 1928 that every African who had been offered land in the NPAs north of the railway line in Matabeleland had declined the offer because the land was 'almost useless'. He warned that the passing of the Land Apportionment Act would not alleviate the land problem in this area, and that unless something was done, 'we are likely to be confronted with a very difficult situation which ... we are quite unprepared to meet at present'. Further confirmation of this warning came from the Gutu District of Mashonaland, where it was reported that Africans were moving without permission from the inadequate reserves into the NPAs without any intention of buying the land.[22] Clearly, a number of pressing problems had begun to emerge even before 1931.

The Land Apportionment Act was duly brought into effect on 1 April 1931, and a new, full-time Native Land Board was immediately set up to administer the NPA as the Land Commission had proposed. The Board comprised Carbutt, the CNC, as *ex officio* chairman; Atherstone, who had just retired and was the High Commissioner's nominee[23] and in fact served on the Board until 1946 when he retired at the age of seventy-five; A. C. Jennings, a member of the Lands Department, who had previously had the thankless task of developing water supplies in the native reserves; 'Wiri' Edwards, who had just retired after holding the post of N/C Mrewa since 1895; and Frank Noble, the Missionary Conference nominee who was the leading Wesleyan minister in Rhodesia following the departure of the dying John White in 1930, and was considered by H. J. Stanley 'a good man, but rather a one-sided and injudicious advocate of native interests'.[24]

Carbutt and Jennings had already drawn up regulations governing the Board's activities. Members were to hold office for three-year terms but could be reappointed, while all applications for land had to be sent to the local Native Commissioner who was to forward them to the Board with a report on each applicant. He was thus in a very strong position to veto 'undesirables'. The Board could make recommendations, nothing more, to the Minister of Native Affairs concerning the inspection and surveying of land and the construction of fences, dipping tanks, wells etc., the costs of which were to be added to and recovered from the price of the land. In subdividing the land, attention was to be paid to its physical characteristics and to the resources and experience of the applicant. The minimum sizes of holdings were fixed as follows: 2,500 Cape square feet for residential plots; 2 morgen for agricultural plots; 50 morgen for other farm holdings and for mixed agricultural and pastoral holdings; and 150 morgen for pastoral holdings. Carbutt regarded these regulations as 'the barest framework to permit the Board to function'.[25]

The Board was immediately confronted by a series of problems which caused it to define its future policy. First and foremost the land had to be subdivided into individual holdings, and water supplies and roads had to be provided in many areas. But the Board commenced its work at the height of the Depression, and the Rhodesian Treasury assigned it only one land inspector, together with a directive that his work was to be 'limited to actual present needs ... and not for the purpose of laying out allotments in advance of applications'.[26] Carbutt promptly protested that it would be quite impossible for one man to cope with all the existing applications; he applied for, and got, a second inspector, and a third was added in 1932. But that was all, so during the first five years of the Board's existence only three officials were engaged on the vital work of survey and subdivision, with the result that the supply was never able to keep up with the demand and the outstanding applications steadily accumulated.

The Board also discovered that there were an estimated 50,000 Africans already living in the NPA, the vast majority of whom had no intention of buying the land since this was 'not in accordance with the Christian spirit'.[27] The Board immediately resolved that it be informed of all proposed movements of people into the NPAs in future, and that no such movements should be sanctioned without the approval of its chairman. But its chairman, Carbutt, was also Chief Native Commissioner and this resolution clearly placed him in a quandry. As CNC he was responsible for moving Africans from the European Area in conformity with the Land Apportionment Act, but since many reserves were by now congested and overcrowded, the possibility of using the NPAs as dumping grounds had obvious attractions. Indeed, Carbutt's predecessor had given an undertaking that Africans who were evicted would be allowed to settle in unalienated parts of the NPA.[28] But as chairman of the Native Land Board, Carbutt's prime task was to press on with the settlement of individual landowners as fast as possible which would obviously entail moving at least a part of the existing NPA population.

Carbutt's initial response was to give preference to his obligations to the Land Board. He informed the S/N Victoria that it was impossible to avoid upsetting some Africans, and that those who did not intend to buy land for which applications had been received would have to be moved, though it was the Board's policy 'to give any man who is already in occupation of land, first refusal to acquire it'. In similar, though more aggressive, vein he told the N/C Melsetter to give African occupants notice to quit, in order 'to force them to make up their minds as to whether they will buy land or not'. But by the end of 1932, when the difficulties of moving large numbers of people were becoming more apparent, the Board considered the possibility of introducing leasehold tenure in the hope that this might obviate the need for wholesale evictions. Carbutt was at first opposed to the idea, arguing that lessees would make no attempt to improve the land, but as further reports of difficulties came in from his Native Commissioners he changed his mind, and pointed out with somewhat dubious sincerity that the Board 'do not wish, if it can be avoided, to drive these Natives away from their ancestral lands', as this would only add to the congestion in the reserves. Leasehold tenure was therefore introduced to the NPA in February 1933, and immediately produced an increase in the number of applicants.[29]

A number of other policy matters were thrashed out in the years 1931–3. The S/N Victoria was very worried that Native Commissioners would have no right of entry onto African farms in the NPA, but was told that the Board possessed this right under the terms of the 'beneficial occupation' clause, while the Legal Adviser advised comfortingly that any African landowner who refused to allow a Native Commissioner onto his farm would be guilty of 'failing to comply with a reasonable request' in terms of the 1927 Native Affairs Act. The position of alien Africans was also discussed, and it was decided that only those who had been in continuous residence in Rhodesia for ten years or more would be allowed to buy land, while no alien who was not resident in Rhodesia prior to the passing of the Land Apportionment Act would be allowed to buy in the future. Carbutt noted that this was necessary if they were not to be inundated with requests from South Africa, and the only real reason for allowing any aliens to buy land was that many of them had rendered good service to the pioneers during the 1890s. After a number of Mfengu had bought land in the Salisbury NPAs, it was decided in 1933 that all applications from aliens should be held up for five years, and at the same time aliens were forbidden to settle in the reserves save in exceptional circumstances. Needless to say—and it is something which still rankles—any 'alien' European arriving in Salisbury was immediately urged to take up land in order to build a whiter Rhodesia. A further problem was that many Africans buying land wished to bring their friends and relatives with them. The Board decided that all tenants who paid rent would have to enter agreements under the Private Locations Ordinance, but that where no rent was charged each case should be decided on its merits. Moffat informed the

Board that while he was opposed to the principle of subletting, the CNC had powers to prevent any excessive squatting.[30]

Thus the Land Board endeavoured to resolve the various problems confronting it, but as we shall see, progress in the NPA was exceedingly slow and did virtually nothing to alleviate the difficulties which were mounting elsewhere in the country.

(iii) The Development of the Reserves

In 1926 the Southern Rhodesian Government appointed a full-time official to study African agriculture and do something about 'the present chaotic conditions' in the reserves.[31] This appointment stemmed from the fact that traditional methods of land rotation cultivation were becoming less and less viable in the face of dramatic population and stock increases, the use of the plough (see table XI) and the evictions from European land, all of which greatly upset the earlier man/land ratios.

TABLE XI

Estimated Number of African-owned Ploughs, 1906–51

1906	692	1931	53,507
1911	3,402	1936	79,015
1916	9,245	1941	108,431
1921	16,913	1946	139,705
1926	27,584	1951	163,492

Robinson has estimated that traditional methods were capable of supporting on average a population of 20 to the square mile, or 32 acres per person.[32] The population figures produced by the 1925 Land Commission, which were certainly underestimates, revealed that while in general the critical level had not been reached (for there were still an estimated 41·9 acres per person in the reserves), in 12 of the 32 districts Africans had less than 32 acres and in a further 9 they would also have less if all the people were moved into the reserves. In the Bulawayo District there was no reserve. Clearly in some districts, as in Kenya at this time,[33] traditional agricultural methods could no longer be sustained. As Garbett writes:

> The movement of villages became restricted or impossible. Land was brought back into cultivation before the soil had a chance to regenerate fully. Grazing areas were also destroyed as the number of stock increased. In some areas land was becoming particularly scarce, fragmentation of holdings

occurred so that individual holdings became smaller and smaller. The land could no longer support this burden and soil degeneration brought falling yields.[34]

Something had to be done.

As far back as 1909, a Native Department conference had called for the establishment of agricultural schools to train Africans in improved farming techniques, and for all revenue derived from the rents of mission and trading sites in the reserves to be assigned to a development fund.[35] It was not, however, until after the BSA Company relinquished its administration that these proposals were implemented.[36] Then the appearance of an article in the Phelps-Stokes Education Report, which asserted that African methods of cultivation had been condemned too hastily in the past and that continuous cultivation should not be enforced without trained advice,[37] led CNC Taylor to ask in 1926 for the appointment of an expert to study African methods and advise on possible changes. In October that year E. D. Alvord, an American missionary who had taught agriculture at Mount Silinda Mission in Melsetter, was appointed 'Agriculturalist for the Instruction of Natives'. His appointment marked the real beginning of the development of the reserves. By 1936, Alvord, 'a textbook representative of muscular Christianity',[38] had a staff of 4 Europeans and 87 Africans working under him whose activities embraced agricultural demonstration work, centralization of the reserves, soil surveys and conservation and irrigation work. A programme was at last under way, on a scale unrivalled in colonies to the north, to revolutionize life in the reserves.

There were two basic objectives. At a theoretical level, it was believed that: 'There must be in the reserves ample opportunity for all the economic, social and political wants of the advancing and progressive natives to be filled. That, in a nutshell, is the secret of a successful native policy.'[39] More practically, and more urgently in the light of the population movements envisaged by the Land Commission and the Land Apportionment Act, it was 'intended to develop the native reserves so as to enable them to carry a larger population, and so avoid, as far as possible, the necessity for acquisition of more land for native occupation'.[40] It was of course not intended 'to stimulate high production of staple cash crops',[41] but this did begin to happen in certain areas with the inevitable consequence that European farmers, as in Kenya,[42] began to criticize the whole policy and the money spent on it.

The first major step in the development programme took place in June and July 1927, when the first African agricultural demonstrators were sent out into the reserves. The scheme was modelled on similar ones in existence in the Transkei and the Southern States of America. The demonstrators were given a three year training in modern agricultural techniques and were then sent into the reserves. They first had to win the confidence of a peasant farmer, and then offer to help him prepare a small 'demonstration plot' of one to two acres and to work it with the aid of modern methods, stressing the virtues of crop rotation, maintenance of soil fertility, etc. It was hoped that each demonstrator would take over ten such plots scattered as widely as possible throughout the reserve. Shortly before harvesting, meetings were held at which Alvord, the Native Commissioner, and the agricultural demonstrator were present, and the local people were invited to see for themselves the results that could be obtained by adopting new methods. It was hoped that the example of the demonstrators would encourage peasant farmers to adopt more intensive methods and that a spontaneous revolution would take place which would ease the growing congestion in the reserves.

Hand in hand with the work of the demonstrators went the policy of centralization, designed in part 'to put a stop to the traditional Bantu [sic] practice of shifting cultivation' and 'to anchor the native to the soil'.[43] Whereas before the European occupation, African arable, grazing, and residential lands had all been clearly defined, after 1890 under 'the peace of the suzerain powers',[44] villages had spread out everywhere, and the extensive use of the plough coupled with a rapidly increasing human and animal population, resulted in lands becoming all mixed up and in frequent destruction of crops by cattle. Alvord's solution, which he called centralization, was simply to return to the pre-colonial system by dividing the reserves into strictly defined arable, grazing, and residential areas, thus enabling them to support a much greater density of population and stock. Where possible, large blocks of arable land were consolidated and fenced off from surrounding grazing lands,[45] while villages were resettled in straight lines as opposed to the earlier clusters in such a way that roads and water supplies could be developed to serve them. The recent experiments of *ujamaa* villages in Tanzania and of 'village regrouping' in Zambia are not dissimilar to this early Rhodesian scheme. Centralization began in 1929 in the Selukwe Reserve, where for some years past the local Native Commissioner had drawn attention to the overcrowded conditions.

Soil surveys, designed as an adjunct to centralization, were begun in 1933 following representations from the N/Cs at Marandellas and Charter. The Assistant N/C Marandellas had suggested that detailed maps of the reserves be drawn up so that suitable arable and grazing lands could be determined with greater accuracy before land was assigned to the various chiefs; while the N/C Charter complained that, with the exception of the Sabi, all his reserves were full up and he was not prepared to allow any more people from other districts to settle in them. Carbutt noted that he could not accept the N/C's unverified statement and that it would be necessary for surveyors to draw up detailed plans of the reserves since Native Commissioners had neither the time nor the technical proficiency to perform the task. If the Land Apportionment Act was ever to be implemented, 'a very careful and complete survey of the Native Reserves is essential with a view to their closer settlement'. Moffat accepted Carbutt's advice and two soil surveyors began work in the reserves in June 1933. They were followed, in June 1936, by a soil conservation officer, after Alvord had warned that unless more attention was paid to the control of erosion the reserves would soon become uninhabitable.[46]

At a Native Department conference in 1927, Carbutt, then S/N Victoria, advocated the reorganization of the reserves to avoid widespread congestion, and the need to persuade Africans to reduce their cattle holdings. A circular was therefore issued in January 1928, urging Native Commissioners to conduct propaganda to this effect, especially after the NPAs became available and the people could sell cattle in order to buy farms. This marked a radical change in policy, for in the past successive Native Commissioners, ever mindful of the events of the 1890s, had paid due deference to the old settler maxim that the loyalty of the Ndebele hung on the horns of their cattle, and therefore it had always been 'an axiom in Native policy to foster cattle-breedings'. The result was an astronomical increase in numbers and by the 1930s, when cattle prices had slumped, serious erosion in many districts. After the Rhodesia Agricultural Union's 1932 Report on Soil Erosion, Native Commissioners stepped up their de-stocking propaganda and Liebig's opened an extract of meat factory at West Nicholson the following year; but Carbutt, as CNC, understandably shied away from compulsory de-stocking. He wrote asking South African officials for advice but they were no wiser than he, and at a Native Department conference in 1935 during which many Native Commissioners drew attention to the steadily deteriorating conditions, he recognized that drastic measures would soon become inevitable though the great objection was that 'if you want to raise trouble amongst the natives that is the quickest way of doing so'. But he had asked for an animal husbandry officer who would tour the reserves, lecturing people on the evils of over-stocking, and warning them that if they did not voluntarily reduce their stock it would only be a matter of time before the Government compelled them to do so.[47]

Finally, the development of water supplies, begun so tardily by the BSA Company, was carried out on a much wider scale than hitherto, particularly in Matabeleland where, as Carbutt admitted, both the reserves and the purchase areas were 'remarkably waterless'.[48] The problem was particularly acute in view of the provisions of the Land Apportionment Act, and in 1931 it was decided to shift the emphasis from the drilling of boreholes which had not yielded the expected results, to the construction of weirs and dams which would be able to store surface water.

Thus a many-sided programme was brought into operation which, it was hoped, would greatly increase the carrying capacity of the reserves, and hence allow them to absorb the many thousands of people who were due to be turned off European land under the terms of the Land Apportionment Act.

(iv) The Squeeze Outside the Reserves

The Land Apportionment Act envisaged that all rent-paying agreements on European farms should cease by 1937, except for those entered into in central Matabeleland prior to the passing of the Act. Thereafter, only labour agreements or agreements carrying no burden at all would be permitted. 'Kaffir farming' would thus be abolished and the absentee landlords forced either to sell or to develop their land. In 1934 Carbutt estimated that some 100,000 Africans would have to be moved in conformity with this policy.[49]

The question was first discussed by Atherstone and the CNC, H. M. G. Jackson, in 1928, when Atherstone objected to Africans being resettled on unalienated Crown Land in the European Area. But, the S/N Bulawayo asked: 'where are the natives ... who have to move at once, to go? The only habitable land [in Gwelo] appears to be Crown Land, on to which the Land Department object to natives moving.' The same problem was raised the following year by the N/C Gutu, who at least had some room in his reserves, and the CNC advised that in their own interests Africans who were given notice to quit should be encouraged to settle where they might expect some security of tenure in the future.[50]

The actual passing of the Land Apportionment Act led to a certain amount of confusion within the ranks of the Native Department. Carbutt himself was 'not at all sure' about the meaning of the Act. He enquired whether new rent agreements could be entered into provided they did not remain in force after 1937, and was told that they could. He therefore instructed the N/C Makoni, who had refused to sanction new agreements, that this was not the correct procedure though the people should be warned of the 1937 deadline. A subsequent query was received from the Assistant N/C Umzingwane, who asked whether the 'protected' status of long-standing rent agreements in his district was affected when farms changed hands, and it was decided that fortuitous circumstances of this kind would not prejudice the right of such tenants to remain after 1937.[51]

Thus the problems of interpretation were gradually ironed out. In general Carbutt was prepared to sanction new rent agreements, especially in districts where there was little room in the reserves, provided it was made clear to the people concerned that they would have to move off European land by 1937. But he refused to endorse any new agreements within twenty miles of the larger towns, fearing that these would only add to the increasingly difficult problems of the urban areas.[52] Such an attitude flew in the face of the prevailing economic reality of an increasing drift to the towns in the wake of mounting rural poverty.

In many districts, and especially in those where the reserves were inadequate, European farmers predictably took the opportunity afforded by the Act to impose harsher terms on their tenants. In 1931 Carbutt pointed out that if he declined to allow agreements which in effect prevented Africans from seeking work away from the farms, they would promptly be evicted and Native Commissioners would frequently have great difficulty finding suitable land elsewhere. In Melsetter, for example, Carbutt felt obliged, against his own inclinations, to continue to sanction the 'traditional' agreements of the district whereby Africans worked on European farms on the *high veld* for three months *without pay*, as the alternative was that they would be driven off into the drought-stricken African areas in the *low veld*. Similarly, in Umzingwane he had to accept stiffer terms as 'an order to quit, would be very embarrassing to this Department'; but in Fort Victoria, where rather more land was available for Africans, he felt able to refuse an agreement which would have tied Africans to the farms completely, describing it as 'a slightly disguised form of slavery'. In Insiza, where there was congestion both in the African areas and on Crown Land, the S/N Bulawayo even approved the movement of Africans from one farm to another, noting that while it would have been preferable to have moved them into the African areas, 'the conditions prevailing in each district must be considered'.[53]

Native Commissioners were therefore able to encourage movements from European farms to the reserves only in districts where there was still room in the reserves; elsewhere they found it impossible to move the numbers who were supposed to go; and they, and the African tenants, were forced to accept the increasingly harsh terms being imposed by the European farmers.

The position of Africans living on Crown Land (formerly unalienated land) in the European Area led to a bitter controversy during the 1930s between the Native and Lands Departments comparable to the earlier struggle over the attack on the reserves in 1908–14. The Land Commission had suggested that Africans on such land should be encouraged to move into the African areas but should be allowed to remain on payment of rent[54] until the land was sold, while the Land Apportionment Act stipulated that they could remain 'on such terms and conditions as the Governor-in-Council may prescribe'.

In 1930 however, R. A. Fletcher, the Minister of Agriculture and Lands, confronted with a number of demands from European farmers that Africans be cleared off Crown Land, asked if the Native Department could define its future policy. The Acting CNC, S. N. G. Jackson, replied that: 'The position in several districts, particularly in Matabeleland, is very difficult owing to the lack of Native Reserves and to the poor or arid nature of many of these.' The Act had taken account of these difficulties and had tried to prevent Africans being made homeless through no fault of their own. He agreed that:

> We should aim at the prevention of the settlement of further Natives on unalienated land ... and that we should, as far as possible, gradually remove those who have so settled ... action on these lines has already been taken in a number of cases, chiefly in Mashonaland where the land question is not so acute. The process of adjustment must be gradual.

Moffat, who had given the Imperial Government an assurance in 1929 that Africans would not be moved from Crown Land, agreed that the position in Matabeleland was difficult and that it was a great convenience to the Government that Africans should be allowed to remain on Crown Land for the present. Subsequent extensive purchases of land by Africans in the NPA might relieve the pressure and, when funds became available, the Government might buy more land for Africans. He could not therefore move Africans simply because Europeans objected to their presence, and he reminded the Lands Department that: 'We live in a country with a large native population. It is our lot and we must put up with it.'[55]

The white farmers were disinclined to 'put up with it' however, and they continually bombarded the Native Department with requests that Africans be moved. The Matabeleland Agricultural Union, which Carbutt himself was later to represent, believed 'that the presence of native squatters on unoccupied Government Farms constituted a menace to the welfare of neighbouring European Farmers', and resolved 'that in view of the enormous permanent damage done to unoccupied Government Farms by Native Squatters the policy of permitting such squatters be investigated immediately with the object of enticing a greater European settlement which is impossible under existing conditions'. Similarly, the Matopo South Farmers' Association complained in 1933 that: 'We appear to have got no further than we were three years ago. In the meantime the position is getting worse and worse, and Europeans living next to the squatters will have to go. If you want European settlers, do please give them a chance. If you don't, say so—and we will then know where we are.' Carbutt's response to such demands was generally to explain that before the reserves could accomodate any large new influx, the development of water supplies would have to be intensified, and in any event preference would have to be given to those who were being forced off European farms.[56]

Notwithstanding such explanations, the Lands Department asked at the end of 1932 whether action could be taken 'soon'. The Acting CNC, tired of his Department being asked to solve a problem not of its making, wrote back with some asperity: 'Will you be good enough to indicate the kind of action you have in mind?' The following year there was another exchange of words when the N/C Insiza asked whether he could leave a number of Africans on Crown Land for another year, as he could find nowhere to put them. At first the Lands Department refused, so that Carbutt was forced to spell out his difficulties once more. Quite apart from the problem of finding land, he said, there had also been a food shortage in the past year. Surveys of the reserves were being made in an attempt to increase their capacity, but these would take time. If he was forced to move the Africans in question, 'the enormous difficulties of the situation will be unduly precipitated, and it will be necessary to ask the Cabinet to consider the whole question of the removal of Natives'. Faced with this virtual ultimatum, the Lands Department backed down, but it was becoming increasingly obvious that some way out of this impasse would have to be found.[57]

(v) The Land Apportionment Act Amended

Population movements on the scale envisaged by the Act were clearly impossible under the existing apportionment of land. Indeed, in the very year the Act was passed, Moffat confessed that there was a need for more land in 'the Matabele country', and in 1932 what were in effect additional reserves were assigned in Bulalima-Mangwe, Umtali, and Umzingwane, following repeated demands from the local N/Cs. Moffat explained to the Legislative Assembly that European farmers in Matabeleland were giving Africans notice to quit, and 'a very difficult position has arisen which might almost become critical. The position is that there is not sufficient land in Matabeleland'. The following year however, Moffat, afraid that his tottering government would incur further criticism, told M.P.s that no more land would be added to the reserves until they had been developed to their fullest capacity. This was clearly an untenable view, for little more than a month later Carbutt told an inter-territorial native affairs conference that the Act could not be carried out until considerable development had taken place in the reserves, and even then he doubted whether they would be able to carry the population envisaged. By August 1933 he had reached the conclusion that 'the Native Reserves of the Colony are inadequate for the accommodation of the indigenous Native population, which have to move into them in terms of the Land Apportionment Act'; a view endorsed in September by the S/N Bulawayo, who urged that: 'The principle of additions to the existing Reserves is one that merits serious consideration of the Government... However much we may accelerate development of Reserves, I am extremely doubtful whether they can absorb the whole of the population for whom provision has to be made.'

By the end of the year Carbutt was even more convinced of this, noting that: 'A few years ago the Native Reserves were considered adequate. Today they are obviously insufficient', and that in Matabeleland in particular, 'huge areas are uninhabitable because of lack of water'.[58]

It was therefore no surprise that when Huggins and Carbutt came to London in 1934 to discuss their ideas for expelling educated Africans to Northern Rhodesia and for removing all Imperial controls over Southern Rhodesia, Carbutt also submitted a memorandum in which he made it quite clear that the Act could not be implemented by 1937. Some 100,000 Africans would eventually have to be moved, but 'it would seem that the implications of the Land Apportionment Act had not been studied or understood in the past, for until recently no adequate preparation had been attempted to provide for the large number of people concerned'.[59] Surveys and the development of water supplies were being carried out, but it was impossible to meet the 1937 deadline, and he therefore proposed, and the Dominions Office agreed, that this be extended to 1941.[60]

Huggins duly passed his Land Apportionment Amendment Act (No. 31) of 1936, which extended the time limit for the abolition of rent agreements to 1941 though it stipulated that where the Minister of Native Affairs was satisfied that there was suitable land available for Africans, he could order the removal of tenants to such land provided reasonable notice was given. This was in accordance with Huggins' policy of 'bringing gradual pressure to bear, so that in 1941, we shall not be faced with the eviction *en bloc* of very large numbers of Natives'.[61]

The new Act was a stopgap rather than a solution to the problem, but the desperate conditions in many parts of the country at least forced Huggins to provide more land for Africans in Salisbury in 1935, and in Bulalima-Mangwe, Insiza, Inyanga, Marandellas, Matobo, Selukwe, and Umtali in 1936.[62] This in turn aroused farming opposition in Parliament, but Huggins informed his critics that the Coryndon and Carter Commissions had not paid sufficient attention to the quality of the land and the availability of water in the areas which they had assigned to Africans. The main reason for buying more land was to enable the Act to be carried out, for he was constantly being asked by European farmers to move Africans. The Government was desperately short of land, but as it was improving conditions in the reserves, so it was moving Africans into them. He hoped by purchasing a little more land from time to time, to complete the movement in 'say, four years', but warned that: 'If eventually it is found that there are so many natives and so little water and we cannot pack the natives into the area set aside under the Land Apportionment Act, it will have to be amended.'[63]

Thus once again the legacy of the Jamesonian era can be seen dominating land policies, in this case making full implementation of the Land Apportionment Act impossible because of the inadequacies of the reserves and the purchase areas. Subsequent policy was much concerned with the rather sterile aim of 'packing the natives into their own areas'.

3 ACTUALITY

(i) White Farmers, Black Peasants

European agriculture in the period 1926–36 was remarkable more for its political than its economic successes. The momentum of previous years was not maintained, and the great Depression brought many white farmers to the verge of bankruptcy.

The comparatively static nature of European agriculture in this period is illustrated by the number of Europeans employed in the industry, which rose from 3,995 in 1926 to 4,172 in 1931 and then dropped to 4,009 in 1936. This was in spite of an increase in the annual expenditure of the Department of Agriculture from £91,874 in 1928–9 to £262,957 in 1936–7. Tobacco enjoyed another brief boom, following an increase in Imperial preference, and production soared from 5,659,809 lbs in 1925–6 to over 19 million lbs the following year and 24,943,044 lbs in 1927–8. But once again, as in 1913–14, Rhodesian tobacco growers had over-reached themselves, for the overseas market was saturated, vast unsalable stocks accumulated in British warehouses, the order books were closed and a great many tobacco farms were abandoned, with some 700 producers, three-quarters of the total, eliminated. As the official history of the industry puts it, 'nearly all the progress of the previous ten years was wiped out in one season'.[64] In response to this collapse, cigarette manufacturers began making a determined, and successful, attempt to penetrate the local African market to the exclusion of the traditional 'Inyoka' tobacco. But immediately there followed a slowing down of mining and industrial activity within the country, and in 1930 South Africa decided to impose a quota system on duty-free tobacco from Rhodesia. These factors, plus the coming of the Depression, resulted in production dropping to 8,644,390 lbs in 1930–1, before picking up again to 22,401,707 lbs in 1935–6. In 1936 the Tobacco Marketing Act introduced greater Government control over the industry with the compulsory registration of all growers, and by giving the minister powers to fix minimum prices to regulate production and control exports.

A similar pattern can be observed in regard to the maize industry, where production rose from 1,393,654 (203 lb) bags in 1925–6 to 1,985,848 bags in 1935–6, and exports rose from 434,592 (200 lb) bags in 1926 to 745,010 bags in 1930. But by the beginning of 1931, with the export price falling from 11/– to 3/4d., most European maize growers were facing bankruptcy. Many increased their acreages in an attempt to offset falling prices, but this led to rampant soil erosion,[65] while their economic plight was worsened by increasing competition from African growers. The Government promptly came to their rescue with the Maize Control Acts of 1931 and 1934 which will be examined shortly, whose main effect was to keep European maize growers on the land though prices remained low. In 1936 maize exports totalled 396,000 bags.

Though the numbers of African-owned cattle continued to increase from 1,197,466 in 1926 to 1,547,623 in 1936, European-owned cattle showed a decrease for the first time dropping from 991,216 to 753,419 in the same period as many white ranchers attempted to jump onto the tobacco boom, or switched to dairying or cotton growing. In 1930 an export market to Britain of chilled and frozen meat was made possible by Rhodesia Railways' acquisition of nine refrigerator wagons,[66] but almost immediately an outbreak of foot-and-mouth disease resulted in a two-year embargo on all agricultural exports, with the exception of tobacco and citrus. All in all, 'the early thirties were years of severe stress and strain for the hard-pressed Rhodesian farmer'.[67]

How did white Rhodesian farmers react to such stresses and strains? As one might expect, they called upon the Government to bail them out and to assist them 'to achieve a return large enough for them to continue farming and live according to "civilized standards"'.[68] Such standards could only be maintained in normal times by paying extremely low wages, and during the Depression many farmers simply stopped paying their African workers altogether.[69] Like European farmers elsewhere at this time, they also raised the spectre of African competition,[70] and feared that unless they were protected from such unfair competition the country would 'surely revert to a native State, as is happening in Nyasaland'.[71] That such fears were taken seriously even at the Colonial Office can be seen from a decision in 1933 to forbid the British Central Africa Company to grow maize in Nyasaland in case this should result in competition for the tottering maize industries of Southern Rhodesia and Kenya.[72] So the European farmers, whose 'methods of cultivation remained inefficient' according to Gann,[73] demanded greater government participation in production and marketing, which resulted in the setting up of Tobacco and Dairy Control Boards and the passing of Maize Control Acts. Moreover, like the Kenya settlers, they resented the very limited attempts by the Government to aid African agriculture,[74] and they were especially hostile to Jowitt's Native Development Department[75] which was promptly emasculated when Huggins came to power. The Great Depression indeed left a deep scar on the white Rhodesian farmers for it was they who provided the largest single group amongst the ranks of the unemployed whites, and many more were only rescued from this fate by a combination of loans from the Land Bank (amounting to over one million pounds in 1934) and a three-year moratorium in 1933 on all instalment payments for farms. In Kenya too, it was the Land Bank which 'helped to maintain impoverished settlers on their farms ... and ensured the continuance of white farming in the colony'.[76]

Perhaps the best illustration of the way in which European farmers sought to protect themselves is provided by the Maize Control Amendment Act of 1934. The Act was highly complex, but broadly speaking it 'discriminated in favour of the small white as against both the larger white and the African grower'.[77] It proved in fact to be a good deal more detrimental to African farmers than similar, and contemporary, pieces of legislation in Kenya and Northern Rhodesia.[78] The pro-settler Governor, Sir Herbert Stanley, pronounced himself 'not a devotee of the principle of maize control, but I regard its introduction ... as a necessity if European maize farmers ... are to be kept on the land'.[79] The African maize growers of the Belingwe District found, however, that whereas they had previously managed to sell some 10,000 bags a year, after the Act they were able to sell none at all.[80] In Mazoe, Africans had once sold maize locally at 6/– to 7/– per bag; after the Act they were obliged to carry it long distances and sell at 2/– to 2/6d. per bag. Not surprisingly, a meeting of the Mazoe Native Board in 1934 expressed its 'grave dissatisfaction'. One speaker asked:

> Why does the Government do everything to help the white farmer and nothing to help us? ... The Government is killing us by this Act which we do not understand. It is made to do good to the white man and harm to us ... Why are not our Native Commissioners consulted before things like this happen and why are we also not consulted? This thing is not fair. It is put on us by force.[81]

The local N/C wrote that: 'Never before during my 30 years service in this Department have I heard natives express themselves so strongly or so openly display a spirit of antagonism to any law as they did to the Maize Control and Cattle Levy Acts.'[82] The antagonism was clearly justified, for even Carbutt concluded that 'it is quite impossible for Natives to benefit in any way' from the Act;[83] while his successor, Charles Bullock, made it clear to Stanley that 'he disagreed entirely with the principle of maize control, and that he had no confidence in the fair-mindedness of the Maize Control Board'.[84] A Government report of 1944 was even more scathing:

> It is difficult to conceive of a principle more inequitable or dangerous than that of deliberately paying to the better-off producers of a State more for a product than is paid to less well-off people in the same State for the identical product. It is the antithesis of assistance according to need and of the universally acclaimed principle of raising rather than depressing the lower classes.[85]

Maize Control was perhaps the most vivid example of the impact of the Depression on African peasant farmers, though the Europeans also successfully pressed the Government 'to decrease the Native production of wheat'.[86] Rather more sober, but none the less revealing, is Arrighi's estimate that whereas in 1903 some 70 per cent of African cash earnings had come from the sale of agricultural produce, in 1932 the proportion had slumped to below 20 per cent.[87] As Carbutt put it: 'From the Natives' personal point of view, the situation is very harrassing: he cannot sell cattle: he cannot get cash for his maize ... and he has great difficulty in obtaining employment, and when he does get it, it is at a reduced rate of pay.'[88] Increasingly, Africans sought refuge in the reserves, where at least there were no rents to pay and they were 'encouraged' to do so by the attitude of most white farmers who, with their farms at a standstill, often changed labour into rent agreements in search of easy cash but in contradiction to the aims of the Land Apportionment Act;[89] and who also demanded, as we have seen, that Africans be evicted from Crown Land to make way for future settlers. What was particularly galling about such evictions was the tiny proportion of European land which was actually being put to good use,[90] and the fact that so much of the land from which Africans were moved lay idle and unused, as happened in Northern Rhodesia too in the 1930s.[91] Thus in Mtoko, 'covetous eyes are always cast on the mile after mile of vacant land from which the Natives have been turned off in the past'.[92] So the reserves became increasingly overcrowded and overstocked, and since it was no longer possible in many areas to live off the land, people were forced to turn more and more to wage-labour—by 1932 over 80 per cent of African cash earnings were coming from this source.[93] Thus a process of involution, of gradually falling productivity modelled closely on the South African pattern, was set in motion, which the attempted 'development' of the reserves and the Native Purchase Areas could do little to check.

(ii) The Native Purchase Area

The Native Land Board began its work of demarcating and selling individual holdings in the NPA at the height of the Depression and the resulting European fears of African competition. Not unnaturally, progress was extremely slow. In the years 1931–6 (as table XII reveals), 548 Africans, only 80 of them from Matabeleland, bought a total of 188,186 acres at a cost of £40,376, giving an average holding of 343 acres at a cost of £74. The average price per acre was 4/3d., but prices ranged from 3/– in Gwaai to 7/6d. in Sabi, and were, according to Jennings, 'in many cases in excess of that charged for similar land in the European Area'. Whereas Europeans bought their farms with a 5 per cent deposit and paid the remainder over a period of nineteen years, Africans had to

TABLE XII

Number and Location of Farms Sold in the Native Purchase Areas, 1931–6
(i) Mashonaland

District	*1931–2*	*1932–3*	*1933–4*	*1934–5*	*1935–6*	*1936*	*Total*
Bikita			5				5
Charter			5	2	6	3	16
Chibi		1				3	4
Chilimanzi							0
Darwin						1	1
Gutu		9	20	22	6	3(−1)	59
Hartley				6	18(−2)	3(−1)	24
Inyanga							0
Lomagundi	2		1			1	4
Makoni		1		3	5(−1)	5	13
Marandellas							0
Melsetter	5	22	11	1	8	18	65
Mrewa		1	(−1)				0
Mtoko						1	1
Salisbury	10	11	12(−1)	5(−1)	8(−2)	4	46
Umtali		1	11	11	3	45	71
Victoria	15	5	22	16	52(−1)	51(−1)	159
Totals for Mashonaland	32	51	85	65	100	135	468

deposit 10 per cent and pay the balance within ten to fifteen years. In addition, Africans were unable to raise mortgages or get loans from the Land Bank. Notwithstanding these great disadvantages, Jennings reported in 1936 that 'instalments of the purchase price are being promptly paid and there are few outstandings'.[94]

The amount of land purchased, though small, is illustrative of what might have happened had previous administrations been willing to allow Africans to exercise their legal right to buy land anywhere. 46,966 acres had been bought on the 'open' market over a period of thirty-five years; 188,186 acres were bought in five years in a period of severe depression.

Progress was, however, much slower than it might have been for a number of reasons. Firstly there was political opposition from Africans, especially in Matabeleland, which recorded only 9 out of a total of 184 applications for land received by June 1931. Explaining the reasons for this, Carbutt wrote:

TABLE XII (contd.)
Number and Location of Farms Sold in the Native Purchase Area, 1931–6
(ii) Matabeleland

District	*1931–2*	*1932–3*	*1933–4*	*1934–5*	*1935–6*	*1936*	*Total*
Belingwe		1					1
Bubi	1	1					2
Bulalima-Mangwe	1				3	2	6
Gwanda					2		2
Gwelo			8	4	8	1	21
Insiza			5		3	30	38
Matobo							0
Nyamandhlovu			2	2	4(−1)	1(−1)	7
Selukwe						3	3
Totals for Matabeleland	2	2	15	6	19	36	80
Totals for Southern Rhodesia	34	53	100	71	119	171	548
Area of Farms (acres)	16,181	25,923	45,269	28,116	35,232	37,465	188,186
Cost of Farms (£)	2,864	5,231	9,577	5,998	7,910	8,796	40,376

I think the Independent Industrial and Commercial Workers' Union had more to do with the attitude of the Matabele Natives towards the Land Apportionment Act than anyone else, because they openly advised Natives not to buy land, which they alleged already morally belongs to them... Whenever I have had a discussion with Matabele on the question of buying land, it has been clear that their attitude towards the Land Apportionment Act is hostile. Should active steps be taken to remove large numbers of Natives from the European areas, I have no doubt we would encounter passive resistance to some degree.

During the early 1930s, the ICU, the Rhodesian Bantu Voters' Association and the Matabele Home Society were all embarrassing the Government by preaching 'the subversive doctrine that the land belongs to the Native and not to the European'. The message scarcely needed to be spelt out, for in Fort Victoria the older people at least believed 'that the land was theirs until they were deprived of it by the European and now the European is making them pay for what by right is still their property'.[95] Such attitudes were scarcely compatible with what the Land Board was trying to achieve.

Equally serious was the problem of the 50,000 African 'squatters' already living in the NPA. Friction between the new owners and these 'squatters' was constant. Prospective purchasers, often with their origins in another part of the country or even outside Rhodesia, were subjected to considerable harassment. In Bulalima-Mangwe it was reported that purchasers were put off by the fact that the land was already closely settled; while at Fort Victoria the S/N was worried by the same problem, for at a meeting in the Mshawasha NPA 'Chief Mapanzure raised the point that as he was the owner of the land why should he purchase it'. This echo of the 'subversive doctrines' of the African political associations was repeated in Insiza, where Chief Maduna who lived in the middle of the Godhlawayo NPA, had his protests upheld and was assured that 'his' land would not be sold during his lifetime and that alienation would accordingly only take place in the outlying parts of the NPA.[96] Nothing could better illustrate the inherent conflict of interests between local peasants and incoming master farmers.

Attempts were made to resolve this conflict in certain districts by the now traditional expedient of moving the 'squatters' into the reserves in the hopes that this would encourage the new African settlers. In 1932 all the inhabitants of the western part of the Mshagashe NPA in Fort Victoria who had not applied for land were removed. The following year 1,000 people were moved in Darwin, 300 in Marandellas, and Chief Gobere and his people in Chilimanzi. In 1935 nearly 500 were moved in Darwin, but here the N/C reported that the people of Chimanda Reserve were tending to settle along the rivers in the NPAs, and as a result 'continual surveillance has had to be exercised to prevent wholesale migration'. The following year in Fort Victoria, however, the N/C was unable to evict the numerous occupants of the Mshawasha NPA because of foot-and-mouth disease, with the result that 'they are continually intefering with, and threatening, legitimate applicants for farms'.[97]

Another major problem was that many of the NPAs required considerable development to make them habitable; water supplies were desperately needed throughout Matabeleland, and new roads were required in many areas. By the end of 1936 only £13,901 had been spent on the provision of boreholes, weirs, and dams, while a mere 100 miles of roads had been constructed.[98] The work was kept to the barest minimum by the prevailing financial stringency, and the results were often disappointing. At Insiza for example, £1,551 was spent on drilling eleven wells, only two of which were successful. Four weirs were then constructed at a cost of £962, but they served only a dozen farm holdings. Inevitably this raised the purchase price of the land. Many Native Commissioners asked in vain for the provision of water supplies; the N/C Gwanda pointed out that the scarcity of water throughout the NPAs was a serious obstacle to their being taken up, and the N/C Nyamandhlovu believed that because of the 'entire lack of surface water' the development of water supplies should precede, and not be dependent on, applications for the land. Elsewhere it was not just lack of water but the quality of the land itself which retarded settlement. Not a single holding had been taken up in Inyanga by 1936, a fact which the N/C attributed squarely to

> the barren nature of some of the areas allocated for purchase by natives. In one of these areas . . . there is not, at present, one native village. In addition to this the areas are far too remote to expect the better class of native to settle in them; add to this factor the hopeless condition of the road and one can hardly wonder that no enterprising natives have negotiated for the purchase of any land.

Two years later he added for good measure that 'they are poorly watered and are said to be malarial'.[99]

More money was in fact spent on buying out white farmers than on developing the land in the NPA. The Government felt itself under 'a very strong moral obligation' to buy out the handful of Europeans who found that their farms were situated within the NPA, provided they would accept reasonable compensation.[100] In practice, many of these farmers held out for high prices and negotiations were protracted. By 1936 the Government had managed to re-purchase some 150,000 acres at a cost of £25,420. Similarly, over half of the 46,966 acres which Africans had managed to buy on the open market before 1930 was included in the European Area under the Land Apportionment Act, and was bought back by the Government at a cost of £5,745, with the owners given the option of acquiring land in the NPA (see Appendix II, pp. 279–82).

One final factor contributing to the lack of development within the NPAs was that the majority of the new owners were urban workers with a little capital who bought land for their retirement and became, at best, 'week-end farmers'. In addition: 'The grant of a Native [Purchase] Area plot was often used as a method of rewarding an African who deserved well of the Government. Such Africans frequently remained in Government service and were therefore unable personally to occupy their plots.' So, following in the European tradition, a pattern of absentee landlordism became established in the NPA. In Salisbury in 1936 the N/C reported few signs of settlement in the Muda NPA where ten holdings had been bought, while an agricultural demonstrator visiting the Rowa NPA in Umtali found that 'nearly all of the farm owners there were itinerating back and forth to jobs in Umtali and the only farming done was done by the wives, who paid no attention whatever to any advice he gave them'. In districts where farms of over 500 acres had been sold, it was found that 'some plot-holders have reverted to the methods of shifting cultivation'. At Insiza, where 38 Africans had bought land by 1936, the N/C acknowledged that: 'The Native Purchase Areas have not solved the problem. The natives who have taken up land are earning fair wages in towns and elsewhere ... 90 per cent are not in personal occupation of their holdings.' All in all, the results were disappointing; 'not all landlords fulfil optimistic expectations as to the magic effect of ownership of land' wrote the CNC in 1939, while neither Lord Hailey nor Governor Evelyn Baring were impressed by what they saw in the NPA in the early 1940s. Belatedly, the Land Board and Huggins decided in 1939 that priority would in future be given to those applicants—and by now there were over a thousand on the waiting list—who agreed to take up immediate occupation of their farms, and only after they had been satisfied would the question of allowing Africans the European privilege of buying farms for retirement be considered.[101] Progress in the NPA thus lagged a long way behind the original expectations of the Land Commission, a fact which no doubt provided some comfort to the hard-pressed white farmers.

(iii) The Development of the Reserves

'Were the reserves to be centres of development producing cash crops in possible competition with white farmers, or were they to remain labour reservoirs, self-sufficient in food crops and refuges for the old and refractory?', asks Steele somewhat rhetorically.[102] The easiest way of answering this question is to look at the amount of money which was spent on 'developing' the reserves. In the year 1940–1, £14,107 was voted for the 'development of agriculture in native [purchase] areas and reserves', a sum which, as Lord Hailey observed, 'seems somewhat exiguous compared with the £208,127 provided in the vote for European agriculture'.[103] This was obviously a good year, for Arrighi estimates that during the war years African agriculture received one-fortieth of the amount voted to the European sector.[104] Confirmation of such parsimony is provided by Governor Baring, who noted in 1943 that the Native Reserves Trust Fund was operating on a budget of about £10,000 of which only about £3,000 came from Government, and he concluded that: 'Insufficient money is spent in the Reserves', and that the number of Europeans attached to Alvord's staff before 1939 was 'almost ludicrously insufficient'.[105] It is not unreasonable to deduce therefore, that while the Southern Rhodesian Government was doing its utmost to foster and protect the growth of the European agricultural sector, it had not the slightest intention of promoting a 'green revolution' in the

African areas. 'Development' was designed primarily to make possible the segregation envisaged in the Land Apportionment Act.

The predominantly Shona-speaking agricultural demonstrators[106] faced innumerable problems in their work. Of the first eleven who went into the reserves in 1927, only three were able to get their full quota of ten plot-holders. In the Selukwe Reserve, Africans were 'very suspicious. Most of them think this is some scheme of the Government to take their land away from them'; while in the Chikwakwa Reserve, Salisbury, they saw it as 'an attempt to test the agricultural potentialities of the reserves with a view to their being exploited for the benefit of the white population.' These identical fears, nurtured not on account of some universal 'peasant conservatism' but based on the past experience of the Company's attack on the reserves and the recommendations of the Coryndon Commission, did not subside with the passage of time. In Gwelo in 1932 there was one rumour that the Government having proved the value of the soil would sell the reserves to Europeans, and another that everyone's lands would be reduced; while the following year it was reported that the demonstration plots would be taxed. In Darwin too, 'most extraordinary rumours were circulated'; the plots would be taken over and the owners forced to surrender their crops to the Government, Africans restricted to small plots only, and taxation would be increased. Finally, an official report of 1944 noted that:

> Some of the Natives, particularly those with a smattering of education, are very suspicious of the motives behind the present drive by the Native Agriculture Department to improve the productive capacity of Native lands. They fear that any success will be a reason for depriving them of portions of the Reserves set aside for them or a ground for refusing their demands, which are insistent, for an extension of the Reserves.[107]

Such suspicions went a long way towards undermining the effectiveness of the demonstration work.

African peasant farmers were also extremely reluctant to abandon their traditional methods of agriculture which, however quaint they might appear to European eyes, at least guaranteed their survival. The element of risk involved in adopting new methods was obviously very great. The demonstrator was a government employee with a guaranteed wage. If his crop failed, he had some security to fall back upon. Not so the subsistence farmer whose entire livelihood was derived from the soil. If his crop failed he might well face starvation. But even if he did adopt the methods used by the demonstrators and thereby increased the size of his crop, there was no guarantee that he would be able to find a market for it. 'Overproduction has proved a disadvantage rather than a blessing in recent years', wrote the N/C Charter in 1932; while the Assistant N/C in the remote Shangani Reserve declared that: 'There is no doubt that the lack of markets in this Reserve gives the native no encouragement to better his methods or increase his crop.' Alvord himself was forced to conclude that:

> The greatest handicap to our efforts to introduce better methods of tillage among reserve Natives is the lack of marketing facilities. In many areas it is impossible for Natives to sell for cash, and they are forced to take salt or cloth for their grain, or they cannot sell it at all ... [this] imposes a hand to mouth existence upon him under which he cannot progress.[108]

These difficulties were compounded by the attitude of European farmers who became increasingly critical of the demonstration work. In 1934, for example, they successfully campaigned for a reduction in the number of demonstrators being trained—for a short while Carbutt imposed a complete standstill on training—and in Fort Victoria, where the demonstrators had encouraged African farmers to grow maize successfully for the first time, Alvord was shunned and treated as a pariah by the Europeans whenever he went to town.[109] Alvord took the view, in words which were neatly excised from one of his annual reports, that European farmers who could not stand African competition 'would do the most good for Rhodesia by moving out'.[110] The Maize Control Amendment Act amply met the demands of the white farmers. In Fort Victoria, prior to Maize Control, 'the demonstration work was really going ahead in leaps and bounds, and in certain areas the demonstrators were unable to cope with the large number of Natives interested in the better methods of farming'. But after the Act all this stopped and the people asked: 'Why should we grow crops and sell them at less than we used to?', and complained: 'Yes, we told you when you first brought demonstrators on to the reserves that they had come to try out the land, and later the Government would either take it or our crops.'[111] An identical feeling was expressed at Matobo where, as a result of the Act, Africans could no longer sell their surplus maize and the Native Board 'wanted to know why Native Demonstrators had been sent into the Native Reserves to teach them modern methods of growing maize'.[112] It cannot have been an easy question to answer.[113]

The policy of centralization also ran into difficulties. It was first adopted in the Selukwe Reserve in 1929 following active propaganda by Alvord, the Native Commissioner, and the demonstrator. To begin with 'innumerable objections were raised against the proposals which would strike at the very root of a system they had been carrying on for many years', but overcrowding was so serious that 14 headmen, with 1,224 people under them, were eventually won over to the idea. The results were so successful that Chief Nhema asked for the whole reserve to be centralized. After Alvord had completed his surveys the headmen assigned arable land to the families under their control; the cattle then had direct access to dipping tanks across the grazing lands and thus no longer tramped over the arable land of other farmers which had been the cause of great friction in the past. By 1933 the N/C could report that the scheme 'has proved a very great blessing', and part of the reason for this was clearly that the objectives of the scheme had been patiently and exhaustively explained to the people.[114]

When it became obvious that the Selukwe scheme was a success, work was begun in other reserves and by 1936 an estimated total of 1,203,637 acres had been centralized, a figure which was doubled by 1938. Five years later the total had almost reached 7½ million acres. But all did not go as smoothly as at Selukwe. Firstly there were a number of personality clashes between Alvord and the Native Commissioners. Several Native Commissioners disliked Alvord because he was an American, a trained scientist, and was encroaching on 'their' territory.[115] There was a major row between Alvord and the Assistant N/C Goromonzi over the centralization of part of the Chindamora Reserve in 1932–3, and the work inevitably suffered as a result. Other Native Commissioners were simply not interested in the demonstration work.[116] In some reserves the very nature of the land proved an obstacle. In the Soshwe Reserve, Marandellas, for example, it was found to be impossible to centralize the reserve properly since there was insufficient arable land to go round, while the grazing lands 'would only be suitable for mountain goats'. Elsewhere, African opposition was strong. In Gwelo, 'the very mention of limiting lands roused a storm of protest', but the scheme was pushed through notwithstanding, as it was in Hartley. By the end of 1933, Alvord had become convinced that 'conditions on some reserves can only be remedied by making centralization compulsory', and as a result an additional agriculturist and two surveyors were added to his staff to speed up the work.[117]

Centralization could in fact only be a success where it was requested by the people themselves following careful explanation from officialdom. But all too often little or no explanation was given—in fairness Alvord was desperately short-staffed—and the scheme was steamrollered through regardless of African wishes and sometimes in the teeth of outright opposition. In such circumstances it was regarded as yet another device for reducing African land holdings.[118]

Other branches of the development programme appeared to raise as many problems as they solved. Soil surveys, which would have been invaluable at the time of the Coryndon Commission, were carried out over a total of 5·8 million acres in 23 reserves in the years 1933–6, and the findings were sometimes alarming.[119] A soil conservation officer, the first appointment of its kind in Africa, was assigned to Alvord in 1936,[120] but once again this merely served to highlight the problem. A commission of 1939 found that contour ridging was urgently needed over 4 million acres of the reserves, that at the existing rate of progress it would take 250 years for this to be done, that most of the grazing land in the reserves was in a state where 'rehabilitation appears almost impossible', and that many of the African areas appeared to be 'heading for ruin'.[121] Attempts to encourage voluntary de-stocking in the face of increasing erosion in the reserves[122] met with a uniformly hostile response. Africans saw no reason to sell at the prevailing low prices, and when they did sell European farmers were quick to complain that 'their' market was being interfered with. When the Government provided grade bulls in Fort Victoria, the people were afraid that it would seize 'all native cattle as soon as they had been sufficiently improved to make it worth while'.[123] A Native Department conference in 1935 learnt that large areas of Bulalima-Mangwe were 'denuded entirely of all vegetation' and were simply 'bare places'. Roads were being washed out and forming into huge *dongas*; also rivers had silted up and were 'one mass of sand'. Hence: 'If conditions go on as they are now, unless very active steps are taken, real measures, large areas will be a howling wilderness in a comparatively short space of time.'[124] Finally, the attempts to develop water supplies were very far from confirming the optimism of the N/C Bulalima-Mangwe, who wrote in 1925 that 'waterless tracts in Reserves will soon become a thing of the past'.[125] There were occasional successes, notably in Mtoko and Gwelo, but these were more than outweighed by the overall lack of success, especially in Matabeleland where it mattered most. In Bulalima-Mangwe itself, only 19 out of 48 boreholes sunk, at a cost of £9,000, had proved effective, while the results in the Semokwe Reserve, Matopo, were 'most disappointing ... costly and futile'.[126] Moreover, by the mid-1930s a further complication had arisen when it was found that overgrazing near conservation works was producing serious erosion, and Native Commissioners were therefore warned to limit the number of cattle watering at each dam or weir. One attempted solution had thus merely produced a further problem.

It was thus obvious by 1936 that conditions in the reserves were generally deteriorating rather than improving and that Alvord and his team, with the very meagre resources made available to them, were basically fighting a losing battle. This in turn meant that the Land Apportionment Act, in so far as it involved the movement of thousands of Africans from European to African land, could not be brought into effect. It also meant that as overcrowding grew and it became less and less possible even to subsist on the land, so more and more Africans would be forced out in search of wage-labour.

(iv) The Movement into the Reserves

In 1941 Huggins told Parliament that in the ten years since the passing of the Land Apportionment Act, an estimated 50,000 Africans had been moved into the reserves.[127] Allowing for the customary vagaries of population figures, this estimate was probably not far from the reality.

Using the CNC's figures, it appears that in the years 1926–35[128] the total African population increased by 30·3 per cent; that in the reserves by 32·2 per cent; that on unalienated land by 36 per cent; but that on alienated European land by only 11·7 per cent.[129] These figures imply that a total of around 30,000 Africans moved off European farms either into the reserves or onto unalienated land. Thus, despite the intentions of the Land Apportionment Act, the movement off European land had actually diminished somewhat for in the previous decade the number moved was around 60,000. The diminution of scale was not for the want of trying of course, but was rather a reflection that the reserves could no longer support 'immigration' of such magnitude. Indeed, there were occasional small movements from the reserves onto European farms caused by overcrowding, or lack of water, or simply the desire to move to better land. These served to illustrate that economic and ecological factors were frequently operating at variance with the wishes of those who had framed the Act. Another reason for the slowing down was that many of the large ranching companies in Matabeleland virtually gave up ranching as a result of the Depression, and turned instead to the much easier business of 'kaffir farming',[130] which at least had the merit of allowing Africans to remain on the land.

Africans naturally resented having to move. In Insiza the N/C reported: 'They have for such a long time been in occupation of alienated lands ... that they have regarded such occupation as a right.' The N/C Lomagundi observed of those who were forced to move in 1933: 'They made every peaceful effort to remain on farms in the locality in which they had lived for very many years past, a locality they were attached to by ties of sentiment, tribal and family history, as well as for economic reasons.' Indeed, such was the strength of these ties that Carbutt believed that if Native Commissioners attempted to initiate large-scale evictions in Matabeleland, 'we would encounter passive resistance to some degree', while the N/C Bubi believed that force would have to be used to make Africans go to the Shangani Reserve, and the N/C Umtali, writing of Chief Umtasa and his 5,500 followers who had been rack-rented by absentee landlords for forty years felt, 'it will require force even to expel them from their ancestral home'.[131] Here, very clearly, lie the origins of the more recent Tangwena affair, and it is interesting that in 1934 Chief Chipunza of Rusape took the unusual step of writing to the CNC:

> I would like to express my grievances in these hard times, as it really comes as a great clash against all of us Natives especially to me, because all my land has been sold to the White farmer. I have no small reserve left for me. Now I am told that the Government wishes to drive all Natives from the farms of the White people. So that I shall have no place where I shall live and sweep the graves of my Fathers. Whereas I have always been thinking as a friend of the British Government from the beginning. I have been a great

> help to the pioneers. When my father was asked to help the White man, by giving them some people to make roads, he willingly sent a number of carriers and Native messengers. He willingly gave this help. When the Missionary came to ask for a site to build his Church and School, although my father had little knowledge of the good of this work, he granted it with all his heart ... When we surrendered to the cruel Shangans and Matabele, they demanded us to be bored in both our ears, then we were free men and counted as one of them. When a hateful Jew got exemption from Rome, he was a free man, counted as one of them (Acts 16 v. 37–39). But when we have surrendered and are baptised and exempted by the British laws, we are told to go into exile and be packed up like swarms of bees in a strange, hilly, dry country, with our wives, children and cattle.[132]

The Native Commissioners who were faced with the thankless task of directing these population movements came increasingly to realize that the only possible solution was to provide more land for Africans. In other words, if the reserves were ever to fulfil the function they were now being called upon to play, they would have to be greatly extended. Only then could possessory segregation be made to work.

The first request for more land, from Gwanda, was received as early as 1926. The following year, the N/C Umzingwane noted that: 'It is now practically impossible for natives, turned off farms, to find land in this district on which to settle.'[133] By 1932 the situation had become sufficiently critical for the Government to buy more land in Umzingwane, Bulalima-Mangwe, and Umtali.[134] Elsewhere, Native Commissioners continued to draw attention to the impossibility or undesirability of implementing the Act. In 1934 the Assistant N/C Fort Rixon, a sub-district of Insiza where over 90 per cent of the African population lived on European land, feared with some justification that:

> The rigid application of the provisions of the Act would result in the loss of almost all native wealth in the form of cattle; the rapid development of a nomadic people moving from employer to employer and gradual disappearance of the last vestiges of tribal control. Some farmers are eagerly anticipating the expulsion of squatters from European areas because they hope it will result in the flooding of the labour market with a consequent fall in wages. It seems likely that their expectations will be realised.[135]

In 1935–6 more land totalling about half a million acres was provided in eight districts,[136] usually in areas already heavily populated. Such land provided a breathing space, but little more. By 1936 most Native Commissioners were being confronted with problems similar to those expressed by the Acting N/C Insiza:

> The thought of even normal yearly increases in any area is a disquieting one; the thought of the transfer of possibly thousands of natives from the European to the inadequate native areas during the next few years is alarm-

ing. More land, much more land, is required for native occupation if the provisions of the Land Apportionment Act are to be carried out ... It seems to me that some of the land now held by Europeans should be given to the natives who will use it, whereas the Europeans have held the land for years without making any use of it.[137]

(v) The 'African Voice'

(*a*) *Introduction*

By 1927 Europeans had long since forgotten their fears of a further African rising comparable to those of 1896, but in that year their complacency was rudely shattered by a strike of 3,500 workers at the Shamva gold mine which was only broken up when troops were despatched to the area.[138] The strike came, as Governor Chancellor admitted, as 'a great surprise to everyone. People in Rhodesia had no idea that natives were capable of such secret and concerted action'.[139] The incident was something of a false alarm, however, for unlike the Copperbelt strikes of 1935 and 1940, it was not followed eventually by the emergence of a strong trade union movement; conditions on the Northern and Southern Rhodesian mines were very different. Less dramatic, but more persistently disturbing for the authorities were the activities of the new, urban based political associations, the recrudescence of the Ndebele royalist movement, and what the Government liked to call 'pseudo-religious sects and factions' which engaged in 'activities antagonistic to the welfare of the Natives and militating against the stability of the State'.[140] There was even an unsuccessful attempt in 1936 to form a branch of Marcus Garvey's Universal Negro Improvement Association.[141]

In the light of conditions discussed in this chapter—the Depression and the persistent movement of thousands of Africans into already overcrowded reserves with a consequent growing dependence on wage-labour—it is hardly surprising that the land question should have formed the major political grievance of the late twenties and early thirties. In 1927 the Acting CNC believed that 'insecurity of land tenure is the basis of the feeling of discontent, intensified by the present drought conditions in Matabeleland and the Coast Fever outbreak';[142] while in 1932 Governor Rodwell observed that 'poor harvests, foot-and-mouth disease, and lack of markets for cattle and maize have hit the natives hard'.[143] Even the old evil of non-payment of wages remained 'a far too frequent occurrence'.[144] At virtually every *indaba*, chiefs complained that they were losing their authority because their followers were being scattered all over the country, and by 1936 the hard-pressed N/C Insiza had come to the conclusion that: 'The Land Apportionment Act needs amendment... as many of the natives will not be in a position to buy land. The wages are so low that a native cannot provide for his family and to have a healthy family it is essential for him to have land on which to produce food for them.'[145]

So the Native Department, the declining quality of whose personnel was becoming yearly more apparent to Governor Rodwell,[146] found itself increasingly challenged as more and more African voices began to be raised. It responded in predictable ways. It attempted to play off one association against another, it hounded the more dangerous leaders, it contemplated the provision of more football pitches, it set up a 'loyalist' association and an official newspaper for Africans and, in an attempt to restrict African politics to a local level and to approved channels, it created native boards in the reserves, these being considered preferable to 'independent associations of Natives, operating without supervision'.[147] The extent of its concern may be measured from the fact that by as early as 1926 the Native Department was afraid to allow further *indabas* to be held in Bulawayo, in case the presence of 'a rabble of employed Natives' might lead to 'irrelevant and undignified interpolations by people unrepresentative of national feeling, over whom the chiefs would exercise no control'.[148] At much the same time, the Nyasaland Government was taking somewhat more sympathetic note of 'an intelligentsia class ... which ... reasons, considers, criticizes, and has passed beyond the stage of being ordered to do things without being told why'.[149]

(*b*) *The Ndebele Royalist Movement*

In Matabeleland the land problem was yearly growing more acute, and Africans complained bitterly that the Government did nothing to protect them from the exactions of the European farmers. In the circumstances, it was not difficult for Rhodes and Albert Lobengula, grandsons of the last Ndebele king, to revive the royalist movement previously headed by Nyamanda and to form an alliance with the Matabele Home Society, founded in 1929.

In 1927, in the wake of the general disappointment with the recommendations of the Land Commission, Albert and Rhodes began collecting money in an attempt to buy 'all land North of the railway and South of the Shangani Reserve and extending Eastwards to the Lower Gwelo Reserve'. This was in essence another attempt to secure a National Home, where all the Ndebele could live together instead of being 'a scattered brotherhood',[150] but it stood no prospect of success in the light of the existing situation and of Government policy which was totally opposed to any resurrection of Ndebele unity.[151] Hence the Matabele Home Society was forbidden to enter the reserves for a period in 1929, Rhodes Lobengula was not allowed to accept the chairmanship of the Rhodesian Bantu Voters' Association or to take up land in a NPA in Matabeleland, though Albert was offered a farm in Fort Victoria.[152] Rhodes' great popularity and his 'political pretensions' were a source of great concern to the Native Department, and in 1932 he was given a fifteen-month suspended sentence, to the chagrin of Carbutt, who wanted him behind bars. Eventually the Rhodesian Government, arguing that 'it would probably be a cheap riddance of him at £2000', paid off his debts and bought him a farm in the Cape—the South African Government had refused to allow him to settle in Natal—on condition that he did not return to Rhodesia. He left in January 1934 and died in the Cape three years later.[153] Albert too fell foul of the authorities. In 1933 he was sentenced to nine months' imprisonment for stock theft, but was released after three months 'as a gesture of good will towards the Matabele people, so that they could join in the celebration of the 40th Anniversary of the occupation of Matabeleland, without that sense of distress which they may have felt, at the incarceration of the eldest grandson of their late King'.[154] Royalist sentiment survived the departure of Rhodes and Albert however, for as late as 1937 the Umzingwane Native Board was calling for the appointment of a 'principal chief' of the Ndebele nation, and for Umzingwane to be made the 'Native Capital of Matabeleland'.[155] The requests met with the inevitable official hostility.

(*c*) *The ICU*

The association which caused the Rhodesian Government the greatest discomfort was undoubtedly the militant Industrial and Commercial Workers' Union, which originated as a branch of Clement Kadalie's parent organization in South Africa but which assumed its independence in 1928 in return for legal recognition by the Government.[156]

The ICU began its operations in Bulawayo but quickly extended to Salisbury and other towns, and then to the alarm of the Native Department began to spread out into the rural areas. Membership increased from 108 in 1928 to 4,910 in 1932, by which time there were thirteen branches.[157] So seriously were its activities viewed that Masoja Ndhlovu, the Bulawayo secretary who was later to be detained in the 1959 Emergency, was granted the rare privilege of an interview with Moffat in 1929, and again in 1932. The ICU was essentially a workers' movement, but no organization operating in Bulawayo could ignore the land question, and it therefore included among its aims the securing of land more suitable than the existing reserves. It also brought a new style and tone to African politics in Rhodesia. Weekly meetings, announced by posters, were held in Bulawayo which attracted audiences of up to 400 and the attention of the C.I.D. The audience heard Ndhlovu proclaim that: 'The land grabbers are taking our country! ... All good land is being taken by Europeans and natives are being driven into the hills and the mopani veld where only animals can live.' He referred to white farmers as 'our greatest enemies ... the greatest labour exploiters. Many natives work on farms for less than 10/– per month. The farmer would be crippled without native labour'. One speaker added that 'if our land was productive we should refuse to work for the white man', while another warned that 'the white man will eventually buy all your cattle and all your land and you will have no place to go... the time is coming when you will all be slaves to the farmers'.[158]

This was all rather too much for the Native Department to swallow, and it began to hound the leadership. Charles Mzingeli, the Salisbury secretary, was forbidden to enter the reserves in Mashonaland and was convicted of libelling 'Wiri' Edwards, the long-serving N/C Mrewa, while Ndhlovu was found guilty of the same offence against Carbutt, whom he described, not without justice, as 'a bad man and an oppressor of natives'.[159] He too, after a successful recruiting drive in 1931–2, was eventually banned from entering the reserves and NPAs in Matabeleland, and was imprisoned for holding a meeting in Filabusi without permission. Thomas Mazula, the ICU's first chairman, was given the option 'offered' to all civil servant members of the ICU, of resigning from the Union or losing his job as a government messenger. He chose to lose his job. Despite such persecution, the ICU continued to operate until 1936 with weekly meetings still being held at Umtali and Penhalonga in 1935, and in general it succeeded in creating 'a rebellious atmosphere in the Reserves, to such an extent that Natives were displaying definite though passive resistance to orders and in one district they went so far as to boycott the Native Commissioner's Office'.[160] It also persuaded many Ndebele not to buy land in the NPA on the grounds that the land already belonged to them, and it made its influence felt even on some of the Government sponsored native boards.

(*d*) *The Native Boards*

The Government responded directly to the success of the ICU by inaugurating native boards in the reserves in 1931 under the chairmanship of the local Native Commissioners. The boards were to comprise both 'tribal' and 'elected' representatives, and would, it was hoped 'provide the politically minded Natives with a safer outlet for his thoughts, than such uncontrolled societies' as the ICU and the Matabele Home Society[161] and, in one district at least, it was thought that they might 'be useful in counteracting the uncontrolled influence of the Watch Tower movement'.[162] The boards might eventually pave the way for native councils modelled on the Transkeian system for which provision had been made in the 1923 Constitution, but here the Rhodesian authorities faced the problem that 'our existing African institutions are not in a fit state to carry out Indirect Rule; although it is possible that they might gradually be revivified, if that should be deemed to be desirable'.[163]

Altogether 39 boards were established in the years 1931–3, and their meetings provide eloquent testimony of what the Depression really meant for rural Africans. Poverty was widespread,[164] wages were low, work was difficult to find, cattle and maize could not be sold, and conditions on farms were often deplorable. Hence there were numerous requests for a reduction in taxation and dipping fees, and for the fencing of reserves because, 'if our cattle stray on to the farms they are impounded and it costs a lot of money to get them released'.[165] As at *indabas* in the past, land grievances were prominent and nearly every board asked at one time or another for additional reserves, most vociferously at Umzingwane where, 'in some instances speeches almost reached the invective'.[166] The Native Commissioners, who chaired the meetings and attempted, not always successfully, to keep a tight rein were unable to do anything to redress the most serious grievances; indeed they were only able to spend £1 per meeting on entertainment which tended to produce 'a feeling of contempt'.[167] Hence many boards withered and died unlamented, though others soldiered on until the end of the 1930s.

Another reason for the failure of the boards in some districts was the extent of ICU influence which was revealed. 'I.C.U. propaganda' was 'apparent throughout the speeches and resolutions' of the 1931 Insiza Board meeting, while in Umzingwane, Ndhlovu, and Mandaba, a member of the Matabele Home Society 'endeavoured to discredit the Board' and 'to persuade the Natives not to have anything to do with the Board as it would be useless, and the resolutions would never reach the Government'.[168] The N/C refused to allow them to address the meeting. At the Filabusi sub-district of Insiza in 1931: 'Although few of the delegates elected by natives were young men, modern aspirations were not found lacking and the majority of the resolutions seemed prompted by I.C.U. influence.'[169] Two years later, one Nduna addressed the Native Commissioner 'in a contemptuous manner' and said 'that as far as he was concerned he would only serve under the chairmanship of Masoja' [Ndhlovu].[170] This view, supported by the powerful Chief Maduna, prevailed to such an extent that the Government was forced to drop the idea of a board, and turn instead to the sterile expedient of 'fostering ... the Matabele Caste system' since 'a more pronounced tribal control would secure better administration than *Vox Populi* methods'.[171]

4 CONCLUSION

The period 1926–36 was one of increasing racial animosity. Europeans were beginning to fear Africans as competitors and were attempting to hinder African advancement, while European farmers took advantage of the paucity of African land in Matabeleland to turn the screw on their tenants. At the same time Africans were becoming increasingly vocal and critical of a land policy which squeezed them from their homes, moved them to distant areas which were generally inhospitable and far from markets, and offered in exchange a few purchase areas of exceedingly dubious value. Indeed by the late 1930s so notorious were Southern Rhodesian land policies, that migrant workers from Nyasaland and Northern Rhodesia had already decided that they wanted nothing to do with any proposed amalgamation of the three territories. Even before the passing of the Land Apportionment Act, the District Commissioner (D/C) at Nkhata Bay in northern Nyasaland, reported that the Lakeside Tonga refused to countenance any further grants of land to Europeans, because 'being widely travelled, they have seen the effects of land alienation in South Africa and Rhodesia'.[172]

So the divorce between the theory and the reality of segregation persisted, indeed increased, for if the segregation which so many white farmers demanded was ever to become a reality they would have to accept a substantial curtailment of their extensive and under-used land holdings. This they were not prepared to accept, and so the dilemma continued, with Africans suffering acutely as a consequence.

NOTES

1. *Report of the Chief Native Commissioner for the year 1933* (Salisbury 1934), 5.
2. The air mail service began in January 1932, and the telephone link followed in December 1933.
3. When asked by the 1925 Land Commission whether Africans 'should have the same right of progress as the European', Huggins replied 'Yes, as long as it is harmless'. ZAH 1/1/1, Evidence of G. M. Huggins to Land Commission, 3 March 1925, 72.
4. D.O. 35/390, Memo by Carbutt, July 1934. He even aired this view in print: C. L. Carbutt, 'The Racial Problem in Southern Rhodesia', *NADA*, **12,** 1934, 6–11.
5. The estimated number of African voters was 53 in 1908, 34 in 1922, 74 in 1930, and less than 130 in 1939. B. A. Kosmin, 'Ethnic and Commercial Relations in Southern Rhodesia: A Socio-Historical Study of the Asian, Hellenic and Jewish populations, 1898–1943', Ph.D. thesis, University of Rhodesia, 1974, 124; M. C. Steele, 'The Foundations of a "Native" Policy in Southern Rhodesia, 1923–33', Ph.D. thesis, Simon Fraser University, 1972, 491.
6. As N/C Belingwe in 1910, Carbutt had proposed a £3 tax on 'idlers'. He advocated the ending of existing rent agreements in central Matabeleland by 1937, though these had been expressly permitted to continue by the Land Apportionment Act. After retirement he represented the Matabeleland Agricultural Union—he was the owner of four farms, totalling 25,595 acres—and endorsed the 'grotesque proposal' that 'the crops which natives should be allowed to grow should be confined to those which do not compete with European-grown crops'. He was accordingly dropped by the Dominions Office as potential 'second string' for the Deputy Chairmanship of the Native Reserves Board of Trustees. D.O. 35/827, Stanley to Harding, 16 September 1937; D.O. 35/820, Stanley to Harding, 15 July 1937.
7. D.O. 35/371, Minute by Bottomley, 27 February 1934.
8. *Report of the Chief Native Commissioner for the year 1933* (Salisbury 1934), 5.
9. Jowitt was a protégé of C. T. Loram and had been prominent in the Natal administration. He was a practising Christian, who maintained close links with the missionaries. Four days after the election of 1933, Huggins placed Jowitt's Department of Native De-

velopment under his control as Minister of Native Affairs. Jowitt subsequently resigned, on finding the new constraints unbearable. Steele, 'Native Policy', 322.

10. D.O. 35/389, Minute by Sedgwick, 27 October 1933.

11. 'The Secretary of State's approval was necessary both for the 1934 [Industrial Conciliation] Act and for the 1937 amendment but, once approval has been given to the legislation, the opportunities for the Secretary of State's intervention have disappeared.' Similarly, 'It is, of course, not practical politics to "disallow" the [Natives (Urban Areas) Accommodation and Registration] Bill because it re-enacts the principle of the 1936 Act'. D.O. 35/845, Minute by Gibson, 15 July 1942; D.O. 35/1167, Minute by Machtig, 29 March 1946.

12. D.O. 63/5, Minute by Davis, 11 May 1928.

13. D.O. 35/486, Minute by Pitblado, 5 November 1935.

14. D.O. 35/486, Minute by Tait, 18 July 1935. Sometimes the whole thing boiled down to a question of semantics, as when Harding suggested with reference to the Industrial Conciliation Bill that 'even if the principle was accepted the wording of the Bill might be improved and made less "anti-native" in appearance'. D.O. 35/845, Minute by Tait, 17 June 1937.

15. D.O. 35/390, Minutes of Meeting in Colonial Office Conference Room, 16 July 1934. Bottomley, permanent under-secretary at the Colonial Office, wrote scathingly that if Carbutt's scheme was carried out, 'Southern Rhodesia would become a European's paradise and the Union Government, profiting by so good an example, would proceed to decant its own native population, with a similar opportunity of servility, into Nyasaland, Tanganyika and Uganda'. D.O. 35/371, Minute by Bottomley, 27 February 1934.

16. D.O. 35/389, Minute by Sedgwick, 7 October 1932. There were dissident views however. H. J. Stanley, soon to become Governor of Southern Rhodesia wrote, somewhat prematurely in 1934, that 'the franchise of the Colony cannot indefinitely be left capable of producing a state of affairs in which the Europeans might become a hopeless minority of the Electorate'. D.O. 35/354, Stanley to Harding, 24 September 1934.

17. Cmd. 5218, *Despatch from the Governor of Southern Rhodesia relating to the Proposed Amendment of the Southern Rhodesia Constitution* (London 1936).

18. R. H. Palmer, 'Land in Zambia', in Palmer (Ed.), *Zambian Land and Labour Studies, Vol. 1*, National Archives of Zambia Occasional Paper 2 (Lusaka 1973), 56–66.

19. Ranger has written the first in a projected series on East, Central, and Southern Africa, covering the period between early resistance and modern mass nationalism. T. O. Ranger, *The African Voice in Southern Rhodesia* (Nairobi 1970).

20. Southern Rhodesia, *Report of the Land Commission, 1925* (Salisbury 1926), 6. A. C. Jennings, the Assistant Director of Native Lands, believed: 'The Native landholders can be regarded as a Native agricultural peasantry and as time goes their production will be very considerable indeed. If the marketing of their produce can be organised and directed in the right channels it should add materially to the national wealth of Southern Rhodesia.' S 1542/L4, Memo by Jennings, 21 November 1936.

21. S 924/G1/1, Secretary to Premier to CNC, 26 September 1927.

22. S 138/21, S/N Bulawayo to CNC, 21 August 1928, N/C Gutu to S/N Victoria, 19 March 1930.

23. The High Commissioner had originally appointed the outgoing CNC, H. M. G. Jackson, but he withdrew in a fit of pique after his brother, S. N. G. Jackson, was not appointed to succeed him, and was passed over by Carbutt.

24. D.O. 35/831, Stanley to Harding, 1 May 1937.

25. S 138/21, Jennings to Secretary to Premier, 19 January 1931. The regulations appeared as Government Notice No. 222 of 3 April 1931.

26. S 138/21, Secretary to Treasury to CNC, 22 May 1931.

27. S 1542/N2, Report of the Insiza Native Board Meeting, 27 March 1931. Similarly, a Zionist church leader 'could not see any authority in the Bible for the sale of land to anybody'. S 1542/M8D, N/C Melsetter to CNC, 9 September 1935.

28. D.O. 63/6, Memo by H. M. G. Jackson, 1 February 1929.

29. S 138/52, CNC to S/N Victoria, 31 December 1931; S 138/21, CNC to N/C Melsetter, 9 November 1931; S 138/81, CNC to Secretary to Premier, 5 September 1932; S 138/21, CNC to Secretary to Premier, 30 November 1932.

30. S 138/21, S/N Victoria to CNC, 24 October 1931, Jennings to CNC, 16 November 1931; S 924/G1/4, Minute by Legal Adviser, 9 November 1931; Government Notice No. 737 of 18 December 1931; S 138/21, CNC to Secretary to Premier, 16 October 1931; S 924/G6/2, Minutes of Native Land Board, 27 July 1933; S 1542/I1, CNC to Secretary to Premier, 21 August 1933; S 138/11, Jennings to CNC, 7 March and 11 April 1932.

31. S 1542/N2, CNC to Secretary to Premier, 11 May 1931.

32. D. A. Robinson, 'Land Use Planning in Native Reserves in Southern Rhodesia', *Rhodesia Agricultural Journal*, **50**, 1953, 328.

33. R. van Zwanenberg, *The Agricultural History of Kenya*, Historical Association of Kenya Paper No. 1 (Nairobi 1972), 12–13.

34. G. K. Garbett, 'The Land Husbandry Act of Southern Rhodesia', in D. Biebuyck (Ed.), *African Agrarian Systems* (London 1963), 190.

35. NUA 5/1/1, Conference of Superintendents of Natives, 16 October 1909.

36. In 1924 the Native Reserves Trust Fund was set up to administer the c. £2,500 per annum derived from mission and trading site rents, which the Company had previously pocketed. The money was mostly spent on roads, water supplies, and the introduction of high grade stock. Two schools were set up, in 1920 at Dombashawa in the Chindamora Reserve, Salisbury District, and in 1921 at Tjolotjo in the Gwaai Reserve, Nyamandhlovu. The schools at first concentrated on homecrafts and other activities which would not arouse European suspicions, and it was not until November 1924 that the first agricultural demonstrators were enrolled. The Company's main efforts appear to have gone into the sinking of a few boreholes in the Gwaai Reserve in 1915 and in some other Matabeleland reserves from 1921. But the situation was little better in Kenya, where 'the work of the Agriculture Department was extended into the reserves for the first time only in 1923'. E. A. Brett, *Colonialism and Underdevelopment in East Africa* (London 1973), 196.

37. H. L. Shantz, 'Agriculture in East Africa', in T. J. Jones (Ed.), *Education in East Africa* (New York 1924), 353–402.

38. L. H. Gann, *A History of Southern Rhodesia* (London 1965), 273. Lord Harlech, who as High Commissioner for South Africa met Alvord in 1943, noted that he 'was champion wrestler and leader of his college American football team in the Far West. His size in collars is 18½ inches. He has no superfluous fat. He has the largest wrists of any man I have ever seen'. D.O. 35/1168, Note by Lord Harlech on a visit to Shiota Native Reserve, 21 May 1943.

39. N. H. Wilson, 'The Development of Native Reserves', *NADA*, **1**, 1923, 88.

40. *Report of the Chief Native Commissioner for the year 1932* (Salisbury 1933), 2–3.

41. *Official Year Book of the Colony of Southern Rhodesia No. 3* (Salisbury 1932), 674.

42. M. P. K. Sorrenson, *Origins of European Settlement in Kenya* (Nairobi 1968), 236, 253.

43. D.O. 35/1169, Baring to Machtig, 15 June 1943; N 3/24/1/4, CNC to Secretary, Department of Administrator, 20 July 1922.

44. W. Allan, *The African Husbandman* (Edinburgh and London 1965), 335.

45. Cattle were 'confined to the grazing areas during the summer and only allowed access to arable areas after harvest'. W. B. Cleghorn, 'Pasture Problems in Native Reserves in Mashonaland', *South African Journal of Science*, **47**, 1950, 141.

46. S 138/52, Assistant N/C Marandellas to N/C Marandellas, 12 May 1931, N/C Charter to CNC, 23 December 1931, CNC to Secretary to Premier, 5 January 1932; 'Report of the Agriculturist, Native Department, for the year 1935', in *Report of the Chief Native Commissioner for the year 1935* (Salisbury 1936), 30.

47. S 235/493, Verbatim report of proceedings at the Conference of Superintendents of Natives and Native Commissioners, 12–16 December 1927, 14–20; S 348, CNC to all Native Department Stations in Southern Rhodesia, 10 January 1928; *Report of the Chief*

Native Commissioner for the year 1935 (Salisbury 1936), 4; S 235/487, Minutes of the Native Affairs Advisory Committee, 23–25 February 1933; S 235/488, Minutes of the Salisbury Senior Native Commissioners' Conference, 27–29 March 1935, 213.

48. S 138/21, CNC to Secretary, Department of Lands, 4 November 1931.

49. D.O. 35/354, Memo by Carbutt, July 1934.

50. S 138/21, CNC to Atherstone, 2 April 1928, S/N Bulawayo to CNC, 21 August 1928, CNC to S/N Victoria, 15 August 1929.

51. S 138/11, CNC to Secretary, Law Department, 13 April 1931, Solicitor General's Opinion No. 143, 15 April 1931, CNC to N/C Makoni, 20 May 1931, Memo by CNC, 4 July 1933; S 138/21, Assistant N/C Umzingwane to S/N Bulawayo, 15 May 1933.

52. S 138/11, CNC to Secretary to Premier, 20 December 1932.

53. S 138/11, CNC to Secretary to Premier, 8 April 1931, N/C Melsetter to CNC, 13 June 1931, CNC to Secretary to Treasury, 24 February 1932, CNC to S/N Victoria, 13 February 1932, N/C Insiza to S/N Bulawayo, 2 May 1931, S/N Bulawayo to CNC, 6 May 1931.

54. The Rhodesian Government decided that from the beginning of 1929 all Africans on Crown Land, in the European and the Unassigned Areas, should pay an annual rent of £1. But CNC Taylor protested against the blanket rate, arguing that Africans in many districts would be unable to pay, and proposing that Native Commissioners be consulted first. This was accepted, and in May 1928 Taylor's successor proposed, on the basis of reports submitted, that Africans in the Bikita, Lomagundi, Ndanga, Sebungwe, and Wankie Districts, and in parts of Darwin, be exempted from the rent and that all past arrears be written off. The Cabinet accepted this, which meant that some 15·1 million of the total 17·8 million acres of the Unassigned Area were exempted, and that only an estimated 15,000 Africans elsewhere were liable for the rent. Nevertheless, the rent remained highly unpopular and, during the Depression years, produced a further exodus into the reserves in districts where this was still possible. S 138/12, Secretary to Cabinet to CNC, 23 November 1927, CNC to Secretary to Premier, 24 November 1927, Secretary to Premier to CNC, 30 January 1928, CNC to Secretary to Premier, 8 May 1928.

55. F 48/N3, Fletcher to Moffat, 3 October 1930, Acting CNC to Secretary to Premier, 13 October 1930, Minute by Moffat, 16 October 1930, Secretary to Premier to Secretary, Department of Lands, 15 December 1930; D.O. 63/6, Memo by Moffat, February 1929.

56. S 1542/R3, Secretary, Matabeleland Agricultural Union, to CNC, 7 October 1933, President, Matopo South Farmers' Association, to Secretary, Matabeleland Agricultural Union, 8 November 1933; S 138/21, CNC to Secretary to Premier, 31 August 1931, CNC to Secretary, Department of Lands, 4 November 1931.

57. S 138/52, Secretary, Department of Lands, to CNC, 2 December 1932, Acting CNC to Secretary, Department of Lands, 12 December 1932, N/C Insiza to S/N Bulawayo, 19 July 1933, CNC to Chief Clerk, Department of Lands, 8 September 1933.

58. S 1542/L1, Minute by Moffat, 10 June 1931; Southern Rhodesia, *Legislative Assembly Debates*, **12,** 3 May 1932, col. 1481; **13,** 29 April 1933, col. 727; S235/484, Minutes of the Native Affairs Conference at Victoria Falls, 8–10 June 1933, 10; S 1542/I1, CNC to Secretary to Prime Minister, 21 August 1933; Hist. MSS. AT 1/2/1/11/1, S/N Bulawayo to CNC, 21 September 1933; S 138/72, Note by CNC on Assistant N/C Goromonzi to N/C Salisbury, 13 December 1933; S 1542/R3, CNC to Huggins, 15 November 1933.

59. Elsewhere he wrote: 'I have never given an undertaking at any time to remove the Natives from Crown Lands by any given date, nor have I ever been instructed by any Minister to do so. When I assumed office as Chief Native Commissioner no steps had been taken, so far as I am aware to enable the provisions of the Land Apportionment Act to be carried out.' S 1542/R3, CNC to Huggins, 15 November 1933.

60. D.O. 35/354, Memo by Carbutt, July 1934. It was also proposed that the Act be amended so that the clause allowing Africans to 'own or occupy' land assigned to them in the urban areas should stipulate that only leasehold tenure be permitted. The Dominions Office agreed that this was not unreasonable, especially as during the discussions Huggins was 'very clear that there would be great difficulty if anything

more was contemplated'. D.O. 35/354, Minutes by Tait and Harding, 19 and 26 July 1934.

61. S 1561/17, Secretary for Native Affairs to Huggins, 5 June 1936. There was no debate before the Bill became law; Huggins simply informed members that is was impossible to meet the deadline, and that the Bill would enable the movement to proceed continuously as the land became available during the next five years. *Legislative Assembly Debates*, **16,** 8 June 1936, col. 2838.

62. The Northern Rhodesian Government did much the same thing in the years 1938–41.

63. *Legislative Assembly Debates*, **16,** 7 May 1936, cols. 1509–10; 28 May 1936, cols. 2427–8.

64. F. Clements and E. Harben, *Leaf of Gold: The Story of Rhodesian Tobacco* (London 1962), 114. The farmer, Rawdon Hoare, passing through Headlands, between Salisbury and Umtali, in the early 1930s, noted: 'On either side stretched abandoned lands, cultivated and prosperous before the tobacco slump four years before. Here and there among the *kopjes* stood houses, fallen and decayed, once the homes of planters who had left them to the mercy of the elements. No sounds of life could be heard, the gay prattle of native labourers having long since departed from those melancholy fields.' R. Hoare, *Rhodesian Mosaic* (London 1934), 130.

65. M. C. Steele, '*Children of Violence* and Rhodesia: A Study of Doris Lessing as Historical Observer', *Central Africa Historical Association*, Local Series Pamphlet **29,** 1974, 3. Hoare wrote in 1934 that: 'Maize land had always been considered a good investment, so the slump of 1930 was a great shock to the country as a whole. £3 and £5 an acre had been paid for a maize farm in the past; to-day, even at 30s. an acre, they would prove difficult to sell.' Hoare, *Rhodesian Mosaic*, 55–6.

66. A. H. Croxton, *Railways of Rhodesia* (Newton Abbot 1973), 172.

67. Federation of Rhodesia and Nyasaland, *An Agricultural Survey of Southern Rhodesia*, Part II *Agro-Economic Survey* (Salisbury 1961), 17. One positive development at this time however was the introduction by Rhodesia Railways of a road motor service. The first, in June 1927, ran: 'From Sinoia to Miami, seventy-two miles away, the centre of the mica mining district. Within two years no less than fifteen road services to feed the railway had been started, of which eight were subsidised by the Government to serve developing areas. Motor lorry services were a completely new feature of life in Rhodesia and quickly proved of immense value in helping farmers to market their produce and obtain their supplies ... The Road Motor Services played a very important role in opening up promising farming country and in providing cheap transport for both agricultural and mining produce, so bringing extra traffic to the rail system.' The mileage of these services rose from 266 in 1927 to 1,626 in 1937. Croxton, *Railways*, 158–9.

68. D. J. Murray, *The Governmental System in Southern Rhodesia* (Oxford 1970), 80.

69. In 1931 there were 357 convictions of Europeans for this crime, compared to 217 in 1913. Kosmin, 'Ethnic and Commercial Relations', 120. On the key importance of low wages, 'the difference between the cost of production and the yield of our maize crop is well known to be small', wrote the Auditor General in 1927. 'Without our native labourer is it not probable that the wealth produced by the maize farmer would not have been produced at all? And though the margin of profit in regard to Tobacco is far higher, would it not be most seriously affected by the substitution of white for native labour if indeed it would be possible to grow the crop at all?' S 480/148. Auditor General to Colonial Secretary, 3 January 1927. I am indebted to Ian Phimister for this reference.

70. As Jack Woddis has observed of European farmers in general: 'Even with the best lands in their possession they have had to be constantly subsidised and aided by governments, and "protected" against African competition by the introduction of various restrictions or limitations on African agriculture, and by the introduction of various discriminatory measures in favour of the European farmer.' J. Woddis, *Africa: The Roots of Revolt* (London 1960), 8. Similarly, Barber concludes that in Rhodesia 'European agriculture

has ... been made a sheltered industry'. W. J. Barber, *The Economy of British Central Africa* (London 1961), 24.

71. Southern Rhodesia, *Report of the Committee of Enquiry into the Economic Position of the Agricultural Industry of Southern Rhodesia* (Salisbury 1934), 30. Evidence submitted to this Committee demanded that 'all natives farming in European areas should be removed to the native areas at once; that no native-produced article should be sold in the European areas and vice versa except under permit'. *Report*, 27.

72. C.O. 525/147, Minute by Shrikdale, 20 January 1933. In Kenya in the 1930s, the colonial Government 'used every possible means at its disposal to maintain European white farming in existence'. R. M. A. van Zwanenburg with A. King, *An Economic History of Kenya and Uganda 1800–1970* (Dar es Salaam 1975), 209.

73. L. H. Gann, *The Birth of a Plural Society* (Manchester 1968), 149. This was confirmed by Governor Rodwell, who wrote in 1930 that many European farmers were: 'At last awakening to the necessity of proper methods of fertility, rotation, and green manuring, but the awakening has come too late. Thousands of acres of the best soil in the Colony have been robbed of their productivity and the owners cannot face the expenditure necessary to restore it.' This was especially so since many maize farmers 'are at the end of their resources and are being carried by the Banks'. D.O. 35/370, Rodwell to Thomas, 17 October 1930.

74. Sorrenson, *Origins*, 236.

75. 'To the farmers', writes Murray, 'the abolition of the Native Development Department became a positive objective. "The Native Development Department", a speaker told the Annual Congress of the Rhodesia Agricultural Union in 1931, "was teaching the natives to grow maize, not to grow *mhunga* and kaffir corn. The Native Department would not be so foolish as to do that sort of thing".' Murray, *Governmental System*, 290.

76. van Zwanenburg with King, *An Economic History*, 289. In 1934 Hoare wrote that: 'In Salisbury to-day the majority of [African] hotel and household servants can be seen riding expensive bicycles, dressed in attire of the latest fashion, while many white men, on account largely of the tobacco slump, plough their way on foot along the dusty roads.' Hoare, *Rhodesian Mosaic*, 65–6.

77. Gann, *Southern Rhodesia*, 298. For a detailed study, see C. F. Keyter, 'Maize Control in Southern Rhodesia 1931–1939: The African Contribution to White Survival', M.A. thesis, University of Rhodesia, 1974.

78. van Zwanenberg, *Agricultural History*, 21; K. Vickery, 'Aspects of Plateau Tonga Economic History', in R. H. Palmer (Ed.), *Zambian Land and Labour Studies, Vol. 3*, National Archives of Zambia Occasional Paper 4 (Lusaka 1977), 70.

79. D.O. 35/842, Stanley to MacDonald, 6 April 1937.

80. S 1542/N2, Report of the Belingwe Native Board Meeting, 13 May 1937.

81. S 1542/N2, Report of the Mazoe Native Board Meeting, 12 and 19 June 1934.

82. S 1542/N2, N/C Mazoe to CNC, 12 July 1934. The Cattle Levy Act increased slaughter fees from 2/6d. to 10/– which, in conjunction with low prices, acted as a strong deterrent against Africans selling their cattle.

83. S 1542/M2, Carbutt to Huggins, 7 February 1935.

84. D.O. 35/842, Stanley to Harding, 21 July 1937.

85. Southern Rhodesia, *Report of Native Production and Trade 1944* (Salisbury 1945), 62.

86. S 1542/A4, Secretary, Rhodesian Wheat Growers' Association, to Director of Native Development, 4 June 1935.

87. G. Arrighi, 'Labour Supplies in Historical Perspective: A Study of the Proletarianization of the African Peasantry in Rhodesia', *Journal of Development Studies*, **6**, 1970, 216. Ranger writes that 'the 1920s saw the triumph of European agriculture over African'. Ranger, *African Voice*, 112.

88. S 1561/38, CNC to Secretary to Premier, 2 September 1931.

89. Labour agreements in Inyanga were said to be 'insufferably severe ... six months of the year at ten shillings a month in return for very limited arable, grazing and residential

rights'. S 235/516, Report of the N/C Inyanga for the year 1938. On personal relations, a visiting official of the Nyasaland Government observed: 'A system of benevolent paternal autocracy still prevails. The law interferes only if a native complains.' Nyasaland Protectorate, *Report on Nyasaland natives in the Union of South Africa and in Southern Rhodesia* (Zomba 1937), 20.

90. In Insiza, where the N/C reported that 'large tracts of land are held by Europeans but nothing is being done with it ... It seems to me', he added, 'that some of the land now held by Europeans should be given to the natives who will use it, whereas the Europeans have held the land for years without making any use of it'. Hist. MSS. AT 1/2/1/11/4, N/C Insiza to S/N Bulawayo, 19 May 1936.

91. Palmer, 'Land in Zambia', 60–2.

92. S 235/514, Report of the N/C Mtoko for the year 1935. In the Shire Highlands of Nyasaland at this time, there was 'a strong feeling of resentment that unoccupied estates should be allowed to lie fallow and undeveloped, while across the boundary the Trust Land native cannot find room to plant his food crops'. C.O. 626/18, Report of the Provincial Commissioner, Southern Province, for the year 1938, 18.

93. The CNC, H. M. G. Jackson, noted in 1930: 'The position now is that £5 no longer means the acquisition of wealth (a cow), quite apart from the depreciated purchasing value of £5. A cow must be dipped: dipping costs money: the children are expected in most localities to go to school: school fees are increasingly exacted: school children are expected to be simply clad: European clothing and European utensils (including ploughs) have become essentials and are no longer luxuries.' S 138/55, Memo by CNC, 27 January 1930.

94. S 1542/L4, Memo by Jennings, 21 November 1936; Steele, 'Native Policy', 447–8.

95. S 1542/M8A, CNC to Huggins, 15 November 1933; S 138/18, N/C Bulalima-Mangwe to S/N Bulawayo, 10 April 1931; S 1542/N2, S/N Victoria to CNC, 8 June 1931.

96. S 138/81, Jennings to CNC, 3 May 1932, S/N Victoria to CNC, 2 November 1932; D.O. 35/371, Rodwell to Thomas, 21 October 1933.

97. S 924/G1/4, Jennings to CNC, 11 April 1932; S 235/511, Reports of the N/Cs Darwin, Marandellas, and Chilimanzi for the year 1933; S 235/514, Report of the Acting N/C Darwin for the year 1935; S 235/515, Report of the N/C Victoria for the year 1936.

98. Boreholes, weirs, and dams were provided in the Chibi, Chilimanzi, Hartley, Salisbury, Bulalima-Mangwe, Gwelo, Insiza, and Nyamandhlovu Districts; roads in Bikita, Gutu, Melsetter, Salisbury, Umtali, Victoria, Belingwe, Bulalima-Mangwe, Insiza, and Selukwe.

99. Steele, 'Native Policy', 453; S 235/513, Reports of the N/Cs Gwanda and Nyamandhlovu for the year 1935; S 235/515, Report of the N/C Inyanga for the year 1936; S 235/516, Report of the N/C Inyanga for the year 1938.

100. F 34, Fletcher to Moffat, 29 December 1930, Cabinet Resolution No. 1781, 8 January 1931.

101. D.O. 35/1167, Baring to Machtig, 5 October 1943; S 235/515, Report of the N/C Salisbury for the year 1936; S 1542/D7, Alvord to Secretary for Native Affairs, 16 March 1939; S 235/515, Report of the N/C Insiza for the year 1936; *Report of the Chief Native Commissioner for the year 1939* (Salisbury 1940), 9; D.O. 35/825, Draft Confidential Report by Lord Hailey on Southern Rhodesia, August 1941; D.O. 35/1167, Baring to Machtig, 14 July 1943; S 1542/L4, Jennings to Secretary for Native Affairs, 16 May 1939; *Legislative Assembly Debates*, **19,** 5 June 1939, col. 1027.

102. Steele, 'Native Policy', 379.

103. D.O. 35/825, Draft Confidential Report by Lord Hailey on Southern Rhodesia, August 1941. In 1936–7, £13,546 was voted for African agriculture, compared to £262,956 for European agriculture.

104. Arrighi, 'Labour Supplies', 220.

105. D.O. 35/1169, Baring to Machtig, 15 June 1943; D.O. 35/1162, Baring to Machtig, 21 October 1944. Baring also believed that 'the great weakness in the very considerable efforts made here to improve native agriculture ... is the lack of Native Administration

authorities inspiring respect among Africans in the rural areas'. D.O. 35/1163, Baring to Machtig, 6 May 1944. Elsewhere in Africa, colonial governments used 'Native Authorities' to push through unpopular programmes of agrarian reform.

106. Baring noted in 1943 that 'only nine out of 106 Agricultural Demonstrators are Matabele ... and few Matabele have received Master Farmers' Badges'. D.O. 35/1169, Baring to Machtig, 15 June 1943.

107. E. D. Alvord, 'Development of Native Agriculture and Land Tenure in Southern Rhodesia', unpublished 1958, 15; S 138/72, Alvord to CNC, 15 November 1927; S 235/505, Report of the N/C Salisbury for the year 1927; S 235/525, Report of the N/C Gwelo for the month June 1932; S 235/526, Report of the N/C Gwelo for the month June 1933; S 235/511, Report of the N/C Darwin for the year 1933; *Report of Native Production and Trade*, 25.

108. S 235/510, Report of the N/C Charter for the year 1932; S 235/513, Report of the Assistant N/C Shangani Reserve for 1935; 'Report of the Agriculturist, Native Development, for the year 1934', in *Report of the Chief Native Commissioner for the year 1934* (Salisbury 1935), 18.

109. Alvord condemned Carbutt's ban as 'a very retrogressive step'. Alvord, 'Development of Native Agriculture', 20, 27.

110. S 138/72, Alvord to CNC, Draft Annual Report for 1928, 14 January 1929.

111. S 1542/M2, Assistant Agriculturist to CNC, 19 January 1935.

112. S 1542/N2, Report of the Matobo Native Board Meeting, 14 June 1937.

113. A few successes were recorded however. In 1929 the first African farmers' associations were founded at Marandellas, Salisbury, and Umtali, which soon developed into co-operatives. In Selukwe, the first area to undergo centralization, the N/C was able to report in 1936 that: 'The practice of cultivating smaller areas, and doing so with method and skill is thoroughly impregnated in the District. No longer is it necessary to hold meetings, and drive modern practice into their minds.' But Selukwe was exceptional, and a rather more typical picture obtained at Salisbury, where 'it is extraordinary that even after 40 years of close contact with the European methods a great number of Natives still continue their old slapdash methods of agriculture'. S 235/515, Report of the N/C Selukwe for the year 1936; S 235/514, Report of the N/C Salisbury for the year 1935.

114. S 235/507, Report of the N/C Selukwe for the year 1929; S 235/511, Report of the N/C Selukwe for the year 1933.

115. Thus the Acting S/N Victoria reacted to the suggestion that the Zimutu Reserve might be centralized in the following terms: 'Mr. Alvord is quite unaware of the fact that the natives arrange the division of land themselves and do it extremely well. If it is ever necessary to adopt his methods I will let him know.' S 170/1161, Acting S/N Victoria to CNC, 16 December 1931. Zimutu Reserve was in fact centralized in 1933.

116. 'It's an awful pity we still have some Native Department Officials who don't take the interest they should in this agricultural Demonstration work. Some never attend a [before harvest] meeting and others don't even bother to notify the natives by a messenger.' S 1542/A4, Assistant Agriculturist to Alvord, 19 May 1939.

117. S 235/515, Report of the N/C Marandellas for the year 1936; S 235/511, Report of the N/C Gwelo for the year 1933; S 235/527, Report of the N/C Hartley for the month June 1934; 'Report of the Agriculturist, Native Department, for the year 1933', in *Report of the Chief Native Commissioner for the year 1933* (Salisbury 1934), 19.

118. A number of writers have commented on centralization. Floyd has noted that the early work was crude in places, with insufficient attention paid to obtaining a suitable ratio between arable and grazing lands with the result that re-centralization was later necessary in some reserves. The Mangwende Commission (in reality Holleman) claimed that it 'changed the character of the traditional Shona village, in that it restricted its mobility and tended to petrify the essentially flexible nature of its membership'. Lord Hailey wrote in 1941 that: 'Though the centralisation policy may itself create new problems in certain other directions, there can be no doubt as to its efficacy as a measure for promoting the conservation of the soil. Observation shows a real improvement both

of grazing and of arable in the centralized reserves, and it does not appear that the policy has encountered any serious opposition among the natives.' B. N. Floyd, 'Changing Patterns of African Land Use in Southern Rhodesia', *Rhodes-Livingstone Journal*, **25,** 1959, 28; Southern Rhodesia, *Report of the Mangwende Reserve Commission of Inquiry* (Salisbury 1961), 17; D.O. 35/825, Draft Confidential Report by Lord Hailey on Southern Rhodesia, August 1941.

119. In the Soshwe Reserve, Marandellas, it was found that nearly all the available land was being cultivated and that the reserve was incapable of meeting the requirements of the population. The land inspector recommended that adjoining land should be added to the reserve and classified as arable land only. This was duly done. In the Umtasa South Reserve, Umtali, it was discovered that maximum capacity had been reached with regard to population, and 'saturation point' with cattle. Fifteen per cent of the arable land had been completely worked out, and the soil would deteriorate unless crop rotation and extensive manuring were made compulsory. As the entire arable area was under cultivation, the reserve had been denuded of all timber. S 235/529, Report of the N/C Marandellas for the month April 1936; S 235/511, Report of the Acting N/C Umtali for the year 1933.

120. Work commenced on irrigation schemes in Melsetter and Umtali, the demonstrators were recalled for an intensive course on soil conservation, and the old rectangular demonstration plots gave way to contoured ones.

121. Southern Rhodesia, *Report of the Commission to Enquire into the Preservation, etc., of the Natural Resources of the Colony* (Salisbury 1939), 15, 42.

122. Alvord had written optimistically in 1928 that with the introduction of intensive farming, 'the serious problems of overstocking the Reserves with cattle . . . will solve themselves'. S 170/1159, Alvord to CNC, 30 March 1928.

123. S 235/504, Report of the N/C Victoria for the year 1926.

124. The N/C Umtali agreed that: 'Things are very, very bad in the reserves. If we go on at this rate we are going to leave this country infinitely worse than we found it.' S 235/488, Minutes of the Salisbury Senior Native Commissioners' Conference, 27–29 March 1935, 199, 204.

125. S 235/503, Report of the N/C Bulalima-Mangwe for the year 1925.

126. As a result of this, the Government decided to buy three farms which had hitherto denied the reserve access to ten miles of the Semokwe river. At Bubi, supplies did not keep ahead of stock increases, the boreholes failed, and there were no good sites for constructing dams and weirs, while the N/C Matobo commented on the 'total inadequacy' of existing supplies and bemoaned the fact that water development had not been started thirty years earlier. *Legislative Assembly Debates*, **13,** 26 April 1933, cols. 503–4; S 138/21, N/C Matobo to S/N Bulawayo, 12 May 1932; S 235/511, Report of the N/C Bubi for the year 1933; S 235/513, Reports of the N/Cs Bubi and Matobo for the year 1935.

127. *Legislative Assembly Debates*, **21,** 19 June 1941, col. 1534.

128. I have not used the figures for 1936 because in that year the method of assessment was altered from the 'rule of thumb' method which had hitherto prevailed. The result was that the figures showed a population decrease between 1935–6! *Report of the Chief Native Commissioner for the year 1936* (Salisbury 1937), 2.

129. The actual figures given were as follows:

	1926	*1935*
Total Population	850,180	1,107,666
Population in Reserves	553,832	732,018
Population on Unalienated Land	113,446	154,372
Population on Alienated Land	159,375	178,053

130. Governor Baring believed that the remedy for this situation was 'to expropriate

the land, re-settle the Natives after the manner of a centralised reserve and enforce soil and pasture conservation'. D.O. 35/1169, Baring to Machtig, 9 June 1943.

131. S 235/515, Report of the N/C Insiza for the year 1936; S 235/511, Report of the N/C Lomagundi for the year 1933; S 1542/M8A, CNC to Huggins, 15 November 1933; S 1542/R3, N/C Bubi to S/N Bulawayo, 26 January 1937; S 1542/L4, Memo by N/C Umtali, 10 October 1937.

132. S 1542/C16, Chief Ishe Chipunza, Rusape, to CNC, 5 April 1934.

133. S 235/504, Report of the Acting N/C Gwanda for the year 1926; S 235/505, Report of the N/C Umzingwane for the year 1927.

134. The amounts were: Umzingwane 67,718 acres, Bulalima-Mangwe 14,427 acres, and Umtali 6,911 acres.

135. S 235/512, Report of the Assistant N/C Fort Rixon for the year 1934.

136.

District	*Acres*
Inyanga	42,300
Marandellas	c. 10,000
Salisbury	6,356
Umtali	42,506
Bulalima-Mangwe	63,599 + 302,000
Insiza	74,320
Matobo	63,500
Selukwe	12,268

137. S 235/513, Report of the Acting N/C Insiza for the year 1935; Hist. MSS. AT 1/2/1/11/4, N/C Insiza to S/N Bulawayo, 19 May 1936.

138. I. R. Phimister, 'The Shamva Mine Strike of 1927: An Emerging African Proletariat', *Rhodesian History*, **2**, 1971, 65–88.

139. D.O. 63/3, Chancellor to Baldwin, 5 October 1927.

140. S 1542/M8B, Acting CNC to all Native Department Stations in Southern Rhodesia, 20 August 1934.

141. The would-be organizer was a Lozi, 'Mutemwa ... alias Shirley Wilson'. The local N/C wrote of him that: 'He is bitten with the idea of forming Associations or Societies. He is an excellent Chef and it is unfortunate he does not confine his activities to cooking.' S 1542/L11, Assistant N/C Bulawayo to S/N Bulawayo, 4 February 1936.

142. S 138/92, Acting CNC to Secretary to Premier, 10 June 1927.

143. D.O. 35/370, Rodwell to Thomas, 23 April 1932.

144. S 1542/A2, CNC to Secretary to Prime Minister, 5 October 1933. (See also note 69 above.)

145. Hist. MSS. AT 1/2/1/11/4, N/C Insiza to S/N Bulawayo, 19 May 1936.

146. D.O. 35/370, Rodwell to Passfield, 18 January 1930; D.O. 35/371, Rodwell to Thomas, 17 October 1932 and 21 October 1933.

147. S 348, CNC to all Native Department Stations in Southern Rhodesia, 21 January 1931.

148. S 138/10, Acting CNC to Secretary to Premier, 25 May 1926.

149. C.O. 525/135, Report of the North Nyasa Native Reserves Commission, 1929.

150. S 138/92, S/N Bulawayo to CNC, 14 July and 26 September 1927.

151. H. M. G. Jackson admitted in 1929 that: 'Our steadfast policy in the past has been to oppose the building up of a unity among the Matabele which would have been a danger; the policy of *divide et impera* was, in effect adopted; and because of our more or less direct rule and scattered Reserves we were able to avoid the evils that followed the Zululand settlement.' S 138/92, CNC to Moffat, 16 November 1929.

152. Carbutt wrote: 'I am not prepared to accede to his [Albert's] application for land, because I am unable to place any confidence in him, and I am not going to give him facilities to entrench himself in Matabeleland as a land holder.' S 1542/L13, CNC to S/N Bulawayo, 14 December 1934.

153. S 1542/L13, CNC to Secretary to Premier, 19 April 1933.

154. S 1020, CNC to all Native Department Stations in Southern Rhodesia, 15 November 1933.

155. S 1542/N2, Report of the Umzingwane Native Board Meeting, 28 January 1937.

156. The Government had earlier deported Kadalie's agent, the Nyasa Robert Sambo, who had arrived in 1927 with the intention of spreading ICU propaganda.

157. Steele, 'Native Policy', 169.

158. S 138/267, Detective Jackson to Chief Superintendent, C.I.D. Bulawayo, 20 April 1930, N/C Gwelo to S/N Bulawayo, 1 April 1930; S 138/55, Detective Moore to Chief Superintendent, C.I.D. Bulawayo, 25 January 1931.

159. Steele, 'Native Policy', 175.

160. S 235/484, Minutes of the Native Affairs Conference at Victoria Falls, 8–10 June 1933, 14.

161. S 1542/N2, CNC to S/N Bulawayo, 18 February 1933.

162. S 1542/N2, CNC to N/C Lomagundi, 5 January 1931.

163. S 1542/A2, Acting Secretary for Native Affairs to Huggins, 10 February 1936. The N/C Marandellas was so worried by the waning influence of the chiefs that in 1931 he provided them with distinctive robes for use on ceremonial occasions. The N/C Mazoe was convinced however that: 'Practically all Chiefs and Headmen are doddering old drunkards with little ambition, activity or initiative. They are certainly of little use in the administrative scheme and cannot be trusted to convey even the simplest orders or instructions to those supposedly under their control.' S 235/516, Report of the N/C Mazoe for the year 1938.

164. At Chipinga, one Dubula Mapanze said: 'We are no longer living as people, we are like baboons, without lands of our own, we have to look for food again in the hills. We have nothing of our own to put in our mouths.' S 1542/N2, Report of the Chipinga Native Board Meeting, 15 January 1932.

165. S 1542/N2, Report of the Hartley Native Board Meeting, 4 November 1931.

166. S 1542/N2, Assistant N/C Umzingwane to S/N Bulawayo, 26 May 1933.

167. S 1542/N2, N/C Inyanga to CNC, 2 June 1933.

168. S 1542/N2, S/N Bulawayo to CNC, 8 April 1931; S 1542/L1, CNC to Secretary to Premier, 8 June 1931, N/C Umzingwane to S/N Bulawayo, 27 May 1931.

169. S 1542/N2, Report of the Filabusi Native Board Meeting, 18 May 1931.

170. S 1542/N2, Assistant N/C Filabusi to N/C Insiza, 13 March 1933.

171. S 1542/N2, Assistant N/C Filabusi to N/C Insiza, 15 June 1933.

172. National Archives of Malawi, S 1/2065/19, D/C Chinteche to Provincial Commissioner, Northern Province, 19 June 1929.

Conclusion

The Land Tenure Act has become one of the prime symbols of the European domination of Rhodesia, and its future is thus inextricably bound to that of the present political system.

British Member of Parliament, 1972.[1]

The previous eight chapters of this book have covered in detail a period of some forty-six years. It is now a further forty years on since 1937, and clearly another book would be necessary to do full justice to the complexities of the land question in recent years.[2] All that can, and will, be attempted here is a very brief outline of main themes, indicating the links between past policies and present realities.

By the end of the 1930s, as we have seen in the previous chapter, the agricultural economy of the Shona and the Ndebele, like that of the Kikuyu and most South African peoples, had been destroyed. What Iliffe terms the struggle between 'the European farmer seeking to reduce the African to a proletarian and the African seeking to retain the maximum amount of economic independence'[3] had been won conclusively by the Europeans. Heavy subsidization, combined with access to and use of political power explain why this was so. Potential white farmers were wooed in Britain and South Africa, offered training on arrival, received Land Bank loans to help establish themselves, and had a wide range of extension facilities placed at their disposal. Moreover with control over the land—legalized by the Land Apportionment Act—came, in varying degree, control over labour, and the ability after 1920 to rely on cheap supplies of local labour was a fundamental prerequisite to the success of European agriculture. As one white farmer of the 1930s put it, the 'relative abundance of labour in Rhodesia is not the least of its charms'.[4] Over time, a 'quasi-feudal' system of labour relations emerged on the farms with African workers totally dependent on their employer for social welfare, including health and educational facilities (rarely provided). Workers were 'allowed' to cultivate small plots on the farm thereby helping to keep wages low, while the farm stores tended to suck wages back thus reinforcing indebtedness and dependence.[5]

The competitiveness of the African peasantry was also reduced, as we have seen, by increasingly forcing them off European land, either by direct eviction or by imposing such a battery of financial and other burdens that they elected to go. Once settled in the increasingly overcrowded reserves they could aspire to become little more than subsistence cultivators—and migrant labourers, prepared to work for the prevailing low wages. In the towns they were in turn harried by the notorious pass laws—paid, housed and fed as single men, and denied the opportunity to lead a normal family life—the social costs of urban development thus being borne by the rural areas. Finally, came the repressive legal mechanisms of the 1930s: the Land Apportionment Act followed, in the wake of the Depression, by the Maize Control Acts and the 1934 Industrial Conciliation Act, which most skilfully imposed an industrial colour bar, so placing yet another obstacle in the path of African advancement. The white farmers and workers, having obtained this position of strength, concentrated thereafter on maintaining it at all costs.

The overall situation, as outlined above, was modified but not fundamentally changed by two important developments during and after the Second World War. Firstly, during the war Rhodesia underwent a process of industrialization in common with other African colonies suddenly cut off from regular contact with their metropoles and forced to manufacture some items which they had hitherto always imported. This industrialization acted initially as something of a safety valve on the land, for it enabled and encouraged thousands of Africans to leave their crowded reserves in search of urban employment and, so they hoped, a more secure future. Thus the number of African men employed in the towns rose sharply from about 45,000 in 1936 to 100,000 in 1946 and to 200,000 by 1956. A second innovation was the post-war agricultural revolution. Up to this time African and European farmers had been using essentially similar technology, though on a different scale. However, the new technological revolution of manufactured fertilizers, herbicides, and pesticides, of efficient motorized machinery, and of new crop strains eventually changed the face of rural Africa decisively in favour of large-scale capital-intensive production.[6]

In Rhodesia the agricultural revolution was marked by the switch from burley and turkish to virginia tobacco, which at last provided—or at least did provide until UDI in 1965—European farmers with the reliable and highly profitable cash crop they had been seeking for the past forty years.[7] European agriculture then entered a period of unprecedented growth: in the years 1937–58 the volume of its output increased by 259 per cent and its value by over 1,000 per cent (see table XIII).[8] The value of tobacco sales rose from £3·9 million in 1945 to £29·5 million in 1960, aided by the continuing practice of financial discrimination, for 'during the period 1945–6 to 1953–4, expenditure on European agriculture amounted to some £12 million as compared with £2 million on African'.[9] At the same time a large influx of new settlers escaping from post-war austerity in Europe descended on Rhodesia, and the white population rose dramatically from 80,500 in 1945 to 219,000 by 1960. Though the majority of the newcomers were attracted by the 'bright lights' of Salisbury and Bulawayo, many did settle on the land, and the number of European men working or owning farms almost doubled from 4,673 in 1945 to 8,632 in 1960.[10] To 'make way' for these new immigrants, recourse was had to the traditional policy of eviction, which for security reasons had lain somewhat dormant during the war years. The bulldozers were moved in and in the decade 1945–55 at least 100,000 people were moved, often forcibly, into the reserves and the inhospitable and tsetse-ridden Unassigned Area.[11] These movements have continued down to the present day.

TABLE XIII

Estimated Gross Value of European Agricultural Output, 1925–65

Year	*£ million*	*Year*	*£ million*
1925	2·0	1946	11·8
1926	2·8	1951	24·4
1931	2·1	1956	38·7
1936	3·3	1961	57·2
1941	5·3	1965	64·3

In terms of land policy, the main effect of this growing white prosperity both in the towns and on the farms, was that the old fear of competition which had so characterized the 1920s and especially the 1930s, began temporarily to recede. During the boom years of the 1950s, when Rhodesia benefited from the creation of the Central African Federation (1953–63), a greater degree of economic 'liberalization' became apparent. This was manifested in the towns in the attempt, within certain carefully defined parameters, to create an urbanized African middle class which, it was hoped, would act as a buffer against the 'winds of change' beginning to blow from below.[12]

In the rural areas, this ploy had its counterpart in the attempt to create a contented, landowning upper peasantry in the reserves by means of the Land Husbandry Act of 1951.[13] This Act, which endeavoured to divide the reserves into individual smallholdings—an immense task at the surveying level quite apart from any other—was supposed to provide people with security of tenure[14] and hence an incentive to maximize production. Now that European farmers were jumping onto the tobacco bandwagon, Africans were required to produce maize—a complete volte-face from the policies of the Depression! But the reserves were simply not capable of supporting the number of people they were expected to support—this had been a matter of deliberate policy in the past in order to procure adequate labour supplies. During the 1950s the African population rose from two to three million, completely wiping out the effects of the substantial drift to the towns. Thus, when surveyors began dividing the reserves up there was instant and widespread opposition, as people away working in the towns returned to find themselves deprived of land, as people had their land holdings reduced, and as a whole host of socio-economic problems cropped up.[15] Moreover a substantial number of the potential cream of the country's emergent farmers, finding themselves landless, crossed the Zambesi into Northern Rhodesia, set themselves up in the Lusaka–Mumbwa–Kabwe 'maize triangle', and subsequently became a vital productive asset to independent Zambia.[16]

By about 1960, land grievances combined with the reduction in urban job opportunities brought about by a recession, had swelled up into nationalism[17] and resulted in the effective abandonment of the Land Husbandry Act.[18] Rhodesia was perhaps atypical in that the rural masses propelled the leaders rather than vice versa, for the urban intellectuals were notoriously slow to join the new political parties. Confronted with what amounted to rural revolt, the white Government of the day determined to take the heat out of the situation by contemplating what to many settlers appeared a revolutionary step—the abolition of the Land Apportionment Act. A commission of enquiry was set up, which duly pondered the 'irrationality' of such protectionism in a period of unprecedented economic growth when many Europeans no longer required it. It also pointed to the fact that such magnanimity on the part of the whites would help to de-fuse the African nationalist movement which had gained strength precisely because of genuine and deeply-felt land grievances. Remove the Land Apportionment Act, the commission (and the Government) reasoned, and white rule could safely be preserved and the country continue to prosper.[19]

The message, however, was not well received by the white electorate, alarmed at trends elsewhere in Africa and by the imminent collapse of the Federation as a result of nationalist successes in Nyasaland and Northern Rhodesia—soon to become Malawi and Zambia. In 1962, in an election contested very largely on the issue of the Land Apportionment Act, the 'populist' Rhodesian Front came to power.[20] The Front represented, at least initially, an alliance of white workers and farmers comparable to that which brought Huggins to power in the 1930s and there has in fact been a return to the policies of that era, reflecting the political and economic uncertainties of the 1960s. The 'liberal' amendments to the Land Apportionment Act were reversed,[21] and segregation on the land—and in the urban areas—has been applied with increasing vigour. This process culminated in the 1969 Land Tenure Act, which finally abolished the Land Apportionment Act, but only to strengthen it by dividing the land in half with 44·9 million acres allocated to each race[22] (see map 5) and by purporting to entrench this division for all time in a new constitution—a somewhat illusory device since the governing party had itself torn up one constitution when

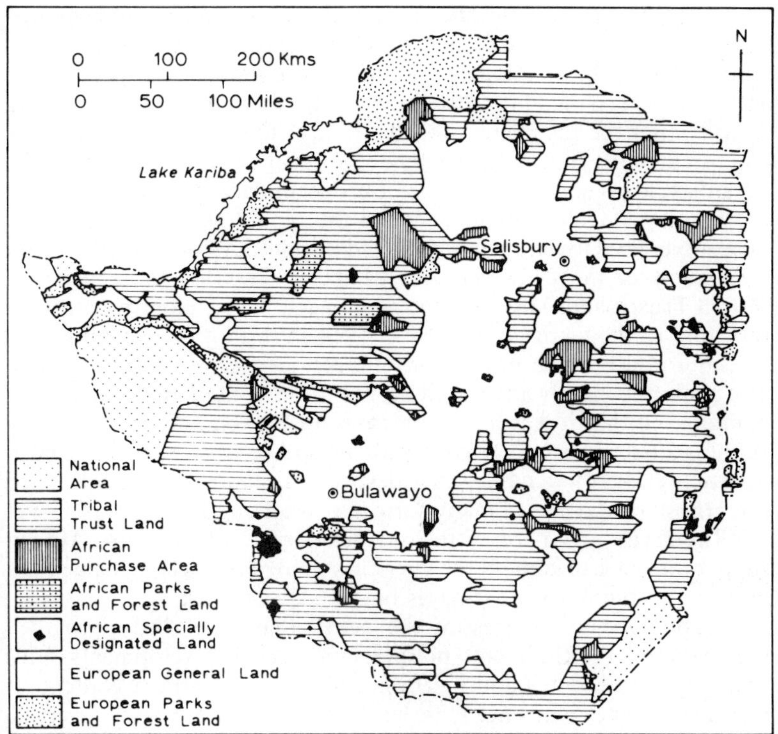

Map 5—Land Apportionment, 1970 (*from Christopher 1971*).

making its Unilateral Declaration of Independence from Britain in 1965.

The Rhodesian Front was acting in direct response to the pressures of African nationalism. In turn, the nationalist movement(s) responded to the pressures of the Front. Orthodox political repression sufficed to contain the orthodox nationalism of the late 1950s and early 1960s—the type of movement which, with the aid of colonial powers rapidly transforming themselves into neo-colonialists, succeeded in bringing political independence to much of the rest of Africa. Since the mid-1960s however and especially since 1972, a new phase opened—that of guerrilla warfare following the pattern of Frelimo in Mozambique.

The fortunes of this war have fluctuated and been greatly complicated by the flurry of diplomatic activity throughout 1975–6, involving South Africa, America, and the 'frontline' African states, aimed at achieving a 'constitutional' settlement. Two points, directly related to the issue of land are, however, worth making. Firstly, the guerrillas initially obtained their greatest popular support in the Centenary, Sipolilo, and Mount Darwin areas in the north-east, where alienation of land to Europeans had taken place only in the past twenty years and the people's resentment was therefore of recent origin. Secondly, it appears that the guerrillas 'obtained from local villagers the names of unpopular farmers in the area and selected their farms for attack ... by attacking isolated farming communities the insurgents hoped to harm the agricultural industry and threaten the effective maintenance of security in rural areas'.[23] The guerrillas clearly sought to drive the Europeans back to the cities, leaving the countryside relatively undefended thus enabling them to mobilize the people. The Government responded by resettling virtually the entire population of the Chiweshe and Madziwa Reserves (now renamed 'Tribal Trust Lands') into 'protected villages'[24] and, more recently, by reverting to the tactics of the early 1960s in setting up a commission to enquire into 'undesirable' and 'unnecessary' racial discrimination. The commission duly advocated the abolition of the Land Tenure Act, pointing out that it was 'the main cause of friction between the races. Witness after witness declared it was the source of all their ills, and it was quite clear to us it has led to widespread discontent and deep-seated resentment on the part of many Africans, Asians, and Coloureds'.[25] Yet the Rhodesian Front, for all the obvious need to obtain some African support in order to contain the guerrillas more effectively, remained unmoved and the Act thus remains on the statute book.

This book began by stressing the fact that land has always provided the lifeblood of Rhodesian politics, and recent developments have amply borne this out. 'Land' has been and is a major issue of contention both around the conference table and in the rapidly escalating guerrilla war in the bush. But with Rhodesia's African population in the region of six million, and with many European farmers badly hit by international sanctions following UDI, often deeply in debt, and increasingly subject to guerrilla attacks, the era of unfettered European domination has clearly come to an end. A variety of political solutions now appear to be possible, though none of them is inevitable. What can however be affirmed with certainty is that the most acute and difficult question confronting the first African, or African-dominated, Government of Rhodesia/Zimbabwe, whatever its ideological hue, will be that of land, bedevilled by its past use as a political and economic weapon by the whites, and by the consequent mythologies to which this has given rise.

The problem will not be an easy one to resolve. The continuing stranglehold of the land division of the 1890s, the fact—exemplified time and again by land legislation—that Rhodesia is part of the Southern African regional economic system, and the lessons to be drawn from the agricultural failures of neighbouring Zambia, will all impose constraints on future land and agricultural policies. That the country possesses enormous potential is not in doubt; that such potential can be harnessed effectively and with social justice remains to be determined.

NOTES

1. M. L. Rifkind, 'Land Apportionment in Perspective', *Rhodesian History*, **3**, 1972, 61.

2. One major thesis covers this period and there are two published theses dealing specifically with the Land Husbandry Act. M. L. Rifkind, 'The Politics of Land in Rhodesia', M.Sc. thesis, University of Edinburgh, 1968; B. N. Floyd, *Changing Patterns of African Land Use in Southern Rhodesia* (Lusaka 1961); M. E. Bulman, *The Native Land Husbandry Act of Southern Rhodesia: A Failure in Land Reform* (Salisbury 1975).

3. J. Iliffe, *Agricultural change in modern Tanganyika*, Historical Association of Tanzania Paper No. 10 (Nairobi 1971), 13.

4. L. Hastings, *Dragons Are Extra* (Harmondsworth 1947), 133.

5. D. G. Clarke, 'The Political Economy of Discrimination and Underdevelopment in Rhodesia with Special Reference to African Workers, 1940–1973', Ph.D. thesis, University of St. Andrews, 1975, 311–20.

6. Q. N. Parsons and R. H. Palmer, 'The Roots of Rural Poverty: Historical Background', in Palmer and Parsons (Eds.), *The Roots of Rural Poverty in Central and Southern Africa* (London 1977), 8.

7. 'The initial impetus to the tobacco industry was undoubtedly the expansion of United Kingdom demand for Rhodesian leaf arising from the post-war dollar shortage. Before the war, the United States accounted for about 70 per cent of Britain's requirements of unmanufactured tobacco ... [by c. 1960] the United States' share of a somewhat larger British market had fallen to about 40 per cent while that of Rhodesia had increased to almost one-third. The mutuality of interests between Britain and Rhodesia led to the negotiation in 1947 of the "London Agreement" under which the United Kingdom manufacturers undertook to purchase two-thirds of the annual flue-cured production, up to a 70-million lb crop, subject to provisos that tobacco of a suitable quality was available at reasonable prices and that there was no appreciable fall in United Kingdom consumption; in return the Rhodesian authorities agreed to institute export controls, which were retained until 1955, to afford United Kingdom buyers an opportunity to purchase their requirements at reasonable prices.' H. Dunlop, *The Development of European Agriculture in Rhodesia, 1945–1965*, University of Rhodesia, Department of Economics Occasional Paper 5 (Salisbury 1971), 45.

8. M. Yudelman, *Africans on the Land* (Cambridge, Mass. 1964), 90. 'In the relatively short space of fifteen years, [1945–60] the poor and backward economy of Southern Rhodesia was transformed into an economy that gave every appearance of being vigorous, dynamic, and expanding.' Yudelman, *Africans on the Land*, 47.

9. Dunlop, *The Development*, 59. The discrepancy in Land Bank loans was much greater. In 1945–55, the first decade in which Africans were able to get loans, less than 70 farmers received a total of under £6,000; in 1958 outstanding Land Bank loans to European farmers totalled nearly £6 million. Yudelman, *Africans on the Land*, 102, 158.

10. Dunlop, *The Development*, 61.

11. A nationalist leader recalled that as a child his grandfather: 'Decided not to comply with the [Land Apportionment] Act and move instead to a "Native Purchase Area", where he could keep most of his herd. In the summer of 1948, then, my grandparents moved with everything they had [from Matabeleland] to the Midlands. More than twenty cattle died on the way and several others succumbed to disease shortly after they arrived due to new types of grass and a different environment.

'The Land Apportionment Act, as you can imagine, meant a great deal of hardship for Zimbabweans. For my grandfather, going to live in a strange area a hundred miles away from his home meant leaving relatives, friends ... everything he knew. It was the same for everybody who was forced to move.

'With my grandparents in the Midlands, our trips to their farm became a major event ... One day, during my first summer there, we went to visit relatives who lived in a reserve near our farm. These people had already been ordered to move to an area in the north—

near the Zambezi escarpment—which was thickly forested and tsetse fly infested. They refused to leave. Most had been born in this reserve, had good houses, well-kept fields, and felt no one had the right to force them out. The land had been the home of their forefathers for generations.

'On our way many police and army trucks raced past us. When we arrived my uncle told us that the Europeans had just arrested the chief, because he told the people to resist. A police truck sped out of the village and we could see the chief and some elders—handcuffed under guard—in the back. Later that day soldiers and police started ordering men to empty their houses and barns. When they refused they were arrested. Soldiers entered their houses and threw everything onto trucks, wrecking a lot of things in the process. Then they did the same with the barns, loading all the tools, grain, etc. into the same trucks. This over, the women, children and old people were put on top of their belongings and driven away. The animals had been rounded up and the boys were ordered to drive the herds north. It was a sorry sight—women, children, old people were weeping, the men arrested, homes set on fire and destroyed.

'Later I heard that these people were just dumped in the Government's assigned area—most of their cattle having died on the long trek. ...

'I really felt pity for the people evicted from their homes in such a brutal manner. I didn't understand why it was done, but I listened to the adults talk about it and they seemed very upset. Everybody opposed the way these people were being treated; the general feeling was one of resentment and hatred towards the government.' O. Gjerstad (Ed.), *The Organizer, Story of Temba Moyo* (Richmond, B.C. 1974), 31–2.

12. Southern Rhodesia, *Report on the Urban African Affairs Commission, 1958* (Salisbury 1958).

13. Floyd, *Changing Patterns*; Bulman, *Native Land Husbandry Act*; G. K. Garbett, 'The Land Husbandry Act of Southern Rhodesia', in D. Biebuyck (Ed.), *African Agrarian Systems* (London 1963), 185–202; K. Brown, *Land in Southern Rhodesia* (London 1959); Southern Rhodesia, *What the Native Land Husbandry Act Means to the Rural African and to Southern Rhodesia* (Salisbury 1955); Southern Rhodesia, *Report of the Mangwende Reserve Commission of Inquiry* (Salisbury 1961).

14. In fact the Government greatly underestimated the security inherent in 'traditional' systems of land tenure. As the Mangwende Report (in effect, the anthropologist J. F. Holleman) noted: 'There is no doubt that the implementation of the Land Husbandry Act has evoked resistances with a strong emotional undercurrent which is closely related to the African concepts of land rights and the security of tenure ... It is probably the mobility or apparent impermanence of individual landed interests in tribal societies and the periodic reverting of individualized holdings to communal use (or no use at all), which lie at the roots of much misinterpretation and under-evaluation of indigenous land rights by colonial administrators in this and other territories in Africa and elsewhere ... What "communal tenure" in indigenous (Shona) society *does* mean, is that because the land and its resources belong to the community, *every full member of this community has an inalienable right to a reasonable share according to his requirements.* For this reason this right is as secure as is a person's membership of the community. In customary law the permanence and inviolability of the land rights of individuals are not conceived (as is ownership in our law) as a relationship to a specific holding in perpetuity, but as a *perpetual relationship with any such unencumbered portion of the land of the community as may be available for individualized occupation whenever required as such from time to time.* Herein lies the *individual's security, that is, in his vested right to claim a share.* If, then, the Native Land Husbandry Act aims "to provide individual security of tenure of arable land and individual security of grazing rights on the communal grazings", this reveals an ignorance of the nature of customary land rights. The African, at any rate, can hardly escape the impression that what the Act generously offers as something special to a qualified member, his own laws had always accepted as the obvious birthright of all. ... *In the Act this security is largely approached from the agronomist's point of view, that is, as a rigid economic (productive) concept within suitably defined legal ramifications; but in Afri-*

can society it is a basic legal right with important but flexible economic and social implications in a dual economy.' Mangwende Reserve Commission, 34–6, 38.

15. Many of these problems were frankly discussed in the Report of the *Mangwende Reserve Commission* (see above, note 14), which was consequently partly supressed by the Government.

16. R. J. Mutsau, 'The Shona and Ndebele Settlements in Kabwe Rural Area, 1953–63', in R. H. Palmer (Ed.), *Zambian Land and Labour Studies, Vol. 1*, National Archives of Zambia Occasional Paper 2 (Lusaka 1973), 41–7; M. Muntemba, 'Thwarted Development: A Case Study of Economic Change in the Kabwe Rural District of Zambia, 1902–70', in Palmer and Parsons, *The Roots of Rural Poverty*, 345–64.

17. As we have seen in earlier chapters, the land question always featured prominently in African political movements down to the mid-1930s. Since land pressures have intensified even more in the past forty years, this trend has naturally continued. Thus, for example, Benjamin Burombo's 1947 African Workers' Voice Association successfully encouraged people to resist Government eviction orders, and the 1957 African National Congress found the Land Husbandry Act 'the best recruiter [it] ever had', and drew much of its support from young urban workers rendered landless by the Act. Subsequent parties placed emphasis on obtaining the political kingdom, with the scrapping of the Land Apportionment Act high on the list of priorities. A particularly useful source is the *Central African Examiner*, but see also: Rifkind, 'The Politics of Land'; J. van Velsen, 'Trends in African Nationalism in Southern Rhodesia', *Kroniek van Afrika*, **4**, 1964, 139–57; T. Bull (Ed.) *Rhodesian Perspective* (London 1967); J. Nkomo, 'The Crucible of Privilege: Southern Rhodesia', *African South*, **3**, 1959, 57–61; J. Nkomo, 'Southern Rhodesia: Apartheid Country', in J. Duffy and R. A. Manners (Eds.) *Africa Speaks* (Princeton, N.J. 1961), 130–43; N. Sithole, *African Nationalism* (Cape Town 1959, revised London 1968).

18. The Secretary for Agriculture wrote in 1962 that: 'The almost complete halt in the Land Husbandry Act, and the need to allow land to be opened up for temporary cultivation, has been caused by political opposition and intimidation, and a reduction in the opportunities for employment.' Southern Rhodesia, *Report of the Secretary for Agriculture for the year 1962* (Salisbury 1963), 39. 'The suspension of the Land Husbandry Act was followed by a period of *laissez-faire* with indiscriminate opening up of new lands by the tribal authorities, abandonment of existing plots, reversion to shifting cultivation and failure to maintain conservation works. Statutory measures were adopted in the late sixties to restore tribal authority in respect of land and to make it more effective.' The 1965 Tribal Trust Land Act 'recognized and re-established traditional tribal authorities as the land authorities in the tribal areas and gave them powers to control the allocation of land in these areas and to enforce conservation methods and the pursuit of good husbandry'. H. Dunlop, 'Land and Economic Opportunity in Rhodesia', *Rhodesian Journal of Economics*, **6**, 1, 1972, 7; G. Kay, *Rhodesia: A Human Geography* (London 1970), 88.

19. Southern Rhodesia, *Second Report of the Select Committee on Resettlement of Natives* (Salisbury 1960).

20. The Rhodesian Front believed 'that as the peoples of Southern Rhodesia differ in many respects, the pattern and principle of racial differentiation in the ownership, use, and tenure of land established under the Land Apportionment Act must be maintained'. Rhodesian Front, *Principles and Policies, 1962* (Salisbury 1962). The Front captured 55 per cent of the vote, compared to the outgoing United Federal Party's 44 per cent.

21. Five and a half million acres, mostly comprising unalienated land in the European Area, was reclassified as Unreserved Land, which people of any race could buy. In addition, any landowner in the Native Purchase Area or the European Area could apply to have his land become Unreserved, and thus transferable to people of any race. Some 681,000 acres were so transferred before the Rhodesian Front put a stop to it in 1963. Also, 4 million acres of the Native Purchase Area and 2 million acres of unalienated land in the European Area, all heavily populated by Africans, were transferred to a 'Special Native Area' to obviate the heavy cost of moving people into the 'correct' land areas.

In 1961 the Special Native Area was combined with the old native reserves to form the newly-designated 'Tribal Trust Lands'. All these steps were intended to be preliminaries to the eventual abolition of the Land Apportionment Act. A. J. Christopher, 'Land tenure in Rhodesia', *South African Geographical Journal*, **53**, 1971, 45–6.

22. The actual division was:

European Area	44,948,300 acres
African Area	44,949,100 acres
National Area	6,617,400 acres

The National Area comprises Hunting and Game Reserves, Lake Kariba, the Wankie and Victoria Falls National Parks and Gona-Re-Zhou, on the south-eastern border with Mozambique. Considerable juggling was necessary to obtain such parity. All the Unreserved Land (5·9 million acres) and a good deal of National Land (3·9 million acres) was transferred to the European Area, which now 'contains eighty-five per cent of all Forests, Parks and Wild Life Reserves placed within the racially grouped areas'. Christopher, 'Land Tenure', 49. The African Area has expanded from its 1930 figure of 29·1 million acres largely as a result of incorporating most of the poor quality 1930 Unassigned Area. The Land Tenure Act also imposed much tighter restrictions on the position of Africans in the European Area, and vice versa, which led to considerable criticism by the Roman Catholic Church.

23. A. R. Wilkinson, *Insurgency in Rhodesia, 1957–1973: An Account and Assessment*, Adelphi Paper 100 (London 1973), 15–16.

24. Catholic Institute for International Relations, *The Man in the Middle: Torture, Resettlement and Eviction* (Slough 1975), 7.

25. Rhodesia, *Report of the Commission of Inquiry into Racial Discrimination 1976* (Salisbury 1976), 9.

APPENDIX I

A District by District Analysis of Land Distribution in Rhodesia 1894–1941

INTRODUCTION

The main aim of this analysis is to provide detailed evidence to substantiate many of the arguments put forward in the core of the book, evidence which is best gathered together and consolidated in an appendix rather than appearing piecemeal in the various chapters and tending to obstruct their flow. The analysis should clearly confirm the crucial importance of the events of the 1890s, and how little the 'balance of power' established by 1902 could be altered thereafter; it should provide ample evidence for a dispassionate appraisal of the work of the Native Reserves and Land Commissions; and finally it should prove of some value to those undertaking regional or local studies of modern Rhodesian history.

The analysis which follows examines the distribution of land between Africans and Europeans in the 32 districts of Rhodesia (19 in Mashonaland and 13 in Matabeleland) in the years 1894–1941. The method employed is to look at each district in turn, discussing the various problems encountered by the Native Commissioners in assigning the initial reserves of 1894–1902; at the various alterations made to those reserves in the years 1907–14 when the BSA Company launched its attack upon them; at the conflicting proposals of the Native Department and Inskipp's Land Settlement Department in 1914–15, and the actual recommendations of the Native Reserves Commission; at the amendments to those recommendations made in 1917–20 as a result of a vociferous campaign of opposition to them; at the additional reserves set aside in four districts in 1924; at the proposals of Native Commissioners to the Land Commission (LC) of 1925 and the recommendations of that Commission; at the subsequent amendments worked out by Taylor and Atherstone in 1926–9, when it was decided to abandon the one million acres of Neutral Areas and replace them with an additional half million acres of Native Purchase Areas; and at the eventual assignments made in the Land Apportionment Act of 1930 and subsequent amendments in the years 1931–41. Reference has not been made to the Special Native Areas which were created during the 1930s; information about them is to be found in chapter 8 (see pp. 208–9, 239 nn. 134, 136).

The data on which this analysis is based comes predominantly from the National Archives of Rhodesia, in particular from the records of the Administrator's Office, the Executive Council, the Land Settlement Department, the Commercial Branch and Estates Office, the Chief Native Commissioner and

District Native Commissioners, the Resident Commissioner, the evidence to the Native Reserves and Land Commissions, and the Schedules to those Commissions and to the Land Apportionment Acts of 1930 and 1941. The individual files are far too numerous to cite. A number of abbreviations have been used in order to prevent tedious repetition and undue length. They are: NRC for Native Reserves Commission, LC for Land Commission, NPAs for Native Purchase Areas, and LAA for Land Apportionment Act. All areas are given in acres. Figures in parentheses denote actual reserves, purchase areas etc.; those without parentheses are recommendations by individuals or commissions which never became a reality.

One further point needs to be made. The areas of many of the reserves given below, especially those for 1902, are mere estimates. At that time topographical knowledge, especially of the outlying districts, was minimal, and the 'boundaries' of many of the reserves were either extremely vague or else quite inaccurate. Of the 16 reserves originally selected in Matabeleland, for example, only 9 had actually been surveyed; the size of the other 7 was admitted to be only 'approximate'. The same applies to Mashonaland, where the areas of the reserves were originally given in square miles, often neatly rounded. The problem was exacerbated by the unknown whereabouts of much technically 'European' land which was lying unoccupied and unsurveyed. When such land was subsequently found to fall within reserve boundaries, as not infrequently happened, the reserves had to be reduced accordingly. For such reasons, one should not look for absolute continuity in the areas of the reserves between 1902 and 1914–15; they may indeed have been altered and if so this is mentioned, but they are just as likely to have remained untouched, and all that has changed are the surveyors' estimates of their size. In cases where district boundaries have been altered and the size, and sometimes the name, of reserves has been affected thereby, this too has been mentioned in the text.

MASHONALAND

Bikita

This district, which lies in the south-eastern corner of Rhodesia, to the east of Fort Victoria, was created in 1920. It comprised what had previously been the eastern half of the Ndanga District and contained three reserves; Bikita (502,000) and Matsai (92,500) which had formed part of the Ndanga Reserve, and Sangwe (67,500) previously part of Ndanga East Reserve.

In 1925 the N/C recommended that two NPAs be assigned. These were enlarged by the LC and included unaltered in the LAA. They were called Mungesi (23,800) and Nyahunda (76,100). The latter comprised land which the NRC had taken away from the Ndanga Reserve in 1914–15. Over half the district was European land.

Charter

The Charter District lies to the south of Salisbury and to the north of Fort Victoria. By 1902 much of the district had been cut up into European farms, and over half a million acres had been granted to two companies, Willoughby's

Consolidated Co., Ltd and the Exploring Land & Minerals Co., Ltd. As a result, the N/C felt impelled to move some 2,000 huts, containing one-fifth of the total population of the district, into reserves, having unsuccessfully asked the administration to re-acquire some of Willoughby's land for a reserve. He created four reserves in all; Naira (111,360), Mangeni (29,440), Umgesi (52,480), and Sabi (1,654,400). A large part of Sabi was uninhabitable owing to the lack of water. Shortly after the reserves had been formally approved by the Executive Council in 1902, the N/C, J. W. Posselt, reported that he now considered them inadequate as the landowning companies were starting to demand rent from their tenants, and he asked in vain for 25,000 acres to be taken from the Exploring Land & Minerals Co., and added to the reserves.

In 1914–15 Posselt stated that the reserves could not be reduced and he asked for an additional 50,000 acres, while Inskipp wanted 555,000 acres taken from the Sabi Reserve and put at the disposal of his Land Settlement Department. Posselt strongly opposed the NRC's original plan of abolishing Narira as well as cutting down Sabi. 'The Sabi is the greatest and most valuable asset the natives possess and their greatest protection and safeguard of the future. Any attempt therefore to diminish its present area would act as a hardship and injustice to future generations.' Africans had come to trust him, and: 'It would be criminal of me to betray that trust by suggesting or consenting to the cutting down or abolition of any of the reserves.'[1] The NRC eventually decided to retain Narira (111,351), Mangene (29,420), and Umgesi (42,470), and to reduce Sabi (1,553,536) by 291,800 to (about 1,261,736) in the form of an indefinite twelve-mile belt along the route of the proposed Odzi–Umvuma railway—which was never in fact built. This proposal brought forth strong protests from the local missionary, A. S. Cripps, who argued that the normal fifty-yard strip would be quite sufficient, and from Posselt, who agreed that the proposed twelve-mile belt was excessive, and who criticized the NRC for showing no inclination to increase the size of any of the reserves. Cripps' continual pressure, combined with the fact that there was no sign of the proposed railway, eventually led the Colonial Office to uphold the protest. They admitted that this was the weak spot in the Report, that the NRC should not have made such an indefinite recommendation, and that had they known that the railway was such a far distant proposal they would never have approved the twelve-mile belt in the first place. It was therefore agreed in 1920 to give the High Commissioner powers to modify the breadth of the belt in order to protect African settlements. In the 1930 LAA the belt was earmarked for a NPA, but because its boundaries were not defined the land could obviously not be sold and in 1936 it was legally reinstated within the reserve.

In 1925 Posselt, who by this time had been N/C Charter for twenty-three years, told the LC that there was little unalienated land remaining in the district. The only possible NPAs were the Sabi belt and two small areas, No. 1 (8,800), which lacked permanent water, and No. 2 (4,088). The retention of the Sabi belt was now 'more necessary than ever before', as considerable numbers of Africans were being moved off farms. There was no available land adjoining the Sabi and Narira Reserves, and 'It is too late to make any re-adjustments in this District'.[2] These proposals were accepted by the LC and were embodied in the 1930 LAA together with two additional NPAs; Mtoro (21,652), added as compensation for survey errors elsewhere, and No. 4 (7,643), which comprised three farms owned by A. S. Cripps. Two Neutral Areas of 88,000 and 9,688 and a further NPA of 66,600, all proposed by Carter and Taylor, were abandoned. By 1941 there were three NPAs in the district, Nos. 2 and 4 having been amalgamated to form a new No. 2 (11,731). Over 60 per cent of the district was African land.

Chibi

In 1897 the N/C Chibi suggested that the whole of the district, which lies on the south-eastern border of Rhodesia, be made a reserve, with the exception of occupied farms. He commented that though the area requested might be excessive, this would allow for future population increase. This was not granted, but in 1900 he successfully applied for extensions to the Chibi and Matibi Reserves; the former because it was far too small, waterless, and very mountainous and Europeans were pegging land in the vicinity, the latter because a large part of it was waterless and uninhabitable. When extended, the areas were estimated to be: Chibi (966,400) and Matibi (3,358,720).

A problem subsequently arose when it was found that the N/C had erroneously regarded the boundary of Chibi Reserve as being the same as the district boundary, and that he had allowed some 7,210 Africans to settle on an area of half a million acres under this misapprehension. In 1912 the N/C and the S/N Victoria met the Africans concerned and proposed that the reserve be extended northwards, but the Imperial authorities were not happy, and the matter was handed over to the NRC.

In 1914–15 Inskipp demanded 300,000 acres of Chibi and the whole of Matibi. The N/C also suggested that considerable reductions could be made, and the NRC decided to reduce Chibi (682,330) by 96,820 to (585,510) and Matibi (3,485,941) by 2,661,345 to (824,596). The land excised from the central part of Matibi, some 1·8 million acres, subsequently formed part of the BSA Company's 2·5 million acre Nuanetsi Ranch. Matibi was thus divided into a No. 1 Reserve in the north-west, and a No. 2 in the south-east.

In 1925 the N/C recommended the Jenya NPA (105,000) and the LC added No. 2 (3,175), comprising a farm lying within Chibi Reserve. These were embodied in the LAA, together with a large Unassigned Area (1,783,000) on the border, though a proposed Neutral Area of 29,800 was dropped. By 1941 Jenya was found, on more accurate survey, to be (98,500). All this meant that about half of the district was in the European Area, while just over a quarter was Unassigned, and just under a quarter was African land.

Chilimanzi

This district lies to the east of Gwelo and to the north of Fort Victoria. Early in 1896 the N/C proposed the creation of three reserves, partly to protect Africans from European farmers, and partly to induce them to come out of the hills where he feared they were hatching trouble. The proposal was not accepted, much of Chief Chirumanzu's land on the *high veld* was taken by Europeans, and eventually two reserves, Serima (115,200) and Chilimanzi (171,520) were created, the latter comprising mostly granite rocks and being suitable, it was said, only for Africans. Gurajena (16,000) was subsequently transferred to Chilimanzi from the Victoria District.

In 1914–15 the N/C was prepared to surrender the southern part of Chilimanzi, of which Inskipp wanted 57,000. The NRC reduced Chilimanzi (275,431) by 40,640 to (234,791), abolished Gurajena (20,177), and retained Serima (47,973). The district also contained 4,091 of the Chikwanda Reserve, Gutu.

In 1925 the N/C proposed two NPAs; Zinyaningwe (42,000), formerly part of Chilimanzi Reserve, and No. 2 (21,100), the former Gurajena Reserve. These were both accepted by the LC, and in the LAA a proposed Neutral Area of 27,800 was converted into an additional NPA, No. 3 (2,726) and an Undetermined Area (15,125). By 1941 Nos. 2 and 3 had been amalgamated to form Mshagashe (23,826). Two-thirds of the district lay within the European Area.

Darwin

In this remote district, first called North Mazoe, in the north-east of Rhodesia bordering on Mozambique, there had been no European penetration by 1902 and consequently no real necessity to demarcate reserves. Five unsurveyed reserves were, however, assigned: Chimanda (640,000), Mshowani (70,400), Chiweshwe (299,520), Madziwa (94,720), and Kandeya (35,840). The N/C believed that no good land should ever be reserved for Africans as they could always adapt themselves to any poor or rocky soil, and while Chiweshwe might appear excessive large tracts of it were totally unfit for habitation.

By 1914–15 the five reserves had still not been properly defined and were scattered about throughout the district. Inskipp wanted to concentrate them into one area of 1,260,000, so as to make white settlement possible elsewhere. The N/C proposed two new reserves, Mzarabani and Chiswiti, and boundaries for the old reserves, noting that 'due attention has been paid to the exclusion of all such land as will in future be useful and suitable for farming and ranching purposes for European settlers'.[3] The S/N Salisbury proposed a new Chimanda Reserve. The NRC duly abolished Chimanda and Mshowani (476,080), reduced Chiweshwe (339,209) by 88,823 to (250,386), retained Madziwa (50,373) and Kandeya (38,521) to which Chiweshwe was joined, and created three new reserves, Mzarabani (297,800), Chimanda (267,100), and Chiswiti (188,800)—the latter two being 'reserve' reserves created at the last minute to allay Imperial fears of a too drastic overall reduction of the reserves. The rearrangement left the district with 1,191,967 acres of reserves, including 98,987 which the NRC claimed, in its statistical tables, to have added to the reserves, but which does not appear in any of the new reserves.

In 1925 the LC accepted the N/C's suggestions and assigned three NPAs: No. 1 (732,000), Chesa (279,400), and No. 3 (13,200), plus an Unassigned Area (51,000), all of which were embodied in the LAA. The N/C remarked of No. 1:

> This may seem a large tract, but it is useless for European settlers: besides being so far from rail-head the land is waterless except... on the Anglo-Portuguese border, and is mostly rocks and hills. Excepting for the land North of the Chimanda Reserve practically the whole is infested with Tsetse Fly.[4]

Some 70 per cent of the district was African land.

Gutu

In this district, which lies to the north-east of Fort Victoria and to the south of Charter, very little land had been alienated to Europeans during the 1890s, so that the N/C had no difficulty in creating the Gutu Reserve (222,720). He felt he had probably chosen more land than was required, but much of it was granite, and it could easily be reduced later if it were found to be excessive. The Chikwanda A, B, and C Reserves (140,800), a majority of which 'consists of massive granite *kopjes*',[5] originally part of Victoria District, was subsequently transferred to Gutu.

In 1907, as part of a series of exchanges, Chikwanda, now estimated to be 258,200, was reduced to 140,330. This was done because the reserve boundaries were found to be very disjointed after the neighbouring white farms had been surveyed. The N/C, who had received many applications from Europeans for the land which was surrendered, agreed to the reduction because of the original underestimation of the size of the reserve. The British Resident Commissioner visited Chikwanda and had no objection to the reduction.

In 1914–15 the N/C suggested that two farms be added to Chikwanda A, B, and C, and the area combined into one reserve. Inskipp agreed but wanted 225,000 of Gutu, which the N/C was only prepared to reduce by 120,000. The NRC duly made Chikwanda A, B, and C (99,943) one reserve and increased it by 95,200 to (195,143), while it reduced Gutu (632,993) by 167,310 to (465,683). 21,870 of Chikwanda lay outside the district; 4,091 in Chilimanzi and 17,779 in Victoria.

In 1925 the LC, accepting the N/C's proposals, assigned three NPAs: Dewure (152,600), Caledon Estate (6,350), and Mazari (3,797), the last being a farm lying within Chikwanda Reserve, plus an Undetermined Area (3,234). Taylor and Atherstone added the Nyazwidzi NPA (68,600) in lieu of Neutral Areas abandoned elsewhere. Dewure and Nyazwidzi both contained land which the NRC had taken from Gutu Reserve. All these suggestions were incorporated into the LAA, though by 1941 Caledon Estate had been merged with Dewure to form the new Dewure (153,200). About 60 per cent of the district was African land.

Hartley

The centre of this district lies some 60 miles south-west of Salisbury on the main road and railway to Bulawayo. In 1900 the N/C complained that 'nearly all the ground has been taken up here before my appointment, and those parts which have been unappropriated have been either too small for reserves or not suitable'.[6] Nonetheless he tried to make his reserves 'large enough for all purposes' on the grounds that they would be easier to reduce than increase in the future, but he added that 'the soil in question is not such as will be hankered after by European occupants on account of its poorness'.[7] He abandoned a projected Hartley Reserve because the soil 'was not as suitable as the ground now selected for native occupation. Also because it was on the Gold Belt partly, and a good deal nearer the Railway and thus of more value to the Government'.[8] He also believed that 'There is always the possibility of a Native Rising and having the Reserves more or less separated would prevent the Natives being so well united in any sudden outbreak, which is the great danger in any Native Rising'.[9] The reserves finally selected were: Gabaza (27,520), Ganga (40,960), Mondoro (561,920), Sanyati (147,200), and Cape Boy (7,680).

In 1909 some 6,350 acres of the southern portion of Cape Boy was exchanged for an equal area to the north. The surrendered land was uninhabited and the exchange was said to meet with the approval of Africans in the reserve.

In 1914–15 Inskipp wanted the whole of Ganga and Gabaza, which were on the route of the projected Salisbury–Enkeldoorn railway, plus 50,000 of Mondoro. The N/C was prepared to surrender Gabaza and the useless, fly-ridden Sanyati, but wished to retain Ganga, Mondoro, and Cape Boy. The NRC abolished Cape Boy (6,699) and Gabaza (27,155), but retained Sanyati (98,770)[10] in the hope that the tsetse fly would move away; Ganga and Mondoro (434,377) were amalgamated, reducing the area by 24,975 to (409,402). Gabaza and the eastern part of Ganga were taken to await the Salisbury–Enkeldoorn railway which, like the Odzi–Umvuma railway through Sabi Reserve, Charter, was never built. Sanyati was still fly-ridden and unoccupied in 1930.

In 1925, the N/C, commenting on the difficulties of obtaining suitable land for NPAs, noted that there were 'miles and miles of land' north of the railway but, except near the rivers, this was waterless, unhealthy, and infested with tsetse fly. He knew of no other area since 'all land has been alienated'.[11] Later in the year his successor proposed three small NPAs: Kutama (2,157), north of the railway, Muda (12,464), and Marirangwe (14,000), formerly part of Ganga Reserve. The LC accepted these and added Msengezi (71,300), also north of the railway, and a fly-ridden Unassigned Area (340,000). These were all embodied in the LAA, though Msengezi was found, on survey to be (68,800). Two Neutral Areas of 23,500 and 73,329 were abandoned. By 1941 Muda and Marirangwe had been transferred to Salisbury District, and Msengezi had diminished, on further survey, to (60,500). Some 80 per cent of the district was European land.

Inyanga

Nearly the whole of this district, which lies on the eastern border of Rhodesia, had been alienated by 1902, and the N/C being unable to select any large unalienated blocks of land simply took what was left. The land was quite unsuitable for reserves, being precipitious, inaccessible, badly watered and generally very poor. There was insufficient land for those who might be turned off European farms in the future. On the 1902 map, the Inyanga reserves were described as 'four isolated reserves' totalling (30,720).

Within a few years the lack of adequate reserves and the imposition of rents by absentee landlords had caused many people to move across into Mozambique, with a consequent loss of revenue to the administration. At first the British Resident Commissioner's request for an additional reserve was turned down but, discovering that the loss of revenue was increasing each year, the BSA Company finally agreed in 1908 to the assignment of the new Scotsdale Reserve (63,496).

In 1914–15 the S/N Umtali, with the approval of the N/C, recommended the retention of Inyanga, the abolition of Mysinyanga, Shitowa, Matisa, and Scotsdale, which was on the Mozambique border, and the creation of a new reserve of about 210,000. Inskipp had no objection to this new Inyanga North

Reserve since one of his inspectors described it as the worst land he had ever seen. The NRC retained Inyanga (20,149), abolished Scotsdale (63,496) and Mysinyanga, Shitowa and Matisa (10,559), and created the new Inyanga North (190,965). The district also contained 41,482 of the Makoni Reserve, Makoni. The previous N/C, D. H. Moodie, who was absent on sick leave at the time, later stated that he would certainly have recommended the retention of Scotsdale, while a subsequent N/C, W. S. Bazeley, was highly critical of the NRC's work:

> When its deliberations had been published and I had had sufficient time to study the question, I became convinced that the Reserves in this district were insufficient. Nominally the area was increased but in reality the gain was small. The Inyanga North Reserve looks well on the map but most of it is barren waterless desert. The Inyanga portion of the Umtasa North Reserve [Umtali District] mainly consists of granite kopjies. Both these new Reserves are too hot for the ordinary high veldt Manyika native and both are bad for cattle. The Inyanga Reserve is too small to be of much use and the soil is poor. The Inyanga portion of the Makoni Reserve [Makoni District] is mountainous and the valleys are too hot and unhealthy. It is moreover practically full. On the other hand the valuable Scotsdale Reserve was surrendered, as well as the small Matiza, Shitowa and Msinyanga Reserves. No attempt seems to have been made to give natural boundaries to the Reserves.[12]

The NRC's recommendations were also criticized by Canon E. W. Lloyd, of St Faith's Mission, Rusape, who pointed out that land lying along the Mozambique border had been left out of the new Inyanga North which had the effect of leaving the reserve without water supplies. In January 1918 the Africans living on this land were exempted from paying rent and the area was regarded as a virtual reserve, but Archdeacon Etheridge had some mission stations there and he felt that the Africans had no security. As a result, the BSA Company finally agreed to include this land within the reserve, which was done in Government Notice No. 340 of 2 July 1920.

The situation in Inyanga remained desperate, however, for 20,000 of the 24,000 Africans lived outside the 'Hopelessly inadequate' reserves,[13] and there was nowhere to resettle Africans evicted from farms. Bazeley had the temerity to suggest that unoccupied European farms might be expropriated, but he was told that this was out of the question. Expropriation was reserved for Africans. Eventually, in Government Notice No. 593 of 7 November 1924, 3,215 acres were added to the Inyanga Reserve and 3,945 to the Makoni Reserve, which was situated in both the Makoni and Inyanga Districts though the Inyanga part was now renamed Manyika, while a new Nyamaropa Reserve (130,490) was created, half of which comprised the former Scotsdale. Bazeley commented that Nyamaropa would be a great help and might accommodate 10,000 people though it was 'very broken country' and could never be of much use to Europeans. The addition to Inyanga was 'useless for European settlement as it consists entirely of rocks, scrub and steep slopes ending in deep gorges. Even the grazing is very poor', while the Manyika (formerly Makoni) addition contained mostly 'high and precipitous cliffs and . . . steep slopes' which no European could make use of.[14]

In 1925 Bazeley proposed two NPAs, No. 2 (49,900) and No. 3 (18,900), and the LC added another of 272,500. This last included a good deal of alienated land, but the cost of expropriation proved too high for the government. It was replaced in the LAA by a small No. 4 (5,905), which was later amalgamated with the Tsonzo NPA, Umtali, and an area of 241,610, of which part comprised the Inyanga No. 1 NPA (96,840), and the remaining 144,770 comprised the Tanda NPA, Makoni. The selection of these additional NPAs had proved extremely difficult, and the expropriation bill had come to £65,000. The 1941 LAA added a new No. 4 (30,588).

The situation in Inyanga, with over 60 per cent of the district in European hands, was not a happy one. As Bazeley wrote in 1924: 'The curses of "Kaffir farming" and absentee landlordism lie like a blight on the Inyanga district. They date from the time when land was distributed haphazard to any individual or company investing capital in the country. Surely it is high time that the errors of 25 years ago were corrected.'[15]

Lomagundi

Lomagundi was a large and sparsely populated district lying to the north-west of Salisbury and extending to the Zambezi border with Northern Rhodesia. The N/C found it difficult to demarcate reserves as so many gold properties were scattered about the district. He believed that as Africans were the original owners of the land, which Europeans had occupied and exploited for their own benefit, large areas of the most suitable land should be set apart for future African needs in view of the rapid population increase which would result from European rule. In all he created ten small scattered reserves: Sipolilo (48,000), Tsheninga (19,840), Zwimba (25,600), Magondi (23,680), Tshanetsa (12,800), Bepura (22,400), Kashankarara (17,280), Tshumsimbi (25,600), Gunduza (16,000), and Dandawe (38,400). One of his successors wrote, however, that these reserves were based on an insufficient knowledge of the country and the people and were 'entirely inadequate'.[16]

In 1913 there were major alterations to the reserves. Sipolilo, Tsheninga, Zwimba, Magondi, and Bepura, then (123,885), were abolished and replaced by a new Zwimba (175,672) and Sipolilo (131,225). A new Urungwe was to be defined when the route of the proposed Zambezi railway was known. The exchange was made in order to consolidate and increase the existing scattered and inadequate reserves, and because an increasing amount of land had been taken up by white settlers since 1911.

In 1914–15 the N/C proposed the abolition of the remaining five small reserves, minor amendments to Zwimba and Sipolilo, and the creation of two new reserves, Urungwe and Magondi, though he noted that 'all the best land has been set aside for farms'.[17] The NRC accepted these proposals, abolished the undefined Tshanetsa, Kashankarara, Tshumsimbi, Gunduza, and Dandawe (105,189), increased Zwimba (175,672) by 28,150 to (203,822), reduced Sipolilo (131,225) by 8,445 to (122,780), and created the new Urungwe (472,412) and Magondi (88,260).

In 1925 the N/C suggested that Africans should not be allowed to buy any land and that Europeans should be free to purchase throughout the district. The LC had the good sense to ignore this advice, and proposed four NPAs:

No. 1 (31,200), No. 2 (55,200), Chitomborgwizi (77,800), and No. 4 (63,800). No. 2 included the land taken from Sipolilo Reserve by the NRC. The LC also proposed an Undetermined Area (9,838) and Unassigned Areas of (3,468,000), largely in the fly-ridden Zambezi Valley, and (748,000) also fly-ridden. All these proposals were embodied in the LAA. In the 1941 LAA 12,382 acres near the new Chirundu bridge across the Zambezi were taken from the large Unassigned Area now (3,455,618), and added to the European Area. Slightly less than half of the district, mostly in the south towards Salisbury, was European land while just over 40 per cent, in the 'fly belt' to the north was Unassigned.

Makoni

This district lies to the south-east of Salisbury and to the west of Inyanga. As early as 1899 the N/C was complaining that 'of course the best land in the District is occupied by farmers, syndicates and companies, and there is very little now vacant'.[18] He assigned two reserves, Makoni (53,760) and Chiduku (314,240), from what he thought was the only land left, much of it being totally unfit for cultivation. But he also believed that reserves should not be made too attractive as this might have an adverse effect on the labour supply. In 1901 his successor added two further reserves, Weya (37,760) and Chikore (40,960), on finding the original selection far too small because of the hilly nature of the ground. He was obliged however to avoid the route of a proposed railway, and to forego his own preference for that of a government surveyor whose choice of land was, he felt, totally unsuitable for a reserve.

In 1914–15 Inskipp wanted about 59,000 of Chiduku and the S/N Umtali agreed to this. The NRC reduced Chiduku (343,584) by 64,660 to (278,924), and retained Weya (54,746), Chikore (71,962), and Makoni and Manica (166,500), which were to be amalgamated and called Makoni. Manica had formerly been part of the Umtali District, while 41,482 acres of Makoni lay within the boundaries of the Inyanga District.

A protest against the surrender of part of Chiduku was made in March 1918 by Canon E. W. Lloyd, his wife, and the Rev. J. H. Upcher of St Faith's Mission. Rusape. Lloyd also criticized the omission of well-watered land from the Inyanga North Reserve, Inyanga. The British Resident Commissioner visited Chiduku with Lloyd, Atherstone, and the local N/C. He found it thickly populated, and though reluctant to depart from the NRC's recommendations without very good reason, believed that the reduction might involve hardship. The High Commissioner then referred the matter to Garraway who had been a member of the NRC, and Garraway agreed that the recommendation had been made on the basis of insufficient knowledge and that it would entail hardship. He therefore proposed that the land be retained within the reserve, which was duly effected in Government Notice No. 337 of 25 June 1920.

In 1925 the N/C proposed four NPAs and the LC accepted three of these: Dowa (35,900), Zonga (11,500) and No. 3 (1,080) which was an African-owned farm, and turned the fourth into an Undetermined Area (3,545). All were included in the LAA, together with the Tanda NPA (144,770), chosen by Taylor and Atherstone in connection with alterations in neighbouring Inyanga. Two Neutral Areas of 19,075 and 4,200 were abandoned. By 1941, 735 acres had been taken from the Undetermined Area, now (2,810), and added to No. 3, now

(1,815), and both of these areas had been transferred to the Umtali District. Over 60 per cent of Makoni lay within the European Area.

Marandellas

Marandellas town lies some 50 miles to the south-east of Salisbury on the main road and railway to Umtali and Beira. The N/C found that most of the European farms in the district were unoccupied, but he endeavoured to select reserves sufficiently large to carry the African population living on these farms should they ever be forced to move off. But 'pacification' in 1896–7 took the form of clearing the road between Salisbury and Umtali and driving Africans away from their homes along the road into the neighbouring hills. When the N/C subsequently came to assign reserves, he did so in the areas into which Africans had been pushed, mistaking them for their traditional homes.[19] The three reserves he chose were: Wedza (304,640), Shiota (217,600), and Soshwe (36,480). Much of Wedza was said to be useless because of its barren hills.

In 1907 an uninhabited area of about 19,050 acres was taken from Wedza and exchanged for an area of 18,344 acres occupied by Chief Soshwe and 1,000 followers. The exchange took place at the request of the chief. In 1911 Shiota and the neighbouring Seki Reserve, Salisbury District, were increased by 23,705. It was thought that the two reserves possessed a common boundary, but a block of 39,579 was found to separate them. This was added to Seki while an uninhabited area of 15,874 was surrendered. The rearrangement was partly for administrative convenience, and partly to include land occupied by Africans within the reserve.

In 1914–15 the N/C stated that the reserves could not be reduced and required no adjustment. Inskipp was informed that Soshwe was quite unsuitable for white settlement and that neighbouring European farmers were dependent upon it for their labour supply. The NRC retained Soshwe (28,488) and Shiota (159,185), but reduced Wedza (260,758) by 53,500 to (207,458), taking away the only part of the reserve which was not mountainous.

In 1925 the Acting N/C reported that there was no land adjoining the reserves suitable for NPAs, but the N/C who was acting as secretary to the LC proposed two NPAs, Ziyambe (80,000) and Chimbghanda (11,108), and three Undetermined Areas (4,233), (6,121), and (8,100). All were accepted by the LC and embodied in the LAA. Ziyambe included land taken from the Wedza Reserve by the NRC, and by the time of the 1941 LAA it had been found, on survey, to be (91,900); while Chimbghanda had been increased to (15,341) as a result of the transfer to it of the former Undetermined Area (4,233). Some two-thirds of the Marandellas District was European land.

Mazoe

A great deal of land had been alienated to Europeans in this district which lies immediately to the north of Salisbury, and in 1898 the N/C wrote that 'our one great difficulty will arise out of our being in some cases compelled to move Paramounts out of their districts on account of the land being taken up by Coy's and farmers'.[20] He selected reserves as close to African ancestral lands as possible, but did not know whether the land had been alienated; if it had, he asked the CNC to select the nearest available land. The reserves eventually chosen were: Chiwaridza (8,320), Bushu (37,760), Chiweshe (227,200), and Negomo (195,200).

In 1910 Bushu was moved further north to coincide with the voluntary movement of the people who had vacated the original reserve.

In 1914–15 the N/C proposed the retention of Bushu, the extension of Chiweshe-Negomo (now one reserve), and the abolition of the small Chiwaridza which was surrounded by white farms and was near the railway line. The NRC wanted to abolish Bushu and Chiweshe-Negomo, but Inskipp had neglected to ask for the former and the latter was too far from the railway. It therefore retained Bushu (33,864), extended Chiweshe-Negomo (247,635) by 38,700 to (286,335), and abolished Chiwaridza (7,054).

In 1925 the N/C reported that 'there is no vacant Crown Land in the Mazoe District and the Native Reserves are surrounded by occupied farms'.[21] Thus the LC was able to recommend only a small Undetermined Area (4,115) which was embodied in the LAA, and by 1941 part of this had become the No. 4 NPA, Salisbury District, and the remainder added to the European Area. CNC Taylor, a member of the LC, noted that consideration was shown to Mazoe Africans by assigning NPAs in neighbouring Darwin, but since Mazoe itself was 'regarded as predominatly white' and was on the *high veld*, 'no provision was made for land to be set aside as a Native Purchase Area'.[22] Nearly 90 per cent of the district lay within the European Area.

Melsetter

Wholesale alienation of land on the *high veld* took place after the arrival of the Moodie Trek in 1893 in this district, which lies on the eastern border of Rhodesia between Bikita to the west and Umtali to the north. The N/C reported that 'the very spots on which the Natives were most thickly situated, were, to a great extent, selected as farms',[23] and in 1896 he therefore proposed that reserves be established while there was still time in order to protect Africans who might be squeezed out in the future. But this was not done until peace was restored to the rest of Mashonaland, by which time the only land which he could find for Chief Musikavanu was dry and insufficient, while the land given to Mutema and Muwushu was rocky and mountainous, and to Mafusi unhealthy and feverish. He at first forgot to provide land for Chief Mutambara, but subsequently remedied this oversight. The 8 reserves selected were: Mutema (134,400), Muwushu (144,000), Mutambara (75,520), Musikwanu (128,000), Sagwenzi (27,520), Mafusi (11,520), Ingorima South (8,320), and Ingorima North (23,040). These reserves were situated almost exclusively in the *low veld*, and the majority of the *high veld* population preferred to remain on European farms and work for three months a year *without pay*, rather than move into them. As Rennie writes: 'The areas of marginal fertility provided a place for the unfortunate or uninfluential African groups during the precolonial period, and were declared Native Reserves in the colonial period.'[24]

In 1914–15 Inskipp wanted the whole of Sagwenzi, Mafusi, and Ingorima North, about 11,600 of Mutambara and 21,000 of Mutema; the local European farmers' association backed this up with a demand that all *high veld* land in the reserves be handed over to Europeans. The N/C was prepared to surrender

Sagwenzi and Ingorima North, both on the Mozambique border and the latter uninhabited, but was opposed to the reduction of Mutambara and favoured an increase to Musikwanu. The NRC abolished Sagwenzi (27,515), which caused great dissatisfaction, and Ingorima North (23,070), while retaining Mutambara (84,662), Mutema (135,175), Muwushu (146,746), Musikwanu (40,354), and Mafusi and Ingorima South (19,832), now one reserve. It would also have abolished Mafusi and Ingorima South, which were on the Mozambique border, had they not been the only *high veld* reserves in the district.

In 1925 the N/C recommended four small NPAs, the only unsurveyed areas left, and the LC accepted three of these: No. 2 (10,124) and two areas of 18,600 and 3,256 which were later amalgamated to form No. 3 (21,856), and which contained part of the former Ingorima North Reserve. The LC added two more NPAs, No. 6 (3,388), which was an African-owned farm, and Sabi (535,500), a low-lying area on the Mozambique border which included the former Sagwenzi Reserve. It also added an Undetermined Area (2,971), while two Neutral Areas of 58,800 and 38,632 were abandoned and replaced by an additional NPA, Tamandayi (9,001). By 1941, 613 acres had been taken from the Undetermined Area, now (2,358), and added to No. 6, now (4,001), while the Mahandarume NPA (16,000) and an Undetermined Area (2,993), formerly part of Umtali District, had been transferred to Melsetter. Just over half the district, and by far the poorer half, was African land.

Mrewa

The N/C, 'Wiri' Edwards, who was in charge of Mrewa from 1895 to 1931, assigned large reserves because of the rocky nature of this district which lies to the north-east of Salisbury, and because of the extensive nature of rotating cultivation. He allowed 15–20 acres per person of land fit for cultivation and adhered carefully to the old tribal boundaries, though he refused to allow Chief Mangwendi and his brother Gatzi who had fought in the 1896–7 Rising to return to their strongholds after its suppression. He also refused to allow a European farm to be pegged in the middle of one of his reserves, as this would have meant pushing Africans into broken country. Four reserves were created: Mangwendi (542,720), Uzumba (483,840), Maramba (111,760), and Fungwi (108,160).

In 1911 an uninhabited area of 64,000 acres of very rich red soil was taken from Mangwendi in return for exchanges made elsewhere.

In 1914–15 Inskipp wanted about 420,000 from the four reserves and Edwards himself was prepared to surrender 77,000 of Mangwendi and 131,000 of Uzumba. He was told by the NRC that these surrenders were inadequate and was asked to suggest further reductions. This he declined to do. The NRC retained Fungwi (153,661) and Maramba (194,721), and reduced Uzumba (502,325) by 56,100 to 446,225 and Mangwendi (593,562) by 217,885 to 375,677, claiming that the N/C had agreed that this could be done without violence to African interests. Edwards subsequently flatly contradicted this assertion, pointing out that 'there has been such a complete destruction of the Eastern part of the Mangwendi reserve that I cannot help thinking some mistake has been made in drawing up the boundaries'. As for the effect on the people, 'the announcement will come as a thunderbolt to them and cause very grave dissatisfaction'. The area in question was thickly populated and he had encouraged Africans to move there after the 1896–7 Rising.[25]

In 1925 Edwards proposed two NPAs, Chitowa (30,600) and Hoyuyu (9,700), which were accepted by the LC and included in the LAA. Chitowa contained a little of the land excised from the Mangwende and Uzumba Reserves by the NRC. About 70 per cent of the district was African land.

Mtoko

In Mtoko, which lies on the north-eastern border of Rhodesia to the east of Darwin and to the north of Inyanga, the N/C asked for 'practically the whole district' (1,802,240) to be made a reserve on account of the lack of water, the poverty of the soil, and the immensity of its useless and unprofitable granite areas.

In 1911, following the discovery of gold and a subsequent influx of white miners, some 100,000 acres were earmarked for European occupation.

By 1914–15 reserves had still not been defined, and the N/C proposed the creation of three, of 2,200, 2,500, and 288,000 acres. Instead the NRC created Mtoko (520,880). The N/C strongly criticized this recommendation, which left half the population outside the reserve which was itself too congested to permit of any large influx. He wrote:

> I feel it my duty to point out that unless the proposed boundaries are amended so as to make the necessary provision for these people, they will be suffering a grave injustice, which will result in discontent amongst the whole population of the district ... without going into statistics which are so often misleading I am of the firm opinion that sufficient ground has not been reserved for the natives of this District. The Mtoko Reserve may appear large, but it is covered with large bare granite hills, and the soil in the intervening spaces is poor and unproductive.[26]

In 1925, when giving evidence to the LC, his successor confirmed that the Mtoko Reserve was nothing but granite *kopjes*, while local chiefs complained at having the best part of their country taken away and being driven into mountainous country where they were being constantly worried by baboons.

In 1917 some 9,000 refugees entered the district following the suppression of the (Shona) Makombe Rising in Mozambique, and two pieces of land on the border, the Mkota (123,400) and Chikwizo (60,400) Reserved Areas, were set aside 'during the Governor's pleasure' in Government Notice No. 243 of 18 April 1924. They were not designated as formal reserves in case the refugees chose to return to Mozambique.

In 1925 the N/C recommended three NPAs, Budja (234,500), No. 2 (47,400), and No. 3 (34,600), commenting that there would soon be insufficient land for Africans in the Mtoko Reserve. He had been obliged to increase the area of the two small NPAs on finding that they contained more granite than he expected. These proposals were duly accepted by the LC and incorporated into the LAA, though by 1941 Budja had been reduced by 5,000 to (229,500), the surrendered area containing government offices, a hotel and a store. Just over half of the district was African land.

Ndanga

This district, on the south-eastern border of the country and lying to the south-east of Fort Victoria was large and sparsely populated, and the N/C asked unsuccessfully for the whole of it to be made a reserve as so much land had been alienated to Europeans in neighbouring Victoria. There were only three occupied white farms in Ndanga and he arranged with the owners that Africans living on them would not be moved. Four reserves were created: Ndanga (926,720), Jiri (424,320), Makouri (122,880), and Nyadjena (40,960). Nyadjena was subsequently transferred to the Victoria District.

By 1909 the CNC Mashonaland wanted large additions to these reserves, because 'at the time when reserves were set aside there was no knowledge of a great portion of the district or of the natives living there';[27] the N/C Ndanga commented that 'the Native Commissioner who originally planned out these reserves had a most rudimentary knowledge of this district'[28] and that some reserves were 'totally inadequate' while others were 'not required at all'.[29] In 1910 the Ndanga Reserve was extended fifteen miles southwards because the earlier N/C's lack of knowledge had resulted in the majority of the people being left outside the reserve. The land added was said to be very mountainous and broken.

In 1914–15 the N/C proposed the amalgamation of Ndanga, Jiri, and Makouri and various amendments so as to increase their total acreage to 1,070,720. Inskipp asked for a modification to this proposal and was opposed to the new Ndanga East Reserve given as compensation for the loss of Sagwenzi Reserve, Melsetter District, as it included excellent agricultural and ranching land. He suggested an alternative area if a new reserve was really considered necessary. The NRC accepted his advice. It created Ndanga East (95,350) and amalgamated Ndanga (639,195), Jiri (201,537), and Makouri (22,604), increasing their acreage by 299,760 to (1,163,096), the reserve to be renamed Ndanga. In 1920 when the Bikita District was carved out of the eastern part of Ndanga, part of both the Ndanga and Ndanga East Reserves fell within the boundaries of the new district, and the area remaining within Ndanga District was approximately Ndanga (824,000) and Ndanga East (40,000).

In 1925 the N/C proposed one NPA, 'but the land is ideal cotton and ranching country ... At the same time there is no other land I can recommend for the purpose'.[30] The LC did not accept his proposal, and so no NPA was assigned in the district in the LAA. Just over half of Ndanga District lay within the European Area.

Salisbury

This district, centred around the capital of Rhodesia, had 'been nearly all pegged out as farms' as early as 1897.[31] The N/C claimed, however, to have secured sufficient land for all the major chiefs with the exception of Seki and Chindamora, and he left the Survey Department to provide them with whatever land was left unalienated. In selecting reserves he attempted to exclude land which would be easily defensible in the event of a further rising.[32] Nine reserves altogether were created: Chikwakwa (47,360), Msana (53,760), Chindamora (176,640), Jeta (21,120), Kunzwi (76,800), Msungu (9,600), Nalire (8,320), Seki

(65,280), and Gwebi (42,240). Seki was thought to contain some farms whose beacons could not be determined. When they were, the farms were to be excised from the reserve.

In 1909 an uninhabited area of red soils was cut off the western part of Chikwakwa and exchanged for four *sand veld* farms, well wooded and watered, near the N/C's station at Goromonzi. This became the Chinyika Reserve (13,504). In 1911 an exchange of land occurred which turned Kunzwi and Msungu into a compact block. The areas exchanged were equal in size and of similar nature and there were only twenty families living on the land surrendered. The exchange may possibly have been motivated by the desire to harass the troublesome Chief Kunzwi-Nyandoro.[33] Also in 1911, the area of Seki and of Shiota Reserve, Marandellas District, was increased by 23,705 acres. It was thought that the reserves shared a common boundary but a strip of 39,579 was found to separate them. This was added to Seki and an uninhabited area of 15,874 was taken from the two reserves.

In 1914–15 the N/C did not think that the reserves should be readjusted or reduced though he was prepared to surrender a small part of Chindamora. Inskipp wanted the whole of Chinyika, Gwebi, Msana, and Nalire, plus 19,000 of Chindamora. The NRC abolished Gwebi (43,035) and Nalire (5,642); retained Chikwakwa (108,578), Chinyika (13,504) and Seki (88,736); and reduced Msana (74,218) by 36,000 to (38,218); Jeta and Chindamora (214,613) by 16,795 to (197,818); and Kunzwi and Msungu (63,877) by 41,350 to (22,527). The names Jeta and Msungu were dropped, and the two reserves were called Chindamora and Kunzwi.

In 1925 the N/C recommended the Shangure NPA (6,773) as 'the only land available'.[34] The land had been part of the area excised from the Kunzwi Reserve by the NRC. The recommendation was accepted by the LC and embodied in the LAA. By 1941 the number of NPAs in Salisbury had grown to four: Muda (12,464) and Marirangwe (16,200) had been transferred from Hartley, and No. 4 (4,176) from an Undetermined Area in Mazoe. Over two-thirds of the Salisbury District was European land.

Umtali

In this district, which lies on the eastern border of Rhodesia between Inyanga to the north and Melsetter to the south, the N/C lamented in 1900 that it was 'particularly unfortunate ... that nearly all the ground had been taken up here before my appointment and those parts which have been unappropriated have been either too small for reserves or not suitable'.[35] He favoured scattered reserves as these would afford less danger in the event of another rising and would moreover facilitate the labour supply. He assumed that reserves were only for those who could not come to terms with the white farmers, and he proposed a £3 rent in the reserves to avoid making them too tempting. He was able to provide reserves for Chiefs Maranke and Zimunya, but not for Umtasa. He hoped that Maranke would be able to cope with any overspill, though parts of his original choice for this reserve had been cut up into farms. The Africans of Umtali, it was said, showed marked antipathy towards moving off land which they had occupied for generations. Four reserves were created: Maranka (584,960), Zimunya (26,240), Umtasa South (12,800), and Manica

(111,360). Chief Umtasa and his Manyika people who had placed themselves under British, rather than Portuguese, protection and had strongly supported the BSA Company in 1893 and 1896, were rewarded with the loss of nearly all their land. The N/C asked the Company to expropriate some European land for them, but in vain. A subsequent N/C spoke of 'the criminal injustice initiated by the British South Africa Company' and wondered, quite erroneously, 'whether there was ever such another disgraceful breach of faith in the whole history of the British Empire'.[36]

In 1914–15 the S/N Umtali suggested that more land be assigned for Umtasa as Umtasa South was far too small, and that Zimunya be abolished and replaced as it was unsuitable. The NRC retained Zimunya (26,245), reduced Maranka (553,968) by 85,100 to (468,868), increased Umtasa South (12,805) by 2,688 to (15,493), the only increase possible, and created the Umtasa North (61,591) which Inskipp regarded as quite unsuitable for European occupation. Manica had been transferred to the Makoni District. In 1930 the CNC wrote that 'the inadequacy of land for the accommodation of Natives ... seems to me to be more marked in Umtali District than in any other'.[37]

In 1925 the N/C recommended four NPAs, three of which were accepted by the LC. They were: Mahandarume (16,000), Rowa (53,597), and Mukuni (39,800), which included land taken from Maranka Reserve by the NRC. His fourth choice was converted by the LC into an Undetermined Area (2,993). A Neutral Area of 71,000 was abandoned and replaced by the Tsonzo NPA (43,033) in the LAA. The N/C later wrote that the LC had greatly underestimated the number of Africans living on alienated land and believed that had it 'been in possession of correct figures it is possible that Umtasa's people would have been better treated in its recommendations'.[38] By 1941 several modifications to the 1930 apportionment had been made. The former No. 4 NPA (5,905), Inyanga District, was added to Tsonzo, which became (48,938); Mahandarume was transferred to Melsetter; the former No. 3 NPA (1,815), Makoni, became the new No. 3, Umtali; a new No. 4 NPA (40,322) was assigned; the Undetermined Area (2,993) was transferred to Melsetter, while another (2,810) was transferred from Makoni to Umtali. Just over half of the Umtali District was in European hands.

Victoria

This district, situated to the south-east of Gwelo and bordered on the south-west by Chibi and on the south-east by Ndanga, was yet another where the provision of reserves was very difficult. In 1898 the N/C reported:

> I do not see that Reserves could be formed so as not to cause great dissatisfaction amongst the Natives, if they had to observe them in the near future, as nearly all the land where the Natives are, within a considerable area [c. 40 miles] of the Town is held by Farmers and Companies granted at a time when the Native Department had not been established.[39]

The N/C therefore found it very difficult to select reserves which would not entail extensive movements of population, and he recognized that 'nothing hurts the Natives more than being taken away from their lands'. As far as possible he chose reserves adjoining European farms so that if Africans were ever moved off they would not have far to go. But he admitted that large parts of the reserves were rocky and unfit for cultivation and that in general they were 'about the worst part of the country, the good land having all been taken up by Farmers'.[40] Ten reserves in all were assigned, though only about 10 per cent of the population of the district actually lived in them: Zimutu (55,680), Nyamarundu (37,120), Gurajena (16,000), Chikwanda (140,800), Charambila (37,760), Mapanzula (33,920), Shumba (57,600), Mlinya (12,800), Mgabi (8,320), and Bere (17,920). Chikwanda which, like the Seki Reserve in Salisbury, contained a number of ill-defined farms which would eventually have to be excised from the reserve, was subsequently transferred to the Gutu District and Gurajena was transferred to Chilimanzi, while Nyadjena (40,960) was moved from Ndanga to Victoria.

In 1914–15 the N/C proposed the retention of Nyamarundu and Zimutu, the extension of Charambila, Mapanzula, Mgabi and Shumba by 50,000, the abolition of Mlinya and Bere, and the substitution of a new Nyadjena for the old reserve. Inskipp agreed to the surrender of Mlinya and Bere and to the Nyadjena exchange, as the old reserve was nearer to the town of Fort Victoria than the new. He considered the proposed extension unreasonable, and was against the retention of Nyamarundu and Zimutu as they abutted sixteen miles of railway line—a rare occurrence for a native reserve. A deputation of European farmers also demanded the abolition of Mlinya and Bere. The NRC duly abolished Nyamarundu (30,478), Mlinya (19,049), and Bere (11,704), retained Zimutu (47,410), created the new Mtilikwe (94,398), substituted a new Nyadjena (78,400) for the old (33,462), and amalgamated and increased by 6,985 Charambila, Mapanzula, Mgabi, and Shumba (94,146), the reserve to be called Victoria (101,131). The district also contained 17,779 of the Chikwanda Reserve, Gutu.

In 1924 the Victoria Reserve was increased by 5,000 acres to compensate for the creation of a leper settlement of the same size at the Morgenster Mission, which was taken from the reserve.

In 1925 the S/N Victoria proposed two NPAs: No. 1 (32,300), which included the old Nyamarundu Reserve, and Mshawasha, 253,700, which included the old Nyadjena Reserve. The LC accepted these and added a No. 2 (9,877). These were duly embodied in the LAA, though Mshawasha was found on survey to be only (106,000), compensation for this loss being given in the Gwanda and Gwelo Districts. By 1941 Nos. 1 and 2 had been amalgamated to form the Mshagashe NPA (42,177) and a new No. 3 (4,380) had been added. Approximately three-quarters of the district was European land.

MATABELELAND

Belingwe

In this district, which lies to the south-east of Bulawayo and to the north-west of Chibi, the N/C had no idea how much land had been granted to Europeans and his first choice for a reserve had to be abandoned when it was found to consist largely of alienated farms. He eventually selected Belingwe No. 1 (253,920) and Belingwe No. 2 (1,512,940). The No. 1 Reserve was reduced by 6,350 in 1902 when a farm of that size was found to lie within its borders.

In 1914–15 the N/C stated that No. 1 should be retained and the S/N Gwelo said the same about No. 2 while Inskipp wanted 137,000 of good ranching land from No. 2. The NRC increased Belingwe No. 1 (177,154) by 82,830 to (259,984) and reduced Belingwe No. 2 (1,005,208) by 158,740 to (846,468).

In 1925 the N/C proposed the Bungowa (154,700) and No. 2 (13,600) NPAs, which were accepted by the LC and embodied in the LAA. Bungowa included some of the land excised from Belingwe No. 2 by the NRC, and it was found, on more accurate survey, to be (105,200) by 1941. Some two-thirds of the district was African land.

Bubi

This district lies to the north of Bulawayo. By 1902 much of southern Bubi, near the town of Bulawayo, had been alienated to companies and only two very small reserves could be assigned in this area: Inyati (7,084) and Insangu (24,146). The 1894 Land Commission had earlier assigned the huge Shangani Reserve (1,917,096) in extremely inhospitable country in the north of the district. The small Ntabezinduna Reserve (26,215) was subsequently transferred to Bubi from the Bulawayo District.

In 1911 Insangu (24,152) was surrendered as part of a major exchange of land in Matabeleland. It had not been occupied for many years and was described as sandy and waterless.

In 1914–15 the N/C had the temerity to request extensions to Shangani, which was vigorously contested by Inskipp who considered the reserve excessive. The S/N Bulawayo was opposed to any reduction of Shangani, but the N/C subsequently agreed to surrender between a quarter and third in the west provided he was given an extension in the south-east. The NRC retained Inyati (7,088) and Ntabezinduna (26,221), the latter being essential as it was the only reserve near Bulawayo, and reduced Shangani (1,632,614) by 545,285 to (1,087,329), though this included a small extension of 31,470 in the south-east as requested by the N/C. The CNC later admitted that Africans disliked Shangani 'because it has a reputation for being unhealthy, and although its area is large, only a small portion of it is habitable, the remainder being forest, growing on Kalahari sand, and quite uninhabitable'.[41]

In 1925 the N/C proposed the No. 1 NPA (995,900), which lay to the west of Shangani and included much of the land excised from the reserve by the NRC. This was accepted by the LC and embodied in the LAA, together with two additional NPAs, No. 2 (110,600) and No. 3 (95,450). The former was taken from a Forest Area in conjunction with a rearrangement in Nyamandhlovu, while the latter was added in lieu of a proposed Neutral Area of 85,485. By 1941, No. 2 had been transferred to Nyamandhlovu; No. 1 was found, on survey, to be (815,900); No. 3, now Inkosikazi, was extended by 20,500 to (115,950); while the Fingo Location (25,824), the subject of much legal wrangling, was added as a fourth NPA. Some 60 per cent of the district was African land, nearly all of it in the north.

Bulalima-Mangwe

This district, which lay to the west of Bulawayo along the Bechuanaland border, contained many occupied farms though in the north the N/C was able to assign the huge Nata Reserve. The British Resident Commissioner pointed out, however, that this was simply an extension of the adjoining Gwaai Reserve and as such was open to the same objections. Reserves were assigned for the Tswana chiefs Mphoeng and Raditladi, though the original selection for Raditladi was altered in 1900 on being found totally unproductive. The reserves assigned were: Mphoeng A (63,480), Mphoeng B Extension (31,702), Raditladi (25,284), Ramaquabane A (88,544), Ramaquabane B Extension (37,963), and Nata (952,200). Initially, the huge Gwaai Reserve (2,422,820) was included in Bulalima-Mangwe and Wankie, but from 1910 it became part of the new Nyamandhlovu District.

In 1914–15 the N/C stated that either the reserves would have to be increased or the administration would have to provide further water supplies. He preferred the latter alternative. He proposed a new Semokwe to replace Ramaquabane which bordered Bechuanaland, was overcrowded and could not be enlarged as it was surrounded by farms. Semokwe should be five or six times the size of Ramaquabane and should include both sides of the Shashani river. Inskipp proposed instead that the Shashani should be the border, as the land on the east bank would probably be required for farms. The NRC retained Mphoeng A and B (95,208), Nata (855,166), and Raditladi (25,290), though the last should be surrendered when the Tswana population dropped below 200; abolished Ramaquabane A and B (126,541) and replaced it with the new Semokwe (278,748). The greater part of the eastern boundary of Semokwe lay along the Shashani river, and the new reserve was not greatly appreciated by the people who were supposed to move into it. In 1918 the N/C took three chiefs from the former Ramaquabane on a tour of inspection. They remarked:

> Never since we have known it has this land been occupied by anything but game and perhaps a few Bushmen ... there is no land fit for ploughing in the area with the exception of here on some river bank, the land in the interior is useless and nothing will ever make it crop-bearing ... the grass is poor except within a short distance of the river or stream beds, where it is very rich indeed, the area is a good one for cattle, but for people to live in is useless, and our answer must be that we cannot move on to this land, we should only come here to die if we did so.

The N/C fully endorsed the chiefs' assessment.[42]

In 1925 the N/C recommended three NPAs: Mambali, originally 29,300 but later extended by Taylor and Atherstone to (77,275), Ramaquabane (54,400) which included part of the former Ramaquabane Reserve, and Samenani (22,500). The LC added a fourth, Maitengwe (423,000), which was situated to the west of Nata Reserve along the Bechuanaland border. All were included in the LAA together with an Undetermined Area (4,233) given, together with the extension to Mambali, in lieu of two Neutral Areas of 96,329 and 25,000. By 1941 Mambali had incorporated the Undetermined Area (4,233), had become (81,508), and had been transferred to the Matobo District, while Samenani was found on survey to be (28,700), and three new NPAs had been created: No. 4 (50,901), No. 5 (180,600), and No. 6 (68,500). Just over half the district, mostly around the main road to Bulawayo, was European land.

Bulawayo

Virtually the whole of this small district surrounding the principal town of Matabeleland and the former capital of the Ndebele nation, had been alienated to Europeans in the rush for land after the 1893 Matabele War. The N/C stated that Africans recognized that all the best land was in European hands and that they had to pay rent to the white farmers. For a while the small Ntabezinduna Reserve (26,215) was situated within the district, but it was later transferred to Bubi.

In 1914–15 the district, covering some 350,000 acres, was still without a reserve. The S/N Bulawayo regarded it as a European area which required no land for Africans.

The same situation obtained in 1925; there was no land available for a NPA and none was assigned in the LAA. The whole district lay within the European Area. By 1941, however, a new No. 1 NPA (67,363) had been created in land formerly a part of Umzingwane District.

Gwanda

This remote district on Rhodesia's southern border with Bechuanaland and South Africa contained a very scattered African population and only one European farmer in 1902, with the result that it was not thought necessary to demarcate any reserves at that time.

In 1914–15 the district was still without a reserve, and both the S/N Gwelo and the S/N Bulawayo felt that there was a need for one. Inskipp successfully challenged the original choice, asking that land of poorer quality be found. He subsequently objected to the eastern boundary of the reserve crossing the Tuli river, and the NRC agreed, in assigning the new Gwanda Reserve (225,411), to demarcate the eastern boundary on the Tuli. The reserve was later described as being 'both inadequate and unsuitable'[43] and 'wholly lacking in water' except along the bank of the Tuli.[44]

In 1925 the LC ignored the N/C's request for NPAs in the northern part of the district and instead assigned two NPAs: No. 1 (1,019,613), and No. 2 (24,227), and an Unassigned Area (278,600), near the Limpopo and Shashi rivers in the south. These were incorporated into the LAA together with three more NPAs selected by Taylor and Atherstone: No. 3 (135,581), No. 4 (52,000), and No. 5 (86,860). The first was provided in lieu of two Neutral Areas of 77,000 and 101,000, and the other two as compensation for the reduction, on survey, of the Mshawasha NPA, Victoria District. By 1941 the five NPAs had been amalgamated and increased by 6,351 from the European Area to form the Tuli NPA (1,324,632), while a new No. 2 NPA (51,400) had been created.

As early as 1928 the N/C pointed out that most of the NPAs were 'waterless and uninhabitable' and that until water was provided, 'the land cannot be used for the purpose proposed'.[45] In 1943 the Governor, Sir Evelyn Baring, noted that the whole of the vast Tuli NPA lacked surface water and the population of 10,000 was concentrated along the banks of the Tuli river. He added that:

> A considerable proportion of this block, perhaps one half, will probably never be inhabitable; it is all low bush veld country. In any case none of it is suitable for division into individual plots since such action would imply the construction of one well per farm and the Government will never be prepared to provide the money.[46]

Some 70 per cent of the district was European land.

Gwelo

The town of Gwelo lies some 100 miles to the north-east of Bulawayo on the main road and railway to Salisbury. Much of the surrounding district was cut up into farms at an early date. In 1896 the N/C believed that 'the people should be left with their original lands, because they were healthier than the lower parts of the [district], and because they were more productive';[47] but his successor in 1899 who actually demarcated the Lower Gwelo (101,568) and Que Que (25,392) Reserves, disregarded this advice and indeed decided to make them 'as small as possible'.[48] He claimed subsequently that Que Que was well watered and ample for its purpose.

In 1914–15 the S/N Gwelo asked for increases to Lower Gwelo and Que Que. Inskipp had no objection as the land added to Lower Gwelo was of little or no value even for ranching, while the Que Que extension was balanced by the reduction of Mondoro Reserve, Hartley. The NRC increased Lower Gwelo (100,535) by 30,090 to (130,625) in order to increase its supply of water, and Que Que (20,572) by 25,820 to (46,392).

In 1925 the N/C, who was by now finding great difficulty providing room for Africans being evicted from farms, proposed three NPAs of 92,300, 104,600 and 50,800, which the LC accepted, although Atherstone was opposed to the last of these, adding an Undetermined Area (11,900). The Undetermined Area was included in the LAA but all the NPAs were altered by Taylor and Atherstone in 1926–9. The first was found, on survey, to be only 86,000 (No. 1); the second, which bordered the Shangani Reserve, was increased to 157,091 (No. 2) in lieu of two Neutral Areas of 40,996 and 19,119; while the third was exchanged for a new area, No. 5 (54,000). Two more NPAs were added, Gokomera (8,776) and Vungu (12,787), the latter being compensation for the reduction, on survey, of the Mshawasha NPA, Victoria District. By 1941 two new NPAs of 142,390 and 18,072 had been added to Nos. 1, 2, and 5, and the whole area was amalgamated and became the Silobela NPA (457,553), while the Undetermined Area had been reduced to (8,598). In 1928–9 the No. 1 NPA was described as 'largely uninhabitable'[49] and 'useless both from an agricultural and a pastoral point of view'.[50] Nearly 90 per cent of the district lay within the European Area.

Insiza

Practically the whole of this district, which lies immediately to the east of Bulawayo, had been cut up into farms, and the N/C suggested that some of it be bought back in order to provide a suitable reserve. This was flatly rejected, but he eventually found some land, only to have it reduced because it clashed in parts with the projected Gwanda railway route. The reserve was called Insiza-Manzamnyama (95,220).

In 1911 Insiza-Manzamnyama was reduced by 16,932 as part of a major re-arrangement of land in Matabeleland. The surrendered land was thinly populated and contained light sandy soils which the Ndebele eschewed in favour of the heavier red soils.

In 1914–15 the N/C regarded the reserve, now known simply as Insiza, as unsuitable, but he was opposed to its abolition as he had assured the people that it would always remain a reserve. He asked for four unalienated farms to be turned into a reserve, but Inskipp firmly opposed the creation of any new reserve in the midst of a district devoted to European settlement. The NRC retained Insiza (64,321) because although it was thinly populated it was surrounded by farms on which there was a large African population. The CNC later admitted that the district was 'badly off with regard to land and that the Insiza Reserve was 'rather small and of poor quality'.[51]

In 1925 the N/C pointed out that: 'The difficulty now is to place the natives on really good soil... position is that practically the whole of the district consists of farms and the result is that the natives are gradually being squeezed out.'[52] He recommended the Godhlawayo NPA (133,500) and No. 2 (9,919), which comprised two European farms lying within Godhlawayo. The LC accepted these, and Taylor and Atherstone added the Gwatemba NPA (69,141) given in lieu of Neutral Areas abandoned elsewhere. By 1941, 2,340 of new land had been added to Godhlawayo, which now incorporated No. 2 and totalled (145,759). Over 80 per cent of the district was European land.

Matobo

Almost the whole of this district which lies directly to the south of Bulawayo, was alienated to Europeans in the years 1893–4. A reserve was selected in the Matopos Hills by the first N/C but his successor was unable to find it, and it had in any event to be abandoned as it contravened the terms of peace issued at the end of the Ndebele Rising. The district was therefore left without a reserve.

In 1911 the new Matobo Reserve (51,432) was created as part of a general exchange of land in Matabeleland. A reserve was necessary because of the increasing number of Europeans settling in the district, and the British Resident Commissioner reported that the soil in Matobo was very rich.

In 1914–15 the N/C asked for a new reserve in the Matopos Hills where the BSA Company had never attempted to collect any rent, and Inskipp offered no objection as the area was infested with baboons and was only traversable by pack animals. The NRC retained Matobo (51,431) and created the new Matopo (124,579). To avoid confusion, Matobo was subsequently renamed Shashani.

In 1925 the N/C noted that 'most of the land adjoining Native Reserves has been taken up by Europeans', and suggested that a number of farms be expropriated in order to create a NPA.[53] The LC rejected this, and proposed only a Neutral Area of 34,020 which, like all the Neutral Areas, was abandoned. The only NPA assigned in the LAA was Mount Sibali (7,259), which was a farm purchased by an African in 1920. By 1941, however, four more NPAs had been added to the district: Mambali (81,508) had been transferred from Bulalima-Mangwe, and the new No. 3 (64,496), No. 4 (57,600), and No. 5 (5,300) had been created in the south of the extended district, bordering on Gwanda. Over 80 per cent of the district lay within the European Area.

Nyamandhlovu

This district, lying to the north-west of Bulawayo, was created in 1910 out of the northern part of Bulalima-Mangwe. It contained the huge and largely worthless Gwaai Reserve (2,422,820) which had been assigned by the 1894 Land Commission.

In 1911, as part of a major exchange of land in Matabeleland, Gwaai was reduced by 816,349 acres around the Victoria Falls railway line. But the surrendered area was waterless, its soil was wretchedly poor, it was unpopular because of a poisonous weed which affected cattle, and it carried a population of only twelve.

In 1914–15 the N/C commented that if the Gwaai were well watered it would be far too large, but he was in any event prepared to surrender its western half. He asked unsuccessfully for the addition of a small area of well watered land. The S/N Bulawayo was opposed to any reduction, but the CNC felt that the western half might be surrendered. The NRC reduced Gwaai (1,377,867) by 877,867 in the west, but 600,000 were promptly returned in the shape of a 'reserve' reserve created to allay Imperial fears of a too drastic overall reduction of the reserves. The revised Gwaai was (1,100,000).

In 1925 the N/C had 'to take into consideration the fact that the best part of the land has already been taken up by Europeans'.[54] He recommended one NPA of 54,600, and the LC added another of 58,700, an Undetermined Area of 16,400, and an Unassigned Area (270,000), which included land excised from the western part of the Gwaai Reserve by the NRC. The Unassigned Area was embodied in the LAA but all the other proposals were altered by Taylor and Atherstone. The NPA of 58,700 was transferred to the Forest Area, and that of 54,600, together with the Undetermined Area of 16,400, were abandoned on being found to contain a poisonous weed. They were replaced by a new No. 1 NPA, of which (26,900) were in Nyamandhlovu and 110,600 in Bubi. By 1941 the 110,600 had been transferred to Nyamandhlovu, but 61,600 had been surrendered to the Forest Area leaving the Gwaai NPA, as it was now called, (75,900). The land was divided almost equally between Africans and Europeans, with the Europeans having slightly the larger half of the assigned land. But the Europeans had virtually all the land in the eastern part of the district near Bulawayo, while Africans were confined to the barren Kalahari sands to the west.

Sebungwe

This large, remote and fly-ridden district bordering the Zambezi in the north-west of Rhodesia was not brought under formal administrative control until 1898. There was no European penetration and consequently no need to assign reserves in 1902.

In 1911, as part of the general exchange of land in Matabeleland, three reserves were technically created in Sebungwe. They were Pashu, Sibaba, and Impampa, each of them shown as a circle on the map and estimated to be 67,729. Care was taken that none actually abutted the Zambezi river. The British Resident Commissioner did not visit the district, but believed that the fact that people had voluntarily settled in the areas concerned pointed to their being suitable. He suggested successfully that their areas be doubled from the size originally proposed by the BSA Company. Shortly afterwards, Africans were moved from the reserves and settled further south as part of a series of anti-tsetse measures.

In 1914–15 Inskipp had no information about the land which the NRC proposed to add to the existing reserves, but in view of the remoteness of the district he considered it unlikely that the land would ever be needed for European settlement. The NRC retained the undefined Pashu (67,729), Sibaba (67,729), and Impampa (67,729), all of them now uninhabited, and created the new Sebungwe (235,800) in the area thought most suitable by the BSA Company's Medical Director. It later added the 'reserve' reserve Omay (660,500) as a sop to the Imperial conscience. The Sebungwe was subsequently described as being 'wild waterless country with no inhabitants',[55] while the reserves in general were thought to be 'of little, if any, use being sparsely inhabited and containing little arable land away from the rivers'.[56] By 1930 only two of the reserves, Impampa and Omay, were inhabited, with a combined population of about 3,000.

In 1925 the LC did not trouble to visit the district and declared virtually the whole of it an Unassigned Area (6,568,700), a proposal endorsed in the LAA. Thus nearly 80 per cent of Sebungwe was left Unassigned; and of the remainder, 17 per cent was African land, and only 3 per cent European land. This was by far the smallest proportion of Euopean land in any district of Rhodesia; the next lowest figure was 25 per cent in Darwin.

Selukwe

This district, which lies to the south-east of Gwelo and to the north-west of Victoria, was well populated and much of it was cut up into farms during the 1890s. The N/C therefore selected a large reserve which he unsuccessfully attempted to have enlarged in 1899. The reserve was called Selukwe (160,816).

In 1914–15 the S/N Gwelo stated that the reserve could not be reduced. The NRC retained Selukwe (158,740), which was by now almost entirely surrounded by farms.

In 1925 the N/C advocated the expropriation of farms surrounding the Selukwe Reserve as most of the owners were absentee landlords indulging in 'kaffir farming'. The LC duly proposed the Tokwe (24,100) and Jobolinko (11,983) NPAs, plus an Undetermined Area of 6,879. All were included in the LAA, though the Undetermined Area was increased to (12,132) in lieu of a Neutral Area of 62,411. By 1941 Jobolinko had been increased by 1,540 from the Undetermined Area and was (13,523), while three additional NPAs had been assigned; No. 3 (5,253), No. 4 (11,122), and No. 5 (3,894). The Undetermined Area had been reduced by 8,746 to (3,386), of which 1,540 had been added to Jobolinko; 5,253 had become the No. 3 NPA, and 1,953 had been 'lost' on faulty survey. Nearly 80 per cent of the district lay within the European Area.

Umzingwane

Practically the whole of this small district lying immediately to the south-east of Bulawayo had been alienated to Europeans, over half of it being in the hands of Willoughby's Consolidated Co., Ltd. The N/C was therefore able to select only one small reserve which had to be reduced by 2,000 acres in 1899 when it was found to include an unoccupied farm. The reserve was called Umzingwane (4,763).

In 1914–15 the S/N Bulawayo said he regarded the district as a European area, and he advocated the surrender of the reserve. But the NRC retained Umzingwane (4,764), for although it was surrounded by occupied farms it was the site of Government offices and no good purpose would be served by its abolition.

In 1925 the N/C observed 'there is no land in this District which is suitable for setting aside for native occupation ... the whole District should be reserved for European ownership'.[57] The S/N Bulawayo disagreed; he thought there was a great need for land in Umzingwane, and on the basis of his recommendation Carter and Taylor proposed a Neutral Area of 95,300. But this was abandoned with all the other Neutral Areas, and no NPA was assigned in the LAA. Over 99 per cent of the district was European land.

Wankie

This remote district in the western corner of Rhodesia, like Sebungwe, was not brought under formal administrative control until 1898. No European had taken up land and there was therefore no need to assign reserves in 1902, though until the Nyamandhlovu District was created in 1910 part of the Gwaai Reserve fell within the boundaries of Wankie.

In 1914–15 the N/C at first favoured the creation of two small reserves, but he found great difficulty in selecting suitable areas. He later proposed one large area, but because of its extremely mountainous nature, only a small proportion was suitable for cultivation. Inskipp had no objection to this, as he was informed that the land was most exceptionally poor. The NRC thus created the new Wankie (317,481). Its capacity was later found to be 'by no means equal to the whole population', as it could only absorb, at most, half of the Africans living outside it.[58]

The situation was sufficiently serious for the Government to set aside the Wankie Additional Reserves A (79,200) and B (93,200), adjoining the main reserve, in Government Notice No. 215 of 11 April 1924. One of Inskipp's inspectors commented on the new reserves, 'no settlement can take place other than possibly an isolated area here and there';[59] while the N/C described 'A' as 'waterless, rocky and barren', and remarked of 'B', 'I have seen no poorer land in Rhodesia'.[60]

In 1925 there was no possibility of assigning NPAs, and the LC proclaimed three Unassigned Areas, (233,000), (3,000,000) and (1,053,000), which were duly embodied in the LAA. Just over half of the district was thus left Unassigned; about 45 per cent was European land, most of it surrounding the Victoria Falls railway line and as yet unsold, and only 5 per cent was African land.

NOTES

1. ZAD 3/2/2, N/C Charter to Secretary, NRC, 15 November 1915.
2. ZAH 2/1/1, N/C Charter to Secretary, LC, 19 March 1925.
3. ZAD 3/2/2, N/C Darwin to S/N Salisbury, 9 July 1915.
4. ZAH 2/1/1, N/C Darwin to Secretary, LC, 13 March 1925.
5. A 3/18/39/3, N/C Gutu to S/N Victoria, 21 May 1913.
6. D.O. 119/586, Report of the N/C Hartley for the quarter ending March 1900.
7. N 3/24/11, N/C Hartley to CNC Mashonaland, 7 July 1900.
8. D.O. 119/586, Report of the N/C Hartley for the quarter ending June 1900.
9. D.O. 119/586, Report of the N/C Hartley for the quarter ending March 1900.
10. The NRC (p. 51) records the area of Sanyati as 98,710, but it is clear from the NRC's statistical tables that the figure should read 98,770.
11. ZAH 2/1/1, N/C Hartley to Secretary, LC, 3 April 1925.
12. A 3/18/39/16, N/C Inyanga to CNC, 31 August 1922.
13. C.O. 417/694, Minute by Davis, 26 July 1923.
14. S 138/196, N/C Inyanga to S/N Umtali, 17 May 1924.
15. S 235/370, N/C Inyanga to S/N Umtali, 21 March 1924.
16. LB 2/1/16, N/C Lomagundi to CNC, 22 October 1915.
17. LB 2/1/16, N/C Lomagundi to CNC, 22 October 1915.
18. N 9/4/5, Report of the N/C Makoni for the month November 1899.
19. R. Hodder-Williams, 'Marandellas and the Mashona Rebellion', *Rhodesiana*, **16,** 1967, 51.
20. N 9/1/4, Report of the Acting N/C Mazoe for the year ending March 1898.
21. ZAH 2/1/1, N/C Mazoe to Secretary, LC, 4 March 1925.
22. F 48/L5, CNC to Secretary to Premier, 23 May 1927.
23. NUE 2/1/2, Report of the N/C Melsetter for the half-year ending September 1897.
24. J. K. Rennie, 'Christianity, Colonialism and the Origins of Nationalism among the Ndau of Southern Rhodesia, 1890–1935', Ph.D. thesis, Northwestern University, Illinois, 1973, 40.
25. A 3/3/20/2, N/C Mrewa to S/N Salisbury, 18 June 1917.
26. A 3/3/20/2, N/C Mtoko to S/N Salisbury, 3 August 1917.
27. L 2/2/117/1, CNC Mashonaland to Director of Land Settlement, 16 November 1909.
28. L 2/2/117/46, Assistant N/C Ndanga to Acting CNC Mashonaland, 31 July 1907.
29. L 2/2/117/46, Assistant N/C Ndanga to S/N Victoria, 4 September 1908.
30. ZAH 2/1/1, N/C Ndanga to S/N Victoria, 14 March 1925.
31. N 9/2/1, Report of the N/C Salisbury for the half-year ending September 1897.
32. P. S. Garlake, 'The Mashona Rebellion East of Salisbury', *Rhodesiana*, **14,** 1966, 10.
33. T. O. Ranger, *Revolt in Southern Rhodesia, 1896–7* (London 1967), 365–6.
34. ZAH 2/1/1, N/C Salisbury to CNC, 12 March 1925.
35. NUA 2/1/3, Report of the N/C Umtali for the half-year ending March 1900.
36. S 1542/L4, N/C Umtali to CNC, 29 September 1938.
37. S 138/21, CNC to Secretary to Premier, 7 August 1930.
38. S 1542/L4, Memo by N/C Umtali, 1 October 1937.
39. N 9/1/4, Report of the N/C Victoria for the year ending March 1898.
40. D.O. 119/586, Report of the N/C Victoria for the quarter ending June 1900.
41. S 1542/N2, CNC to Secretary to Premier, 13 April 1931.
42. A 3/3/20/3, N/C Bulalima-Mangwe to S/N Bulawayo, 23 May 1914.
43. A 3/3/20/3, CNC to Secretary, Department of Administrator, 23 June 1920.
44. L 2/2/122, N/C Gwanda to S/N Bulawayo, 22 July 1919.
45. D.O. 63/5, N/C Gwanda to S/N Bulawayo, 10 January 1928.
46. D.O. 35/1169, Baring to Machtig, 9 June 1943.
47. LO 5/6/7, N/C Gwelo to CNC Matabeleland, 30 November 1896.

48. L 2/2/117/40, N/C Gwelo to CNC Matabeleland, 20 May 1899.
49. S 138/21, S/N Bulawayo to CNC, 31 August 1929.
50. S 138/21, N/C Gwelo to S/N Bulawayo, 15 August 1928.
51. S 1542/N2, CNC to Secretary to Premier, 13 April 1931.
52. ZAH 1/1/2, Evidence of N/C Insiza to LC, 28 March 1925, 597.
53. ZAH 2/1/1, N/C Matobo to Secretary, LC, 18 March 1925.
54. ZAH 1/1/2, Evidence of N/C Nyamandhlovu to LC, 28 March 1925, 577.
55. S 235/515, Report of the N/C Sebungwe for the year 1936.
56. S 138/206, N/C Sebungwe to S/N Bulawayo, 22 March 1924.
57. ZAH 2/1/1, N/C Umzingwane to Secretary, LC, 17 March 1925.
58. A 3/20/3, S/N Bulawayo to CNC, 7 July 1920.
59. N 3/24/4, Land Inspector Boyes to F. W. Inskipp, 6 May 1922.
60. N 3/24/4, N/C Wankie to CNC, 26 September 1923.

APPENDIX II

List of Farms Owned by Africans in 1925

The following list[1] provides details of the fourteen farms, totalling 46,966 acres, which Africans had managed to buy by 1925, despite the refusal of both the BSA Company and the Southern Rhodesian Government to honour the law which clearly stipulated that 'A native, may acquire ... land on the same conditions as a person who is not a native'. Information, where available, is given about the size of each farm, the name of the owner and his nationality, the amount he paid for his farm and what happened to it under the Land Apportionment Act of 1930. The list is arranged chronologically, according to year of purchase.

1. Maya and Gwabu, who were both Shona (Rozvi), bought 25 acres of the Riverside Agricultural Lots, six miles from Bulawayo, for £270 in 1898. They bought the farm from wages they had earned during the Matabele War. By 1910 the whole farm was under cultivation; they had built brick houses, sunk wells, used irrigation and planted orchards. They owned mules, donkeys, carts and wagons, and grew barley, oats and vegetables which they often sold to neighbouring European farmers, and from which they made a good deal of money. The land became part of the European Area under the LAA, and the owners were paid £880 in compensation.

2. Tom Zonzo and five other Zulu missionaries of the American Board Mission at Mount Silinda bought six sub-divisions of the farm Emerald, totalling 3,386 acres, in the Melsetter District, for £190 in 1902. The farm was bought from the former missionary F. W. Bates who, on being found in bed with a Zulu girl at the mission, was sent on leave and not invited to return. Under the LAA the farm became the No. 6 Native Purchase Area, Melsetter District, and after most of the original Zulu owners left the country, c. 1930, it gradually passed into the hands of local Shona (Ndau) farmers.

3. The Rev. M. Dipulela Makgatho and David Mogale bought 89 acres of the Riverside Agricultural Lots, six miles from Bulawayo, from Willoughby's for £436 in 1904. Makgatho was a Sotho minister of the African Methodist Episcopal Church, who 'set out to establish a series of AMEC schools which would provide the Ndebele with modernizing education under African control'.[2] He opened a school at Riverside and professed himself well satisfied with

his farm when giving evidence to the 1925 Land Commission. However, the land became part of the European Area under the LAA, though he was paid £1,137 in compensation.

4. Jacob Mulibalini, a Sotho, together with two other Sotho and a Shangaan, bought the farm Erichstal, 14,202 acres, in the Victoria District, for £1,000 in 1907. The land became part of the European Area under the LAA, but the owners were given 11,656 acres in the Mungesi NPA, Bikita District, in exchange, and paid £2,118 in compensation.

5. Ephriam Morudu and nine other Sotho bought the farm Niekerk's Rust, 3,249 acres, in the Victoria District, for £900 in 1909. The land became part of the European Area under the LAA, but the owners were given 5,228 acres in the Dewure NPA, Gutu District, in exchange, and paid £374 in compensation.

6. John Hongwe and five others, all of them Shona (Karanga) teachers from the Dutch Reformed Church Mission at Morgenster, bought the farm Rugby, 3,247 acres, in the Victoria District, for 100 head of cattle in 1911. They had tried unsuccessfully to buy land from the BSA Company in 1909. Under the LAA the farm was included in the No. 2 NPA, Victoria District, later named Mshagashe.

7. Frank Sixubu, a Zulu missionary of the Anglican Church who had served the Mashonaland Mission since 1891, bought the farm Waterfall Induna, 618 acres, seven miles from Salisbury, for £400 in 1911. He was able to pay for the farm by selling some cattle, which were then fetching high prices. By 1925 he was employing eight full-time labourers and was 'drawing upon the rents of fourteen squatter families'.[3] He was cultivating about ten acres, and was using the remainder to graze his 50 head of cattle and 20 donkeys. He earned £10 per month from the sale of wood, and was very glad that he had bought the farm. It became part of the European Area under the LAA, however, and it is probable that Sixubu was bought out before the Act came into force.

8. Thomas Mazinyani, a Sotho, bought 6 acres of the farm Trenance Plot, about six miles from Bulawayo, for £150 in 1916. On this small plot he built a house worth £200 and employed one full-time labourer. He was glad he had bought the land and told the Land Commission that he wanted more. Though a Sotho, Mazinyani 'completely identified himself with the Ndebele and was accepted by them as a member of the Enhla caste'.[4] He supported the Ndebele royalist movement under Nyamanda and became a prominent member of the Rhodesian Bantu Voters' Association. It was he who told the Land Commission: 'I do not see why the Subjects of any one King should be separated. Seeing that all the natives are ruled by the British Government there should be no distinction in regard to their being able to purchase land.'[5] Mazinyani's farm became part of the European Area under the LAA, and he was paid only £187 in compensation.

9. Albert Nxale, probably a Xhosa, bought 40 acres of the farm Trenance Plot, about six miles from Bulawayo. The date of the purchase and the price paid

are not known. The land became part of the European Area under the LAA, and it is probable that Nxale was bought out before the Act came into force.

10. George Nyangazonke, probably an Ndebele, bought the farm Stutterlingen, 7,258 acres, in the Matobo District, for £3,000 in 1920. He bought it because Europeans were continually impounding his cattle. Under the LAA the farm became the Mount Sibali NPA, Matobo District.

11. Kohle Sekani, probably an Ndebele, bought sub-division 'A' of the farm Guswini, 1,000 acres, in the Bulalima-Mangwe District, for £300 in c. 1920. The land became part of the European Area under the LAA, and was exchanged for 1,058 acres in the Ramaquabane NPA, Bulalima-Mangwe District.

12. Madhloli Kumalo, a nephew of Lobengula, bought the farm West Junction, 6,417 acres, in the Nyamandhlovu District, for £2,400 in 1921. Madhloli was a leading ally of Nyamanda in the Ndebele royalist movement, and later became a member of the Rhodesian Bantu Voters' Association. He bought the farm largely because he was tired of being moved from place to place by European farmers. He paid for part of it by selling 500 head of cattle, but in 1925 felt unable to pay off the remainder. He cultivated the land and grazed cattle, and also sold timber to the saw-mills, which sometimes brought him £70 a month. Five villages were established on his farm, but, unlike Frank Sixubu, he exacted no rent or labour dues from them. The land became part of the European Area under the LAA, but the Government paid off Madhloli's debt of £1,048 and exchanged his farm for 4,233 acres in the Gwaai NPA, Nyamandhlovu District.

13. The Shona (Manyika) Chief Makoni bought the farm Mbobo Vale, 6,350 acres, in the Makoni District, for about £1,000 in 1922. The land in question was 'the ancestral home of the Makoni chiefs, and the tribe decided to purchase it rather than have the chief and his family in danger of being removed to the reserve'.[6] Under the LAA the farm became part of the Zonga NPA, Makoni District.

14. Kawadza, a Shona (Manyika), bought sub-divison 'A' of the farm Buffalo Bush, 1,079 acres, in the Makoni District, for £750 in 1922. He had not finished paying off the farm by 1925, though he was growing and selling a good many mealies. Under the LAA the farm became the No. 3 NPA, Makoni District.

CONCLUSION

Thus of the fourteen farms, totalling 46,966 acres, purchased by Africans on the theoretically 'open' market before 1925, seven were bought by black Rhodesians, and seven by black South Africans. Nine of these farms, totalling 25,646 acres, were placed in the European Area under the LAA, while the remaining five, totalling 21,320 acres, became part of the Native Purchase Area.

NOTES

1. This list is compiled on the basis of two, slightly different, 'schedules of land owned by natives', dated 1926, in files S 96 and Hist. MSS. AT 1/2/1/10. Further information is contained in the reports of the Native Land Board, the Chief Native Commissioner and District Native Commissioners, in the evidence to the Land Commission, and in T. O. Ranger, *The African Voice in Southern Rhodesia* (Nairobi 1970).
2. Ranger, *African Voice*, 42.
3. Ranger, *African Voice*, 59.
4. Ranger, *African Voice*, 92.
5. ZAH 1/1/2, Evidence of T. Mazinyani to Land Commission, 30 March 1925, 683.
6. *Report of the Chief Native Commissioner for the year 1922* (Salisbury 1923), 2.

SELECT BIBLIOGRAPHY

1 Theses

BEACH, D. N., 'The Rising in South-Western Mashonaland, 1896–7', Ph.D. thesis, University of London, 1971.

BECK, J. H., 'The Chinyika Reserve, Southern Rhodesia. A Geographical Study', M.A. thesis, University of London, 1957.

CHANOCK, M. L., 'British Policy in Central Africa, 1908–26', Ph.D. thesis, Cambridge University, 1968.

CLARKE, D. G., 'The Political Economy of Discrimination and Underdevelopment in Rhodesia with Special Reference to African Workers, 1940–1973', Ph.D. thesis, University of St. Andrews, 1975.

COBBING, J. R. D., 'The Ndebele under the Khumalos, 1820–96', Ph.D. thesis, University of Lancaster, 1976.

DUIGNAN, P. J., 'Native Policy in Southern Rhodesia, 1890–1923', Ph.D. thesis, Stanford University, 1961.

FAGE, J. D., 'The Achievement of Self-Government in Southern Rhodesia, 1898–1923', Ph.D. thesis, Cambridge University, 1949.

HASSING, P. S., 'The Christian Missions and the British Expansion in Southern Rhodesia, 1888–1923', Ph.D. thesis, The American University, 1960.

HODDER-WILLIAMS, R., 'The Development of Social, Economic and Political Attitudes in a European Community, 1890–1968', draft thesis.

JOHNSON, R. W. M., 'The Economics of African Agriculture in Southern Rhodesia: A Study of Resource Use', Ph.D. thesis, University of London, 1968.

KEYTER, C. F., 'Maize Control in Southern Rhodesia 1931–1939: The African Contribution to White Survival', M.A. thesis, University of Rhodesia, 1974.

KOSMIN, B. A., 'Ethnic and Commercial Relations in Southern Rhodesia: A Socio-Historical Study of the Asian, Hellenic and Jewish populations, 1898–1943', Ph.D. thesis, University of Rhodesia, 1974.

LEE, M. E., 'Politics and Pressure Groups in Southern Rhodesia, 1898–1923', Ph.D. thesis, University of London, 1974.

MACKENZIE, J. M., 'African Labour in South Central Africa, 1890–1914 and Nineteenth Century Colonial Labour Theory', Ph.D. thesis, University of British Columbia, 1969.

MARGOLIS, W., 'The Position of the Native Population in the Economic Life of Southern Rhodesia', M.A. thesis, University of South Africa, 1938.

MCGREGOR, R., 'Native Segregation in Southern Rhodesia. A Study of Social Policy', Ph.D. thesis, University of London, 1940.

MCHARG, J., 'Influences contributing to the Education and Culture of the Native People in Southern Rhodesia from 1900 to 1961', D.Ed. thesis, Duke University, 1962.

MOYANA, H. V., 'Land Apportionment in Rhodesia 1920–1960', Ph.D. thesis, Columbia University, 1975.

NDANGA, H. J., 'The Labour Problem in Southern Rhodesia, 1896–1904', M.A. thesis, University of London, 1970.

PALMER, R. H., 'The Making and Implementation of Land Policy in Rhodesia, 1890–1936', Ph.D. thesis, University of London, 1968.

PHIMISTER, I. R., 'History of Mining in Southern Rhodesia to 1953', Ph.D. thesis, University of Rhodesia, 1975.

RENNIE, J. K., 'Christianity, Colonialism and the Origins of Nationalism among the Ndau of Southern Rhodesia, 1890–1935', Ph.D. thesis, Northwestern University, 1973.

RIFKIND, M. L., 'The Politics of Land in Rhodesia', M.Sc. thesis, University of Edinburgh, 1968.

ROONEY, M. G. B., 'European Agriculture in the History of Rhodesia, 1890–1907', M.A. thesis, University of South Africa, 1968.

SAMKANGE, S. J. T., 'The Establishment of African Reserves in Matabele Land, 1893–1898', Ph.D. thesis, Indiana University, 1968.

STEELE, M. C., 'The Foundations of a "Native" Policy in Southern Rhodesia, 1923–33', Ph.D. thesis, Simon Fraser University, 1972.

TAYLOR, J. J., 'The Native Affairs Department in Southern Rhodesia, 1894–1914', Ph.D. thesis, University of London, 1974.

VAN ONSELEN, C., 'African Mine Labour in Southern Rhodesia, 1900–1933', Ph.D. thesis, Oxford University, 1974.

WARHURST, P. R., 'Rhodesia and her Neighbours, 1900–23', Ph.D. thesis, Oxford University, 1970.

2 Books and Pamphlets

ALLAN, W., *The African Husbandman* (Edinburgh and London 1965).

ANDREWS, C. F., *John White of Mashonaland* (London 1935).

ARRIGHI, G., *The Political Economy of Rhodesia* (The Hague 1967).

BARBER, J. P., *Rhodesia: The Road to Rebellion* (London 1967).

BARBER, W. J., *The Economy of British Central Africa* (London 1961).

BARKLIE, J., *The Title Tangle in Southern Rhodesia* (Bulawayo 1913).

BATTEN, T. R., *Problems of African Development, Part I: Land and Labour* (London 1954).

BAXTER, T. W., (Ed.), *Guide to the Public Archives of Rhodesia, Vol. 1: 1890–1923* (Salisbury 1969).

BAXTER, T. W. and BURKE, E. E., *Guide to the Historical Manuscripts in the National Archives of Rhodesia* (Salisbury 1970).

BERTIN, H., *Land Titles in Southern Rhodesia* (Salisbury 1912).

BOURDILLON, M. F. C., *The Shona Peoples* (Gwelo 1976).

BOWMAN, L. W., *Politics in Rhodesia: White Power in an African State* (Cambridge, Mass. 1973).

BRELSFORD, W. V. (Ed.), *Handbook to the Federation of Rhodesia and Nyasaland* (London and Salisbury 1960).

BROOMFIELD, G. W., *Colour Conflict: Race Relations in Africa* (London 1943).

BROWN, K., *Land in Southern Rhodesia* (London 1959).

BROWN, W. H., *On the South African Frontier* (New York 1899).

BUELL, R. L., *The Native Problem in Africa, Vol. 1* (New York 1928).

BULL, T. (Ed.), *Rhodesian Perspective* (London 1967).

BULLOCK, C., *The Mashona and the Matabele* (Cape Town 1950).

BULMAN, M. E., *The Native Land Husbandry Act of Southern Rhodesia: A Failure in Land Reform* (Salisbury 1975).

CAIRNS, H. A. C., *Prelude to Imperialism* (London 1965).

CARY, R., *Charter Royal* (Cape Town 1970).

CATHOLIC INSTITUTE FOR INTERNATIONAL RELATIONS, *The Man in the Middle: Torture, Resettlement and Eviction* (Slough 1975).

CLEMENTS, F., *Rhodesia: The Course to Collision* (London 1969).

CLEMENTS, F. and HARBEN, E., *Leaf of Gold: The Story of Rhodesian Tobacco* (London 1962).

CLUTTON-BROCK, G. and M., *Cold Comfort Confronted* (London and Oxford 1972).

CREIGHTON, T. R. M., *The Anatomy of Partnership* (London 1960).

CRIPPS, A. S., *An Africa for Africans* (London 1927).

—— *How Roads were Made in the Native Reserves of Charter District, Mashonaland, 1934–5* (London 1936).

—— *The Sabi Reserve* (Oxford 1920).

CROXTON, A. H., *Railways of Rhodesia* (Newton Abbot 1973).

DAVIES, M. A. G., *Incorporation in the Union of South Africa or Self-government: Southern Rhodesia's Choice, 1922* (Pretoria 1965).

DAY, J., *International Nationalism* (London 1967).

DENOON, D., *Southern Africa since 1800* (London 1972).

DICKSON, R. H. B., *Native Policy in South Africa and Southern Rhodesia, 1830–1938* (Umtali 1938).

DREW, A., *Drew's Articles on Native Affairs* (Salisbury 1921).

DUNLOP, H., *The Development of European Agriculture in Rhodesia, 1945–1965*, University of Rhodesia, Department of Economics Occasional Paper 5 (Salisbury 1971).

DU TOIT, S. J., *Rhodesia Past and Present* (London 1897).

EVANS, I. L., *Native Policy in Southern Africa* (Cambridge 1934).

FLOYD, B. N., *Changing Patterns of African Land Use in Southern Rhodesia* (Lusaka 1961).

FORD, J., *The Role of the Trypanosomiases in African Ecology* (Oxford 1971).

FOX, H. W., *Memorandum containing Notes and Information concerning Land Policy, with accompanying Papers and Maps* (London 1912).

—— *Memorandum containing Notes concerning the Development of Estates and Industries of the British South Africa Company, with accompanying Papers and Maps* (London 1914).

—— *Memorandum on Constitutional, Political, Financial and Other Questions concerning Rhodesia* (London 1912).

—— *Memorandum on Problems of Development and Policy* (London 1910).

—— *Memorandum upon Land Settlement in Rhodesia, with accompanying Papers and Maps* (London 1913).

—— *Notes concerning the Cases Submitted to the Judicial Committee of the Privy Council with relation to the Unalienated Land of Southern Rhodesia* (London 1915).

FRANCK, T. M., *Race and Nationalism* (New York 1960).

GALBRAITH, J. S., *Crown and Charter* (Berkeley, Los Angeles, and London 1974).

GANN, L. H., *Central Africa: The Former British States* (Englewood Cliffs, N.J. 1971).

—— *A History of Southern Rhodesia* (London 1965).

GANN, L. H. and DUIGNAN, P., *Burden of Empire* (London 1968).

—— *White Settlers in Tropical Africa* (Harmondsworth 1962).

GANN, L. H. and GELFAND, M., *Huggins of Rhodesia* (London 1964).

GJERSTAD, O. (Ed.), *The Organizer, Story of Temba Moyo* (Richmond, B.C. 1974).

GRAY, R., *The Two Nations* (London 1960).

GREEN, J. E. S., *Rhodes Goes North* (London 1936).

HAILEY, W. M., *An African Survey, revised 1956* (London 1957).

HANCOCK, W. K., *Survey of British Commonwealth Affairs, Vol. II*, Part 2 (London 1942).

HANNA, A. J., *The Story of the Rhodesias and Nyasaland* (London 1960).

HARRIS, J. H., *The Chartered Millions* (London 1920).

—— *The Greatest Land Case in British History* (London 1918).

HARRIS, P. S., *Black Industrial Workers in Rhodesia* (Gwelo 1974).

HASTINGS, L., *Dragons Are Extra* (Harmondsworth 1947).

HAW, R. C., *No Other Home* (Bulawayo 1961).

HENSMAN, H., *A History of Rhodesia* (London 1900).

HEWETSON, W. M., *Race Contact in Southern Rhodesia* (Salisbury 1926).

HILLER, V. W. (Ed.), *A Guide to the Public Records of Southern Rhodesia under the Regime of the British South Africa Company 1890–1923* (Cape Town 1956).

HOARE, R., *Rhodesian Mosaic* (London 1934).

HOLE, H. M., *The Making of Rhodesia* (London 1926).

—— *Old Rhodesian Days* (London 1928).

—— *The Passing of the Black Kings* (London 1932).

HOLLEMAN, J. F., *African Interlude* (Cape Town 1958).

—— *Chief, Council and Commissioner* (Assen and London 1969).

—— *Shona Customary Law* (Cape Town 1952).

HONE, P. F., *Southern Rhodesia* (London 1909).

HUGHES, A. J. B., *Development in Rhodesian Tribal Areas: An Overview* (Salisbury 1974).

—— *Kin, Caste and Nation among the Rhodesian Ndebele*, Rhodes-Livingstone Paper No. 25 (Manchester 1956).

JOHNSON, F., *Great Days* (London 1940).
JOHNSON, R. W. M., *The Labour Economy of the Reserve*, University College of Rhodesia and Nyasaland, Department of Economics Occassional Paper 4 (Salisbury 1964).
JOLLIE, E. T., *The Real Rhodesia* (London 1924).
JONES, N., *Rhodesian Genesis* (Bulawayo 1953).
KADALIE, C., *My Life and the I.C.U.* (London 1970).
KAY, G., *The Distribution of African Population in Southern Rhodesia: Some Preliminary Notes*, Rhodes-Livingstone Communication No. 28 (Lusaka 1964).
—— *Rhodesia: A Human Geography* (London 1970).
KEATLEY, P., *The Politics of Partnership* (Harmondsworth 1963).
KING, P. S. (Ed.), *Missions in Southern Rhodesia* (Bulawayo 1959).
KNIGHT-BRUCE, G. W. H., *Memories of Mashonaland* (London 1895).
KUPER, H., HUGHES, A. J. B. and VAN VELSEN, J., *The Shona and Ndebele of Southern Rhodesia* (London 1954).
LEYS, C., *European Politics in Southern Rhodesia* (Oxford 1959).
LONDON GROUP ON AFRICAN AFFAIRS, *Memorandum on Projected Legislation affecting Rights and Liberties of Africans in Southern Rhodesia and Kenya* (London 1936).
LONEY, M., *Rhodesia: White Racism and Imperial Response* (Harmondsworth 1975).
MAIR, L. P., *Native Policies in Africa* (London 1936).
MASHONALAND FARMERS' ASSOCIATION, *The Native Question* (Salisbury 1902).
MASON, P., *The Birth of a Dilemma* (London 1958).
—— *Patterns of Dominance* (London 1971).
—— *Year of Decision* (London 1960).
MASSELL, B. F. and JOHNSON, R. W. M., *African Agriculture in Rhodesia: An Econometric Study* (Santa Monica 1966).
MLAMBO, E., *Rhodesia: The Struggle for a Birthright* (London 1972).
MNYANDA, B. J., *In Search of Truth* (Bombay 1954).
MOFFAT, R. U., *John Smith Moffat* (London 1921).
MTSHALI, B. V., *Rhodesia: Background to Conflict* (New York 1967).
MURRAY, D. J., *The Governmental System in Southern Rhodesia* (Oxford 1970).
NIELSEN, P., *The Black Man's Place in Africa* (Cape Town 1926).
—— *The Matabele at Home* (Bulawayo 1913).
ODLUM, G. M., *Land Settlement* (London 1905).
OFFICIAL DELEGATES REPRESENTING THE SETTLERS OF THE ORANGE RIVER COLONY, *Report on Rhodesia* (London 1909).
OLIVIER, S. H., *The Anatomy of African Misery* (London 1927).
OLIVIER, S. P. (trans. Boggie, J. M.), *Many Treks made Rhodesia* (Cape Town 1957).
O'MEARA, P., *Rhodesia, Racial Conflict or Coexistence?* (Ithaca and London 1975).
ONSLOW-CARLETON, W. M., *Land Settlement Scheme for the Matabele* (Cape Town 1910).
PALLEY, C., *The Constitutional History and Law of Southern Rhodesia, 1888–1965* (Oxford 1966).
PALMER, R. H., *Aspects of Rhodesian Land Policy, 1890–1936, Central Africa Historical Association*, Local Series Pamphlet **22**, 1968.
PALMER, R. H. and PARSONS, Q. N. (Eds.), *The Roots of Rural Poverty in Central and Southern Africa* (London 1977).
PARKER, F., *African Development and Education in Southern Rhodesia* (Ohio 1960).
PASSMORE, G. C., *Local Government Legislation in Southern Rhodesia Up to 30th September, 1963*, University College of Rhodesia and Nyasaland, Department of Government (Salisbury 1966).
PERHAM, M., *African Apprenticeship* (London 1974).
POSSELT, F. W. T., *Fact and Fiction: A Short Account of the Natives of Southern Rhodesia* (Bulawayo 1935).
RANGER, T. O., *The African Voice in Southern Rhodesia* (Nairobi 1970).
—— (Ed.), *Aspects of Central African History* (London 1968).
—— *Revolt in Southern Rhodesia, 1896–7* (London 1967).

RANSFORD, O., *The Rulers of Rhodesia* (London 1968).
RHODESIA INFORMATION SERVICE, *Land Apportionment in Rhodesia* (Salisbury 1965).
RHODESIAN INSTITUTE OF AFRICAN AFFAIRS, *Land and its Apportionment in Southern Rhodesia* (Bulawayo 1961).
RHODESIAN LANDOWNERS' AND FARMERS' ASSOCIATION, *Report of Commission of Rhodesian Landowners, Farmers etc., on Land Titles* (London 1897).
RICHARDS, H., *Next Year will be Better* (London 1952).
ROBERTSON, W., *Rhodesian Rancher* (London and Glasgow 1935).
RODER, W., *The Sabi Valley Irrigation Projects*, University of Chicago, Department of Geography Research Paper No. 99 (Chicago 1965).
ROGERS, C. A. and FRANTZ, C., *Racial Themes in Southern Rhodesia* (New York 1962).
ROLIN, H., *Les Lois et l'Administration de la Rhodésie* (Bruxelles 1913).
SAMKANGE, S., *On Trial for my Country* (London 1967).
—— *Origins of Rhodesia* (London 1968).
SCHREINER, O., *Trooper Peter Halket of Mashonaland* (London 1897).
SCOTT, L., *The Struggle for Native Rights in Rhodesia* (London 1918).
SELOUS, F. C., *Sunshine and Storm in Rhodesia* (London 1896).
—— *Travel and Adventure in South-East Africa* (London 1893).
SHAMUYARIRA, N., *Crisis in Rhodesia* (London 1965).
SHAPIRO, M. J., *The Burning Question of Rhodesia* (Salisbury 1913).
SITHOLE, N., *African Nationalism* (Cape Town 1959, revised London 1968).
—— *Obed Mutezo* (Nairobi 1970).
SONIUS, H. W. J., *Rhodesia: Een Dilemma van Ras en Grond* (Leiden 1966).
SOUTHERN RHODESIA, *Handbook for the Use of Prospective Settlers on the Land*, 6 editions (London 1924–35).
—— *Official Year Book of the Colony of Southern Rhodesia*, Nos. 1–4 (Salisbury 1924–52).
——*Statistical Year Book of Southern Rhodesia 1938* (Salisbury 1938).
STAUB, P., *African Land Hunger in Southern Rhodesia* (Salisbury 1962).
STEERE, D. V., *God's Irregular: Arthur Shearly Cripps* (London 1973).
STENT, V., *A Personal Record of Some Incidents in the Life of Cecil Rhodes* (Cape Town 1970).
STOKES, E. and BROWN, R. (Eds.), *The Zambesian Past* (Manchester 1966).
SUMMERS, R. and PAGDEN, C. W., *The Warriors* (Cape Town 1970).
TABLER, E. C., *The Far Interior* (Cape Town 1955).
THOMAS, T. M., *Eleven Years in Central South Africa* (London 1873).
THOMPSON, C. H. and WOODRUFF, H. W., *Economic Development in Rhodesia and Nyasaland* (London 1954).
THOMPSON, J. G., *The Soils of Rhodesia and their Classification* (Salisbury 1965).
THOMSON, H. C., *Rhodesia and its Government* (London 1898).
TODD, J., *Rhodesia* (London 1966).
—— *The Right to Say No* (London 1972).
TREDGOLD, R. C., *The Rhodesia that was my Life* (London 1968).
VAMBE, L., *From Rhodesia to Zimbabwe* (London 1976).
—— *An Ill-Fated People* (London 1972).
VAN ONSELEN, C., *Chibaro: African Mine Labour in Southern Rhodesia 1900–1933* (London 1976).
WEINMANN, H., *Agricultural Research and Development in Southern Rhodesia, 1890–1923*, University of Rhodesia, Department of Agriculture Occasional Paper 4 (Salisbury 1972).
—— *Agricultural Research and Development in Southern Rhodesia, 1924–1950*, University of Rhodesia, Series in Science 2 (Salisbury 1975).
WEINRICH, A. K. H., *African Farmers in Rhodesia* (London 1975).
—— *Black and White elites in Rural Rhodesia* (Manchester 1973).
—— *Chiefs and Councils in Rhodesia* (London 1971).

WILKINSON, A. R., *Insurgency in Rhodesia, 1957–1973: An Account and Assessment*, Adelphi Paper 100 (London 1973).
WILLS, A. J., *An Introduction to the History of Central Africa* (London 1964).
WILLSON, F. M. G., PASSMORE, G. C. and MITCHELL, M. T., *Holders of Administrative and Ministerial Office 1894–1964 and Members of the Legislative Council 1899–1923 and the Legislative Assembly 1924–1964*, University College of Rhodesia and Nyasaland, Department of Government Source Book Series 3 (Salisbury 1966).
—— *Source Book of Parliamentary Elections and Referenda in Southern Rhodesia, 1898–1962*, University College of Rhodesia and Nyasaland, Department of Government Source Book Series 1 (Salisbury 1963).
WILMER, S. E. (Ed.), *Zimbabwe Now* (London 1973).
WINDRICH, E., *The Rhodesian Problem* (London and Boston 1975).
WISE, C. D., *Report on Land Settlement in Southern Rhodesia* (London 1906).
WODDIS, J., *Africa: The Lion Awakes* (London 1961).
—— *Africa: The Roots of Revolt* (London 1960).
YOUNG, K., *Rhodesia and Independence* (London 1967).
YUDELMAN, M., *Africans on the Land* (Cambridge, Mass. 1964).

3 Articles and Unpublished Papers

ALLAN, W., 'African Land Usage', *Rhodes-Livingstone Journal*, **3**, 1945, 13–20.
—— 'Changing Patterns of African Land Use', *Journal of the Royal Society of Arts*, **108**, 1960, 612–29.
ALVORD, E. D., 'Agricultural Demonstration Work on Native Reserves', *Department of Native Development*, Occasional Paper 3, 1930.
—— 'Agricultural Life of Rhodesian Natives', *NADA*, **7**, 1929, 9–16.
—— 'Development of Native Agriculture and Land Tenure in Southern Rhodesia', unpublished 1958.
—— 'The Great Hunger', *NADA*, **6**, 1928, 35–43.
—— 'The Progress of Native Agriculture in Southern Rhodesia', *The New Rhodesia*, **15**, 1948, 18–19.
ANDERSON, C. A., 'Development of Water Supplies in Native Reserves', *NADA*, **3**, 1925, 74–7.
ANON, 'Soil Conservation Advisory Councils', *Rhodesia Agricultural Journal*, **32**, 1935, 132–3.
—— 'South Africa: The Southern Rhodesia Land Commission', *Round Table*, **17**, 1927, 632–42.
AQUINA SR. M. [Weinrich, A. K. H.], 'The Social Background of Agriculture in Chilimanzi Reserve', *Rhodes-Livingstone Journal*, **36**, 1964, 7–39.
ARRIGHI, G., 'Labour Supplies in Historical Perspective: A Study of the Proletarianization of the African Peasantry in Rhodesia', *Journal of Development Studies*, **6**, 1970, 197–234.
—— 'The Political Economy of Rhodesia', *New Left Review*, **39**, 1966, 35–65.
AYLEN, D., 'Conserving Soil in the Native Reserves', *Rhodesia Agricultural Journal*, **39**, 1942, 152–60.
BAZELEY, W. S., 'First Principles of Native Policy', *NADA*, **13**, 1935, 47–51.
—— 'Townships in the Native Area', *NADA*, **17**, 1940, 81–4.
BEACH, D. N., 'Afrikaner and Shona Settlement in the Enkeldoorn Area, 1890–1900', *Zambezia*, **1**, 2, 1970, 25–34.
—— 'Ndebele Raiders and Shona Power', *Journal of African History*, **15**, 1974, 633–51.
—— 'The Politics of Collaboration: South Mashonaland, 1896–97', University of Rhodesia, Department of History, Henderson Seminar No. 9, 1969.
—— 'Resistance and Collaboration in the Shona Country, 1896–7', University of London, SOAS/ICS African History Seminar, 1971.
—— 'The Shona and Ndebele Power', University of Rhodesia, Department of History, Henderson Seminar No. 26, 1973.

BEACH, D. N., 'The Shona Economy: Branches of Production', in Palmer, R. H. and Parsons, Q. N. (Eds.), *The Roots of Rural Poverty* (London 1977), 37–65.

—— 'South Charter: An Example of Intensive Settlement', University College of Rhodesia, Department of History Seminar Paper, 1968.

BECK, J. H., 'Yafele's Kraal', *Geography*, **45**, 1960, 68–78.

BEVAN, Ll. E. W., 'The Education of Natives in the Pastoral Pursuits', *NADA*, **2**, 1924, 13–16.

BHEBE, N. M. B., 'Ndebele Trade in the Nineteenth Century', *Journal of African Studies*, **1**, 1974, 87–100.

—— 'Some Aspects of Ndebele Relations with the Shona in the Nineteenth Century', *Rhodesian History*, **4**, 1973, 31–8.

BIRKENHEAD, EARL OF, 'The Southern Rhodesia Land Case', in Birkenhead, *Famous Trials of History* (London 1926), 207–15.

BLAKE, J. Y F., 'Native Rhodesia', *National Review*, **30**, 1897, 217–25.

BOND, W. E., 'Soil Conservation and Land Use Planning in Native Reserves in Southern Rhodesia', *Tropical Agriculture*, **25**, 1948, 4–13.

BOWKER, S., 'A Scheme for Segregation Areas', *Contemporary Review*, **117**, 1920, 546–53.

BRODERICK, G. E. P., 'Some suggestions Towards the Development of a Native Policy in Southern Rhodesia', *NADA*, **17**, 1940, 77–80.

BURKE, E. E., 'Mazoe and the Mashona Rebellion, 1896–97', *Rhodesiana*, **25**, 1971, 1–34.

—— 'Twenty-eight Days in 1890: Two Reports by Lieut.-Colonel E. G. Pennefather', National Archives of Rhodesia, *Occasional Paper 1*, 1965, 21–40.

CARBUTT, C. L., 'Communal Land Tenure', *NADA*, **5**, 1927, 42–5.

—— 'The Racial Problem in Southern Rhodesia', *NADA*, **12**, 1934, 6–11.

CHANCELLOR, J. R., 'Progress and Development of Southern Rhodesia', *Journal of the African Society*, **28**, 110, 1929, 149–54.

—— 'Southern Rhodesia and its Problems', *Journal of the African Society*, **26**, 101, 1926, 1–6.

CHIKEREMA, J. R. D., 'ZAPU's Land Policy', *Zimbabwe Review*, **1**, 6–7, 1966.

CHIVANDA, C. G., 'The Mashona Rebellion in Oral Tradition: Mazoe District', University College of Rhodesia, Department of History, undergraduate seminar paper, 1966.

CHRISTOPHER, A. J., 'The European Concept of a Farm in Southern Africa', *Historia*, **15**, 1970, 93–9.

—— 'Government Land Policies in Southern Africa', in Ironside, R. G. (Ed.), *Frontier Settlement* (Edmonton 1974), 208–25.

—— 'Land Policy in Southern Africa During the Nineteenth Century', *Zambezia*, **2**, 1, 1971, 1–9.

——'Land tenure in Rhodesia', *South African Geographical Journal*, **53**, 1971, 39–52.

—— 'Recent Trends in Land Tenure in Rhodesia, 1961–70', *Geography*, **56**, 1971, 140–4.

CLARKE, D. G., 'Land Inequality and Income Distribution in Rhodesia', *African Studies Review*, **18**, 1975, 1–7.

CLEGHORN, W. B., 'Pasture Problems in Native Reserves in Mashonaland', *South African Journal of Science*, **47**, 1950, 141.

COBBING, J., 'The Evolution of Ndebele Amabutho', *Journal of African History*, **15**, 1974, 607–31.

—— 'Historical Materialism and the Nineteenth Century Ndebele', University of Rhodesia, Political Economy Research Seminar No. 11, 1974.

—— 'Lobengula, Jameson and the Occupation of Mashonaland 1890', *Rhodesian History*, **4**, 1973, 39–56.

COLQUHOUN, A. R., 'Matabeleland', *Proceedings of the Royal Colonial Institute*, **25**, 1893–4, 45–103.

COLSON, E., 'The Impact of the Colonial Period on the Definition of Land Rights', in Gann, L. H. and Duignan, P. (Eds.), *Colonialism in Africa 1870–1960*, Vol. 3, *Turner, V. (Ed.), Profiles of Change: African Society and Colonial Rule* (Cambridge 1971), 193–215.

CRIPPS, A. S.,' African Land Tenure', *NADA*, **4,** 1926, 96–101.

—— 'An Africa of the Africans', *International Review of Missions*, **10,** 1921, 99–109.

——'A Difficult and Delicate Operation', *NADA*, **2,** 1924, 98–106.

—— 'Dispossession of the African', *East and the West*, **20,** 1922, 211–26.

—— 'Native interests in Southern Rhodesia and the Renewal of the Rhodesian Charter', *Contemporary Review*, **106,** 1914, 537–44.

—— 'Native Rhodesia's Now or Never', *South African Quarterly*, **5,** 1923, 6–9.

—— 'Native Rhodesia's Now or Never', *NADA*, **1,** 1923, 44–51.

—— 'Native Rights under a new Government in Southern Rhodesia', *South African Quarterly*, **4,** 1922, 5–7.

—— 'A New Native Affairs Act in Southern Rhodesia', *Contemporary Review*, **132,** 1927, 721–6.

—— 'The Reserves Commission in Southern Rhodesia', *Contemporary Review*, **117,** 1920, 553–6.

—— 'Southern Rhodesia and her Native Reserves', *South African Quarterly*, **6,** 1924, 3–8.

DANCKWERTS, J. P., 'Technology and the Economic Development of African Agriculture in Rhodesia', *Rhodesian Journal of Economics*, **4,** 4, 1970, 17–30.

DAVENPORT, T. R. H., 'Rhodesian and South African policies for Urban Africans: Some Historical Similarities and Contrasts', *Rhodesian History*, **3,** 1972, 63–76.

DAVIS, C. S., 'The Amandabele Habitat', *NADA*, **12,** 1934, 74–9.

DUNLOP, H., 'Land and Economic Opportunity in Rhodesia', *Rhodesian Journal of Economics*, **6,** 1, 1972, 1–19.

—— 'Land Policy in Rhodesia 1945–69', University of Rhodesia, Political Economy Research Seminar No. 2, 1974.

ECKERSLEY, W. A., 'Notes in Eastern Mashonaland', *Geographical Journal*, **5,** 1895, 27–46.

EDMONDS, J. A., 'A Pioneer's View of Farming in Southern Rhodesia', *The 1820*, October 1936, 33–5.

EDWARDS, J. A., 'Colquhoun in Mashonaland: A Portrait of Failure', *Rhodesiana*, **9,** 1963, 1–17.

EDWARDS, W., 'The Wanoe', *NADA*, **4,** 1926, 13–28.

—— 'Wiri', *NADA*, **37,** 1960, 81–101; **38,** 1961, 5–21; **39,** 1962, 19–44.

FLETCHER, P. B., 'A Revolution in African Agriculture', *Optima*, **6,** 1956, 55–9.

FLOOD, D., 'The Jeanes Movement. An Early Experiment', *NADA*, **10,** 3, 1971, 13–25.

FLOYD, B. N., 'Changing Patterns of African Land Use in Southern Rhodesia', *Rhodes-Livingstone Journal*, **25,** 1959, 20–39.

—— 'Land Apportionment in Southern Rhodesia', *Geographical Review*, **52,** 1962, 566–82.

FULLER, C. C., 'Notes on (a) Education, and (b) Land', *NADA*, **1,** 1923, 28–9.

GALBRAITH, J. S., 'Engine without a Governor: The Early Years of the British South Africa Company', *Rhodesian History*, **1,** 1970, 9–16.

GANN, L. H., 'The Southern Rhodesian Land Apportionment Act, 1930: An Essay in Trusteeship', National Archives of Rhodesia and Nyasaland, *Occasional Paper 1*, 1963, 71–91.

GANN, L. H. and DUIGNAN, P., 'Changing patterns of a White Elite: Rhodesian and Other Settlers', in Gann and Duignan (Eds.), *Colonialism in Africa 1870–1960*, Vol. 2. *The History and Politics of Colonialism 1914–1960* (Cambridge 1970), 92–170.

GARBETT, G. K., 'The Land Husbandry Act of Southern Rhodesia', in Biebuyck, D. (Ed.), *African Agrarian Systems* (London 1963), 185–202.

GARBETT, G. K. 'The Rhodesian Chief's Dilemma: Government Officer or Tribal Leader?', *Race*, **8**, 1966, 113–28.

GARLAKE, P. S., 'The Mashona Rebellion East of Salisbury', *Rhodesiana*, **14**, 1966, 1–11.

GELFAND, M., 'Migration of African Labourers in Rhodesia and Nyasaland (1890–1914)', *Central African Journal of Medicine*, **7**, 1961, 293–300.

GILCHRIST, R. D., 'Rhodesia's Place in the Native Problem', *Journal of the African Society*, **32**, 126, 1933, 135–9.

GLUCKMAN, M., 'African Land Tenure', *Rhodes-Livingstone Journal*, **3**, 1945, 1–12.

—— 'Studies in African Land Tenure', *African Studies*, **3**, 1944, 14–21.

GOOD, K., 'Settler Colonialism in Rhodesia', *African Affairs*, **73**, 290, 1974, 10–36.

GOPALAKRISHNAN, P. K., 'Land Relations and Social Change in Africa', in Prasad, B. (Ed.), *Contemporary Africa* (Bombay 1960), 108–21.

GUSSMAN, B. W., 'Industrial Efficiency and the Urban African: A Study of Conditions in Southern Rhodesia', *Africa*, **23**, 1953, 135–44.

HAMILTON, P., 'The Changing Pattern of African Land Use in Rhodesia', in Whittow, J. B. and Wood, P. D. (Eds.), *Essays in Geography for Austin Miller* (Reading 1965), 247–71.

—— 'Population Pressure and Land Use in Chiweshe Reserve', *Rhodes-Livingstone Journal*, **36**, 1964, 40–58.

HARRIS, J. H., 'Native Labour: Success after Thirty Years', *Contemporary Review*, **156**, 1939, 296–303.

HENDERSON, I., 'White Populism in Southern Rhodesia', *Comparative Studies in Society and History*, **14**, 1972, 387–99.

HERSKOVITS, M. J., 'Some Property Concepts and Marriage Customs of the Vandau', *American Anthropologist*, **25**, 1923, 376–86.

HOARE, R., 'Native Questions in Southern Rhodesia', *Dublin Review*, **194**, 1934, 246–57.

—— 'Rhodesian Jottings', *Cornhill Magazine*, **150**, 1934, 467–76.

HODDER-WILLIAMS, R., 'Afrikaners in Rhodesia: A Partial Portrait', *African Social Research*, **18**, 1974, 611–42.

—— 'The British South Africa Company in Marandellas: Some Extra-institutional Constraints on Government', *Rhodesian History*, **2**, 1971, 39–63.

—— 'Marandellas and the Mashona Rebellion', *Rhodesiana*, **16**, 1967, 27–54.

HOLE, H. M., 'Native Rhodesia: A Rejoinder', *National Review*, **30**, 1897, 354–9.

—— 'Rhodesian Natives and the Land', *Ways and Means*, **6**, 1920, 18–25.

—— 'The Rise of the Matabele'. *Proceedings of the Rhodesian Scientific Association*, **12**, 1913, 135–51.

HOLLEMAN, J. F., 'Some "Shona" Tribes of Southern Rhodesia', in Colson, E. and Gluckman, M. (Eds.), *Seven Tribes of British Central Africa* (London 1951), 354–95.

—— 'Town and Tribe', in Smith, P. (Ed.), *Africa in Transition* (London 1958), 62–70.

HOOKER, J. R., 'The African Worker in Southern Rhodesia: Black Aspirations in a White Economy', *Race*, **6**, 1964, 142–51.

—— 'Welfare Associations and Other Instruments of Accommodation in the Rhodesias between the World Wars', *Comparative Studies in Society and History*, **9**, 1966, 51–63.

HOWMAN, R., 'Report on Urban Conditions in Southern Rhodesia', *African Studies*, **4**, 1945, 9–22.

HUGGINS, G. M., 'Outline of Native Policy', *South Africa*, **183**, 1934, 82.

—— 'Southern Rhodesia and Native Affairs', Address to the Empire Parliamentary Association, 27 July 1939.

—— 'Southern Rhodesia: Recent Progress and Development', Address to the Empire Parliamentary Association, 18 July 1934.

—— 'A Vital African Problem: and the Need for a Definite Policy', *African Observer*, **2**, 1935, 18–25.

HUGHES, A. J. B., 'Tribal Land Tenure—An Obstacle to Progress?' *South African Journal of African Affairs*, **1**, 1971, 56–73.

HULEC, O., 'Some Aspects of the 1930s Depression in Rhodesia', *Journal of Modern African Studies*, **7**, 1969, 95–105.

IBBOTSON, P., 'Urbanization in Southern Rhodesia', *Africa*, **26**, 1946, 73–82.

JACKLIN, E. R., 'The Maize Control Amendment Act No. 17 of 1934', *Rhodesia Agricultural Journal*, **31**, 1934, 487–95.

JACKSON, H. M. G., 'The Natives of Southern Rhodesia: Their Position after Ten Years under Responsible Government', *African Observer*, **1**, 1934, 19–23.

JENNINGS, A. C., 'Improved Housing for Urban Natives', *Proceedings and Transactions of the Rhodesia Scientific Association*, **38**, 1941, 129–36.

—— 'Irrigation and Water Supplies in Southern Rhodesia', *South African Journal of Science*, **24**, 1927, 21–9.

—— 'Land Apportionment in Southern Rhodesia', *Journal of the Royal African Society*, **34**, 136, 1935, 296–312.

—— 'Land Settlement Problems and Irrigation in Southern Rhodesia', unpublished 1925.

—— 'The Native Area', *NADA*, **10**, 1932, 74–7.

—— 'Water Supplies in Native Reserves', *NADA*, **2**, 1924, 32–3.

—— 'Water Supply Development in Native Reserves', *NADA*, **1**, 1923, 7–9.

JOHNSON, R. W. M., 'African Agricultural Development in Southern Rhodesia: 1945–60', *Food Research Institute Studies*, **4**, 1964, 165–223.

—— 'An Economic Survey of Chiweshe Reserve', *Rhodes-Livingstone Journal*, **36**, 1964, 82–108.

JOLLIE, E. T., 'Land and the Native in British Africa: The Southern Rhodesian Experiment', *American Geographical Society Special Publication* **14**, 1932, 178–91.

—— 'Native Administration in Southern Rhodesia', *Journal of the Royal Society of Arts*, **83**, 1935, 973–85.

—— 'Southern Rhodesia: A White Man's Country in the Tropics', *Geographical Review*, **17**, 1927, 89–106.

—— 'Southern Rhodesia's Native Policy', *United Empire*, **28**, 1937, 336–41.

JORDAN, J. D., 'Zimutu Reserve: A Land-Use Appreciation', *Rhodes-Livingstone Journal*, **36**, 1964, 59–81.

KAY, G., 'Changing Patterns of African Population in Zambia and Rhodesia', *South African Journal of African Affairs*, **2**, 1972, 19–31.

—— 'South-Central Africa: European Settlement and Economic Development', in Prothero, R. M. (Ed.), *A Geography of Africa* (London 1969), 264–324.

KEIGWIN, H. S., 'An Educational Experiment', *South African Journal of Science*, **18**, 1921, 172–82.

—— 'Native Development', *NADA*, **1**, 1923, 10–17.

—— 'Segregation', *NADA*, **2**, 1924, 52–7.

KINLOCH, G. C., 'Changing Black Reaction to White Domination', *Rhodesian History*, **5**, 1974, 67–78.

KOSMIN, B. A., 'The Inyoka Tobacco Industry of the Shangwe People: A Case Study of the Displacement of a Pre-Colonial Economy in Southern Rhodesia, 1898–1938', *African Social Research*, **17**, 1974, 554–77. This has been revised for inclusion in Palmer, R. H. and Parsons, Q. N. (Eds.), *The Roots of Rural Poverty* (London 1977), 268–88.

—— 'On the Imperial Frontier: The Pioneer Community of Salisbury in November 1897', *Rhodesian History*, **2**, 1971, 25–37.

LAWTON, C., 'Development and the African', *Crossbow*, **3**, 1960, 31–4.

LEE, E., 'The Trade Union Movement in Rhodesia, 1910–24', *Rhodesian Journal of Economics*, **8**, 1974, 215–37.

LEGGATE, W. M., 'Some Observations on the Economic Position of the Native in Rhodesia', *South African Journal of Science*, **24**, 1927, 80–7.

—— 'Southern Rhodesia: Some Problems of Native Development and Trade', Address to the Empire Parliamentary Association, 27 November 1929.

LEROUX, A. A., 'African Agriculture in Rhodesia', *Rhodesia Agricultural Journal*, **66**, 1969, 83–9.

MACKENZIE, J., 'The Chartered Company in South Africa', *Contemporary Review*, **71**, 1897, 305–28.

MACKENZIE, J. M., 'African Labour in the Chartered Company period', *Rhodesian History*, **1**, 1970, 43–58.

—— 'Chartered Africans: Colonial Office, Settlers and BSA Company, Rhodesia, 1890–1923', University of London, Institute of Commonwealth Studies, *Collected Seminar Papers on The Societies of Southern Africa in the 19th and 20th centuries, Vol. 4* (London 1974), 77–86.

—— 'Colonial Labour Policy and Rhodesia', *Rhodesian Journal of Economics*, **8**, 1, 1974, 1–15.

—— 'Red Soils in Mashonaland: A Re-assessment', *Rhodesian History*, **5**, 1974, 81–8.

—— 'Trade and Labour: The Interaction of Traditional and Capitalist Economies in Southern Zambezia, 1870–1923', University of London, ICS Postgraduate Seminar, 1975.

MACMILLAN, W. M., 'The Development of Africa: Impressions from Rhodesia', *Political Quarterly*, **3**, 1932, 552–69.

—— 'Southern Rhodesia and the Development of Africa', *Journal of the African Society*, **32**, 128, 1933, 294–8.

MAGUIRE, R., 'Rhodesia', *Journal of the African Society*, **22**, 86, 1923, 81–95.

MAIR, L. P., 'Modern Developments in African Land Tenure: An Aspect of Cultural Change', *Africa*, **18**, 1948, 184–9.

MAUFE, H. B., 'Presidential Address on the Soils of Southern Rhodesia and their Origin', *Proceedings of the Rhodesia Scientific Association*, **14**, 1915, 15–26.

MAUND, E. A., 'Mashonaland and its Development', *Proceedings of the Royal Colonial Institute*, **23**, 1891–2, 248–70.

MOFFAT, H. U., 'Southern Rhodesia: Its Interests and Problems', Address to the Empire Parliamentary Association, 29 June 1932.

MOYANA, H. V., 'Land and Race in Rhodesia', *African Review*, **5**, 3, 1975, 17–41.

MOYO, P. H., 'Native Life in the Reserves', *NADA*, **3**, 1925, 47.

MTSHALI, B. V., 'Land—The Crucial Factor in Rhodesian Politics', *World Justice*, **9**, 1967–8, 7–21.

MUTSAU, R. J., 'The Shona and Ndebele Settlements in Kabwe Rural Area, 1953–63', in Palmer, R. H., (Ed.), *Zambian Land and Labour Studies, Vol. 1;* National Archives of Zambia Occasional Paper 2 (Lusaka 1973), 41–7.

NEWTON, F. J., 'Southern Rhodesia', *United Empire*, **16**, 1925, 82–93.

NKOMO, J., 'The Crucible of Privilege: Southern Rhodesia', *Africa South*, **3**, 1959, 57–61.

—— 'Southern Rhodesia: Apartheid Country', in Duffy, J. and Manners, R. A. (Eds.), *Africa Speaks* (Princeton, N.J. 1961), 130–43.

NOBBS, E. A., 'The Native Cattle of Southern Rhodesia', *South African Journal of Science*, **24**, 1927, 328–42.

OATES, A. V., 'Some Pasture Problems encountered in the Native Areas of Matabeleland', *South African Journal of Science*, **47**, 1951, 327–9.

OLIVIER, S. H., 'Native Land Rights in Rhodesia', *Contemporary Review*, **130**, 1926, 145–51.

O'NEILL, J., 'Habits and Customs of the Natives of Mangwe District, South Matabeleland', *Zambesi Mission Record*, **4**, 1910–11, 35–9, 106–13, 146–51, 187–94.

—— 'Native Reserves in South Rhodesia', *Catholic Magazine for South Africa*, **29**, 1918, 535–42.

PALMER, R. H., 'The Agricultural History of Rhodesia', in Palmer, R. H. and Parsons, Q. N. (Eds.), *The Roots of Rural Poverty* (London 1977), 221–54.

—— 'Johnston and Jameson: A Comparative Study in the Imposition of Colonial Rule', in Pachai, B. (Ed.), *The Early History of Malawi* (London 1972), 293–322.

—— 'Red Soils in Rhodesia', *African Social Research*, **10**, 1970, 747–58.

PALMER, R. H., 'War and Land in Rhodesia', *Transafrican Journal of History*, **1**, 2, 1971, 43–62.

—— 'War and Land in Rhodesia in the 1890s', in Ogot, B. A. (Ed.), *War and Society in Africa* (London 1972), 85–107.

PARKER, F., 'African Community Development and Education in Southern Rhodesia, 1920–1935', *International Review of Missions*, **51**, 1962, 335–47.

PERHAM, M., 'The Story of Ndansi Kumalo of the Matabele Tribe, Southern Rhodesia', in Perham, *Ten Africans* (London 1936), 63–79.

PHIMISTER, I. R., 'Alluvial gold mining and trade in Nineteenth-Century South Central Africa', *Journal of African History*, **15**, 1974, 445–56.

—— 'Peasant Production and Underdevelopment in Southern Rhodesia, 1890–1914', *African Affairs*, **73**, 291, 1974, 217–28. (This has been revised for inclusion in Palmer, R. H. and Parsons, Q. N. (Eds.), *The Roots of Rural Poverty* (London 1977), 255–67.

—— 'Precolonial Gold Mining in Southern Zambezia: A Reassessment', *African Social Research*, **21**, 1976, 1–30.

—— 'Rhodes, Rhodesia and the Rand', *Journal of Southern African Studies*, **1**, 1974, 74–90.

—— 'The Shamva Mine Strike of 1927: An Emerging African Proletariat', *Rhodesian History*, **2**, 1971, 65–88.

POLLAK, O. B., 'Black Farmers and White Politics in Rhodesia', *African Affairs*, **74**, 296, 1975, 263–77.

—— 'The Impact of the Second World War on African Labour Organization in Rhodesia', *Rhodesian Journal of Economics*, **7**, 3, 1973, 121–37.

POWYS-JONES, L., 'The Native Purchase Areas of Southern Rhodesia', *Journal of African Administration*, **7**, 1955, 20–6.

PRESCOTT, J. R. V., 'Overpopulation and Overstocking in the Native Areas of Matabeleland', *Geographical Journal*, **127**, 1961, 212–25.

—— 'Population Distribution in Southern Rhodesia', *Geographical Review*, **52**, 1962, 559–65.

PRESTAGE, P., 'The Kraal Family System Among the Amandebele', *Zambesi Mission Record*, **1**, 1901, 442–6.

RANGER, T. O., 'African Reaction and Resistance to the Imposition of Colonial Rule in East and Central Africa', in Gann, L. H. and Duignan, P. (Eds.), *Colonialism in Africa 1870–1960, Vol. 1, The History and Politics of Colonialism 1870–1914* (Cambridge 1969), 293–324.

—— 'The Historiography of Southern Rhodesia', *Transafrican Journal of History*, **1**, 2, 1971, 63–76.

—— 'The Last Word on Rhodes?' *Past and Present*, **28**, 1964, 116–27.

—— 'The Rewriting of African History during the Scramble: The Matabele Dominance in Mashonaland', *African Social Research*, **4**, 1967, 271–82.

—— 'State and Church in Southern Rhodesia, 1919–1939', *Historical Association of Rhodesia and Nyasaland* [subsequently Central Africa Historical Association], Local Series Pamphlet **4**, 1961.

RENNIE, J. K., 'The Private Locations Ordinance (1908) and the Melsetter Labour Agreements', unpublished 1967.

RICHARTZ, F. J., 'Habits and Customs of the Mashonas', *Zambesi Mission Record*, **2**, 1905, 508–13.

RIFKIND, M. L., 'Land Apportionment in Perspective', *Rhodesian History*, **3**, 1972, 53–62.

ROBINSON, D. A., 'Land Use Planning in Native Reserves in Southern Rhodesia', *Rhodesia Agricultural Journal*, **50**, 1953, 327–33.

—— 'Soil Conservation and Implications of the Land Husbandry Act', *NADA*, **37**, 1960, 27–35.

—— 'The Work of Agricultural Demonstrators in Southern Rhodesia', *Tropical Agriculture*, **31**, 1954, 109–11.

RODER, W., 'The Division of Land Resources in Southern Rhodesia', *Annals of the Association of American Geographers*, **54**, 1964, 41–58.

SAMPSON, H. C., 'Soil Erosion in Tropical Africa', *Rhodesia Agricultural Journal*, **33**, 1936, 197–205.

SELOUS, F. C., 'The History of the Matabele, and the Cause and Effect of the Matabele War', *Proceedings of the Royal Colonial Institute*, **25**, 1893–4, 251–90.

SCOTT, P., 'Migrant Labor in Southern Rhodesia', *Geographical Review*, **44**, 1954, 29–48.

SHANTZ, H. L., 'Agriculture in East Africa', in Jones, T. J. (Ed.), *Education in East Africa* (New York 1924), 353–402.

SHAW, F. G., 'The Chartered Company and Matabililand', *National Review*, **26**, 1896, 786–97.

SHROPSHIRE, D., 'Native Development in Southern Rhodesia', *Journal of the African Society*, **32**, 129, 1933, 409–23.

SHUTZ, B. M., 'European Population Patterns, Cultural Persistence, and Political Change in Rhodesia', *Canadian Journal of African Studies*, **7**, 1973, 3–25.

SIMONS, H. J., 'Race Relations and Politics in Southern and Eastern Africa', in Linton, R. (Ed.), *Most of the World* (New York 1949), 271–330.

SIMS, G., 'Paladin of Empire: Earl Grey and Rhodesia', *Central Africa Historical Association*, Local Series Pamphlet **26**, 1970.

STEAD, W. H., 'The Organisation for Land Management in Native Reserves in the Colony of Southern Rhodesia', unpublished 1948.

STEELE, M. C., '*Children of Violence* and Rhodesia: A Study of Doris Lessing as Historical Observer', *Central Africa Historical Association*, Local Series Pamphlet 29, 1974.

—— '"With Hope Unconquered and Unconquerable ...": Arthur Shearly Cripps, 1869–1952', in Ranger, T. O. and Weller, J. (Eds.), *Themes in the Christian History of Central Africa* (London 1975), 152–74.

STIGGER, P., 'The Emergence of the Native Department in Matabeleland, 1893–1899', unpublished 1974.

—— 'The Membership and Proceedings of, and the Evidence before, the Land Commission of 1894', unpublished 1974.

—— 'Volunteers and the Profit Motive in the Anglo-Ndebele War, 1893', *Rhodesian History*, **2**, 1971, 11–23.

SURRIDGE, F. H., 'Matabeleland and Mashonaland', *Proceedings of the Royal Colonial Institute*, **22**, 1890–1, 305–31.

SYKES, R., 'A New Way with the Rhodesian Native', *South African Catholic Magazine*, **28**, 1918, 445–50.

TABERER, W. S., 'Mashonaland Natives', *Journal of the African Society*, **4**, 15, 1905, 311–36.

TAYLOR, G., 'Review: Agriculture in East Africa by H. L. Shantz', *NADA*, **3**, 1925, 86–90.

TAYLOR, H. J., 'The Amandebele, and other Tribes of Matabeleland', *Proceedings of the Rhodesia Scientific Association*, **6**, 1906, 22–32.

TAYLOR, J. J., 'The Origins of the Native Department in Southern Rhodesia, 1890–98', University of Rhodesia, Department of History, Henderson Seminar No. 7, 1968.

THOMAS, O., 'Land Settlement and Colonization of Rhodesia', *Empire and the Century*, 1905, 557–74.

TOWNSEND, E. R., 'Land Settlement in Rhodesia', *South Africa*, **65**, 1905, 555–6.

VAN ONSELEN, C., 'Black Workers in Central African Industry: A Critical Essay on the Historiography and Sociology of Rhodesia', *Journal of Southern African Studies*, **1**, 1975, 228–46.

—— 'The 1912 Wankie Colliery Strike', *Journal of African History*, **15**, 1974, 275–89.

—— 'The Role of Collaborators in the Rhodesian Mining Industry 1900–1935', *African Affairs*, **72**, 289, 1973, 401–18.

—— 'Worker Consciousness in Black Miners: Southern Rhodesia, 1900–1920', *Journal of African History*, **14**, 1973, 237–55.

VAN VELSEN, J., 'Trends in African Nationalism in Southern Rhodesia', *Kroniek van Afrika*, **4**, 1964, 139–57.

WHITE, J., 'The Rationale of the Missionary Conference of Southern Rhodesia', *NADA*, **2**, 1924, 67–9.

WHITEHEAD, R., 'The Aborigines' Protection Society and White Settlers in Rhodesia, 1889–1930', University of London, Institute of Commonwealth Studies, *Collected Seminar Papers on The Societies of Southern Africa in the 19th and 20th Centuries, Vol. 3* (London 1973), 96–109.

WHITTLESEY, D., 'Southern Rhodesia—An African Compage', *Annals of the Association of American Geographers*, **46**, 1956, 1–97.

WILLOUGHBY, J. C., 'The Alarm in Matabeleland', *New Review*, **14**, 1896, 703–12.

WILSON, N. H., 'The Development of Native Reserves', *NADA*, **1**, 1923, 86–94.

—— 'The Future of the Native Races of Southern Rhodesia', *South African Journal of Science*, **17**, 1920, 136–50.

—— 'Native Political Movements in Southern Rhodesia', *NADA*, **1**, 1923, 17–19.

WOODS, G. G. B., 'Matabele History and Customs', *NADA*, **7**, 1929, 43–9.

4 Official Publications

(i) Southern Rhodesian Reports

BRITISH SOUTH AFRICA COMPANY, *Reports on the Company's proceedings and the Condition of the Territories within the Sphere of its Operations* (London 1889–97).

—— *Reports on the Administration of Rhodesia* (London 1897–1902).

Annual Reports of the Chief Native Commissioner[*s*] (Salisbury 1903–62}.

Report of the Select Committee on Native Administration (Salisbury 1899).

SOUTH AFRICA, *South African Native Affairs Commission, 1903–5, Vols. I, IV and V* (Cape Town 1905).

Report of Native Labour Enquiry Committee (Salisbury 1906).

Report of the Native Affairs Committee of Enquiry, 1910–11 (Salisbury 1911).

Report by H. S. Keigwin, Esquire, Native Commissioner, on the suggested Industrial Development of Natives (Salisbury 1920).

Report of Native Labour Committee of Enquiry, 1921 (Salisbury 1921).

DEPARTMENT OF LANDS, 'Memoranda on Land Settlement Policy', mimeo. (Salisbury 1925).

Report of the Land Commission, 1925 (Salisbury 1926).

'Report of the Native Labour Enquiry Committee', mimeo. (Salisbury 1928). [in file S 235/426].

Report on Industrial Relations in Southern Rhodesia (Salisbury 1930).

Report of the Committee of Enquiry into the Economic Position of the Agricultural Industry of Southern Rhodesia (Salisbury 1934).

Report of the Commission of Enquiry into Certain Sales of Native Cattle in Areas Occupied by Natives (Salisbury 1939).

Report of the Commission to enquire into the Preservation, etc., of the Natural Resources of the Colony (Salisbury 1939).

'Secretary for Native Affairs' Memorandum and Plan for the Development and Regeneration of the Colony's Native Reserves and Areas, and for the Administrative Control and Supervision of the Land occupied by Natives', mimeo. (Salisbury 1943).

'Secretary for Native Affairs' Report on the Question of Native Housing and the Implementation of the Land Apportionment Act in the Urban Areas of the Colony', mimeo. (Salisbury 1944).

'Report on a Survey of Wages, Housing and Living Conditions of Africans employed in Plumtree, Southern Rhodesia by Percy Ibbotson', mimeo. (Bulawayo 1944).

Report of Native Production and Trade 1944 (Salisbury 1945).

Report to the Minister of Agriculture and Lands on the Agricultural Development of Southern Rhodesia by Professor Sir Frank Engledow (Salisbury 1950).

The African in Southern Rhodesia, No. 3: Agriculture (Glasgow 1952).
What the Native Land Husbandry Act means to the rural African and to Southern Rhodesia (Salisbury 1955).
'Report of the Select Committee on the Development of Unimproved Land, 1956', in *Votes and Proceedings of the Legislative Assembly, Third Session, Eighth Parliament, 1956*, 105–17 (Salisbury 1956).
Report of the Urban African Affairs Commission, 1958 (Salisbury 1958).
FEDERATION OF RHODESIA AND NYASALAND, *Agricultural Policy in the Federation of Rhodesia and Nyasaland. Report to the Federal Minister of Agriculture by The Federal Standing Committee on Agricultural Production in collaboration with Professor Sir Frank Engledow, C.M.G., F.R.S.* (Salisbury 1958).
First Report of the Select Committee on Resettlement of Natives (Salisbury 1959).
Second Report of the Select Committee on Resettlement of Natives (Salisbury 1960).
'A Note on the Economics of African Development in Southern Rhodesia with Special Reference to Agriculture', mimeo. (Salisbury 1960).
FEDERATION OF RHODESIA AND NYASALAND, *An Agricultural Survey of Southern Rhodesia*, Part 1 *Agro-Ecological Survey*, Part II *Agro-Economic Survey* (Salisbury 1961).
Report of the Mangwende Reserve Commission of Inquiry (Salisbury 1961).
Report of the Advisory Committee on the Development of the Economic Resources of Southern Rhodesia with Particular Reference to the Role of African Agriculture (Salisbury 1962).
Report by the Constitutional Council on the Land Apportionment Act, 1941 (Salisbury 1964).
Report of the Constitutional Commission, 1968 (Salisbury 1968).
Proposals for a New Constitution for Rhodesia (Salisbury 1969).
A Guide to the Land Tenure Act (Salisbury 1970).
Agro-economic Survey of South-western Matabeleland, Report by the Agricultural Development Authority (Salisbury 1972).
Agro-economic Survey of Northern Matabeleland, Report by The Agricultural Development Authority (Salisbury 1973).
Agro-economic Survey of Central Matabeleland, Report by The Agricultural Development Authority (Salisbury 1974).
Report of the Commission on Enquiry into Racial Discrimination 1976 (Salisbury 1976).

(ii) British Reports

C. 8130, MATABELELAND, *Report of the Land Commission of 1894, and Correspondence relating thereto* (London 1896).
Cd. 1200, SOUTHERN RHODESIA, *Correspondence relating to the Regulation and Supply of Labour in Southern Rhodesia* (London 1902).
Cd. 2028, SOUTHERN RHODESIA, *Correspondence relating to the Proposed Introduction of Indentured Asiatic Labour into Southern Rhodesia* (London 1904).
Cd. 7509, SOUTHERN RHODESIA, *Papers relating to a Reference to the Judicial Committee of the Privy Council on the Question of the Ownership of Land in Southern Rhodesia* (London 1914).
Cd. 8674, SOUTHERN RHODESIA, *Papers relating to the Southern Rhodesia Native Reserves Commission, 1915* (London 1917).
Special Reference as to the Ownership of the Unalienated Land in Southern Rhodesia, Report of the Lords of the Judicial Committee of the Privy Council, delivered on the 29th July, 1918 (London 1918).
Cmd. 547, SOUTHERN RHODESIA, *Correspondence with the Anti-Slavery and Aborigines Protection Society relating to the Native Reserves in Southern Rhodesia* (London 1920).

Cmd. 1042, *Native Reserves in Southern Rhodesia, Despatch to the High Commissioner for South Africa transmitting the Order of His Majesty in Council of the 9th November, 1920* (London 1920).

Cmnd. 4964, RHODESIA, *Report of the Commission on Rhodesian Opinion under the Chairmanship of the Right Honorable the Lord Pearce* (London 1972).

Index